C. GORDON BELL *with* JOHN E. McNAMARA

HIGH-TECH VENTURES
THE GUIDE FOR ENTREPRENEURIAL SUCCESS

ADDISON-WESLEY PUBLISHING COMPANY, INC.
Reading, Massachusetts • Menlo Park, California • New York
Don Mills, Ontario • Wokingham, England • Amsterdam • Bonn
Paris • Milan • Madrid • Sydney • Singapore • Tokyo • Seoul •
Taipei • Mexico City • San Juan

Many of the designations used by manufacturers and sellers to distinguish their products are claimed as trademarks. Where those designations appear in this book and Addison-Wesley was aware of a trademark claim, the designations have been printed using initial caps.

The publisher offers discounts on this book when ordered in quantity for special sales. For more information please contact:

Corporate & Professional Publishing Group
Addison-Wesley Publishing Company
Route 128
Reading, Massachusetts 01867

Library of Congress Cataloging-in-Publication Data
Bell, C. Gordon
    High-Tech ventures : the guide for entrepreneurial success /
C. Gordon Bell with John E. McNamara
    p. cm.
    ISBN 0-201-56321-5 (hardback)
    1. High technology industries—Management. 2. New business
enterprises—Management. 3. Entrepreneurship. 4. Computer
industry—Management. 5. Computer software industry—Management.
    I. McNamara, John E. II. Title
    HC79.H53B45 1991   90-25717
    620' .0068—dc20   CIP

Cover design by Hannus Design Associates
Cover photographs by Kurt R. Hulteen, Lisa LaForge, and John W. Wait
Text design by Kenneth J. Wilson
Set in 10 point Palatino

ISBN: 0-201-56321-5

Printed on recycled and acid-free paper
Third Printing, December 1991
3 4 5 6 7 8 9–AL–9594939291

CONTENTS

PREFACE

High-Tech Ventures is written primarily for those who are creating the future high-tech world by designing, building, and marketing innovative products. It is equally useful for board members, investors, attorneys, accountants, consultants, and others who are intimately involved in new ventures. These readers, plus students of the start-up process and other voyeurs, will find here a quantitative evaluation method, which includes a set of rules for examining a company and comparing it with an "ideal" organization.

The analytical approach presented in *High-Tech Ventures* differs considerably from the anecdotes, testimonials, and confessions so commonly found in today's autobiographies and case studies. Case studies are by no means ignored in this book, however, since the evaluation rules have been generated from actual cases and an entire chapter is devoted to case studies. But the diagnostic method described here is much broader than the approach employed in typical case studies, which focus on a particular discipline—such as marketing, finance, or management—to enable readers to understand a situation that aptly illustrates a flaw or an exemplary action. In contrast, the diagnostic method presented in this book enables users to examine all the critical dimensions that affect a new venture, which could very well reveal multiple flaws in the company. Furthermore, the diagnostic provides a consistent methodology for analyzing and comparing cases.

Although *High-Tech Ventures* is designed to serve embryonic entrepreneurial firms, the guidelines given here are equally useful for large-company intrapreneurs (individuals within big, established organizations who are creating new businesses). These pioneers must deal with the same technologies, products, markets, and general environmental rules as entrepreneurs. All too often, however, intrapreneurs' suggestions are rejected because the new products they propose either do not fit within the current business or threaten the status quo. Thus, start-ups are the main arena for innovation in the world market of information processing, even though the basic technology and product ideas often originate in a research laboratory or a large company.

As suggested above, most of this book outlines a diagnostic method that can be used to assess the health of a high-tech venture. The idea of developing a tool for diagnosing start-ups evolved over a period of nearly ten years. The possibility first presented itself when I was vice president of engineering at Digital Equipment Corporation (DEC). In that position, I defined rules for testing the management, team, market(ing), product position, and product development in an internal DEC guide for managers, "Heuristics for Building Great Products." Since then, I have been involved with about twenty start-ups, including Ardent Computer Corporation (now Stardent Computer, Inc.); Encore Computer Corporation; MIPS Computer Systems, Inc.; Silicon Compiler Systems Corporation (now Mentor Graphics Corporation); Silicon Graphics, Inc.; and Visix Software, Inc.

My observations in these ventures—typically, from the vantage point of a technologist and product architect—have, over the course of a long collaboration, been merged with the marketing, sales, and strategic insights of Heidi Mason, founder and, until recently, chief executive officer of Acuity, a strategic marketing and public relations firm in Silicon Valley. Our research has been encapsulated into a series of guidelines, which take the form of questions or rules, known as the Bell-Mason Diagnostic.

The Bell-Mason Diagnostic constitutes a rule-based, human-applied, expert system. Its more than six hundred rules are gleaned from experience and research in start-ups and established organizations. Review and feedback from peers supplemented the original work, and testing performed on high-tech companies both by ourselves and by Coopers and Lybrand provided a cross-check. Finally, the diagnostic was licensed to Coopers and Lybrand for use in assessing high-tech start-ups.

As mentioned earlier, the rules reflect the diagnostic's view of an ideal company, with which an organization can compare itself. These rules take the form of objective questions (e.g., regarding the existence and content of certain plans and processes) that can be used to gather verifiable information from key people in the company. Formal assessment of a firm includes the following elements: a review of written plans, an evaluation at the company's site (to secure more detailed documentation and simply look at the organization and its progress), analysis of the information that has been collected, preparation of a written assessment, and a feedback session with the principals in the firm. Such a formal assessment should be conducted by a team of two or three individuals who are familiar with the technology and the product and who have a general knowledge of marketing and sales, organization, control, and finance.

The Bell-Mason Diagnostic can also be used informally. Anyone starting a high-tech venture, or contemplating joining a start-up, can read the diagnostic and answer the questions contained therein to test whether the company is healthy.

Although the diagnostic's rules have been posited, reviewed, and tested, the user is free to change or weight them to assess special situations, to perform a more detailed analysis of a particular type of organization, or to emphasize certain dimensions. For example, accounting and legal firms might add more rules in the cash, finance, and control dimensions.

Futurists may be interested in reading *High-Tech Ventures* simply to learn more about high information technology, including the products, market, and trends. People who suffer from "technolophobia" and "graphophobia" to such an extent that they are frightened by simple graphs and shudder at logarithmic scales are welcome to skip over the graphs in this book and concentrate on the text.

Although the preceding paragraphs imply that the Bell-Mason Diagnostic was developed through a simple evolutionary process, it wasn't quite that simple. When Heidi Mason and I first tried to apply a small set of rules to diagnose a start-up, we discovered that the rules were inadequate and that, to be effective, they would have to vary in detail with time, just as a new venture's circumstances vary with the passage of time. We found that we had to precisely define the stages and substages through which a start-up passes in order to create detailed rules that would be appropriate for each stage. In general, a start-up has two planning stages: the concept stage (stage I) and the seed stage (II). These precede the heavily funded product development stage (III) and the even more expensive market development stage (IV), when the company invests in manufacturing and distribution. Finally, if all goes well, the firm enters the steady-state stage (V).

In addition to the five time-dependent stages, there are twelve dimensions, or aspects, that can be used to evaluate any company. The combination of five stages and twelve dimensions raises the possibility of a sixty-chapter book! However, two simplifications have been made herein. Namely, only the first two stages, concept and seed, are discussed in detail, since the viability of an entire venture is most often determined during these initial, critical stages, and a number of the chapters cover more than one dimension. Chapter 2, for example, deals with three dimensions: the CEO, the team, and the board of directors. The business plan dimension is discussed in Chapter 3; cash, financeability, and control, in Chapter 4; technology, in Chapters 5 and 6; manufacturing, in Chapter 7; the product, in Chapter 8; and marketing and sales, in Chapter 9. The entire Bell-Mason Diagnostic is explained in Chapter 10, which includes a set of general, time-independent questions that can be used to evaluate a company on a cursory basis at any stage in its development.

No simple, one-line formula such as "hire good people" or "build an irresistible and unique product" will ensure the success of a high-tech venture. However, being able to answer all the diagnostic's questions affirmatively is a good start! Although in developing the questions, every effort was made to emphasize each of the company's twelve dimensions equally and to give equal weight to the concept and seed stages, a few of my own biases have probably crept in, especially with regard to people, cash, manufacturing, and marketing.

The following subsections provide a brief overview of some of the critical determinants of a start-up's health.

PEOPLE

Since a start-up is a fragile, embryonic organization, it is at the mercy of its chief executive officer, the latest great American cowboy. Companies fold or perform poorly as a result of CEO failure more often than they do from any other single cause. Common failings include the inability to manage, to hire and fire, and to make good and timely judgments. Managers from large organizations are especially dangerous, since they are often incapable of performing basic functions without the plethora of resources available in a big company. Various sins such as greed, sloth, and egoism can also kill an otherwise potentially healthy venture.

I have seen too many CEOs with brittle egos who will do almost anything to be considered right and who constantly place themselves ahead of their team members and their organization. These individuals—second CEOs, in many cases—are likely to abandon a company that they themselves caused to fail. Ironically, their departure is often cushioned by a "golden parachute."

CASH

From study and experience, I have come to believe that too many entrepreneurs have, in the past, had access to too much capital to fund too many marginal-technology companies marketing "me-too" products. Furthermore, these entrepreneurs have frequently felt that they could afford to skip the seed stage and go directly to the market development stage. Throughout the book, I will attempt to show why this is a very risky strategy.

Early profitability is stressed in almost every chapter because, in a successful venture, early profitability lessens or eliminates the need for further use of investor cash. Profit is habit-forming—and so is loss. This bias comes from studying successful start-ups. Each time the issue of profitability is raised in the book, I try to present the underlying theory of its importance. For example, an unprofitable company cannot become self-sustaining and will therefore eventually cease to exist.

MANUFACTURING

It is essential for a start-up to determine whether another company is in a better position to manufacture (or market) the start-up's product. If so, the start-up must form a key strategic partnership with this firm rather than trying to reinvent the wheel by developing its own proprietary technologies, markets, and distribution channels. All too often, however, time, greed, and ego prevent a start-up from seeking such relationships.

MARKETING

Most companies regard marketing as something of a black art, and none of the organizations analyzed by the Bell-Mason Diagnostic came close to the ideal in this area. Marketing is inherently the most difficult dimension to plan, execute, and measure, because the long time span between an action and its result makes it hard to determine the correlation between the two. Furthermore, there is the classic uncertainty over whether a product's success can be attributed to the quality of the product or the quality of the marketing effort. Both a great product and great marketing are essential!

Companies that fail are, for the most part, those that are unable to deal with the complexity of technology and the fast pace of technological change while simultaneously growing as organizations. Start-ups operate in an undefined, high-risk environment, in an emerging market. Some unsuccessful firms cannot meet the challenge of defining a product; others try to create customers in markets for which no market model exists.

Successful start-ups, in contrast, manage to prevail over the inherent risks and the challenge of technological complexity. They are able to increase their size, define their product or products, and create their market. The success of these ventures would seem to suggest that start-up experience is a prerequisite for establishing a viable organization. There is an apparent paradox, however: many of the firms that created new industries—Apple Computer, DEC, Microsoft, and Sun Microsystems—were begun by entrepreneurs who had no previous experience in founding a company.

Starting a high-tech company is more difficult today than ever before, because most of the classes of computers and software, as segmented by price, have already been developed and are being marketed successfully. Furthermore, in the early 1990s, less venture capital is likely to be available for new ventures. These factors, while discouraging, do not toll the death knell for the start-up process. They merely mean that entrepreneurs and venture capitalists are going to be a lot more careful.

Keeping an established high-tech company running successfully is also more difficult today than ever before. A number of readers have argued, for example, that the best-selling book *In Search of Excellence* (Peters and Waterman, 1982), which studied some of our nation's most successful firms, was flawed because several of the companies described therein later became less successful. Not so! The methodology presented in *High-Tech Ventures* clearly demonstrates that a growing firm in an emerging market can easily get into trouble—or out of trouble—at any time and in any number of ways.

A case in point is the "palace revolt" that occurred at a profitable, growing New England start-up, prompting the board to replace the successful CEO, which, in turn, eventually resulted in a poor merger. Likewise, a very large company can become complacent and overly bureaucratic, or its health can be jeopardized by an inappropriate organizational structure. In 1990, DEC is suffering both from having held on to its single VAX product vision for too long and from the displacement of minicomputers by personal computers and workstations. Each of the twelve dimensions of the Bell-Mason Diagnostic includes at least one fatal flaw, which, if manifested at any stage of a company's life, can spell disaster! *High-Tech Ventures* also includes many case studies and vignettes that illustrate this capacity for sudden failure or success.

This book does not present advice or step-by-step details on what to do and how to do it when founding a company. Instead, it posits a new way of examining embryonic firms and emerging businesses via the Bell-Mason Diagnostic, which constitutes a guide and a checklist for the start-up process. (Checklists are powerful tools that every engineer and marketing manager should learn to use.) The book also contains a wealth of information about the computing industry. As an assessment tool, it can help readers determine whether they are ready to start a company, or launch a new project within their present company, and provides a model for doing so. Thus, *High-Tech Ventures* tells readers whether they understand the "how-to" books, because it is, in effect, a "should-be" book. (Those who are interested in the "how-to" books will find a number of good ones listed in the annotated bibliography.)

In a way, founding a company or becoming involved with a start-up is like participating in an exciting sport: the risks are great, but so are the rewards. Carrying the analogy a step further, I might add that before engaging in any sport, it's always a good idea to learn as much as possible about it—by studying the winners and the losers, the smart moves and the fatal accidents. *High-Tech Ventures* will help readers do exactly that. Good luck!

ACKNOWLEDGMENTS

I would like to thank the following reviewers for providing significant input: Paul Baran, Steve Blank, Sally Browning, Henry Burkhardt, Bob Chinn, Steve Coit, Elizabeth

Corcoran, John Doerr, Alison Elliott, Mary Jane Forbes, Ted Johnson, Karen Mathews, Pamela McCorduck, Sesha Pratap, David Salzman, Michael Schrage, John Shoch, Bert Sutherland, and Bill Taylor.

Major contributions were made by the following individuals: Ronna Alintuck, who contributed to both the Gateway story and the marketing chapter; Adam Bosworth and Eric Michelman, who provided the Analytica story; Mark Duncan, of Askmar, who provided many of the figures in Chapter 5; Barry James Folsum and Bonnie Johnson, who offered feedback on the book and applied the Bell-Mason Diagnostic at Focus Systems; Prabhu Goel, who contributed to the Gateway story; John Grillos, who contributed to the financing chapter; Lowell Hawkinson and Bob Moore, who provided the Gensym story; Jeff Kalb, who provided the MasPar story; Bob Keeley, who tested the use of the diagnostic on his classes in entrepreneurism at Stanford; Vinod Khosla, who provided the Sun Microsystems business plan; Dave Nelson and Bill Poduska, who provided the Apollo business plan; Matt Sanders, who contributed the basic ideas for the manufacturing chapter; Arthur Spinner, who contributed to the board of directors section; and Suhas Patil, who provided the Cirrus Logic story.

Gwen Bell made many suggestions, through discussion and detailed editing, and was also a constant source of encouragement.

Coopers and Lybrand deserves special thanks. Bob Stavers of the San Jose office helped create the Bell-Mason Diagnostic and make it work on real companies. Cheryl Suchors of the Coopers and Lybrand National High Tech Group in Boston worked with Bob to champion the diagnostic and license it throughout Coopers and Lybrand.

The book could never have been written without Heidi Mason's collaboration, which resulted in the Bell-Mason Diagnostic.

I gratefully acknowledge the following for their kind permission to reprint or adapt some of the artwork that appears in this book: Askmar (Mark Duncan), The Gartner Group, Harvard Center for Information Policy Research (Anthony G. Oettinger, John F. McLaughlin, Anne Louise Antonoff), Hewlett-Packard (Frank Ura), Intel Corporation, International Data Corporation, and the IEEE Scientific Supercomputer Subcommittee.

I would especially like to thank the staff at Addison-Wesley for their encouragement and dedicated involvement in the book, specifically: Kate Habib, assistant editor; Perry McIntosh, production manager; Peggy McMahon, production coordinator; Leslie Morgan, marketing manager; Linda O'Brien, director of technical sales; John Wait, editor-in-chief, for many ideas and much helpful editing; and Susan Cohan for copyediting.

Chapter 1

INTRODUCTION: THE FORMATION OF HIGH-TECH COMPANIES

As we move into the 1990s, entrepreneurial self-determination continues to release vast amounts of human energy and drive the formation of "start-up" companies based on a wide variety of technologies and applications. These emerging companies create a variety of new products, ranging from relatively simple hardware and firmware components to complete computer systems, which often offer as much as fifty times the performance or performance/price advantage of products produced by long-established firms. In bringing a new product to market, the engineering and overall organizational productivity of the start-up can be ten to fifty times greater than with a large, existing firm.

High-tech start-ups follow the basic process outlined in Figure 1.1. (Readers familiar with programming will immediately recognize that the process is formatted just like a computer program, which seemed appropriate in the present context. Readers unfamiliar with programming should have no trouble understanding the material either, since it can simply be read as ordinary text.)

Let's begin by considering the first few lines of this high-tech start-up "program":

```
Start  a  high-information-technology  company
if  frustration  is greater than  reward
      and greed  is greater than  fear  of  failure
      and a  new  technology/product  is  possible  then
```

```
Start a high-information-technology company
if frustration is greater than reward
        and greed is greater than fear of failure
        and a new technology/product is possible then
        begin
                exit (job);
                get (tools to write business plan);
                write (business plan);
                get (venture capital);
                start (new company);
                get (space, people, product development tools,
                     UNIX license);
                sell (product idea); design (product);
                market&sell&produce (product);
                while new company is not profitable then
                        wait; get (more $);
                sell (new company);
                retire; wait; restart;
                if entrepreneur wants to do it again then
                        start (another high-information-
                                technology company) else
                start (new venture capital company);
        end;
```

Figure 1-1. Simple "Program" for Starting a High-Information-Technology Company.

The founders of the new companies discussed later in this book are typically people who, for a number of reasons, were frustrated with their previous job. On the one hand, they felt compelled to keep the job because they needed the paycheck and wanted to stay in touch with people and advancements in their field. On the other hand, the fact that their frustration exceeded the rewards they expected to receive from their employer tended to push them to leave the firm.

When it comes to starting a new company, this "push" effect is necessary, but not sufficient—at least, not by itself. Thousands of people are frustrated in their present job and yet never strike out on their own. Two additional ingredients are required: having a cash motivation that exceeds one's fear of failure and being able to envision a new technology or product that can serve as the basis for a viable enterprise. These latter two ingredients are the "pull" to form a new company.

Thus, the "if" underlying the creation of a new firm is a combination of the "push" to leave an old company (involving such considerations as bureaucracy, lethargy, politics, and frustration) and the "pull" to form a new company (involving such considerations as a new product, superior technology, recognition, and financial reward). Throughout each succeeding generation of technology, new companies have formed from the interaction of these two forces, which appear to be of equal importance. Furthermore, it is not uncommon for the same individual to experience the push and pull effects several times in his or her career, leading to the formation of several start-ups. For example, Gene Amdahl, Seymour Cray, Steve Jobs, Gordon Moore, Bob Noyce, and Bill Poduska each founded more than one new company, most of which are discussed in greater detail later in the book.

Now let's continue with the next segment of the high-tech start-up "program" presented earlier in the chapter:

```
begin
        exit (job);
        get (tools to write business plan);
        write (business plan);
```

Once the decision has been made to start up a company, the first step is to write a business plan. Occasionally, entrepreneurs do manage to write business plans while they are still part of another organization. In the case of most successful companies, however, a small core of founders leave their jobs and write a detailed business plan on a full-time basis. This process typically takes from three to twelve months, depending on the technology, market uncertainty, product complexity, and manufacturing process.

The standard planning tools used to create the business plan are a personal computer and a spreadsheet program. The importance of the spreadsheet program is that it enables the new company's founders to develop a business plan that offers investors large, but plausible returns. As with all powerful tools, though, spreadsheets are subject to misuse, and the market is littered with hundreds of business plans that tout completely unreasonable and unjustifiable financial numbers. As a result, it is not surprising that high-technology business plans are often perversely described as "that place in time and space where the rubber meets the blue sky."

Because of the range of technologies a new company might utilize and the variety of approaches it could take to structure its program, there are no hard-and-fast rules governing the creation of a business plan. Still, experience shows that short plans are better than long ones, not only because they are easier for investors to read and understand but also because they force the entrepreneurs to think in an orderly fashion.

Because new companies require significant capitalization, the founders must now:

```
        get (venture capital);
```

They do this by taking their business plan to venture capital firms, friends, and relatives in an attempt to obtain funding. This process consists of rounds of courtship with venture capitalists, during which the plan is refined, interviews are conducted to select core personnel, and some ad hoc engineering conceptualization is done to refine the product design and marketing approach. Alliances to achieve additional funding may also be formed at this time. Despite all these efforts, of every hundred business plans that are submitted to a given venture capital company, only about thirty result in a first meeting, ten receive a more detailed review, and less than one gets funding. In 1989, roughly fifteen hundred companies were funded by venture capital firms.

If funding efforts are successful, the founder and his or her core personnel will:

```
start (new company);
```

This is also the point at which additional people leave their jobs to form the nucleus of the new firm.

In order for the fledgling organization to become fully operational, the founders must now:

```
get (space, people, product development
        tools, UNIX license);
```

At this stage, the new company's founders have to acquire the basic tools needed for product development. In the early 1980s, systems companies purchased a VAX, a copy of UNIX, and a license to operate, develop, and sell it as the standard operating system. In the 1990s, a collection of Sun workstations, Apple Macintoshes, or IBM-compatible PCs is likely to substitute for the VAX.

Now that the new firm is in business, it proceeds to:

```
sell (product idea);design (product);
market&sell&produce (product);
```

The sequence of events—sell, design, and build—is very important. The product development process starts with attempts to sell the product idea to potential customers. This provides critical feedback for the design (although it can also produce an unbuildable product specification). The founding team typically spends between twelve and twenty-four months developing a product, often making sales agreements with traditional companies that are unable to develop new products in a timely manner. The start-up then begins to market, sell, and produce its product.

Marketing, sales, and production are extremely important, since these are the activities that determine the new company's profitability, which is the subject of the next segment of our high-tech start-up "program":

```
while new company is not profitable then
        wait; get (more $);
sell (new company);
```

If the new venture does not at first achieve profitability, investors are asked to provide additional funds, dilute the company, and wait patiently for success. If profitability is still not achieved, the start-up must cease operations, merge with another firm, or be acquired. Merger or acquisition (although on more favorable terms) are also possible outcomes of the success scenario, which is discussed below.

With a high-growth (or simple) product and plan, the company may become profitable after only a few quarters of sales. After the start-up has sustained its profitability for several quarters (a "stair-step" pattern of revenue growth), it can either remain in private hands, "go public" with an initial public offering (IPO), or be acquired. Although some firms do continue to be privately held for many years, this discussion assumes that one of the start-up's paramount goals is to gain substantial amounts of additional operating capital—in which case, going public or being acquired is the appropriate course of action.

Going public can wreak havoc with the company's operations, since it demands the full, ongoing attention of already-overworked key personnel. The focus of operations temporarily shifts from sales and service to the task of auditing strengths and weaknesses. Nevertheless, going public is financially beneficial, both for the firm and for its employees and investors. The company gains capital with which to expand its operations, and the founders may realize substantial financial rewards. For example, if an idea results in the founding of a high-tech business that subsequently becomes successful and goes public (the odds of this happening are about six in a million), the dominant founding entrepreneur can receive an average of $6.5 million (Nesheim, 1988).

Although the rags-to-riches scenario of a start-up and its founders' prospering via an IPO is attractive, this is not how the majority of new companies gain additional capital. Instead, the most common method is for the start-up to be acquired by a successful firm, usually in the same area of expertise, which enables the start-up to avoid the trauma of going public and coming under public scrutiny. In 1989, for example, 149 companies (worth $2 billion) in the PC field were acquired, whereas only 18 companies (worth $300 million) went public via an IPO.

I strongly recommend staying private and independent as long as possible and avoiding the inevitable urge to go public. Public investors are rarely interested in a firm and its technology, products, and market. Instead, most tend to be interested only in stock appreciation. Public investors, in short, are not truly investing in a company; they are merely renting one until a better opportunity comes along.

Now that the start-up has become successful, a number of possible scenarios present themselves:

```
retire; wait; restart;
if entrepreneur wants to do it again then
        start (another high-information-
                technology company) else
        start (new venture capital company);
```

How the start-up has obtained additional financing (i.e., by going public or by being acquired) may affect what happens to the founder and/or to the company. In the case of a firm that goes public, the founder may be exhausted from the effort that was required to start the company and sustain it through the public offering, and very often chooses to leave. In the case of a firm that is acquired, the founder may find it distressing to no longer be his or her own boss and to (once again) be part of a large organization. Furthermore, the new owners sometimes consider the founder's job as CEO of the acquired company to be redundant. Either way, his or her departure is likely.

A handful of founders have attempted to take extended vacations or retire at this point in their lives, but they often find it impossible to wind down from the excitement of the start-up process. They discover that they have become more enmeshed in the creation effort than they originally thought. Such individuals may reenter the start-up arena as venture capitalists, ready to advise others, or they may choose to "do it again," founding yet another start-up company.

Prospective investors and employees of firms that have recently gone public or been acquired should note that a company's value often peaks at this point. Although, ideally, the enterprise has now achieved what might be termed steady-state operations and has reached the point of being able to develop new products and sustain its profitability, the departing founder(s) may have built an organization with little lasting value. The company may be locked into a product architecture that has no way of becoming self-sustaining. A successful track record up to the point of IPO or acquisition, then, is no guarantee of future success. Which brings us to the

```
end;
```

Now that readers are familiar with the preceding simplified "program" for starting a high-tech company, it is time to consider a more detailed scenario. The "program" shown in Figure 1-2 not only expands upon the simplified program but also divides the creation of a start-up into five stages:

- *Stage I—Concept:* The founders develop an idea and create a plan for a company that will implement that idea. They either seek funding for a seed stage to further test and refine the idea, or they go directly to the product development stage.

- *Stage II—Seed:* The idea is refined, and a detailed plan for the company is created.

- *Stage III—Product development:* The product is developed and tested by users.

- *Stage IV—Market development:* The product is sold, and the company becomes profitable, thereby proving its viability.

- *Stage V—Steady state:* Investors and founders achieve liquidity as the start-up either goes public, merges with another company, or continues its operations while remaining in private hands.

```
The spark to start a new company
if an idea for a technology/product/service company exists
    and frustration is greater than reward in current job
    pain
    and greed is greater than fear of start-up's failure gain
    and financial and emotional support for start-up exist then
begin

  I.  Concept stage:
      exit (job); find (team);
      get (spreadsheet tools); write (plan); find (investors);
      if plan has low risk then
          go to product development stage;

 II.  Seed stage:
      exchange (stock in company for cash from friends and venture
      capitalists);
      recruit (superstar start-up team);
      while company is on plan and money is in bank do
          begin verify (technology, product, market, business);
          refine (plan);
          if seed stage is done and plan is still good then
                  go to product development stage;
          end;
      the following occurs if out of money or the plan is missed
      if company is still viable and investors are willing then
          continue seed stage else
                  sell (company) or close (company);

III.  Product development stage:
      exchange (stock in company for cash from investors);
      recruit (superstar development team);
      get (space, development tools, software licenses);ᵃ
      while company is on plan and money is in bank do
          begin sell (product idea); specify (product);
          develop (product); a market-driven productᵇ
          build (first product prototypes); via manufacturing
          test (product, internally); alpha testing
          manufacture (first products); manufacturing begins
          test (product, externally); beta testing
          announce (product);
          go to market development stage;
          end;
      if company is still viable and investors are willing then
          continue product development stage else
                  sell (company) or close (company);
                                                         (continued)
```

(continued)

```
    IV.  Market development stage:
         exchange (stock in company for cash from investors);
         recruit (superstar sales team);
         while money is in bank do
             begin sell (product); produce (product);
                 deliver (product); the business cycle
             if company is profitable for six quarters then
                 go to exit and cash in; steady state
             end;
         if company is still viable and investors are willing then
             continue market development stage else
                 sell (company) or close (company);

    V.   Steady-state stage:
         Exit and cash in: Company is sold to achieve liquidity.
             sell (company for sales revenue X 20, to public or to
                 another company);
             continue (company);
             retire and return (entrepreneurs);
             if entrepreneurs are not tired then
                 start (next company) else
                 go to venture capital company;

    end; completion of start-up program
```

[a]In the early 1980s, the development tool was VAX, and the system plan was to design a product to "beat VAX" with a UNIX-based system. In the late 1980s, the development tool was a Sun workstation, a Macintosh, or an IBM-compatible PC. The software license depended on the product: UNIX, Macintosh, MS-DOS, or OS/2. In 1990, it's DOS with Windows and UNIX.
[b]Finis Conner, CEO of Conner Peripherals, characterizes his market-driven product planning and development philosophy as "sell, design, and build."

Figure 1-2. Detailed "Program" for Starting a High-Information-Technology Company.

As the company grows, it proceeds according to a plan, which allows it to move from one stage to the next by obtaining funds from its investors in exchange for stock. During the course of each stage, the firm does one of two things:

- Achieves its goals for the current stage and advances to the next stage

- Misses its planned goals or runs out of money

In the second case, the firm becomes subject to the "if" statement at the end of each stage of the start-up "program." If the investors believe the company is still viable and are willing to proceed, then the company continues with the stage. If not, it is sold or closed.

This book focuses primarily on the first two stages, concept and seed, since these form the foundation of any new enterprise. In both of these stages, the start-up's viability is determined by the interaction of as many as twelve different dimensions:

- People—i.e., the CEO, team and culture, and board of directors (discussed in Chapter 2)

- Business plan (Chapter 3)

- Cash, financeability, and control (Chapter 4)

- Technology (Chapters 5 and 6), manufacturing (Chapter 7), and product (Chapter 8)

- Marketing and sales (Chapter 9)

In the chapters indicated in the preceding list, a set of rules (in the form of questions) is presented for each of the twelve dimensions. These rules can be used to test the new company's readiness to leave the concept stage and/or seed stage. In Chapter 10, the rules for each dimension are summarized, and readers will learn how to apply the Bell-Mason Diagnostic to test a start-up's ability to meet the requirements for long-range success with respect to each dimension. Although, in the following chapters, the application of the diagnostic is discussed in detail for only the concept and seed stages (i.e., the first two, most critical stages), the diagnostic can, of course, be applied to an organization throughout all five stages of its growth.

CONCLUSION

This chapter has introduced the two basic concepts involved in examining a start-up: that start-ups are sequential in nature (i.e., a new firm passes through five discrete stages) and that all aspects of a company are important and must be considered in assessing a new venture's health. The relationship between these two basic concepts was illustrated in "computer-program" format in Figure 1-2, which presented a series of statements, grouped according to stage, with each statement involving one or more of the twelve dimensions.

The first of the twelve dimensions, "people," is also the most important, as readers are about to learn in Chapter 2.

Chapter 2

THE PEOPLE

People, people, people.
    —Arthur Rock

It is often said that the three most important factors in real estate are "location, location, and location." Likewise, the three most important factors in the formation of start-up companies are "people, people, and people," because it is the people who lead the firm and have ultimate responsibility for its success. The key personnel are the chief executive officer (CEO) and those immediately adjacent to him or her in the reporting structure—i.e., the board of directors above the CEO and the team of direct reports below him or her. Although the board of directors has the ultimate fiduciary responsibility for the company, it is the CEO who is responsible for leading the firm, since the CEO leads the team members, who, in turn, lead the vital functions of engineering, manufacturing, marketing, and sales.

The requirements for the board, the CEO, and the team change somewhat as a company matures, and a person or group of people who may have been right for one stage of a firm's development may not be right for another stage. Each of the following sections starts by presenting the time-independent general requirements for a given position—beginning with the most important of these positions, that of CEO—and then discusses possible flaws and more specific requirements, including how these requirements may change between the concept stage and the seed stage.

THE CEO: LEADER, COACH, MANAGER, AND "STANDARDS SETTER"

The CEO sets all the standards for the company, including coaching, decision making, delegation, effort, egalitarian behavior, energy, ethics, hiring, honesty, leadership, management style, quality, thoroughness, and working style—i.e., the complete A-to-Z range of attributes that form "the corporate culture." The CEO, in short, is the firm's heart or "clock," which drives every event.

Academics, biographers, and autobiographers have written a great deal about the personal characteristics required to start a company and become its first CEO. Silver (1985) believes that the typical entrepreneur is a happy, creative, insightful, guilt-laden twenty-seven- to thirty-three-year-old who is a good communicator, comes from a middle-class home with an absent father, had a deprived childhood, is married or divorced, and can focus intensively for long periods of time.

It should be noted that wealth was not among the characteristics just specified. Not only does Silver not require it, but both White (1977) and I believe that "being wealthy is a significant handicap" to an entrepreneur because success isn't absolutely essential for wealthy people, and they are therefore not driven by an urgent need to acquire and preserve cash. In the words of Jim Hammock, president of Silicon Compilers (acquired by Mentor Graphics), "When we started up, the company was all any of us had. We simply had to make it work. Often, fear of failure was our strongest driving force." It is possible to create the appropriate fear of failure in a wealthy person, however, and thus overcome the "handicap of wealth," by having that person invest a significant portion of his or her net worth in the new venture.

The CEO must have a very high energy level and be completely dedicated to the company. Dedication means that the CEO should not be involved in more than one or two outside organizations, since excessive outside involvement is irresponsible and places his or her firm at significant risk. On the other hand, neither should the CEO be overzealous—trying to do everything personally. Rather, the CEO must be able to hire creatively, understand the responsibilities of every team member, and delegate tasks appropriately. If the CEO is the founding entrepreneur, and is an inventor or marketing visionary but not a manager, he or she may wish to delegate a majority of the tasks through an intermediary manager—a chief operating officer (COO). Under these circumstances, Silver (1985) advises hiring a manager who is older and more formal, who has a great deal of energy and heart, and who is both practical and thorough. Typically, a good manager for this position is a former corporate achiever with a nonegocentric mind-set who became dissatisfied with his or her environment.

Having both a COO and a CEO in a start-up involves a number of potential dangers, however. This is essentially a "two-in-a-box" style of management, and the

COO and CEO may try to perform the same tasks, tripping over each other while increasing costs and slowing decision making. Alternatively, the CEO may delegate too much responsibility. Ideally, the CEO should rely upon the COO as one of the chief members of the team to whom tasks can be delegated, but the CEO should never delegate his or her primary responsibility, which is driving the company.

Another way to get into difficulty is to have a chief operating officer who manages internal affairs while the CEO sells the company in various ways. Such an arrangement stresses "selling" as a CEO's most important skill and thereby biases the choice of a CEO, by limiting the field to candidates with a sales background. Unfortunately, such individuals often find themselves incapable of hiring outside the sales specialty and hence tend to populate the company with salespeople. Although a CEO (and the rest of the team) should have some sales ability, the need for such ability pales in comparison with the need for him or her to understand finance, control, marketing, and products. Further, unlike a salesperson, who leads and manages individuals, a CEO must create, lead, and manage *teams* of individuals. In short, I believe that those involved in a start-up should think very hard before selecting a salesperson or sales manager as a CEO.

Over time, I have concluded that the chief executive officer is typically the weakest dimension of a start-up. The CEO holds a position of great influence, since systems and controls for running the company smoothly are not yet in place. Resource limitations compel the CEO to wear a number of hats, frequently in areas where he or she has little expertise. One of the important hats is often that of mediator, because intrateam disputes can have immediate (and possibly devastating) bottom-line ramifications. The fledgling organization's inordinate dependency on the CEO places a great deal of power and responsibility in this individual's hands— perhaps more than he or she has ever exercised. Some CEOs get drunk on this power, while others become frightened and paralyzed. Good CEOs are able to maintain a certain measure of detachment and perspective and understand the need to drive the organization.

The following list presents some key personal qualities exhibited by effective CEOs. Readers are encouraged to rely on their own experience and intuition when weighing them.

- *Intelligence and energy:* CEOs need intelligence so they can identify and prioritize problems and set direction, and they need extraordinary stamina and commitment because everyone in the company takes his or her lead from above. When it comes to these two qualities, the higher a CEO's level of intelligence and energy, the better.

- *Integrity, quality, and working habits and environment:* CEOs must be honest and open in dealing with everyone, inside as well as outside the company. They must set a personal example that translates into both corporate and product quality.

- *Openness:* CEOs who encourage an "open-door" policy, invite suggestions for change and solutions from anyone, anywhere, and who are willing to openly acknowledge their strengths and weaknesses tend to be good, honest leaders. They have no "hidden agendas" and demonstrate a realistic, appropriate pride in their accomplishments. They usually get things done through the natural processes of building interpersonal respect and recognizing competence.

- *Background:* Good training and good role models, or mentors, are two of the most common attributes of effective CEOs. The problem is that the great companies don't let their people escape. Thus, many of the available CEO candidates may be the products of an inferior corporate background and inferior professional role models. The best alternatives are often "virgin" candidates with no preconceived company concept.

- *Team-building skills and ability to delegate:* These attributes, which are actually closely related to the team dimension, involve the CEO's personal ability to create, motivate, and drive the team in a productive and organized way.

- *Ego and humility:* Excessive ego or lack of ego can lead CEOs either to consistently fail to delegate authority and responsibility, or to chronically overcommit or undercommit to accomplish personal and company goals. CEOs must therefore be able to restrain, but not eliminate, their personal and professional pride. The accuracy of the CEOs' assessment of the company's (and their own) strengths and weaknesses gives an indication of their true humility.

Just how critical is CEO selection? Dennis Gorman of Sevin Rosen found that over 90 percent of the companies backed by his firm that went public were still headed by the original CEO, whereas 25 percent of the companies that failed or were floundering had retained the founding CEO.

In summary, James Swartz, past chairman of the National Venture Capital Association, describes five attributes that a CEO needs to "win a venture capitalist": leadership, vision, integrity, openness, and dedication.

CEO FLAWS

CEOs' flaws are legendary, as countless newspaper and magazine articles have chronicled with delight. Some CEOs have been victimized by technology's moving more slowly than they anticipated; others have met their fate at the hands of a fickle buying market; still others have simply been losers. Unfortunately, the authors of newspaper and magazine stories tend to simplify the issues by concentrating on single events or single flaws and do not provide a holistic view. Book authors, in contrast, have more time for research and more space to tell the story. As a result, some books do provide a balanced picture of the right attributes, and many book-length biographies and analyses present case studies illustrating effective CEO performance.

The flaws summarized in the following subsections are, in effect, the reverse of the virtues listed above. Since no one is perfect, the CEO is likely to exhibit at least one of these flaws to some degree. How the start-up deals with a CEO's flaws is very important, because a company that is weak in other dimensions may find these flaws to be fatal. A flawless CEO is a rare phenomenon; however, Ken Olsen[1] (Rifkin and Harrar, 1988) comes as close to this ideal as any CEO with whom I have worked, and his record of success is legendary.

Low Energy, Low Intelligence, and/or Low Integrity

The CEO may have either a low energy level (slow clock) or an inadequate time commitment, low intelligence (what might, in computer lingo, be termed a slow central processing unit, perhaps coupled with a small 640K memory), and/or questionable ethics. This type of CEO tolerates nonegalitarian behavior, low quality standards, poor work habits, and unrestrained company spending.

The criticality of the CEO as the standards setter—the individual who establishes the company's clock—was discussed earlier. Almost all the dimensions encompassed in this flaw, ranging from intelligence and work habits to ethics, have come up in "judging" every CEO I know. A particularly annoying flaw for start-ups is the CEO who treats the fledgling company as if it were a large, solidly established firm, demanding all the perks. Individuals of this sort are readily identifiable, since they insist on a large salary, absolutely must fly first class, require a carte blanche expense account, and tend to be found quibbling over (or modifying) their original compensation agreements with the company. Arrogance and greed drive such CEOs to milk the very firms they were hired to nurture.

My own biases are clear: only become part of a venture led by a hardworking, extremely intelligent, and highly ethical individual who knows how to establish a dynamic, open company culture and can manage, lead, and sell.

---

1. Digital Equipment Corporation started in 1957 and ran well under Ken Olsen's leadership until the mid-1980s, when the advent of other forms of computing began to stall the company. Product revenues for 1990 declined from the previous year, and in the fourth quarter, the firm was unprofitable.

Inability to Sustain the Cheerleader Role

The CEO may lack the stamina, energy, and ability to continually sell employees, customers, and investors, throwing in the towel when the company fails to take off. Given the brutal environment of a start-up, the CEO can never abdicate his or her job as head cheerleader.

Inadequate Hiring Skills

The CEO may be unable either to make first-rate hires or to deal with the inevitable hiring mistakes. Because this type of individual simply doesn't know how to test for and hire top-quality people, he or she often just hires former cronies, placing more stock in allegiance than in competence. The company must continually seek and hire only the best candidates. If the CEO is unable to accomplish this, then "pygmy hiring" sets in and the quality of the firm's personnel enters a downward spiral.

Poor Managerial and Team-Building Skills

The CEO's lack of managerial and team-building skills can manifest itself in numerous ways. The company may operate in a state of continual chaos; the CEO may reserve all control and decision making for himself or herself, thereby preventing any of the subordinates from managing or developing; or the CEO may work all issues one-on-one so that a team never has the opportunity to form and team problem solving never occurs. This type of CEO may create either a "political" environment in which every decision hinges on the selling power of individual personalities or a bureaucracy in which decisions take forever to be made.

The CEO who places a high value on "being liked by everyone" will probably create an environment in which staff-level decision making is impaired or futile. At the other extreme is the tyrant who insists on taking and keeping control of every area of the company personally, thereby impeding all progress. The CEO sometimes does this overtly, by delivering imperial mandates at staff meetings; but he or she can also achieve the same effect covertly, by allowing many issues to be left unresolved. In the latter case, the CEO then avoids confrontation by "solving" these issues outside of staff meetings, without buy-in from the parties who are most affected.

Above all, the CEO has to understand the fundamentals of leadership and management. He or she must be able to delegate, form a team, and get the team to make extraordinary commitments.

Inability to Build a Team or Keep a Team Together

It is sometimes possible to detect a lack of team quite readily. A venture capitalist I know simply asks a direct question of a team member. If the CEO interrupts with an answer, he suspects that the company is driven from the top down and lacks a viable team.

When the founder and CEO is unable to keep the team together, he or she may be ousted by a "palace revolt" and replaced by a series of ill-conceived, board-controlled actors and actions. For example, I know of a company that built real-time laboratory computers based on the first 32-bit microprocessors. After two years, when the firm was just beginning to reach its peak sales and was becoming profitable, a "palace revolt" prompted the board to replace the existing CEO. The new CEO came from a very large computer company but was a sales-oriented individual with no experience in the laboratory market area or in product development. The organization subsequently declined to the point where it was forced to merge with another floundering firm. Guess who the winner(s) were: (a) investors; (b) the founding CEO; (c) the new CEO, who received a "golden parachute"; (d) all the founders and employees; (e) customers; (f) none of these.

Inability to Sell the Company to the Financial Community:
The "Short-Socks Test"

A start-up may fail to secure funding for many reasons, not all of which are necessarily relevant to the firm's viability. The following is a case in point: After visiting an entrepreneur, a New England venture capitalist commented to his associate that the company wouldn't be funded. "Why?" asked the associate. Replied the capitalist: "Because the president was wearing short socks." Although I'm sure that lots of California firms have obtained funding despite their founders' wearing no socks at all, the basic principle still applies: when an entrepreneur is initially seeking financing, first impressions really count—perhaps more than they should.

Regardless of whether the precise reason for the CEO's inability to sell the start-up to the board and the investors is trivial (e.g., failing the "short-socks test") or substantive (e.g., not being a sufficiently persuasive advocate for the company), his or her shortcoming will manifest itself through financing problems for the firm and a lack of belief in and/or support for the CEO. This flaw really involves an inability to manage the board and the investors. It is perhaps the most rapidly fatal flaw of all those discussed, and its cost is quite simple: the CEO loses his or her job when an impatient board finds it isn't getting the response it believes it needs.

CEO RULES

In some cases, a company is founded by an entrepreneur who has a technical or marketing idea and who then serves as the acting CEO during the firm's seed stage, even though he or she may lack many of the required qualifications. This is a risky way for a company to start out, because it may subsequently be forced to hire a new CEO in order to reach more advanced stages of its development, and the transition to the "real" CEO can prove traumatic. Changing CEOs is similar to performing a heart transplant: it takes a long time to find a compatible donor, the operation is lengthy and complex, the body requires a long period of healing and adjustment afterward, and there are no guarantees that the procedure will ultimately be successful. It would be much better to search for an appropriate CEO from the outset, using the rules in this subsection as guidelines.

Does the CEO candidate possess the levels of intelligence, energy, ethics, and quality that are required to establish the clock and culture for the proposed company?

Although this rule can be stated explicitly, it is never really answered explicitly. It is answered implicitly, however, by everyone—employees, investors, strategic partners, or customers—who becomes associated with a particular start-up. Despite its being wholly subjective, this rule tests the overall quality of a CEO candidate by evaluating the individual as the prospective leader of the environment that he or she proposes to create.

To satisfy this rule, the CEO candidate must provide solid evidence and references that testify to his or her past accomplishments. In particular, if a prospective CEO has run another company and has led in the definition of its culture, then the new firm is likely to be similar to his or her previous one. As the start-up ends the seed stage, it will become increasingly clear to the employees, investors, strategic partners, and customers—as well as to the CEO himself or herself—whether the CEO was well chosen.

A second, less subjective rule should also be applied to the concept stage selection of a CEO:

Has the CEO demonstrated management, team-building, and leadership ability involving product development, in a resource-constrained environment, and on a do-it-from-scratch (e.g., start-up) basis?

This rule really has three parts, since being able to manage, team-build, and lead are all highly critical skills. Without managerial skills, the CEO will be unable to establish any standards of commitment and follow-through. However, as discussed earlier, the CEO could satisfy this aspect of the rule by delegating management tasks to a COO, provided the company can afford the extra staff and there's a clear understanding that the CEO is in charge. The second part of the rule tests whether the CEO has experience in technology and product development. The final part tests his or her ability to operate with constrained resources. Ideally, the prospective CEO will have gained that skill during a previous start-up, but a person who has begun a small enterprise within a large company might be an alternative candidate, albeit a risky one.

Can the CEO articulate and sell the company vision to attract the financing, engineering, and other key talent needed for the (advanced or predevelopment) seed stage?

The final rule for the concept stage evaluates the CEO's ability to act as a salesperson in order to obtain seed stage financing and recruit outstanding employees so that the seed plan can be carried out.

Does the CEO have extensive experience in management, and has he or she demonstrated competence in product development, marketing, and sales by adhering to the principal objectives of the seed plan?

This rule provides a simple test based on the CEO's most recent accomplishments during the seed stage. Given the seed stage requirement of translating unique technology into a product specification, it should be easy to determine whether the CEO has in fact been successful in leading the company to this point.

Is the CEO a leader and team builder across departments, and can he or she lead/manage the team and help attract key personnel at various phases of the product development stage? This will be necessary in order for the company to start building all the required functions.

This rule looks beyond accomplishments during the seed stage and examines the likelihood that the CEO can continue to be an effective leader and manager during the firm's future stages of growth. It is a rule that is often violated, because many entrepreneurs do not have the time to receive management training (or to gain its equivalent in terms of practical experience) before they begin running a company. It is hard for an inexperienced CEO to manage a fledgling firm and get funding at the same time. Michael Dell of Dell Computer and Bill Gates of Microsoft were inexperienced CEOs who succeeded, but they did not have to obtain traditional funding, which is fortunate, since their youth and lack of experience might have made it difficult.

Has the CEO been successful in attracting financing, recruiting key employees, and finding directors for the board?

The ultimate proof of the CEO's selling ability is whether key individuals have signed up at the seed stage. There should be a "backlog" of people wanting to be involved in the company.

Does the CEO have insight into the content, scheduling, and management interdependencies of engineering and marketing in the early phases, and of manufacturing and sales in the later phases?

In order for the CEO to build a team, he or she must understand the motivation of the various functions and know how to get the team's members to work together and resolve the conflicts that will inevitably arise. A good test of the CEO's skills in this regard is whether both engineering and marketing have agreed to the product specification by the end of the seed stage.

Can the CEO function actively as a company missionary in preselling, negotiating strategic alliances, and lining up codevelopment partners during the product development stage?

As noted earlier, a CEO must be able to sell the company to investors and the financial community. Beyond that, however, he or she must also be able to sell to customers and potential partners. In some cases, the "ideal" selling target is a strategic partner who can invest in the new venture.

THE TEAM AND COMPANY CULTURE: THE PARTS MUST FUNCTION AS A WHOLE

> Lack of team is the number one company killer.
> —John Shoch

Although teamwork is a critical aspect of an organization of any size, it is especially important in a start-up. Teamwork is like a tree, with communication as its trunk and with mutual respect and recognition of common goals as its major root structures. The leadership necessary to nurture teamwork starts with the CEO and his or her direct reports, each of whom leads a team effort within a particular functional group. Although each direct report/group is measured independently, the groups must realize that they form a team and that the results of the total team are what count. There can be no such thing as saying "Your end of the boat is sinking."

Without integrated team effort, the company will be unable to understand and resolve all the critical issues that cross organizational boundaries. Some of the issues (financial compensation, working environment, product quality) require the mutual efforts of several groups, whereas others (product pricing, materials sourcing) can be resolved by special pairwise relationships between groups.

Table 2-1 lists some crucial tasks that call for high levels of formal cooperation and coordination.

To achieve the level of teamwork required to form and grow a successful company, it is important that the top-level team (direct reports to the CEO) consist of high-quality individuals with measurable experience and expertise. The head of the start-up's engineering department must have proven expertise in the company's technology/product domain; in addition, he or she must be able to perform a function, such as design or analysis of some portion of the design. The top-level team must also be "do"-oriented rather than "management"-oriented. Each member must be able to "play" several positions on the team that reports to him or her rather than just managing the team. This requirement implies specific kinds of competence and serves to ensure that:

- Members of the top-level team have an appropriate level of competence, ruling out bureaucrats who come from large companies and possess the necessary credentials on paper but often lack actual competence

- The department head really knows what's going on in the department, since he or she functions as an active participant instead of just serving as the "boss"

- The organization is lean right from the start, since it does not have the separate line (brawn) and staff (brain) components characteristic of many large, "fat" companies

A top-level team that passes these tests demonstrates competence, and competence is the basis for respect. Respect among the collected heads of the various groups will ensure that they function as an integrated team rather than as a collection of egocentric or warring individuals.

Even though the team operates in an integrated manner, each of its members still has his or her own contributions to make. The measure of a team's success is how the contributions that its members make through their individual roles combine to produce an overall result that is greater than the sum of the separate contributions,

Table 2-1. Tasks Requiring Teamwork.

Task	Involved Organizations
Define the product for customers	Engineering/marketing
Manufacture the product	Engineering/manufacturing
Control the order-to-product flow	Sales/manufacturing
Provide marketing information and establish order flow	Marketing/sales
Resolve customer problems	Service/manufacturing/ engineering
Meet corporate and departmental operating and financial objectives	All departments/financial organization
Maintain a commitment to corporate quality	All departments

due to the synergistic effect of teamwork. Table 2-2 summarizes the unique roles played by various individuals as members of successful teams in some well-known start-ups.

RESPECT FOR EMPLOYEES AND THEIR PERSONAL TIME

The new company's attitudes about how people will be treated begin to develop during the seed stage. One of the most important and visible of these attitudes involves the work ethic, as embodied in the firm's working hours. A start-up must strike an appropriate balance so that participants can have a life beyond the firm. The successful start-up is often staffed with twenty-five- to thirty-five-year-olds whose families, including young children, can't understand why they never see their parents. It is unreasonable to establish a company culture in which, from the outset, employees are routinely expected to work over eighty hours during six- or seven-day weeks. One reason why a firm should avoid overscheduling its employees is that it will have no slack—nothing to fall back on when the inevitable real crises arise. However, the main reason for avoiding overscheduling is that burnout can occur when employees work at such a pace for two to three years.

Hundred-hour weeks are inevitably required in even the best-managed start-ups, but they should be the exceptions. In many new companies, staff members find themselves working at least part-time on Saturdays, and it is not uncommon to hear

Table 2-2. Roles of Key Individuals in Several Well-Known Start-ups.

Company	Person	Roles
Apple	Jobs	Founder, driving entrepreneur, and product visionary
	Wozniak	Founding engineer and product designer
	Markula	Cofounder and source of financing and business expertise
	McKenna	PR, unofficial member of executive staff, and board of directors
	Rock	Funding and board of directors
	Scott	First president
Microsoft	Gates	Founding technical leader and visionary
	Allen	Technical Cofounder
	Balmer	Engineering operations
	Shirley	Business, marketing, and operations
Apollo	Poduska	Founder and company leader
	Nelson	Product visionary
	Greata	Product design
	Spector	First president until steady state
	Vanderslice	Second president, bureaucrat, sold floundering company to Hewlett-Packard
Intel	Grove	Operations
	Moore	Overall visionary
	Noyce	Visionary and external spokesperson
Lotus	Kapor	Founding president and product visionary
	Manzi	Second president, during steady-state growth
Sun	Khosla	Founding entrepreneur and first president
	Bechtolscheim	Hardware product designer
	Joy	Software product designer and UNIX visionary
	McNealy	Manufacturing, with transition to president
	Lacroute	Operational management

investors remarking about the number of cars in the firm's parking lot on evenings and weekends. In short, the start-up has a responsibility to establish reasonable expectations with regard to work load and to clearly communicate those expectations to job candidates before they join the organization.

RESPECT FOR THE INVESTORS' CASH AND THE COMMITMENT TO PROFITABILITY

The firm's attitudes about spending are another key part of its culture. Ideally, the start-up should have a virtual reverence for cash, minimize spending (this includes keeping salaries down), and maintain a clear focus on profitability. Investors respect a new company that borders on being miserly. In contrast, they worry about a company whose employees rake in high salaries and fill the parking lot with expensive cars when the venture is not yet profitable.

I recently visited a chronically unprofitable company whose employees have created a culture in which profit is disdained as if it were an unethical concept. The organization, staffed with many talented artisans, came from a government-funded research laboratory and now builds creative animation software, which it must sell in order to survive. This firm must ultimately change if it hopes to remain viable, since even the most gullible investors reach the point where their patience wears thin and their purse snaps shut.

TEAM FLAWS

Because a team can be undermined by almost anyone on it, the responsibility for a team's success lies with every one of its members. Whether or not those involved can operate as a team depends on such factors as the extent to which they share a vision of how to build a lasting company, the competence of the individual team members, the team members' respect for one another, and the CEO's leadership skills. Since a discussion of all possible team flaws could fill an entire book, this subsection describes only some of the most common ones.

A Mercenary Team

The problem with building a team using entrepreneurial mercenaries is that the members' motivation will be questionable. If the team's aim is simply to make a quick buck rather than to develop a unique technology and form a lasting company, difficulties will soon ensue. A similar flaw, forming a company with a questionable motivation, is discussed in Chapter 3, "The Business Plan."

Conflicting Egos and Lack of Respect

In some cases, certain key participants, including the CEO, may be so egocentric that the CEO cannot form them into a viable team. The first test of a group's ability to work effectively together as a team is when it has to prepare the company's business plan and make trade-offs among various functions. If there is a problem with conflicting egos and lack of respect, the team may simply fall apart at the concept stage or the seed stage because of its members' inability to get along while preparing the plan. Alternatively, the team may break up during a later stage of the company's life, when the stakes are much clearer and the pressure for teamwork is even greater.

Lack of mutual respect is usually at the root of this flaw, although the problem may give the outward appearance of ego conflict between the involved individuals. It is common in high-tech organizations to find a lack of respect between marketing and engineering personnel, which is almost certain to prevent effective teamwork. Every possible effort must be made to overcome this flaw because although mutual love is not a criterion for team membership, mutual respect certainly is.

TEAM RULES

The team is more than the sum of the founders or those who report to the CEO. Although the CEO is ultimately responsible for the company culture, the entire team must embody it. Team members must help define and promulgate the culture throughout the firm by their actions. The likelihood of forming a successful team can be analyzed by applying the rules presented in this subsection.

> **Do the two or three people currently "on board" at the concept stage have the critical experience and expertise in technology/product/market development?**

The first rule tests whether the team has the individual and collective professional capabilities to start up. Unless each member exhibits an outstanding level of professionalism, the company does not have a solid foundation, and the lack of competence and mutual respect is likely to prevent the formation of a team.

> **Is there evidence that the founders can function as a team?** *Tests:* **Have they worked together productively for three to six months? Do they respect one another?**

The second rule checks for what might be termed "teamness" at the concept stage. Without solid professional competence on the part of each member, the team will not function cooperatively to solve the inevitable conflicts, such as disagreements between engineering and marketing over the product requirements. This rule also tests how compatible and comfortable the individuals are with one another in terms of whether they can engage in joint problem solving and trust one other to manage their respective areas. The simple tests include the team members' having worked with one another long enough to be certain that they can build a company together. Some investors insist on the team's having worked together either in a previous job or for at least six months on the current start-up.

Does the team's orientation reflect an appropriate balance between "doing" and "managing" that will enable it to begin establishing an action-oriented culture? *Tests:* **Can each of the top-level team's members "play" one or more positions on his or her team as opposed to just managing a team of players? Has the team managed comparable undertakings before?**

This rule requires each member to function both as an individual contributor and as a manager. Unlike managers in large, established companies, managers in start-up firms invariably spend significant amounts of their time personally performing their department's function, so they should be technically capable. On the other hand, they should also possess managerial skills, since it is hoped that the company will ultimately grow to the point where they will function primarily as managers. It is, of course, difficult to find technological creativity and sound managerial ability in the same person. Whenever technologically creative individuals discover that they are weak in management, their first priority should be to hire their own boss.

Do the reputations of the concept stage team serve to attract a first-rate engineering team along with the critical marketing resources necessary to achieve seed stage and product development stage objectives?

The team must have the individual and combined reputations (in terms of skill, charisma, etc.) that will enable them to hire the critical people who will actually form and carry out the company's main functions.

By the end of the seed stage, are the core leaders for the technology development, product development, critical-process manufacturing, and marketing functions on board? Are they operating as an integrated team of six to eight people?

This rule, which provides yet another assessment of team formation, is tested continuously during the seed stage, when the team members have an opportunity to work together for several months—a vital step in team building. It is extremely important that the founders be able to function as a team. If they show mutual respect and the CEO is a good leader, chances are they will form a successful team.

By the end of the seed stage, have hiring criteria been established? Is a systematic recruitment method in place?

Although each of the functions is responsible for recruiting in its respective area, having companywide standards is also important to ensure that the first employees are operating according to a single set of principles in establishing the company culture. In start-ups, it is very easy to erect arbitrary walls and create different classes of corporate "citizens" based on the way individuals are rewarded by various managers. No matter how hard a firm may try, salary and stock ownership are likely to become widely known. Although egalitarianism is not mandatory in order for a start-up to be successful, rewarding on the basis of skill makes for a happier environment.

By the end of the seed stage, if innovative manufacturing processes are required (such as in semiconductor or disk manufacturing), is an experienced manufacturing leader with a core team of functional specialists on board?

If the company must undertake a manufacturing-intensive development process, then the manufacturing leader must be part of the key hiring and team-building effort right from the start.

By the end of the seed stage, have team members defined their desired corporate culture? Is it compatible with what can reasonably be expected, both from the company's people and in terms of the overall professional working environment in the firm's geographic area?

All companies attempt to create a corporate culture that is uniquely their own. The two key aspects of culture that must be defined at the outset are how the company will treat its employees and how it will manage cash (the ever-present symbol of its investors).

Interested readers can find many books and articles that discuss the culture-formation process and/or analyze the culture of specific companies. Deal and Kennedy (1982), for instance, have described various aspects of corporate culture, including the case of Tandem Computers, which has the highest regard for its employees and is well known for its creative, healthy environment and its nearly unique culture. Rogers and Larsen (1984) have described the culture of Silicon Valley, and their work is required reading for anyone starting a venture there. And finally, *In Search of Excellence* (Peters and Waterman, 1982) is the best-known book on the subject.

THE BOARD OF DIRECTORS: REVIEWERS, COUNSELORS, AND COMPANY MISSIONARIES

The board of directors has the ultimate fiduciary responsibility in a company and thus the ultimate responsibility for selecting the CEO. However, once the board has chosen a CEO, its members should function only as reviewers and counselors rather than trying to run the CEO's company for him or her. The only time the board collectively, or its members individually, should play an active role in the firm's day-to-day operations is during those rare periods when the position of CEO is vacant. Arthur Spinner of Hambro International Venture Fund summarizes the relationship between the CEO and the board like this: "If you are a venture capitalist [on a board] and you want a company to run, go start one yourself."

Spinner also cautions, "If you are an entrepreneur and you need direction rather than support, you should not be running a company; you should be working with one." However, at various stages of the start-up's development, the CEO may have occasion to call on the board for review and counsel. Assistance may be required initially in obtaining financing and later in taking a company public. Advice may be needed in such areas as product and market development or selling to key customers. The wisdom of experience may be useful in dealing with control and operational problems. In each case, the board may provide its advice and counsel by asking hard questions and may help the firm achieve a more realistic perspective by offering an alternative point of view.

Choosing board members is a critical process, because some may become directors for life, and each must be considered a vital part of the company. Unfortunately, the composition of a board is frequently linked to financing, because many venture capital firms make funding contingent on their being granted a board position. In such cases, the member is often unable to make any contribution beyond cash. Selecting board members based on their ability to come up with money or work harmoniously with the CEO is usually a bad idea; rather, board members should be selected based on the expertise that they can contribute. Even then, it will be rare for a board member to have a broad range of applicable expertise unless he or she has run a similar organization. I believe that a start-up should avoid choosing board members who have not participated in the operation of a company or who possess only a single area of expertise, such as the ability to raise money (unless it is unquestionably clear that they can bring in cash easily).

Cautions have also been expressed about board members whose sole area of expertise is the law. According to Gladstone (1988), many venture capitalists feel that "practicing lawyers make poor directors of small businesses" because "businessmen . . . will help reach a consensus . . . [whereas] lawyers do not bring harmony to the boardroom."

A homogeneous board should be avoided, since this type of board is unlikely to have the perspectives that a new company needs in such diverse areas as operations, finance, technology, marketing, and consulting. A start-up whose board consists of six near-clones is a recipe for disaster, because each member has the same limited outlook. In fact, Spinner even argues that it is helpful for a board to have at least one "renegade of sorts who will consistently play devil's advocate."

In contrast, a heterogeneous board is the ideal (although heterogeneity should not be carried to the point where board members cannot work together harmoniously or communicate effectively). Such a board will find it easier to engage in a variety of activities, ranging from simply serving as a support structure to shaping external perceptions of the company (as Ben Rosen did for Compaq and Lotus). It might also be useful to enlist members who have experience in working with troubled firms and increasing their valuation.

The start-up should select board members who can spend the time necessary to learn about the company's business, its products, its competitors, and its customers. They should understand the business well enough to detect danger signs and recognize opportunities. Thus, people with time to do the job right may be much more valuable than well-known individuals who already sit on a dozen or so other boards.

When selecting board members, quantity should be considered in addition to quality. Rosenstein et al. (1989) did a study of 162 start-ups in the northern California, Boston, and central Texas areas, which revealed that board size tends to increase as a company progresses from stage to stage in its growth process. (See Table 2-3.)

Of the 162 companies studied, the average board had 5.6 members, of whom 1.7 were internal members, 2.4 were venture capital principals, 1.2 were venture capital staff, and 1.8 had various other backgrounds. As companies grow, so do their boards, and large, established firms have a mean board size of 13 persons.

The rather large representation of venture capital people on the boards surveyed may be cause for concern, given the caution voiced earlier. However, it should be remembered that the caution was against selecting board members exclusively as sources of cash. If the company can find venture capitalists who have demonstrable

Table 2-3. Board Size Versus Growth Stage.

Stage	Average Board Size	Standard Deviation
Seed	3.7	0.50
Start-up	5.0	1.24
Financing rounds 1, 2, and 3	6.0	1.50
Financing round 4	6.0	1.40

expertise, they can make a valid contribution to the board. For example, in addition to providing financing, these individuals can serve the firm in such capacities as the following:

Developing the firm's original strategy	Monitoring operations
Acting as a sounding board	Monitoring financial performance
Recruiting and/or replacing the CEO	Evaluating market plans
Recruiting (other than the CEO)	Establishing customer contacts
Securing debt financing	Developing new strategy
Securing equity (outside of venture channels)	Serving as an interface with vendors
Serving as an interface with investor groups	Assisting with crises

The value added by venture capitalists in performing these functions (as perceived by the CEOs) was also tabulated in the Rosenstein et al. study. The study concluded that venture capitalist board members made worthwhile (but not outstanding) contributions, with the greatest contributions being made in the earlier stages of company development. Also, no correlation was found between how well the firm was doing and the CEO's assessment of its board, although the ordering of the perceived value of each function did change slightly. Other functions performed by the board were listed, too (evaluating product/market opportunities, formulating marketing plans, developing compensation plans, and assisting in the initial public offering [IPO]), but these were deemed to be of negligible help. Steve Coit of Merrill, Pickard, Anderson, and Eyre suggests that the venture capitalists on the board are really the vice presidents in charge of financing and the IPO.

In order to maximize the board's usefulness, the CEO must know how to manage the board. For instance, the CEO should always raise issues rather than adopting a defensive position. He or she should take care to meet the board's expectations, which means exceeding the requirements of the plan. Being prepared, especially for the very first meeting, is essential. The agenda should include information about progress and a summary of key issues that need to be dealt with. In addressing key issues, the CEO should propose a plan for review as opposed to asking for advice. The CEO who asks for advice will get it, and the CEO who does so too often will find that the board or one of the directors is running the company.

Board meetings should be conducted in an atmosphere of openness. Both Spinner and I believe that the company's vice presidents should attend board meetings to make them aware of the board's views on various issues and to give the board insight into the company's management team, one of its most important assets. In contrast, CEOs who guard access to the organization are likely to be either hiding something or insecure. In exchange for the CEO's policy of openness, the board should deal with the CEO fairly and honestly, without wasting his or her time on petty matters. Board members must realize that the CEO's time is a precious resource, which they should conserve.

BOARD FLAWS

Individual competence is at the root of having a great board of directors, just as it was a key factor in having a great team. Not utilizing a competent board is merely a lost opportunity, but certainly not a fatal flaw. The most serious flaw in this dimension is simply having board members who are unable to contribute to the company, either because they lack an understanding of the industry or because they possess no knowledge and have only an ordinary level of intelligence. (The inexperienced venture capitalist usually falls into the latter category.)

One of the CEO's most important jobs is to keep the board appropriately informed and involved in the firm. Thus, the company must have a relatively competent and cohesive board of a manageable size (about six or fewer members). When the company goes out of control by missing its plan and board members are surprised, the board oftentimes becomes involved in day-to-day operations.

The balance of this subsection describes typical board-related problems that every start-up must guard against.

An Investor-Heavy Board with No Industry Experience

A board can have a very negative effect on productivity if it demands that the company conduct its operations in a way that pleases the board instead of in a way that will help the firm become a successful provider of goods or services. An especially naive board composed of individuals who have had scant operational responsibility or who have a very limited understanding of the industry is likely to have a net negative effect by creating "make-work." One such board that I know of contains a member who has no product, market, or technology experience and is unable to make any valid contribution. Rather than having this individual tutored "off-line," roughly 30 percent of the board meetings are spent in his education.

A Board That Runs the Company

As noted above, when a board finds itself surprised by missed plans or faced with operational uncertainty, it may get involved in the day-to-day management of the firm, usurping the functions of the CEO and his or her team. A board that exhibits this flaw is the riskiest type of board for the CEO to face, because it is just a step away from firing the CEO.

No External Product/Market Review

Although the company's product/technology should routinely be subject to outside review as the start-up develops its business, this may not be occurring because of such factors as (1) an uninformed or inexperienced board, (2) the lack of a technology advisory board (TAB) or customer advisory board (CAB), or (3) operational negligence on the part of the CEO and his or her team.

Every company needs an appropriate review mechanism to help direct its efforts. In the case of an established firm, customers automatically provide such a review through the marketplace. In contrast, a start-up is like a newly launched missile, in that it must first be aimed in the right general direction and its trajectory must then be continually corrected in midcourse if it is to reach the intended destination. If board meetings are held only sporadically and communication with the board is erratic and ad hoc, the board is typically out of control.

BOARD OF DIRECTORS RULES

A formal board of directors is usually established with the first round of investment. Although investors will naturally want to make sure the company is in control and help it achieve its goals, granting board membership to inexperienced investors (or to any other inexperienced individuals) won't help the firm in the long run.

During the seed stage, the board should be structured to review the start-up's product and market plans in order to provide advice that will ensure the birth of a healthy company. A customer or technical advisory board should also be established during this stage.

The following are the key questions that the start-up must address in setting up its board of directors and its CAB or TAB.

Have board members with expertise in the key strategic areas outlined in the business plan been identified to serve during the seed stage and later stages?

Although it is inappropriate to have a full-scale board of directors during the concept stage, the company's founders should have some idea of whom they would like and should have approached these individuals as the funding is finalized. During the seed stage, the board will no doubt be composed of the two or three founders and one or two investors. Since the goal of the seed stage is to reduce risk and plan the start-up, it is worth having this critical sounding board to weigh ideas about the start-up's future direction.

During the concept stage, formal technology advisory and customer advisory boards are probably inappropriate. However, if the company is entering an area where the technological risks are especially high or where certain critical strategic partnerships must be formed as part of the start-up process, it is prudent for it to be working with a small group of key outsiders who will ultimately advise and assist the firm during the seed stage and later stages.

Is a technology and/or customer advisory board in place by the end of the seed stage?

This rule about having a functioning technology and/or customer advisory board by the end of the seed stage is related to the preceding rule about having identified potential board members with expertise in key strategic areas. It is becoming increasingly common for start-ups to have a TAB and/or a CAB composed of experts who understand the technology and advise the company on the formation of the development team, reviewing the status of the technology and the competitiveness of the proposed products. I recommend a single board composed of both builders and users that meets regularly and whose members play an active role in advising the firm, including serving as paid consultants.

The CEO must attend TAB meetings because they perform a critical review function and provide feedback that the start-up may not get in any other fashion, since its potential customers are often unwilling to tell the company's marketing staff the truth about their products. Also, the market input may get garbled as it passes through various individuals who are grinding their own axes and who may be unable to communicate effectively with engineering. A TAB should be free to conduct its critical review of the company's technical and applications directions without restrictions that may hamper its effectiveness. No topic should be off-limits, including how the firm designs products, to whom it sells, or how it conducts its business.

By the end of the seed stage, does the board include members who have appropriate operational experience related to product and market development in addition to the investor representatives?

At the seed stage, the board is likely to be overstaffed with investors whose only function is to keep an eye on their money. An ideal board would contain no more than two investors, the CEO, and one or two outsiders. The two investors should have previous operational experience in related businesses. The outsiders should have experience in the product, service, or market area and should have invested enough through sweat or equity to ensure that they are involved and concerned.

In 1990, most venture capital companies are staffed with people who have had successful operational experience. This reflects a change in the composition of these firms that occurred in response to the often-expressed criticism that they were staffed with fresh MBAs who had no previous experience in operations or in the industry. Although being lucky in a few previous deals is a necessary prerequisite, it is not in itself a sufficient qualification.

CONCLUSION

The CEO of a new start-up was lamenting to his board about the difficulty of hiring. A wise venture capitalist advised: "It's not only hard; it's your only job, because if you are successful, everything else is easy." The top-level people—the CEO, the team responsible for carrying out the major functions, and the board of directors—constitute the start-up's three most important dimensions.

The CEO establishes the standards for the company and serves as its team leader. The vice presidents for engineering, manufacturing, marketing, and sales are the "CEOs" for their respective functions. This top level of management must operate as an integrated team and "drive" the organization to achieve its business plan and establish a healthy company culture. The CEO reports to the board of directors, where the ultimate fiduciary responsibility for the venture rests. In the ideal firm, the board merely helps and advises the CEO and company rather than participating actively in the start-up's management.

Chapter 3

THE BUSINESS PLAN: A ROAD MAP AND A SCORECARD FOR THE FUTURE

The dream is what I look for more than anything else.
—Matsuda-san, Kubota Limited

Investors usually take the advice given in Chapter 2 and study the people associated with a proposed company very carefully before making a commitment, since they realize that a great team with a great product can recover from substantial adversity, including the setbacks caused by a faulty business plan. This is not to say that a great team and a great product don't need a great business plan, however, because the plan serves both as a road map for guiding the company's current operations and as a scorecard for subsequently determining how well those operations met their objectives.

The business plan serves many critical purposes. It is:

- A set of guidelines for operating the company

- The standard of record against which the firm expects its results to be measured

- A sales brochure directed at potential investors (although the downside and the risks the company faces must also be covered)

- A place where the founders can describe their vision for the firm

Because of the unlimited range of technologies and market approaches that a start-up can employ in creating a market and a company, there are no hard-and-fast rules governing the size, creation, and contents of a business plan. Experience shows, however, that short plans (ten to thirty-five pages) are better than long plans. Short plans are easier for potential investors to read and comprehend, since significant points are made quickly and succinctly and can be readily understood within the context of the overall plan. Furthermore, because it is quite difficult to create a good short plan, the process of doing so forces the entrepreneur and his or her team to think in an organized way. Entrepreneurs who are unable to make a case for their proposed new venture within a handful of pages need to do more homework. Finally, unless a plan is short, it cannot be easily referenced and updated as a working document.

The business plans written by Bill Poduska—a founder of Prime, Apollo, Stellar, and Stardent—have all been short and successful. In 1983, he offered the following format for a successful business plan containing no more than ten pages:

- *Summary* (one page).

- *Market brief:* Who will buy and why—characterized as a new or existing product type, for a new or existing market. (Poduska favors a new product for an existing market.)

- *Product brief:* The what, why, and how of building the product.

- *People:* The who of building the product, the rule being to use only grade-A, experienced individuals.

- *Financial projections:* Both a statement of a practical strategy that can yield high, yet realizable returns and a tool that can be used as the operational yardstick.

In many ways, the ability of a CEO and his or her top-level group to write a good business plan is the first test of their ability to function as a team and to run their proposed company successfully. If a firm's founding CEO can't understand, build, and operate the financial model for the company's business, he or she should not be the CEO. If the team has trouble writing a simple business plan, which is the first step in running a business, then it's quite likely they won't be able to make any plans, and they should give up the idea of starting a company until they get their act together (which may mean forming a different team).

Despite the importance of a good business plan, a few companies have managed to become successful without the benefit of such a plan. For example, Gateway (discussed in Chapter 11) succeeded with no written plan. In some circumstances, individual entrepreneurs can also get away without a business plan. I recently advised an engineer who had a working product prototype to simply make a data sheet, price the product at four times his cost, and then sell a few to see how users like the product. If the results seem promising, he should then get a partner who can handle the business aspects of founding a company.

Early in the planning process (i.e., at the concept stage), the company needs a financial model that makes sense, showing how it can become profitable and stay profitable. This model of the profit and loss statement, balance sheet, and cash flow is just as important as the plan for designing and selling the product. Founders should "hang it up" right at this point if they see no way to create a viable model based on reasonable assumptions about costs, prices, and market sizes, because the initial business model is probably the most optimistic one the company will ever have.

Surprisingly few variables drive the financial model. The key ones are:

- Fixed assets and overhead costs, such as rent, telephones, and equipment

- Variable costs based on head count, together with associated overhead (e.g., equipment, insurance, travel), for the fixed components of the organization—research and development, manufacturing, marketing, sales, and administration

- Variable costs for manufacturing the product, including work in progress and inventory

- Average selling price, sales productivity, order-gestation time, accounts payable, and cost per salesperson

- Requirements for cash to fuel the enterprise

THE COMPANY VISION

The company's vision of its future is the most import part of the business plan. Without a dream, the firm is unlikely to excite either itself or potential investors. It should be possible to state the vision with equal facility in a single sentence, a paragraph, or a slide show; the vision should be articulated in the plan; and finally, it should be embodied in the product or demo. At each level, more should be revealed so that investors, customers, and the press maintain their interest in the product and want to see even more. For example, Ardent has a demo of its graphics supercomputer that displays a simulated American flag waving in the breeze. The resolution and clarity of the demo's graphics prove that the supercomputer is fully capable of delivering the 100 million floating point operations per second that the simulation requires.

Digital's "VAX strategy," which guided the company throughout the 1980s, is an example of a simple, yet powerful vision offered by an established firm:

> Provide a set of homogeneous, distributed-computing-system products based on the VAX-11 so that a user can interface, store information, and compute, without reprogramming or extra work from the following computer sizes and styles:
>
> - via [a cluster of] large, central (mainframe) computers or networks;
>
> - at local, shared departmental/group/team (mini) computers [and evolving to PC clusters];
>
> - with interfaces to other manufacturers and industry standard information processing systems; and
>
> - all interconnected via the local area Network Interconnect [Ethernet] in a single area, with the ability of interconnecting the Local Area Networks (LANs) to form Campus Area and Wide Area Networks.

The essence of the strategy was described in just a single page, and the entire document (including the rationale and details) was only seven pages long. The detailed plan was updated annually to reflect the tactics needed to respond to changes in the marketplace and technology. The plan's simplicity enabled over a hundred thousand employees and customers to understand and support the company's effort.

BUSINESS PLAN FORMATS

All recommended formats for business plans include Bill Poduska's five components, listed earlier in the chapter: summary, market, product, people, and financial projections.

Beyond these basic components, various authors recommend specific options and structures. Gladstone (1988), for example, presents a strong argument for starting with a capsule presentation (i.e., a summary), followed by a section entitled "The Business and Its Future." This section is probably the most extensive, because it covers such topics as the nature of the business, history and future, uniqueness, product/service, customers, industry and market, competition, marketing, production, labor force and employees, subcontractors, equipment, property and facilities, patents and trademarks, research and development, litigation, government regulation, conflicts of interest, backlog, insurance, taxes, corporate structure, and detailed résumés. Gladstone also recommends separate sections describing the financing, risk factors, return on investment, and exit (how the investors obtain liquidity).

White (1977) presents a number of heuristics about generating a quality plan that will pass seven hurdles in the funding, from initial evaluation to financial evaluation and final negotiation. He recommends that the plan include sections on the history of the start-up, its manufacturing methods, quality assurance and reliability, money-leveraging strategies, proposed distribution of ownership, and founders' stock incentives. He also suggests an extensive set of appendixes that examine how the proposed company will be managed, including the use of management by objectives.

Nesheim (1988) proposes two more sections (in addition to Poduska's five)— one dealing specifically with strategy and milestones and the other dealing with operations, including engineering, manufacturing, finance, and administration.

BizPlanBuilder (JIAN, 1988) is a ten-point format that can be run on a PC or a Macintosh. It provides a plan outline that anyone can build on directly simply by editing the plan file, filling in the answers to critical questions, and completing a spreadsheet. BizPlanBuilder's ten points supplement Poduska's format by adding situation audit, objectives, and manufacturing sections; separating the topic of marketing into two subtopics: analysis and strategy; and ending with a summary. Although BizPlanBuilder is more suitable for lower-tech companies, its usefulness can be expanded by adding a product development section. With this tool and pruning, an author can develop a twenty-five- to fifty-page plan (not including financials and appendixes). BizPlanBuilder can also be used to check any business plan and make sure it covers all vital areas.

Content is the key to a good business plan, regardless of whether that content is prepared manually or with the assistance of a spreadsheet program. Venture capitalists rightfully complain about the quality of writing in plans. Thus, a plan should be written so clearly that any of your friends or relatives who don't work in the high-tech field could easily understand it. Authors should not be lulled into complacency by the nifty presentation possibilities of desktop publishing, spreadsheets, and graphics. Venture capitalists and funders will not grade the plan according to its thickness or sparseness, according to its flashiness, or according to whether all possible questions (even irrelevant ones) have been answered. They will grade a plan according to its integrity and the ability of the company's founders to back up absolutely every statement made in the plan.

SUCCESSFUL PLANS

Having gone to considerable lengths to describe model formats for drafting business plans, I must admit that all three of the successful plans discussed below differ from the models in certain respects. However, they all show major elements of the model formats, and they demonstrate the variety of approaches that can prove successful.

THE APOLLO BUSINESS PLAN (JANUARY 8, 1980)

Figure 3-1 shows Bill Poduska's business plan for Apollo (referred to as "Nuco" in the figure). In addition to the summary, market brief, product brief, and people brief, over half of the handwritten document (six pages) consisted of a five-year financial plan. The financial section included such information as the projected profits and losses, a proposed balance sheet, and the scheduled head count (the key cost-control item in a start-up). The financial plan was used as a blueprint throughout the self-funded seed stage, while the three key technical founders worked on the product concept. Four months after the business plan was written, the first round of funding closed, having raised $1.6 million, which represented 60 percent of the value of the company. The Apollo business plan was brief because it assumed readers would be completely familiar with the computer marketplace and understand what is required for development. The plan was thus designed to convince both founders and funders of the company's viability. It contained no near-term milestones (which is at variance with the recommendations made earlier in the chapter), only the first ship date. No other plan was made.

Nuco is formed to create a Profitable, Major Computer Company which Manufactures and Sells, High-Technology, Low Price Computer Systems.

- *Profitable* means 20% Pretax and 10% After-Tax.

- *Major* means $50 million in 5 years, poised to grow to $1 billion in an orderly way.

- *Manufacture and Sell* includes Design, Fabrication, Direct Sales and Distribution, Installation, and Service—Nuco will sell both hardware and software.

- *High-Technology* means the explosive technology of the 1980's including LSI Processors, Large Memory Systems, Extensive Mass Storage, Highly Interactive Human Interface, and High-Bandwidth Network for Distributed Data Processing.

(continued)

(continued)
- *Low Price* means under $20,000 for a Personal Computer System to $70,000 for a Central Computer System.

II. *Overview of The Business Plan*

A. *Marketplace*

The *Marketplace* for Nuco is the community of users who now use Time Shared Systems. These users want and demand high levels of performance, functionality, and interaction in order to increase human productivity. But the era of Time-Sharing is ending. With the rapid decline in the cost of computer hardware, it is no longer necessary to share the cost of a large computer among many users, who then suffer the inevitable delays and poor response of a shared system. The future will be dominated by powerful Personal Computer Systems designed to maximize individual productivity. These systems will be integrated into a unified, but distributed computing system by a high-bandwidth network. This Network will also include Central Computer Systems which provide great computing power as well as support for large central files, and sharing of expensive peripherals.

B. *Product*

The *Product Line* consists of two basic product systems: 1. a Personal Computer System and 2. a Central Computer System. A typical installation would have several PCS systems in a network, roughly one per computer professional. A larger system might have one or more CCS systems attached for greater throughput.

Recent advances in computer technology now make such systems economically feasible. The most important of these advances are:

1. LSI Processors: Both Custom Gate-Array LSI and Standard 16/32 bit Processors and Peripherals.

2. 64K RAM: Making extensive Local Storage Practical.

3. Fixed Media Disk: Winchester Technology making 30-60 MB of Mass Storage per PCS Economically Feasible.

4. UNIX et al.: Software Technology to Provide Highly Interactive User Oriented Services.

5. Network Technology: High Speed Local Networking to Distribute the Resources while Maintaining a Community of Users.

The Technology Advances have not gradually emerged but are dramatically coming available in the period mid-1980 to mid-1981. Thus the timing of this Venture is most appropriate and Nuco could achieve a dominant position in the marketplace.

C. *Business Plan*

The *Business Plan* is structured to rapidly enter the marketplace and to grow to a volume of $50 million in year 5. The Model Plan has the following salient characteristics:

Yr	Rev.	Earn's	Paid in cap.	Comments
1	000	-900	1694	Design Products, Build Organization
2	2060	-1339	3574	Build Sales Rapidly, Continue Product Development
3	8230	-240	7129	Build Volume, Breakeven Q4, Public Offering
4	21666	2547	7189	Build Profits, Sustain Volume, Reduce Costs
5	53164	6509	7239	Sustain Growth and Profit Rates, Introduce 2nd Generation Products

The *Marketing Organization* is structured for very rapid growth in Year-2 and will continue to operate a high expense level. Promotion and Merchandizing of the product are crucial to reaching such a vigorous marketplace and will be heavily funded. Expectations are that 65% to 75% of sales will be generated by a direct commissioned sales force, and about 25% to 35% [of] sales will be generated by distributors, dealers and/or representative[s]. European Sales operations will be initiated early and will account for 20% to 30% of sales in Year-2. Software OEM [original equipment manufacturer] buyers; i.e.

(continued)

(continued)

companies which buy Nuco products, add software, and resell; may become an important sales mechanism. Field Engineering and Service are part of the Marketing function to insure rapid response to customer needs.

D.   *Financial Plan*

The *Financial Plan* for Nuco is to finance the rapid growth of the business by Equity and limited Debt. The Model Plan calls for investments of $3.0 to $3.5 million in the first two years, and a Public Offering . . . in the third year. The Venture Capital is to be raised in several steps with one or two lead investors in the beginning. Additional rounds of financing are planned every 6-9 months which will include up to six additional investing firms.

Founders and early employees will be offered stock purchases at very attractive prices. Such stock will vest to the employee over a four or five year period prorated quarterly. Some founders and board members may also participate in early rounds of financing on an equal basis with the investing companies. The Model Plan uses debt sparingly in the first several years in anticipation of forbidding[ly] high interest rates. However, debt may be used more aggressively with favorable conditions up to about a 1:1 Debt/Equity ratio.

Figure 3-1.   The Apollo (Nuco) Business Plan. (Reprinted with permission from Bill Poduska.)

SUN MICROSYSTEMS SEED PLAN (FEBRUARY 12, 1982)

An outline of the six-page Sun Microsystems seed plan is shown in Figure 3-2. This plan is interesting because it is, in principle, exactly in line with the idea of a seed stage business plan. Using this plan and seed stage funding, the company went directly to break-even within a few months. One element of the plan is unusual, however—namely, the fact that the first product marketed was a university "laboratory product" (from Stanford).

AUTODESK

The Autodesk File (Walker, 1987) contains Walker's first working paper proposing the company in January 1982 as well as other key documents covering until 1988. Autodesk was funded ($59,030) by its founders, a group of talented programmers who built applications programs and marketed them through retail dealers whom

Mission statement: "Develop, manufacture, market, and support graphics workstations for the OEM CAD/CAM marketplace. Evolve a family of compatible graphics workstations. Maintain lead with the best cost/performance product on the market."

Objectives for four months: "Take current laboratory product to market, begin to develop [a] workstation, assemble [a] team, build a plan, and obtain financing."

Tentative two-year plan.

Product: The Sun workstation, including key competitive advantages. (This section also covered standards and current availability.)

Market: OEM workstations.

Summary of marketing approach.

Competitors.

Patents and other rights.

Current team.

Appendix A: Costs.

Appendix B: Financial requirements until May 1982.

Appendix C: All the tasks, with dates and resources.

Appendix D: Staffing for sixteen months.

Figure 3-2. Outline of the Sun Microsystems Plan. (Reprinted with permission from Vinod Khosla.)

they knew. The company vision was that a PC revolution would occur and that this group would simply capitalize on it. One of the firm's first products was AutoCAD, a program for architectural and engineering design. One of the founders' major goals was for the venture to be profitable from the start, and Autodesk did essentially achieve profitability during its first year of operation. When Autodesk went public in June 1985, each $1 initially invested was worth $165, and in mid-1990, the firm's value was over $1 billion. Given Autodesk's success, and the orderly but unorthodox way in which the company was started and funded, readers are urged to study Walker's book and to be equally creative.

BUSINESS PLAN FLAWS

The company's business plan is important because it is used in such a variety of ways—as everything from an informal contract to the ultimate scorecard. The plan's main purpose is to serve as a blueprint for operating the firm (Chapter 4 discusses how the plan is used as a control mechanism).

There are many reasons why entrepreneurs feel compelled to write unattainable plans. In some cases, the firm is attempting to pander to the greed of potential investors and ends up producing a plan that is not only immoral but also potentially illegal. In other cases, the company is simply fooling itself and its investors through ignorance and incompetence. Hence, one of the most serious flaws is to start a venture by accepting major product development financing without having an adequate development plan—a plan that could have been written had the company taken the time for a seed stage.

The following subsections present some common plan-related flaws and describe a number of classic cases of flawed firms whose difficulties stemmed from poor business plans.

UNREALISTIC PLANS

Proceeding according to an unrealistic plan is one of the greatest risks a start-up company can take. Two frequent causes of unrealistic plans are investor greed and technology miscalculation.

Start-ups often prepare absurdly aggressive and optimistic plans, which have a very low likelihood of success, just to maximize the company's perceived dollar value. In succumbing to venture capitalist greed ("Show us a plan that creates a $100 million company in five years") and funding requirements ("We don't put less than $X million into a deal"), the company establishes expectations that cannot be met. In 1990, the canonical business plan projects revenues of $50 million in five years. Such "plans" are often the product of misused spreadsheet technology and venture capital funding patterns rather than being the result of careful, realistic planning by the company's founders.

Greed may continue to dominate even after a company fails to meet its initial business plan and requires additional funds. In such cases, the plan is often revised to project even higher revenues, in order to prevent the firm's valuation from being lowered. This spiral continues, with accelerating expectations, until the funders at last tire. When the funders do tire, the valuation is finally corrected for the next funding round, and the organization and its management are restructured to operate at a substantially reduced scale.

Table 3-1. Example of Company Valuation at Variance with Actual Performance.

Round	Price/Share [a]	No. of Shares [c]	$s/Round [b]	Company Valuation [b]	Total Raised [b]
12/83	0.3300	0.42	0.140	0.14	0.14
7/84	1.0000	7.70	7.700	—	—
common	0.0100	2.60	0.026	10.70	7.90
9/86	2.0000	3.20	6.400	29.80	14.30
3/88	0.3000	10.80	3.200	8.00	17.50
8/89	0.0750	20.00	1.300	4.20	18.80
7/90	0.0125	240.00	3.000	3.70	21.80

[a] In dollars.
[b] In millions of dollars.
[c] In millions.

I speak from firsthand experience, since I once invested in a company whose operations aptly illustrate the spiral-of-accelerating-expectations scenario. This firm, whose funding history is shown in Table 3-1, was even backed by a foreign government.

Table 3-1 illustrates a typical case of a company's valuation getting out of line with its actual performance. The price of the stock rose initially, while the firm developed its technology and first product, led by the founding president, a technologist. The second president, a former CEO, was then brought in to run the company "professionally." He was able to sell stock at $2 a share and proceeded to spend the company's funds by buying another firm and investing in several products that were orthogonal to the primary venture's technology, marketing and sales expertise, and general business. The third president operated a demoralized and disorganized firm for two years while the original product slowly gained market acceptance.

In 1989, one of the company's venture capitalists took over as president, reduced expenses to a minimum, and delegated responsibility for planning and operations. Finally, the firm started selling in sufficient volume to attain profitability. The plan on which the July 1990 funds were raised was to finally become profitable and then sell the much-devalued company for several tens of millions of dollars, thereby allowing the last round of patient (or foolish) investors to attempt to make a severalfold return in order to rapidly recoup their original investment.

Although the company was founded during a period of bountiful capital, common sense would rule out a venture that required multisite international operations from the outset. What looked like a sure money maker—with compelling technology and engineering, backed by government funding, and having a built-in home custom market—was derailed by the existence of too many agendas (multisite international operations, custom and standard products, doing research contracts) and other management-related factors. The early investors' stake was diluted by the fact that they did not continue investing in the company in the final financing rounds. The early founding employees (common stockholders) have negligible equity except through common stock that was issued in the final round. Despite these shortcomings, however, the firm did have sound technology and a viable product.

DOING RESEARCH AND CALLING IT PRODUCT DEVELOPMENT

Figure 3-3 is derived from the financial data of a company that was formed in the early 1980s to build a human input device. The figure compares the actual operating revenue (the plain in the foreground), which rose to nearly $6 million per year during the first four years, to the ever-increasing mountain range of plans in the background, which represents the firm's dreams for its sales. The first two-year plan projected sales of over $10 million, even though market forecasts in the 1980s (still unrealized in the early 1990s) for the product showed sales in the billions of dollars. The second and third plans, which enabled $15 million to be raised, projected $40 million in revenue. Finally, in order to make the last two financings of over $11 million, projections of more than $50 million in sales were required. Altogether, $38 million was raised over a period of seven years. The question the company still faces is, if and when the technology matures to the point where it can serve a large market, will the firm be able to respond, or will some other competitor, such as IBM, come in and take it all?

More recently, a new company announced its intention of introducing a computer that accepts handwritten input. The questions associated with its product/market viability are exactly the same as those for the firm shown in Figure 3-3: (1) can the company be kept under control while its product is sold to an infant market willing to pay high prices for a new technology product, and (2) will the required technology mature rapidly enough for the product to decline in price sufficiently to make it attractive to a broad, general market?

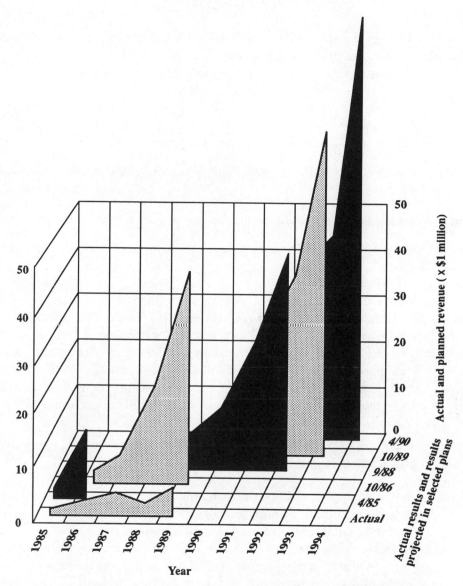

Figure 3-3. From the Plain of Revenue Reality to the Mountains of Dream Plans.

LOSING TOUCH WITH REALITY

A plan contains both a spending stream (reality) and a revenue stream (a desire). When the two streams diverge significantly, a new plan is needed. Here are a few popular rationalizations for why the two streams may have diverged:

- "All our expenses are on plan. We do have a 'top-line' problem, however." (When a company fails to meet its revenue plan while proceeding with its expense plan, the difference shows up immediately on the bottom line.)

- "We're selling the right quantities, but the discounts are much higher than expected."

- "We're selling and people are buying, but we still can't produce the product."

- "We've met our hiring and spending plan, but the product still isn't quite ready to ship."

The common thread running through all these rationalizations is the (mis)belief that the plan is more real than the tangible results. This form of dishonesty occurs when the company refuses to face the facts that it sees in hiring, schedules, costs, sales, etc.; believes that the plan is reality; and views the actual facts as anomalies (expressed by parentheses or minus signs) that will eventually go away. The frequent result is that the CEO and board refuse to create a new plan, and the company goes blissfully on, runs out of money, and returns to the investors with an even more aggressive plan, as shown in Figure 3-3.

LACK OF A SUSTAINING TECHNOLOGY OR PRODUCT

The most common flaw of a high-tech business plan is to center the plan on a "one-shot" technology or product, without providing for subsequent products. Such a plan may be able to validly project a market victory for the first product, but it has no enduring vision for the company and no strategy for how the company will win in the long term. A firm has no lasting advantage if it is based on a transient product or on a distribution scheme designed simply to fill a niche left by a dominant supplier.

When integrated circuits first appeared on the market in the 1960s, a huge number of minicomputer ventures sprang up, ready to do battle with the existing suppliers, pinning their hopes on their first (and only) product. A majority suffered from the lack-of-sustaining-technology flaw and failed. A similar situation has occurred more recently, with the first computers that utilize RISC (reduced instruction set computer) technology. In this case, companies have formed to exploit a particular technology in an existing, filled marketplace where all the players are ultimately likely to catch up, and have been doing so.

The lack-of-sustaining-technology flaw is also discussed in Chapter 5 ("Technology and Engineering"), Chapter 6 ("The Technology Balance Sheet"), and Chapter 8 ("The Product"), since it is also a technology flaw and can cause a flawed product idea, thereby resulting in the creation of a flawed company.

QUESTIONABLE MOTIVATION

Business plans flawed by questionable motivation (and no product vision) are written by:

- Chronic entrepreneurs who start many companies but do not build organizations that last

- Entrepreneurs who start a company to "get even" with a competitor (usually a former employer)

- Entrepreneurs who want produce a *perfect* "Product X" in a field of fifty companies that already build a "Product X"

Most business plans exhibiting the questionable-motivation flaw result from a need to satisfy the ego and personal desires of the founder(s). Chronic entrepreneurs enjoy starting ventures but lack the determination to stay with a small firm and nurture it into a larger, healthier, and more successful one. These people get high on the rush of excitement associated with any start-up, including that of a hot dog stand. Although they can be useful in the start-up process, they are unlikely to build the infrastructure of a lasting company. Another questionable, but nonetheless frequently observed, motivation is to start a firm in order to compete against a former employer. In such cases, revenge rather than vision is the driving force, and failure is the usual result. The third questionable motivation, perhaps the most common of all, is a form of technical arrogance—the not-invented-here syndrome. In this scenario, engineers enter a crowded field to build an incrementally better product. Naive arrogance of this sort accounts for most start-up failures, including the failure of many of the one hundred firms that were founded to build minicomputers.

SKIPPING THE SEED STAGE

Skipping the seed stage could be called a "lack-of-refinement" flaw. By rushing into the product development stage without a seed stage business plan, the company is relying completely on the untested assumptions made in the concept stage business plan. Because its plan lacks the refinements normally incorporated during the seed stage, the firm faces higher market and development risks. The results are usually the same: it costs more, takes longer, and requires more resources to market the product (which may then fail the market test). Skipping the seed stage is especially apt to be fatal if the founders haven't done a similar product before and the proposed product involves a significant amount of development that relies on several technological breakthroughs.

MULTIPLE AGENDAS

During the operation of a company, new ideas frequently emerge, and the firm may allocate resources to these new endeavors. If the new endeavors are outside the main thrust of the company's principal business, even a well-established organization may run into trouble. For example, in the 1970s, Control Data Corporation (CDC) acquired a wide range of businesses to become a conglomerate. It also tried to reform education by investing hundreds of millions of dollars in the development of the Plato Computer Aided Instruction system at the University of Illinois, operated inner-city factories, and promoted trade with Russia to fight the cold war. It even had a hydroponic garden on one of its buildings. These multiple agendas eventually had an adverse effect upon CDC's core business—computers.

For a start-up, the pursuit of multiple agendas is particularly troublesome, since it spreads the fledgling firm's already-thin resources even thinner. Start-ups cannot afford to try to become conglomerates. Furthermore, a start-up that follows "other trails" after creating the seed stage business plan is usually on morally and legally shaky ground, because that plan is a contract that the company has made with its investors.

TWO OR MORE START-UPS IN ONE

Most successful ventures began with one idea and product: Intel with memory chips, Microsoft with a Basic compiler for Altair, Apple with a home computer board, NCR with cash registers. Divisionalization and a multiplicity of products came *after* profitability and established success.

An organization founded to conduct two parallel and independent projects, each of which might in itself be the basis for a company, faces a high probability of failure. In effect, two start-ups are being managed under the umbrella of one firm. Such a plan is predicated on greed and a naive misunderstanding of the difficulty of starting a company. For one thing, two projects usually cost just about twice as much as one. For another thing, redundancy does not result in a lowering of the company's risk. In fact, dual projects involve considerably more than twice the risk (the risk may be as much as the square of the number of projects per firm).

The multiple-start-ups flaw can manifest itself in either of two ways:

- The company may engage in top-down, or backward, integration as a system supplier to reduce product cost before a business exists. For example, the firm may attempt to develop all the components that it could buy and therefore be unable to concentrate on what it intends to sell.

- The company may engage in bottom-up, or forward, integration from a component technology. For example, the firm may have a new and unique component whose sale could be the basis for a successful company, but the firm tries instead to capture the "whole market" by using the component to make systems.

An interesting example of a company exhibiting the top-down, or backward-integrating, flaw was Cydrome.

Cydrome.   Cydrome was formed in 1983 and produced an impressive minisupercomputer that exploited parallelism by executing several instructions at once. The computer consisted of a numeric portion and a UNIX front end (for communicating with users, networks, and managed files). The front end was similar to UNIX-based multiprocessors available from Arete, Encore, and Sequent. As a founder of Encore, I attempted to convince Cydrome to use an Encore computer for the firm's front end, because it could save time and about $15 million in development costs by doing so. However, Cydrome's management felt that the Encore machine was too costly and that Cydrome could make contributions in front-end design.

Development of the numeric part went well, but the front end was late and proved to be more costly than anticipated, causing the total system to be late and less competitive. Thus, Cydrome exhibited the classic top-down, or backward-integrating, flaw by devoting resources to developing something the company could have bought rather than concentrating on its principal field of expertise, which was the numeric portion of the machine. Unfortunately, the flaw was fatal, since Cydrome folded after five years.

A good example of the bottom-up, or forward-integrating, flaw can be seen in the case of Vitesse.

Vitesse.   Vitesse began as a manufacturer of gallium arsenide (GaAs) circuits, for which a small market existed. Vitesse then funded the development of a computer to exploit the circuits it had developed. When problems arose with GaAs circuits in terms of cost, size, and availability, the computer division switched to complementary metal oxide semiconductor (CMOS) technology. Fortunately, the firm recognized its mistake in time, closed the computer division, and switched back to its roots, manufacturing GaAs semiconductor parts.

A third example of the multiple-start-ups flaw is Modular Advanced Design, a company that exhibited some elements of both bottom-up, or forward, integration and top-down, or backward, integration.

Modular Advanced Design (MAD) Intelligent Systems.   MAD is a Silicon Valley start-up funded to build a workstation that would use rule-based systems to access knowledge bases and databases. It began by building (rather than purchasing) an ordinary PC as its workstation base. It then implemented a new (rather than an existing) version of LISP, which it integrated with its own design for a database. Finally, it built the shell, a rule interpreter, which it considered to be its proprietary and unique technology.

Having thus exhibited the top-down, or backward-integrating, flaw by developing components that it could have bought, MAD then proceeded to exhibit the bottom-up, or forward-integrating, flaw by trying to use its unique component (the rule interpreter) to make systems and thereby capture the "whole market." To take the product into a variety of markets, MAD had to build operational prototypes of several applications, a very expensive and resource-draining process. In 1990, the company is selling financial-services software products written in C.

Although a company that concentrates on what it does well may start smaller, the likelihood of its success will be four times greater than for the company that tries to do everything. When Digital Equipment Corporation was funded in 1957 with $70,000 from American Research and Development, for 70 percent ownership of the firm, its plan was to start by developing transistorized digital modules and eventually develop computers. In the first year, it was profitable based on sales of the modules. In 1960, it introduced a computer that used the modules.

As readers will see in the following examples of MIPS and VPL, it is possible to avoid both the multiple-start-up and the one-shot-technology/product flaws by going deeply into technology, and it is also possible to develop and maintain the technology base by establishing partnerships with other companies. But as the Gyration example will illustrate, such a plan is not easy to sell to investors because it implies a lack of focus.

MIPS Computer Systems, Inc.   MIPS was successful because it developed RISC-technology microprocessor chips on which to base its computer board and system products. MIPS knew that making a great computer meant starting with the silicon and having the best chips, unlike the first RISC companies—Pyramid (now a MIPS customer) and Ridge (defunct). In 1985, MIPS initially designed and sold chips, boards, and systems. By 1988, it was no longer selling chips but instead licensed chip designs to semiconductor companies for a license and royalty fee. By 1990, it became a supplier of systems and applications software that it and third-party software suppliers created. In this way, MIPS users had a single standard, providing a large market for software suppliers.

VPL. VPL started up to build a "virtual-reality" system that allows a user wearing a special helmet with displays for each eye to "walk through" a three-dimensional space. Navigation is controlled by head movement and by a special glove. The company needed a program for displaying a 3-D space, so it wrote Swivel 3D and licensed it to Paracomp. In the short term, the market for Swivel 3D is substantially larger than for any virtual-reality product. VPL also designed a simplified glove for Nintendo games. Although the helmet and glove are sold as components, the vision for the company is still to create a virtual-reality system.

Gyration.   Gyration started up to make a 3-D pointing device—in essence, a 3-D mouse (perhaps it might be termed a "bat"). The founder, a successful entrepreneur, hired a graduate fresh out of Stanford who invented a revolutionary gyroscope. Their patented invention reduces both the cost and size of gyros by large factors while increasing their accuracy and stability. The company has both the need and the opportunity to become a significant gyro manufacturer because it has created a breakthrough component. As an enabling technology, Gyration's invention could replace many existing gyros, and it could form the basis for fundamental new products such as television remote controllers, 3-D pointers, and controllers for industrial manipulators, mobile robots, and vehicle navigation units.

In the summer of 1990, the venture capital community was reluctant to fund Gyration, however, because every venture capitalist knows that software is "in" and that all low-cost, volume-produced products have to be designed and manufactured in Japan. The venture capital community offered Gyration the following recommendations, despite the fact that, paradoxically, it is also unwilling to fund the proposed course of action:

- First, the venture capital community urged an initial, unlikely plan under which the company would build and sell computer pointing devices—a potential, but currently nonexistent future market that no one can prove will actually materialize. In fact, at this stage, companies should focus on only one application.

- Second, it ruled out other, equally feasible product applications areas because companies producing components are even less in vogue than companies entering new markets. Conventional wisdom says that components sell at a lower price and have a diffuse market.

Under the second operational plan, Gyration will prove the efficacy of its technology by building the pointing device product while at the same time selling gyros for every potential new application. American military vendors, who want and need a gyro (e.g., for use in low-cost, small, smart missiles) are too bureaucratic to allow themselves to invest in or use the new technology. Meanwhile, Japanese component and system suppliers are happy to fund the company and to get the rights to build small, accurate, inexpensive gyroscopes.

Gyration intends to make both the technology and the company successful. In the process, the country and infrastructure that supported Gyration's invention may reap none of the rewards—except through products purchased from foreign firms. A sad, but typical scenario. Stay tuned for further developments.

BUSINESS PLAN RULES

Although there are stories of business plans being written while entrepreneurs are part of another organization, this is not the norm. Furthermore, writing a plan while one is part of another organization is immoral and potentially illegal, and should never be done!

Another warning: Although investors and other reviewers may sign nondisclosure statements, a start-up's business plan will nonetheless end up as a public document and will be seen both by its traditional competitors and by others who are starting up with similar ideas. Therefore, the founders should avoid including excessively detailed and critical information about development schedules, stockholders, budgets, market projections, marketing approach, proprietary products, or proprietary processes. Such details can be presented verbally on a "need-to-know" basis in the course of the due-diligence process.

In the case of successful companies, a small core of founders leave their jobs and write a complete business plan on a full-time basis. Finishing the plan typically takes from three to twelve months, depending on technology, market uncertainty, complexity of the product, and complexity of the manufacturing processes. To determine whether they have written an effective concept stage business plan, the founders should ask themselves the following question:

Is the plan's summary of technology, product, market, and formal business plan development short (six to ten pages, excluding appendixes), and does it contain the following elements?

- **Statement of the proposed company's vision, mission, and business**

- Product concept (what the product is)

- Technological uniqueness that will sustain the firm beyond the initial product

- Rationale (why people will buy)

- Gross estimates of the target market (who will buy)

- Simple "market map" (how the product will be sold)

- Plan for reaching the seed stage, with objectives and milestones

- Outline of a financial plan for the company

- Resources, in terms of dollars and people

All nine parts of this question must be answered, and the answers must be detailed enough for the concept stage. Of the nine parts, the plan for reaching the seed stage is especially important, since this is fundamentally what investors are buying during the concept stage round of financing. Thus, the concept stage plan is both the first draft of a traditional business plan (which convinces investors of the company's potential) and a "plan for a plan"—i.e., a plan for the company's "real" business plan.

Near the end of the seed stage, the start-up prepares for entry into the product development stage. One of the tasks that must be accomplished at this point is to upgrade the concept stage business plan to a seed stage business plan. To determine whether they have succeeded in performing this upgrading, the founders should ask themselves the following questions:

Has the concept stage plan been updated, expanded, and confirmed as a result of the seed stage? Is the plan now twenty to thirty pages long (not counting the financial appendixes)? Does it contain the following elements?

- Statement of the proposed company's vision, mission, and business

- Product concept (what the product is)

- Technological uniqueness that will sustain the firm beyond the initial product

- Rationale (why people will buy)

- **Gross estimates of the target market (who will buy)**

- **Simple "market map" (how the product will be sold)**

- **Financial plan and details of company ownership**

- **Description of the firm's people and operating philosophy**

- **Key milestones in product development and company growth**

The first six items on this list are the same as those for the concept stage business plan, and the overall plan has a fundamentally similar format. The major difference is that earlier assumptions have now been verified, and the company should have enough information to more accurately plan the development of the product and the market.

In addition to the items on the preceding list, the founders need to ask themselves a few other questions about the seed stage business plan. Several of these questions partly overlap the items on the list but are sufficiently important to warrant examining them in greater depth.

Does the company have a formal financial plan that includes the strategy and timing of present and additional funding rounds, types of backers being sought, etc.?

To support the financial information in the business plan, the company should have a position statement about its intended method of financing and a "sketch plan" schedule of the financing requirements for the first five years.

Does the plan clearly demonstrate that the company is sustainable and verify the assumptions initially made at the concept stage? (E.g., is the technology implementable, is the engineering plan valid, and has the firm determined why customers will buy?)

Technology and market verification were carried out during the concept stage. The seed stage business plan simply has to present convincing arguments for why the company is sustainable.

Does the plan refer to a detailed plan for the next stage of the start-up (the product development stage), including a list of objectives, a schedule with milestones, and allocations of the required financial and human resources?

Although the seed stage business plan need not contain details of the product development stage, except for a few key dates (the completion times of the four phases of the product development stage), the company should have a development plan. As will be discussed in Chapters 5 and 6, the creation of a start-up company has a technology dimension in addition to the business plan dimension being discussed here. If a development plan is not available during the seed stage, both the technology and business plan dimensions of the start-up process don't measure up to the ideal.

Are the product development times, product cost, product performance, and external risks (component or process) clearly identified, and are they accounted for in the plan's funding?

A business plan should not identify risks merely so the company can tell investors that a potential problem materialized as predicted. Rather, the plan must contain adequate backups and contingency provisions to enable the firm to deal with the problems. If the company has made no plans for creatively managing the problems that will surely arise, the product introduction schedule and the product cost will be adversely affected. The inevitable result of missing the schedule and blowing the product cost is dilution of the company and reduction of market share.

At the seed stage, the founders need not state every possible risk with the rigor that is normally required in the prospectus of a company about to go public. However, they definitely must indicate all foreseeable problems that may affect the plan's outcome, if only to defend themselves against potential lawsuits.

CONCLUSION

A company must always have a single vision and a common business plan, for without this guiding focus, it will be directionless. (Imagine, for example, that instead of consistently sailing west, Columbus had asked his officers and crew each morning which way they felt like sailing that day!) Although such a plan can be changed, one and only one plan must exist at any given time, and everyone in the organization must be trying as hard as possible to carry out that plan.

The business plan serves many purposes: first, it is the document that the company uses to secure funding; second, it is the plan for operating the company; and finally, it is the yardstick against which the company is measured.

The company's vision is a statement of its image and trajectory within an industry, reflecting the essence of what it is attempting to be. Such a vision must be incredibly simple. In fact, the larger the firm grows, the simpler the vision must become. Apple, Digital, IBM, Lotus, Microsoft, and most recently, Sun Microsystems all used single product lines around which to rally resources and focus effort.

In short, the company that has a well-thought-out vision and a truly effective business plan understands the purpose of its existence and knows where it is going, how it intends to get there, and how it will demonstrate that it has accomplished what it set out to do.

Chapter 4

CASH, FINANCEABILITY, AND CONTROL

A company's financial health is determined by three factors:

- *Cash:* the funds that the firm has on hand or can obtain rapidly (i.e., in less than three months)

- *Financeability:* the company's ability to raise cash in the short term (i.e., in three months or longer) and in the long term (i.e., over the life of the firm)

- *Control:* the company's ability (going substantially beyond simple financial control) to operate according to a plan that specifies income, spending, and overall results

The following sections examine these three determinants of a start-up's financial health and present the flaws and rules applicable to each one.

CASH: FUEL TO GET TO THE NEXT MILESTONE

> Cash is more important than your mother.
> —Al Shugart

> Inadequate cash for growth is the number two killer.[1]
> —John Shoch

Cash is a crucial resource, because only cash can buy the fledgling company time to search for answers to such hard questions as: When will a viable business plan be ready? When will the technology work? When will the product work? What is the market for the product? How long will customers take to decide to buy the first product, and when will they and their colleagues buy more? When will customers pay cash for the product?

In many ways, cash and time are opposite sides of the same coin, since time sometimes "buys cash." With time, a critical problem can be solved so that a product can become operational or go from unacceptable to great. Also, with time, a customer may pay a bill, a large order can come in, or more financing can be obtained. Nearly all failed companies claim that if they had simply had more cash and had not run out of money, the venture would have worked. On the other hand, cash can also prolong the inevitable demise of ill-conceived, cash-rich firms.

Ideally, the company will at all times have more cash on hand than what is called for in the business plan—i.e., the company will be "above plan." Having adequate cash permits the firm to control the timing of its next request for financing, such that the request is made when it is in a strong negotiating position. For example, the cash available during a start-up's product development stage must last through the alpha-testing phase, so that investors will be convinced that the product is sound and will therefore regard the company's next round of investment as worthy of a higher valuation.

In contrast, lack of cash could put the company in the unenviable position of needing money immediately in order to meet its payroll. When the firm is thus pressed to the wall, its negotiating position is nil, and investors and bankers can make the price of money almost anything they want, including below the price of the previous round of financing. Sy Kaufman of Robertson Stephens, when counseling a company about the need to accelerate its funding plans, stated: "The pain caused by running out of money is just unbelievable and unbearable. Don't ever let this happen to you."

A company in the market development stage can find that lack of cash is the primary limitation on its growth and success. Banks are usually unwilling to

---

1. Lack of team is the number one killer.

provide a line of credit to unproven ventures and are unlikely to make loans against collateral that consists merely of accounts receivable and customer purchase orders. Lending money to established small businesses with a good cash flow is usually much more profitable for the banks and does not involve the risks inherent in trying to understand a complex industry. There are exceptions, however, and some banks in high-tech areas (such as the Silicon Valley Bank) are aggressive pioneers in making conventional and equity-backed loans to start-ups.

Having adequate cash and negotiating additional financing from a position of strength also permit the start-up to grow without giving up substantial ownership to the investors. Nearly all the companies with which I have been involved have pursued this goal. Unfortunately, in order to achieve this goal, the CEO and the CFO (chief financial officer) are often forced to spend almost full time looking for money, even in firms that fund their growth primarily through their existing investors.

In short, start-ups face the same financial paradox that individuals do when dealing with banks: "The only time you can borrow or raise money is when you don't need it."

CASH FLAWS

Three of the following four flaws involve a lack of cash. If the start-up doesn't have enough cash, it may be unable to get off the ground or advance to the next stage; and if an already-established company burns off its cash by being out of control, its board of directors may take over active management of the firm. The final flaw involves having too much cash, which, surprisingly enough, can also be detrimental to a start-up's health.

Inability to Pay the Founders During the Concept Stage

Perhaps the most common cash flaw a start-up can exhibit is simply having no way to support its founders while they make a creditable business plan. Thus, the fledgling organization is faced with a dilemma: a plan must be written, but the founders cannot leave their present jobs without support, nor can they write a plan while they are part of another company. The only way out of the dilemma is to have one of the founders write the plan while not working for an existing firm.

Having Inadequate Cash to Move to the Next Stage

In either the seed stage or the product development stage, the start-up may have inadequate cash to move to the next stage and demonstrate the firm's competence or efficacy. This flaw can also manifest itself at a later stage in the company's growth if it fails to deliver on its product or market development promises.

The Investor-Run Company

If the start-up's cash declines to the point where investors repeatedly have to put in more money on an emergency basis, they—rather than the CEO, CFO, and team—can end up running the firm. When this happens, investors may keep the purse strings very tight, doling out funds one phase at a time in an operational fashion and even making such decisions as when to buy parts in order to make the first prototype. This is an inherently poor way to run a company.

Having Too Much Cash

As noted above, being cash-poor can stifle a firm's development. It might therefore seem as if there would be no such thing as having too much cash. But the cash-rich organization runs the risk of becoming careless. The company may start off on-plan but then slip into operating in a sloppy fashion that will ultimately require a major adjustment.

Although the public ridicules the extravagance of some large, wealthy companies, small start-ups may exhibit equally foolish spending habits. The on-plan venture that has much more cash than it needs can easily get into trouble, because it is quite likely to begin spending without the appropriate planning. John Grillos—former CEO of SPSS and Tesseract and venture capitalist at Robertson, Stephens & Company in San Francisco—describes this condition as "financing-induced brain damage." A cash-rich company is prone to acquiring many bad habits, including inadequate control of spending, unwillingness to continually prune growing expenses (including people), and a general inability to run lean and mean. In short, all organizations, regardless of their size, must watch their outlays.

Some good spending habits for start-ups that are almost never practiced by large companies include such tactics as planning trips wisely and in advance to save time and money, not booking business class, choosing reasonably priced accommodations (e.g., Days Inns), and buying nonmatching, used, or auctioned-off furniture. Most important, salaries must be based on value to the company and performance rather than on traditional salary-hierarchy formulas. Suhas Patil, founder of Cirrus Logic, believes that the founders establish a start-up's salary standards and argues that the pay scale for hiring should be governed by need and performance, not by hierarchy.

There is some evidence to support the idea that less money is better. Objectivity, a Silicon Valley firm building an object-oriented database, studied a number of software companies and found that many of the most successful did not have a significant amount of venture financing in their early years. The Objectivity team hypothesized that the absence of a large bankroll forced these organizations to behave in several ways that tended to promote their success:

- Smaller projects had to be undertaken to get products to market sooner, reducing development risk.

- Development teams remained small and focused, an approach widely believed to be most effective for software.

- Product definition and development were often customer-funded, which ensured that the resulting products would meet real market needs.

- Getting to market sooner with useful products enabled the companies to establish a lead in the race for market share.

CASH RULES

When it comes to starting a venture, "cash is king." Without cash, there is no company. During the concept stage, the founders can trade off their personal time for cash, but once full-time employees are hired, cash is required to fuel the firm. The following rules test whether, at each stage, the organization has met its objectives and has enough cash to carry itself through to the next stage.

During the concept stage, do the founders have sufficient (usually personal) time and cash to be able to write the business plan for the seed stage?

The only mechanism for funding the concept stage, during which the first plan is developed, is the founders themselves. They must be capable of sustaining themselves while they write the seed stage plan and look for seed or start-up financing. Having adequate time and cash for this indeterminate period, which may last up to a year, is essential. At this first stage, out-of-pocket, personal cash is synonymous with financeability.

Have the founders obtained the cash to execute the seed stage plan?

The preceding two rules test whether the company has the cash and time to start up. Without funds or some way to support the founders during the concept and seed stages, the firm will be unable to get off the ground.

By the end of the seed stage, has the seed stage funding been sufficient to enable the start-up to meet its objectives and milestones for that stage? Does the company still have enough cash on hand to sustain itself for a period of up to three months while it pursues product development stage financing?

At the completion of the seed stage, the start-up may require more time to search for additional cash than was originally anticipated. For this reason, the company should always be in the position of having up to a three-month supply of funds in reserve. Furthermore, it should be understood that receiving a commitment for funding is not the same as having cash in hand, since several months can elapse between agreement and the actual availability of funds.

FINANCEABILITY: VIABILITY THROUGH THE ABILITY TO RAISE CAPITAL

Nowhere is the expression "timing is everything" more applicable than in financing a new venture. The principal measure of financeability is the ability to raise capital in a timely fashion at a fair market value. Furthermore, raising capital in a timely fashion is not a problem that the start-up will face only once. Rather, it is an ongoing process, because the more successful the firm, the more additional capital it will need to sustain its growth. Even with continued and increasing profitability, a company's capital requirements will rise sharply, especially if it is operating in a capital-intensive field such as manufacturing (e.g., semiconductors or disks), in which large amounts of cash are needed to finance plant and inventory expansions.

Financeability is perhaps the most difficult dimension to measure, since it depends both on circumstances that are entirely beyond the company's control (exogenous factors) and on circumstances that the company can directly control (indigenous factors). The exogenous factors that affect financeability include the following:

- The condition of the overall economy, together with the apparent market for the firm's proposed product or service

- The number of competing companies engaged in businesses similar or identical to that of the start-up

- The financial community's current health and willingness to fund the business sector

- The desire of a given source of funds to be in a particular industry sector

The indigenous factors on which financeability depends include the following:

- The company's ability to operate according to its business plan

- The competitiveness of the product (i.e., the product position) and the likelihood of the firm's achieving its planned results

- The organization's ability to create a competitive market in which investors will find the company attractive

- The company's perceived intangible value, including any synergy with other companies in an investment portfolio

- The return that the firm offers its investors on their investment

During any round of financing, the company's valuation is determined by all of the factors in the preceding lists, together with the vicissitudes of the negotiating process. The best way for a new venture to get a high valuation is to offer investors a great company and then have lots of firms that want a piece of the deal, such that the offering is oversubscribed. Attracting a large number of buyers is also a good way to ensure that they are not illegally colluding to establish the price of the offering.

Two calculations are especially important in determining the company's valuation:

- The cost that was required for the start-up to attain its current position, compared with the cost required to finance a similar company to a similar point

- The expected return

The former calculation is critical, because if a company is founded on a great idea that is both simple to implement and offers a high expected return, other similar companies will probably be formed. (Remember Silver's [1985] axiom for the venture business: "Anything worth doing is worth duplicating.") The possibility of other similar firms being funded will tend to drive down the valuation of each of the individual firms.

The expected return is also an important consideration in valuation. It should increase in proportion to risk and will vary depending on where the company is in its growth process. Several books on entrepreneuring (such as Gladstone, 1988) discuss the process of determining appropriate valuations based on the expected return. Although in the 1980s, venture capital firms average about a 22 percent annual return, the contributions of the various companies in their portfolios may vary widely. For example, Saratoga Venture Finance (Nesheim, 1988) estimated that in a typical venture capital portfolio, only 10 percent of the investments were substantial winners, with 6 percent returning 50 percent annually and 4 percent returning over 100 percent annually. Winning investments such as these offset the investments in firms that go bankrupt (60 percent!).

Given these statistics, it is easy to see why venture capital firms need to pick as many winners as possible and avoid paying too much for either the winners or the losers. Silver (1985) offers some advice to assist these firms in valuing a company appropriately. He starts by looking at the firm during five risk periods—product development, manufacturing, marketing, management, and growth, which roughly correspond to our stages—while applying three laws of venture capital:

1. Accept no more than two risks per investment.

2. Valuation = $P \times S \times E$, where P is the size of the problem being solved, S is the elegance of the solution, and E is the entrepreneurial team; the S factor is further defined to be:

    $S = B \times T$, where B is the Business Plan, and T is the technology.

3. For companies where the above formula yields comparable results, invest in the big-P companies because the public market will accord them unreasonably high valuation, irrespective of S and E.

Silver looks at the following eight DEJ (demonstrable economic justification) factors in determining the value of S and P:

1. Existence of qualified buyers.

2. Existence of qualified sellers.

3. Homogeneity of buyers.

4. Large number of buyers.

5. Lack of institutional barriers to selling.

6. Word of mouth is principal form of advertising.

7. Optimum price/cost relationship.

8. Whether invisibility of the new company can be maintained.

In 1990, many entrepreneurs are saying that venture capital has turned itself inward and operates more like a bank, with venture capitalists being unwilling to finance an enterprise unless it has a proven operational prototype, orders in hand, and a guaranteed market. In fact, in the case of Gyration (page 53), the venture community is unwilling to invest in what may be a breakthrough technology even though the company already has a bank line of credit to build prototypes.

SOURCES OF CAPITAL

Two major sources of capital exist: self-funding and external funding. Although self-funding is by far the preferred method, as Gateway (see Chapter 11) and Microsoft have shown, if that approach is not possible, the company will have to seek a financial partner. To do so, it must establish criteria for a desirable partner and decide on a financing strategy; otherwise, it will waste a great deal of time searching for the "golden goose." The selling and final negotiation processes determine the terms for the "deal" with the start-up's financial partner.

Self-Funding

I strongly recommend some form of self-funding, if at all possible. Self-funding permits the founders to spend more time on their business plan and on product development without having to devote major amounts of time to wooing financial backers. Self-funding also fosters a strong sense of discipline with respect to spending control, shortens the time it takes to reach the market, minimizes extraneous marketing and sales overhead, and keeps the firm from being overly concerned with product elegance. On the one hand, a self-funded company does sacrifice some of the advantages that venture capital or other investors can offer. On the other hand, it avoids burdening the board with three or four venture capitalists who lack any understanding of the product or market—a surefire recipe for disaster.

Self-funding has been quite successful for a number of companies, especially software firms. One example, described more fully in Chapter 11, is Dragon Systems. Dragon was founded in 1982 by Jim and Janet Baker and has become a leader in speech-recognition products. The company, which bootstrapped its financing without outside investment, is employee-owned, wholly supported by customer revenues, and net-profitable.

External Funding Sources

Although the preceding subsection emphasized self-funding, and this chapter in general has focused on venture funding, there *are* other sources of cash, and all should be pursued with equal vigor. White (1977) presents a relatively large list of sources, including the aforementioned self-funding and venture capital options.

The important sources, arranged roughly in order of growth stage, are:

1. The founders' savings, including borrowing on assets

2. Family and friends

3. Formal investment groups, including venture capital concerns and companies that specialize in the private placement of stock

4. Foundations

5. Grants and small-business loans from various government agencies, such as the National Science Foundation's SBIR (Small Business Innovative Research) contracts for transforming technology into products

6. Having the company's employees buy equipment and lend it to the firm

7. Obtaining the firm's capital equipment through bank loans and leasing companies

8. Forming research and development partnerships with investment companies to do incremental development

9. University endowments

10. Large companies that enter into a venture-investment phase and pension funds

11. Strategic partners that are potential customers and want early access to the start-up's product

12. Strategic partners that are manufacturers whose products would be enhanced by the start-up's product

13. Strategic foreign investors that want access to technology, ranging from simple distribution to complete rights, through manufacturing

14. Foreign governments, companies, and banks that might be interested in building a local joint subsidiary to produce or market the start-up's product

15. Banking institutions that invest working capital based on firm orders

16. Equipment suppliers and vendors that may help a new company get started

17. Customers, including other start-ups, that may pay in advance for product or for a development contract (i.e., use someone else's venture capital)

18. Going public or being acquired by a larger, more cash-rich company

There are, however, some reservations that founders should keep in mind when considering funding from some of these sources. For example, funding from "family and friends" may be desirable during the concept and seed stages. However, these people will also be called on to provide emotional support during those periods, and it may be too much to ask them for their capital as well.

In the case of venture funding, it is common for venture capitalists to invest in companies that run out of money and to do so at prices substantially lower than previous rounds. These financing rounds are called "cram downs" or "washout rounds," and they have the effect of devaluing the previously issued stock. Even if the start-up ultimately succeeds, early investors are unlikely to get their money back. This possibility is another reason why it is critical for the founders to think twice about taking money from their family and friends.

The third funding source on the list—"formal investment groups, including venture capital concerns and companies that specialize in the private placement of stock"—also has its potential dangers. When it comes to securing funds, there is no such thing as "easy money" or "dumb money." The oft-written-about private placement specialists who obtain funding from doctors and dentists are seldom able to deliver either in time or on reasonable terms. Furthermore, many of these investors can be naive and dangerous. The founders should remember that the start-up makes a contract with every source of funds and therefore has a contractual obligation to succeed—an obligation that nonprofessional investors may take quite literally. Although when all is going well, as in the case of an initial successful financing, everyone is a friend, when things are *not* going so well, nonprofessional investors are likely to turn on the start-up and its founders. Naive investors tend to build up expectations based on hope rather than on the start-up's business plan. When the financial results do not live up to such inflated expectations, the investors conclude that the company has failed.

Finding a Financial Partner

If self-financing is not possible, founders might be well advised to consider reviewing the list presented in the preceding subsection with an eye to identifying financial-partnership possibilities, keeping in mind the cautions just voiced about family, friends, and naive investors. John Grillos has provided the following helpful guide to the selection process by listing ten attributes of a desirable financial partner. According to Grillos, the ideal prospective partner:

1. Fits the financing model and strategy for the company

2. Has valuation expectations consistent with [those of] the current owners

3. Has resources to play its role in the strategy—i.e., has "deep pockets"

4. Has a philosophy that fits with [that of] the company and its current owners

5. Can aid in future financing

6. Has liquidity preferences consistent with [those of] the current owners

7. Can afford to take the loss if the business fails ([which] may rule out family and friends)

8. [Is] nice to work with and is likely to be with you when the chips are down

9. Understands the business

10. Can contribute [more] than [just] money: consulting, sales, contracts, board membership, joint venture and strategic partnerships

PRESENTING YOUR CASE
TO A PROSPECTIVE FINANCIAL PARTNER

Almost every entrepreneur who finds venture capital funding advises that the first few contacts are a learning experience and that they will probably result in turndowns until the entrepreneur's story comes together. Mike Hackworth, former CEO of Signetics and current CEO of Cirrus Logic, notes:

> You have to tell the story of a company in [the] language of the business you're in. But it has to be done in such a way that the financial person can picture it. That means defining—up front—risks, milestones, and critical dependencies. The market content is more important than anything; the capitalists assume the technology is there. Further, investors are interested in getting to know you.

One way for the founders to plan, and subsequently present, a financing strategy is to pattern it after the strategies of successful ventures that have something in common with their own firm. In many cases, the people responsible for successful financing strategies are more than happy to talk about, and relive, their previous successes. Also, they are likely to want to invest in the proposed start-up if the founders can demonstrate that what they're doing now is similar to what the established company did earlier.

As for how long this process will take, the founders should be advised that financing is more complex and time-consuming than they could ever have dreamed. In 1990, the most optimistic scenario for a "perfect" company seeking venture financing is that it will take a minimum of three months from the time a preliminary business plan is available until the cash is in the bank. The amount of time required depends on such factors as the number of investors involved in the deal, the financing round (first, second, third, etc.), and the existence and seriousness of any differences of opinion between the entrepreneur and the investors concerning the appropriate valuation. Until there is agreement on the value of the company, there can be no deal. The incredible time demands of raising money clearly engender poor behavior and always prompt the firm to go after more money than is actually needed. This phenomenon is known as Kleiner's law: "When the hors d'oeuvres are passed, take two."

Funding becomes very complex in later rounds, when the terms for the liquidation of the company (it either fails, goes public, or is purchased), based on the current round and all previous rounds, are written into the financing.

HOW MUCH FUNDING AND HOW MANY ROUNDS?

The amount of funding and the number of rounds are very difficult to determine, since in each case, the total varies substantially between labor-intensive enterprises such as software companies and capital-intensive efforts such as disk or memory companies. Midway between these extremes is the computer systems firm. By 1990, a well-run, successful computer systems firm typically required about $50 million before it achieved profitability. Having $50 million to spend does not guarantee success, however, because many companies spent that amount (or more) but still failed. ETA (1983-1989) had an average of four hundred employees and probably spent on the order of $200 million before it was closed, having shipped a dozen supercomputers. Trilogy spent nearly $300 million and never could get its technology to work, let alone ship a computer.

For software companies, self-funding is best if the founders can manage it. In the case of small software projects involving a single team of five working for two years, only a few million dollars may be required from start to profitability. In the case of large software projects involving half a dozen teams of five, a minimum of $10 million may be required to reach profitability. In 1983, Lotus spent $6 million to launch its 1-2-3 spreadsheet and thus preempt competitors.

As for the number of rounds required, a company rarely achieves profitability with just one or two financing rounds, and the norm is more like three or four rounds. The funding model advocated herein assumes at least four rounds: seed;

product development with alpha testing; beta testing until market calibration; and market development, including profitability until the steady-state stage is reached.

FINANCEABILITY FLAWS

When a company has trouble obtaining funding, it is often hard to determine whether the problem involves a lack of financeability or whether potential investors believe the firm is inadequate in one of the other dimensions, such as people, product, or plan. This section deals with the most common exogenous and indigenous flaws involving the financeability dimension per se rather than financeability problems that stem from a start-up's inadequacies in other areas.

One major exogenous flaw is a dearth of capital in the overall market caused by a lack of confidence in the economy, region, product, or market. For example, one large New York- based venture capital company has gone from having a third of its investments in New England in 1985 to having less than a tenth of its investments in that region in 1990. During the same period, in contrast, its investments in Silicon Valley have risen from a third to over half. Another serious exogenous flaw is the existence of a crowded product area in which the start-up is one of many "me-too" players.

One major indigenous flaw can arise when the company first starts up if the entrepreneur and investors cannot come to terms about a fair market value for the firm. Another major indigenous flaw can manifest itself in later stages when several rounds of financing have been required because the company failed to meet its plans; in this case, investor fatigue sets in, and the investors finally say "no." The firm is then closed, and its assets are sold.

A Dearth of Capital

Unlike most of the other flaws discussed in this book, having the supply of capital dry up is almost completely beyond the company's control. Rather, it is caused either by an overall economic shift toward recession or by a shift in investment strategies away from certain technology sectors. The result is that no funding is available, and the start-up's founders will just have to wait until a more favorable time.

An Overly Crowded Product Area

Like the dearth-of-capital flaw, the entry of too many firms into the product area is primarily the result of circumstances beyond a company's control. This problem is common, however, because lots of people often come up with the same idea at the same time. It should be obvious that entering the market with a "me-too" product under these circumstances is dangerous. Unfortunately, even entering such a market with a compelling technological advantage may be unsuccessful, since investors are often wary of a market they consider to be overcrowded.

As an example, I recently looked at a radical (yet simple) disk design that halved the number of parts required. Although building a radical new disk structure is risky, the cost advantage was quite compelling. Many firms, including current disk companies, had examined the patented design and felt fairly certain that it would work. Despite all these favorable factors, no venture capital company or industrial partner would fund the start-up. They wouldn't even fund a seed stage effort to examine the design in more detail, evidently because they felt that the disk field was already full and that it would therefore be impossible for the new product to take market share away from the entrenched leaders.

Failure to Come to Terms with Potential Investors

Although in a few rare cases, the entrepreneur and investors feel equally pleased with the valuation placed on a company when a round is closed, the norm is for disagreements to arise over the firm's valuation. The line between fairness and exploitation is thin enough that such disagreements can stop the negotiating process, and a potentially profitable venture may fail to obtain funding. In most of these cases, the problem stems from the entrepreneur's having an overly inflated view of the start-up's value, and it's just as well that the firm doesn't form. In other cases, the entrepreneur goes on to self-fund the company and is better off without external funding.

Investor Fatigue Resulting from the Start-up's Failure to Exhibit Integrity or Self-Control

The final flaw—a start-up's lack of integrity or self-control—brings us full circle to a scenario dominated by indigenous factors. When it comes to financing, the combined advantages of luck, positive exogenous factors, and a good product can be totally counteracted by a company's lack of integrity or by its inability to control or sell itself. Once these shortcomings become apparent to investors, they can be expected to lose patience with the firm and withdraw their financial support.

FINANCEABILITY RULES

At any stage of a new venture's growth, the issue of financeability essentially boils down to the basic question of whether the firm got the financial support it needed in order to continue. The rules presented in this subsection are aimed at testing the start-up's financing readiness and its quality in the minds of potential investors. For example, it is critical to have the right experts "bless" the company. A knowledge-able expert's personal financial backing and commitment to spend time count far more than words coming from a paid consultant.

Are the present plan and people sufficiently compelling to facilitate raising capital for the seed stage (usually $100,000 to $1 million, depending on the company's scope) at the desired price level and also produce a waiting list of additional investors who want to be part of the start-up round?

Getting financing for the seed stage is, by definition, the only real test of whether the concept stage has been successful. Independent of whether the company has obtained seed stage funding, the following two rules diagnose the likelihood of its successfully achieving concept stage financeability.

Has the start-up gained the support of at least three reputable, known outside individuals—persons whose backing would tend to lend credence to the technology, product, market, and company concept?

The venture must have the support of at least three respected individuals who are willing to attest to the company's efficacy and the feasibility of its proceeding to the seed stage. It is helpful at this point if the outside sources are also willing to invest their personal capital and time.

By the end of the concept stage, are the critical founders prepared to commit to a full-time effort during the seed stage?

This second rule for the seed stage tests whether those founders who might be considered critical have made a commitment to carrying out the seed plan on a full-time basis. After all, the founders are what the company is selling as a start-up. Their commitment is usually conditional on obtaining funding—i.e., if the funds for the seed stage arrive, the founders will leave whatever they're doing and begin to develop the plans for the company. However, if the founders are not personally committed, it is unlikely that investors will be either. In effect, seed stage investors are buying both a potential idea and a team.

Have the formal business plan and seed stage proved salable, such that an excess of investors have signed up to provide financing for the next stage

(i.e., product development) at the sought-after price, resulting in an overcommitment of funds?

The principal proof of financeability is as simple as it was for the seed round: the company got the money.

Was the financing sought at the end of the seed stage in line with the objectives, milestones, and resources required to complete the product development stage?

Ideally, enough funds should be obtained to complete all phases of the product development stage, including beta testing. For large development projects, however, two or more funding rounds may be required merely to finish the product. The first nonseed round just covers the product specification, basic design, construction, and preliminary alpha testing. A second round would cover beta testing and the first few months of the market development stage.

When the company starts up (i.e., at the end of the seed stage), is its valuation in line with reality as compared to similar endeavors?

The most convincing plan is to present a comparison with other, similar ventures. Depending on the capital market and the firm's perceived market position, the valuation will be disproportionately higher or lower by factors of more than 3 (or about an order of magnitude between the highest and lowest valuations) for a comparable stage. The CEO or financial person should understand how other companies have done and use this information to set realistic valuation goals across the board.

Is the funding picture (in terms of availability of funds, state of the economy, and market and product segment) adequate to sustain the company's need for capital? *Test:* **Is the product and/or market area still sufficiently unique and "in fashion," or has the once-"hot" area suddenly become "cold" because of an overabundance of suppliers or a long market-gestation time?**

During the seed period, the funding picture can suddenly become unfavorable for the start-up through no fault of its own. Funds can dry up for many reasons, including investors' receiving requests for cash from companies they started earlier that are now doing poorly. For example, a semiconductor start-up may place heavy demands on cash just when the economy and spending take a downturn.

CONTROL: DOING WHAT THE COMPANY SAYS IT WILL DO

> Income 20 pounds, expenses 19 pounds, 19 shillings, and 11 pence—result happiness. Income 20 pounds, expenses 20 pounds and 1 shilling—result misery.
>
> —Charles Dickens

A system is under control when it is operating predictably by producing outputs in response to a variety of inputs. The most important element of being "in control" is first and foremost having a plan that describes the relationship between resource inputs (time, cash, people, etc.) and outputs (specifications, products, paying customers, profit, etc.). Without this critical plan (described in Chapter 3), there can be no control because there is no standard of measure. The second most important element of control is simply operating the company in such a way as to ensure that it meets its plan and changing the plan appropriately when exogenous factors dictate the need for change. In addition to financial control, it is equally important for the firm to achieve qualitative control, by employing such techniques as management by objectives (MBO).

THE PROFITABILITY HABIT

The preceding sections of this chapter have emphasized the importance of cash and have shown that cash depends on successful rounds of financing. In turn, successful rounds of financing depend on credibility. To achieve credibility, a company must be in control of what it is doing: it must be able to make a plan and operate according to that plan. Furthermore, when conditions change, as they will if products or markets shift, the company must able to adapt quickly. Any firm that wishes to sustain its profitability must operate according to the following maxim:

> Profit is habit-forming. So are losses. Therefore, be profitable from the outset.

PLANNING: THE KEY TO CONTROL

In order for an organization to be in control, it must measure its operations against a plan. A high-quality company will have a high-quality plan, and that plan will be a key document for keeping the enterprise in control. A company whose plan is infeasible or not believed is a company that is inherently out of control. A firm with no plan at all is *really* out of control and should consider itself to be in a stage of unfettered research.

FINANCIAL MANAGEMENT OF THE INPUT AND THE OUTPUT

The financial portion of the plan is a major part of the firm's control dimension. A company's financial operations have two basic components: the input side and the output side. The input side is the cash generated by the financing rounds. The key test of input-side control is whether the chief financial officer understands the plan and is in control of spending the company's cash according to that plan. To achieve control, the company must establish control mechanisms for hiring (salaries and stock), consulting personnel, other temporary personnel, benefits, office expenses, capital equipment, purchasing, travel, and entertainment. The output side is the firm's production of goods and services. The key test of output-side control is whether the company produces its contracted output—e.g., completing projects, delivering against purchase orders, and building the agreed-upon products at the right price and on schedule.

To achieve control of the input and output sides of the company's finances, every part of the organization (and nearly every individual) must plan, operate according to the plan, and adapt to changing conditions. The best, and perhaps the only, way to achieve this sort of control is to establish formal systems whereby every individual makes weekly objectives that support the overall plan and reports on them. Management by objectives, management by exceptions, or some other control scheme is necessary.

The organization's people can learn to plan and operate by the numbers if they are required to measure themselves against a concrete numeric standard. For example, I measure an engineering group's planning ability by a single number, the schedule fantasy factor (SFF), which is calculated by dividing the actual time it takes to achieve a given milestone by the planned time for achieving that milestone.

MANAGEMENT COMMUNICATIONS AND CONTROL

The company must hold staff meetings and minutes should be taken to chronicle the topics discussed and the resulting "action items." The easiest way to tell how a firm operates is to examine the minutes of its staff meetings and review the reports of each critical function. Are these meetings held on a regular basis? Does interfunction communication occur? Is the performance of each function tracked? Are critical issues identified and resolved? Does the company somehow deal with every crisis rapidly and efficiently, or is it in a constant state of crisis because problems rarely get resolved?

Decision making must be rapid, yet not precipitous. I believe that every major decision should be made over at least a one-day period, with time allocated for reconsideration. When changes in the situation necessitate changes in the company's plan, the new plan must be carefully thought out and appropriate in light of the new situation; otherwise, the plan is foolhardy.

The key to planning is easily stated (as I did at Digital in 1973): "He who plans, does." The only way to achieve total commitment to carrying out a plan (control) is for everyone responsible for the plan's execution to participate in its formation. The staff knows when it has a decision or a plan that it can implement, and will commit to such a plan. In contrast, the staff usually recognizes an unrealistic and ill-conceived plan, and will not give it their full commitment; the plan will then have to be remade.

THE LINK BETWEEN PROFITABILITY AND CONTROL

Concern for profitability is the basis of control. As noted earlier, profit is habit-forming. Concern for it must therefore pervade the organization from the day the doors are opened and the company starts spending money. Everyone has to understand that every dollar spent must ultimately be repaid by product revenue.

Although profitability, like quality, has to come from the top, it must also be ingrained in every single individual in the organization. It is to every employee's benefit to keep profit in mind, because a chronically unprofitable company is generally an unhappy place in which to work. In particular, the founding team knows that the firm is being fundamentally dishonest and deceiving itself if it must keep creating a succession of new plans to convince investors that profitability is just around the corner. Furthermore, this dishonesty is likely to repeat itself, since an unprofitable company must return to its funding sources over and over again for more cash. Each trip to the investors will be increasingly unpleasant and very time-consuming, because the investors will ask nagging questions about those earlier plans for profitability. Also, unless the CEO has a stranglehold on the firm, through ownership or technology blackmail, sustained unprofitability will ultimately cost his or her job.

An often-successful way to improve the chances for profitability is to delegate the responsibility for it below the CEO. Thus, several people share the responsibility, and the CEO merely helps them achieve the desired goal. This argues for a quasi-divisional structure, a technique used during Digital's period of greatest growth (1966- 1984). During that time, the company was organized around a collection of about twenty "product lines," which were responsible for various market segments. The segments included professionals (e.g., laboratory, engineering, industrial control, commercial); customers (e.g., government, small business); buying channels (e.g., original equipment manufacturer [OEM], components, retail); and products (e.g., DECsystem-10). This structure allowed a series of closed loops to control the allocation of resources and the delegation of profit responsibility. With the advent of the VAX architecture, all customers were buying similar products. The opportunity to differentiate the product and to address the respective markets diminished, and the organization abandoned the product-line structure in favor of a more traditional functional organization. Profitability then depended upon overall control of every organization. In 1990, DEC once again began to reorganize around a product-line structure in order to be able to delegate control and responsibility for profitability.

CONTROL FLAWS

As noted earlier, control involves having a good plan and carrying it out. Conversely, control flaws involve having a poor plan and/or being unable to carry it out. The planning flaws range from having a foolish plan to having a plan that the company is not confident it can execute. Although the control flaws usually stem from shortcomings in the way the organization manages itself, the firm may be doing everything it thinks is right and still fail to meet its sales projections. Other control flaws range from having total anarchy to being overly bureaucratic. The CEO and team are at the heart of a start-up's (in)ability to be in control.

Trying to Operate with a Plan That Has Lost Touch with Reality

A company may continue to spend according to an operational plan that has become unrealistic, oblivious of the fact that it is failing to meet important milestones. Although unrealistic plans were discussed in Chapter 3, "The Business Plan," this flaw is worth mentioning in the present context as well, because it is also related to the control dimension, a relationship best illustrated with the following true story.

In early May 1990, I attended a Dutch-treat dinner celebrating the end of the seed stage for a company about to enter the office automation market. The team had performed admirably during the concept stage and had come up with a good plan for a product and a company. The CEO had obtained advice from a small group of competent friends in the industry (called the KBOD, for "kitchen board of directors") and had conducted numerous interviews with potential strategic partners and customers to help develop the product specification during the eight-month concept stage.

When the firm proceeded to the seed stage, it continued promoting the product, working on selecting early beta sites, writing draft manuals, etc. However, it had created a complete fantasy. On the one hand, the company appeared to have a lot going for it. It had a team with a board (KBOD), a product spec, a demo (which it came to believe was the product), a process for improving the product, customers, and a support team. The only thing the company lacked was an actual product. Worse yet, it continued to be unable to hire a person to be responsible for building the product. The firm was spending its precious seed money and time (using up credibility with its investors by jeopardizing its seed plan) to do work that was irrelevant at that stage. It was simply addressing the wrong problems, and the various parts of the organization were out of synchronization with one another. Furthermore, by broadcasting its plan widely, the company was giving competitors, both potential start-ups and existing firms, an opportunity to build the product first. Fortunately, the company recognized the flaw and by fall that year was on track with two product developers who produced a great prototype to use in closing the product development funding.

Having No Measures or the Wrong Measures

A company is, and gets, what it measures. A firm that operates with no measures or with the wrong goals or measures is likely to produce either nothing or the wrong thing. Each part of the organization, especially engineering, must have appropriate measures, such as schedule and product quality. The Ardent product development story (page 122) illustrates a case in which focusing on a single product-performance metric nearly proved fatal for the company. Every department that concentrates on just one metric to the exclusion of all others runs the risk of being similarly flawed. For example, a customer service organization may assess its performance only in terms of an overall customer service index and not bother measuring the myriad factors that are reflected in that rating, such as response time, mean time to failure, and number of outstanding errors.

Inadequate Financial Control

When a company operates without adequate financial control, it may embark on a spending spree not covered by its operational plan. For example, one CEO went out and bought an expensive computer-aided design (CAD) system, using 15 percent of the start-up funds, as his first executive act. It was a system that his engineering team neither wanted nor needed. Later on, the firm purchased an expensive tester that it could have rented. The organization was never brought under financial control because the investors were always willing to provide additional funding in return for promises.

Overly Bureaucratic Planning and Decision Making

The opposite of an out-of-control organization is an organization controlled so tightly that it cannot spend enough time generating output. Instead, it wastes valuable time adhering to procedures that require needless forms and approvals, appearances before committees and working groups, etc. Although bureaucracy usually goes hand in hand with large organizations, start-ups can often evolve rapidly into ungainly bureaucracies. Because engineers frequently complain about bureaucracy, one would expect a venture led by engineers to be streamlined and efficient. This is not necessarily the case, however. In practice, engineers are inherently the world's greatest bureaucrats because they are so good at designing organizations and processes.

Lack of Support for the Plan

The only way to ensure a company's commitment to the operating plan is to have its entire staff participate in making the plan. Any other planning approach will result in an out-of-control situation. Thus, companywide support for the plan is a necessary condition (though not a sufficient one) for achieving control.

Top-Level Flaws in Planning and Decision Making

Planning and decision-making flaws that originate at the top can take several forms. An autocratic CEO or department head may insist on being involved in every decision. An anarchic CEO or department head may fail to make timely decisions, believing instead in the "Bo Peep" school of management ("Leave them alone and they'll come home . . . "). A mercurial CEO or department head may make decisions capriciously because they are fun to make, oblivious to the fact that all the decisions must then be remade. Or a top-down CEO or department head may make a plan that lacks "buy-in" from those who will be responsible for its implementation.

I know of one CEO who was a fine leader and salesman for the company but possessed all of the above-mentioned traits to some degree. This individual made certain decisions in an autocratic and mercurial manner, was unaware of some important decisions, was inconsistent about management practices, and made top-down plans and pronouncements that no one could believe in or carry out. I know another truly anarchic CEO who was simply dumb, perhaps lazy, and an inept manager and leader, but he didn't possess any of the above-mentioned flaws. This may have made him somewhat less dangerous, because his team rallied and was able to manage itself.

Experiencing a Major, Unexplained Slip in the Plan

The company's credibility is established by how well it meets its commitments—i.e., how successfully it achieves its plan. A major slip can occur, though, when the assumptions about a product or market turn out to be invalid, and the firm then attempts to recover or respond to the new information. Slipping the schedule during the seed stage is not a fatal flaw if it happens for good reason, since during the seed stage, the organization is still permitted to engage in open-ended work (including advanced development and market research).

However, such a slip raises a couple of important questions: Is everyone in the company operating according to some formal schedule and management by objectives? Is everyone informed about the firm via effective staff meetings during which review, direction setting, and problem identification/resolution take place? If these questions cannot be answered affirmatively, the slip could be the first sign that the organization is operating in a potentially open-ended fashion.

CONTROL RULES

The following rules provide the guidelines for evaluating whether a new venture is in control at both the concept and seed stages. In these early stages, it is difficult to determine whether or not a company is in control. In fact, at the concept stage, the only real indicator is whether the CEO and individual team members have a history of being able to perform their respective functions in a controlled fashion. At the end of the seed stage, however, the firm's ability to control itself can be measured in terms of how it performed during the seed stage.

At the concept stage, does an examination of the founders' reputation and past achievements disclose solid evidence that they are capable of accomplishing the following?

- **Hiring top-quality people**

- **Demonstrating technical and marketing expertise**

- **Producing successful products and planning effectively**

- **Achieving schedule milestones and meeting budgets**

Although control is hard to measure at the concept stage because there does not yet exist an actual company with committed resources, a diligent effort should be made to ascertain whether the founders have run comparable firms successfully in the past and whether the group is likely to be able to meet its own timetables, both for the seed stage and for subsequent stages. Thus, it behooves a start-up to accurately record its progress in achieving the goals to which it has committed itself. This gets the company into the habit of clearly understanding and continually monitoring its own abilities and accomplishments so that it can be "in control" during later stages.

Did the team meet its timetable for making the seed plan?

By the end of the concept stage, a preliminary estimate can be made of whether the company is likely to be able to meet its commitments and remain in control. If the firm can't plan effectively enough to create its seed plan on time, there is little reason to expect successful results from any other activities that require planning.

Has the company been operating according to an overall plan, and has that plan been changed only minimally during the seed stage?

The first part of control is having a plan. The second part is sticking to that plan.

Were seed stage objectives met without major milestone slips? If milestone slips did occur during the seed stage, were the backers' expectations managed and recast to their satisfaction such that they are willing to continue investing during the product development stage?

The new venture's track record during the seed stage is likely to be the best predictor of its future performance.

Does everyone in the company operate according to some formal schedule and MBO? Is everyone informed about the company via effective staff meetings during which review, direction setting, and problem identification/resolution take place?

The firm's credibility is first established during the seed stage, based on how well it meets its commitments. However, a major slip can occur if the assumptions about a product or market prove invalid and the company attempts to recover or respond to the new information. As mentioned above, slipping the schedule during the seed stage is not a fatal flaw if it occurs for good reason, but an inability to answer these two questions affirmatively could be the first indication that the organization is starting up in a potentially open-ended, out-of-control fashion.

Does the company have a controller, or a control mechanism, with budgeting, hiring, and spending processes in place to manage cash for both the current and next stage and control its spending as it enters the product development stage?

When the company opens as a full-scale entity, it is likely to be flush with a large amount of cash ($5 million to $10 million). At this point, there will be an enormous pent-up demand to hire direct and support staff and buy equipment, parts, and computer resources. Unless the firm has controls in place or is operating according to a detailed budget, it can easily begin spending vasts sums right away for critical items and thus find itself out of control from the moment it starts up.

CONCLUSION

Cash, financeability (the ability to get more cash), and control (the ability to produce results, including profit, with the cash and resources a company has) are all interrelated.

Without cash, the venture cannot proceed beyond the "kitchen table" planning stage. At least one founder must be self-supporting while the business plan for the seed stage is written. Later on, when the founders have spent several months in the seed stage planning the company and writing the business plan, the start-up must have a large enough cash cushion to wait out a period of at least three months while financing is sought. However, even if an enterprise has the necessary cash cushion, if it lacks control, its cash will ultimately decline to zero and the firm will be unfinanceable.

Without financeability, a company cannot continue to implement any plans or vision that it may have. Financeability is determined by both exogenous and indigenous factors. Although the firm can only respond to what it believes are the exogenous factors, it has total control over the indigenous factors—its business, as embodied in the technology it selects, the product it builds, its plan, its people, and other dimensions. The best guarantee of financeability is for the start-up to be in control and to have adequate cash through planning and profitability. Getting out of control and starting to deplete cash will put the venture on a downward spiral.

Control is the start-up's combined ability to make an effective overall business plan and then be able to operate in such a way as to achieve the plan. Control is measured quantitatively by how closely the company's actual operations match its plan in both the expenses and revenues lines on the profit and loss statement. Control is also measured qualitatively by how the company manages itself with respect to the objectives it has established for products, employee satisfaction, service, etc. Being in control is at the heart of preserving cash and financeability. But being in control is moot if the company is out of cash and not financeable.

Chapter 5

TECHNOLOGY AND ENGINEERING

The technology and engineering dimensions of a high-tech venture are so important that it takes two chapters to describe them fully. This first chapter covers the role of technology in product development, technology progress in logic and memories, and various aspects of technology creation and transfer. The following chapter covers technology and engineering flaws and presents the "technology balance sheet," a framework for analyzing a company's technology and engineering.

The technology dimension is reflected by a firm's ability to assimilate and utilize scientific and engineering knowledge as embodied in components, processes, and the "know-how" of its people. The engineering dimension is reflected by its ability to produce specifications (or actual information in the case of software) for a manufacturing organization. Since technology is the basis for engineering, technology will be discussed first, starting with its role in product development.

TECHNOLOGY

The technology needed to develop products can come from a range of sources. When technology emerges solely from science and engineering, the technology is pushing products into the market. In contrast, when technology is required in order to satisfy needs, the market is pulling to create technology. One difficulty with new technology is its acquisition. I firmly believe that the best way (and in some cases, the *only* way) to transfer technology is to transfer the people associated with the creation of that technology. Because technology is rarely measured, many companies start up without knowing how much technology they need, how long it will take to acquire it, or how much it will cost. The founders of a new venture must understand the firm's technology well enough to measure it. The following subsections should help them achieve that level of understanding.

TECHNOLOGY PUSH AND MARKET PULL

Product development is usually characterized as involving either technology push or market pull. According to the technology-push model, products originate with a flow of ideas that starts in research, progress through advanced development and product development, and ultimately reach the customer. According to the market-pull model, products originate with customers, who specify their requirements to a marketing organization, which, in turn, tells a development organization what to design and build, with research and advanced technology playing only a minor role. Strictly speaking, neither of these two models is correct, even for limited classes of products. Companies that operate exclusively according to either of these models are doomed to fail, because product and market responsibility must be disseminated throughout the entire organization in order for top-quality products to be created.

During the past decade, every company has attempted to characterize itself as "market-driven." Unfortunately, that often translates to *"marketing-department - driven."* In such a firm, the marketing department talks to some users and comes to the engineering organization with a comprehensive list of requirements for the proposed product. The list is inevitably embellished with marketing's own ideas about how the product should be designed, since many high-tech marketing personnel are also former engineers. Products that are specified in this fashion have the following predictable attributes:

- They are priced lower than all current competitors.

- Their performance is greater than that of any existing product.

- Their features and functions represent the total of those of all existing products.

- They possess unique, discriminating features designed to enable them to "knock off" other products, often by differentiating themselves just enough to allow government buyers to avoid competitive procurement.

- The desired delivery time is yesterday.[1]

---

1. Marketing wants it yesterday, engineering will have it tomorrow, and science is still working on it.

Engineering is expected to design and specify a product that satisfies these requirements and conforms to the original design provided by the marketing department. This approach to designing and building a product ignores technology and engineering innovation. Worse yet, it relegates the engineering organization to the role of a nonthinking automaton that simply builds products in response to what other companies produced several years ago. Without question, a firm driven solely by its marketing department is fatally flawed. The following two stories, the first apocryphal and the second true, illustrate the potential perils of basing a product on marketing ideas that lack sufficient engineering input.

Let's start with Ken Olsen's tale of a revolutionary new wallpaper remover. According to Ken, a marketing person approached an engineer one day with an idea for a very powerful wallpaper remover that, when applied, would immediately take the paper off, leaving the wall spotless and ready to paint. The impressed engineer exclaimed: "Great, let's build a plant to manufacture and sell it. We'll get rich! What's in it?" Replied the marketing person: "Darned if I know. I thought up the idea. You tell *me* what's in it and design the plant to manufacture it!"

Then there's the tale of the "recording whiteboards." In early 1986, just before the arrival of "recording whiteboards" from Japan, I was asked to become involved with a concept stage venture that proposed to manufacture such a product. The start-up wanted advice about its design. Two marketing people, with virtually no technical background, had identified the need for the product and had just spent six months investigating the market for it. They presented a plausible case for why it would be such a great product: who would buy at various prices, how many they would buy, and how it would be sold. We then got into how the product would be built and what it would cost. It turned out that the marketing people who originated the idea had little understanding of technology and cost. After a few phone calls, we ruled out their approach (using conductive fiberboard) because of its resolution and questionable reliability. I described a scroll-scanning approach, made possible with new photodiode arrays that were part of the fax revolution. They felt that this would be too expensive and too complicated. Fortunately, Japanese manufacturers introduced the product I described before the company was able to obtain funding or hire gullible engineers who might have been tempted to try its flawed approach.

These stories are not intended to absolve engineering from all blame, though. Firms driven solely by their engineering departments can fail because of an inability to satisfy the customers' needs and are therefore also flawed.

The successful start-up must strike a balance between marketing and engineering. Striking a balance, however, does not mean eliminating legitimate and healthy competition between the two organizations. Each organization must fulfill its responsibility with wholehearted commitment and a high level of drive. The conflict that inevitably arises when engineering's product definition clashes with marketing's requirements often produces precisely the spark needed to generate premier products. The most appropriate roles for the engineering and marketing organizations, and for the CEO, can be summarized as follows:

- *Engineering:* The engineering organization must acquire the technology and the engineering talent. It must then design the product to meet the cost and schedule goals at the highest possible quality level.

- *Marketing:* The marketing organization must identify the product requirements, including what (the price, performance, features, and functions), why (the buying rationale, expressed in terms of benefits), and who (precise customer/application profiles).

    In the last stages of development, marketing must also deliver the necessary support material for the resulting product, so that the sales organization can generate profitable orders.

- *CEO:* The CEO must arbitrate conflicts and deadlocks between engineering and marketing to arrive at a common product and marketing plan and ensure that each group carries out its respective responsibilities.

TECHNOLOGY PROGRESS

Technology progress, which can occur in both an evolutionary and a revolutionary fashion, results from two basic factors: (1) the increased density of semiconductors and magnetics and (2) the quest to build and exploit computers with new applications. Additional factors that drive progress include all the forms of research, development, and manufacturing.

Revolution and Evolution

Figure 5-1 shows two models of progress (Gomory and Schmitt, 1988). One model is a "ladder" of scientific revolution based on important milestones in computer technology, while the other is a "wheel" of evolution based on continuous refinement of a basic design or process. The "rungs" of scientific revolution are somewhat arbitrary. Furthermore, the dates given are for the introduction of a particular technology into computers, not for the initial availability of the technology itself. For example, vacuum tubes were used in radios long before 1944. These observations aside, the most interesting aspect of the ladder is that it shows no computer-technology revolutions

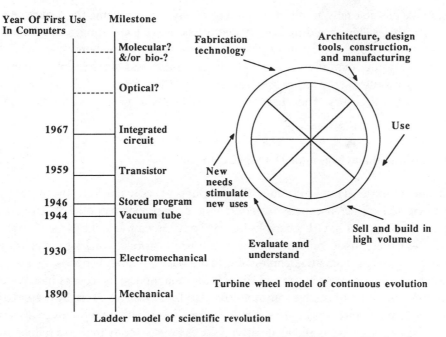

Figure 5-1. Revolutionary (Ladder) and Evolutionary (Wheel) Models of Technology Progress

since the introduction of integrated circuits in 1967. Although optical technology (now used extensively in communications) may eventually find its way into computers, products based on this technology are unlikely to appear during the 1990s, since there is a substantial delay between laboratory development and product introduction. I quantify the typical laboratory-to-product lag like this: roughly a decade (or one technology generation) usually elapses between the time a significant laboratory invention occurs and the time that invention is used to any significant extent in products.

Despite the fact that marketing organizations often use the term *revolution* to describe new products or developments in computing, *evolution* is a more realistic word, because progress is generally based on well-established technology and a set of design principles. In particular, circuit and memory technologies (i.e., the technologies involving the physical components that actually process and store information) are the key determinants of a computer's performance and cost, and during the past twenty years, progress in these technologies has been considerably more evolutionary than revolutionary. Unfortunately for the United States, which excels in revolutionary inventions, Japan excels in evolution.

The cycle of evolution in computer technology is driven by the interaction of many processes. New basic materials and circuits, along with advances in fabrication technology, make possible new architectures and new ways of producing the next computer. The process of selling, building in higher volumes, using, evaluating, and understanding computers raises aspirations for the next cycle of evolution. Some of these factors involve computer manufacturers, some involve users, and some involve the formal study of computers in computer-science courses. With the advent of increased capabilities comes the discovery of new uses and needs, which unleashes more funds to fuel the next cycle.

Semiconductor and Magnetic Density Evolution

Many developments have permitted the computer to evolve rapidly, the most important being density increases in semiconductors and magnetics. Although improvements in these technologies have been evolutionary (i.e., conforming to the "wheel" model in Figure 5-1), their impact on computer architecture and applications has paved the way for revolutionary changes (i.e., conforming to the "ladder" model) in those areas. At the present rates of progress in semiconductors and magnetics, the cost of hardware for computers of the type and size commonly used today will be near zero by the end of the century. Semiconductor people often make the analogy that "If cars evolved at the rate of semiconductors, we would all be driving Rolls Royces today that go a million miles an hour and cost $0.25." The difference lies entirely in the technology: Maxwell's equations governing electromagnetic radiation, which moves at the speed of light, versus Newton's laws governing the motion of objects with mass, which move at far slower speeds.

The integrated circuit was invented in 1958, the year when discrete transistors first started being used in computers. Every year from 1958 until about 1972, the number of transistors per die doubled. Starting in 1972, the number began doubling only every year and a half, or increasing at roughly a rate of 60 percent per year, resulting in a factor of 100 improvement each decade. Gordon Moore of Intel posited two laws based on this phenomenon:

- *Moore's law (1964):* The density of chips doubles every year.

- *Moore's law (1975):* The density of chips doubles every 1 $\frac{1}{2}$ years.

In recent years, the use of memory circuits that require only one transistor per bit stored (plus some capacitance) have made bits per chip rather than transistors per chip a more interesting measure, but density has continued to double every year and a half, which means that it quadruples every three years. This three-year pattern is illustrated by these statistics on the number of bits per chip and the year in which each chip was introduced: 1K (1972), 4K (1975), 16K (1978), 64K (1981), 256K (1984), 1M (1987), and 4M (1990). The following equation applies (note that *t* equals the current year):

$$\text{Number of bits/chip} = 1K \times 2^{(t - 1972)/1.5}$$

This trend seems likely to continue until the year 2000, when extrapolation suggests that a single memory chip will store 256 million bits. The 256-million-bit figure may be slightly optimistic, however, since Meindl (1987) predicts that growth will slow down from 60 percent to between 20 percent and 35 percent beginning in 1992–1998. However, Meindl sees 20 percent to 35 percent growth persisting for another twenty years, in which case, a single die will store between 1 trillion and 100 trillion bits.

Both this past history and the future of the entire industry can be seen in the following graphs. The first graph (Figure 5-2), based on data from Intel, shows the number of transistors per die for various-size memories and microprocessors during the period 1970–1990 and projects the growth in density through the year 2000. The graph indicates a logarithmic increase in density over time. This has allowed computers to operate faster while costing less, because of the following two rules:

- The smaller everything gets, approaching the size of an electron, the faster the system behaves.

- Miniaturized circuits manufactured in a batch process tend to cost nothing to produce after the factory is in place.

The cost impact of the increased densities shown in Figure 5-2 is reflected in Figure 5-3, which shows changes in the relative cost of scientific computing from 1950 to 2000. The cost has declined over five orders of magnitude during that period, representing a price drop of 20 percent per year.

Not all of the cost benefits of increased memory chip density have translated into a reduction in system cost, however. Some of the cost benefits have translated into larger memories, since the advances permit a given computer to have more memory for a constant price. In the forty-five-year period shown in Figure 5-4, primary memories have grown by over six orders of magnitude, representing an increase in size at the rate of 35 percent per year.

In summary, the semiconductor density evolution has been extremely dramatic. It has spawned whole new classes of computers, new computer systems, new companies, and new opportunities, many of which are discussed later in the chapter.

However, semiconductor memories are only one part of computer memory systems, which can be thought of as a hierarchy (Figure 5-5). Information pertaining to

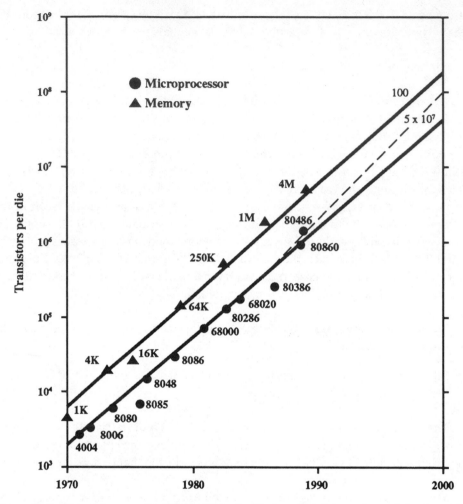

Figure 5-2. Transistors per Die Versus Time for Various-Size Memories and for Several Intel Microprocessor Chips. (Courtesy of Intel Corporation.)

a present computation is stored in fast registers that are part of the central processing unit (CPU), while recently referenced information is held in cache memories. Information referenced less often is stored in primary (semiconductor array) memories. Infrequently referenced information is stored using electromechanical technologies that record information on magnetic disks, magnetic tape, and electro-optical media. Although each lower level in this technological hierarchy is characterized by slower access times, the cost per bit stored is correspondingly lower. Technology progress at all levels of the hierarchy has driven down the price of computing systems memory, as indicated in Figure 5-6.

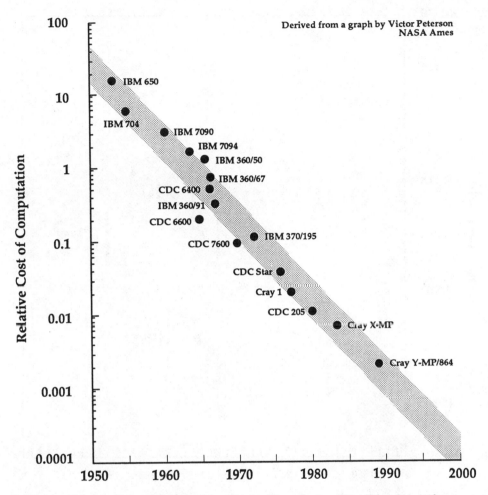

Figure 5-3. Relative Cost of Computation Versus Time for Leading-Edge Scientific Computers. (Courtesy of Askmar. Reprinted with permission.)

Just as increasing transistor density has improved the storage capacity of semiconductor memory chips, increasing areal density[2] has directly affected the total information-storage capacity of disk systems. Figure 5-7 shows lines of constant areal density for disks and tapes. Notice that IBM's 1957 disk file, the 350 RAMAC, recorded about 100 bits along the circumference of each track and each track was separated by 0.1 inch, giving an areal density of 1,000 bits per square inch. In early 1990, IBM announced that one of its laboratories had stored 1 billion bits in 1 square inch. This technology

---

2. The amount of information that can be stored per unit area.

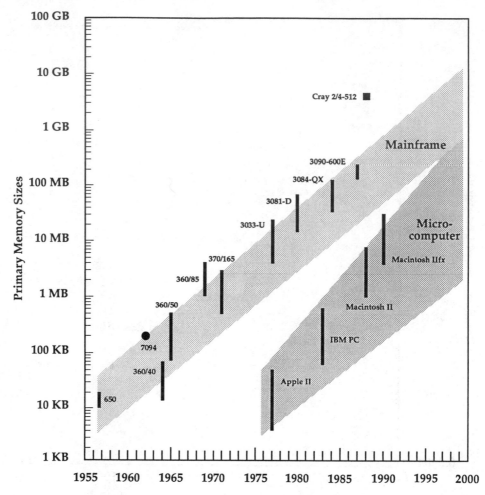

Figure 5-4. Primary Memory Size Versus Time for Mainframes and Microcomputers. (Courtesy of Askmar. Reprinted with permission.)

progression of six orders of magnitude in thirty-three years amounts to a density increase at a rate of over 50 percent per year.

Increases in areal density have led to magnetic storage systems that are not only cheaper to purchase but also cheaper to own, primarily because the density increases have markedly reduced floor-space requirements (which are a substantial item of expense in many environments). Figure 5-8 shows changes over time in the amount of information that can be stored in various-size disk memories. The first disk files occupied over 2 square meters of floor space but held only 5 megabytes of information.

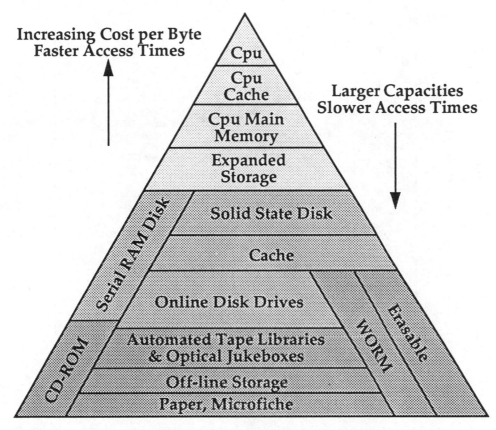

Figure 5-5. The Various Technologies That Form the Computer Memory Hierarchy.
(Coutesy of Askmar. Reprinted with permission.)

By the mid-1960s, large disks occupied less than a square meter of floor area. With the introduction of 8-inch-diameter disks (not shown in the figure) in the mid-1980s, six 500 megabyte disks could be rack-mounted in a cabinet occupying 1 square meter of floor area, a twelve hundred- fold improvement over the early disks.

Modern $5\frac{1}{4}$-inch and $3\frac{1}{2}$-inch drives can be mounted within a workstation, and without such high-density disks, the modern workstation environment would be impossible. In 1990, a $2\frac{1}{2}$-inch 20-megabyte disk drive occupies an area of less than 10 square inches at a height of less than half an inch, permitting the disk to be mounted

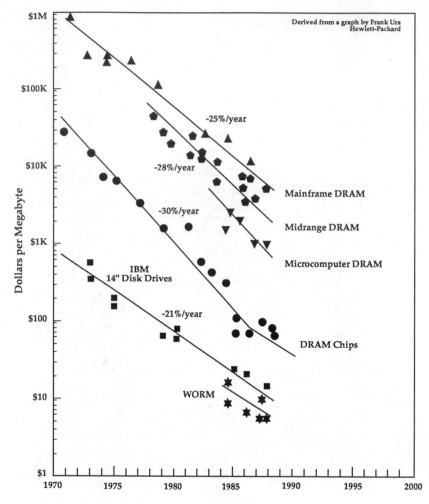

Figure 5-6. Price of Primary (Dynamic RAM), Secondary (Disk), and Tertiary (Write-Once) Memory Versus Time. (Courtesy of Frank Ura, Hewlett-Packard.)

entirely on a printed circuit board and thereby making laptop and notebook-size PCs possible. Soon, electro-optical disk technologies will provide a gigabyte of disk memory at the cost of a compact audiodisk, making it economically feasible for PC or workstation users to have roughly four hundred thousand pages of pure text or ten thousand pages of pure image data instantly available. In short, along with semiconductors and display devices, disks have been a key enabling technology for a number of computer classes, including PCs, workstations, and laptops.

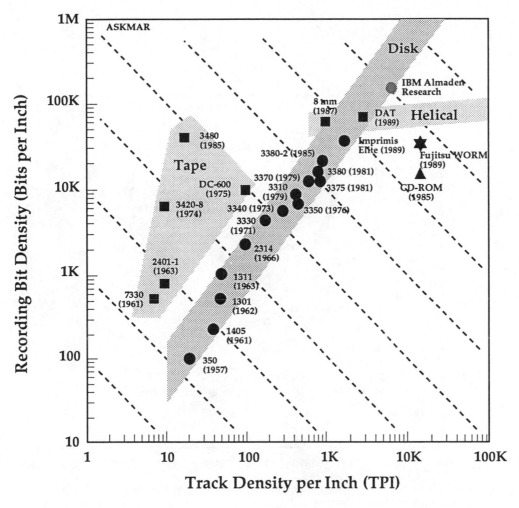

Figure 5-7. Density for Various Secondary (Disk) and Tertiary (Tape) Memories. (Courtesy of Askmar. Reprinted with permission.)

THE ROLE OF TECHNOLOGY PROGRESS IN FORMING START-UPS

In the previous subsection, technology progress was said to be the result of two factors: the increased density of semiconductors and magnetics, and the quest to build and exploit computers with new applications. That is perhaps a simplistic view, however, because the synergistic relationship between start-ups, established companies, research labs, and academia plays an equally important role in technology progress. Defining

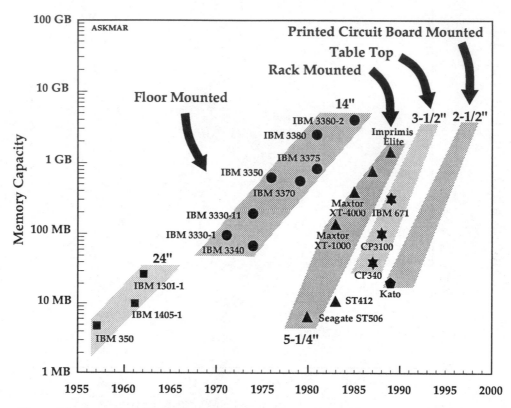

Figure 5-8. Secondary (Disk) Memory Capacity Versus Time. (Courtesy of Askmar. Reprinted with permission.)

that relationship is a bit like addressing the "Which came first, the chicken or the egg?" question, because established companies, research labs, and academia create advances in technology, which provide the impetus for the formation of start-ups. Start-ups then create additional advances in technology, which are further researched and developed by established companies, research labs, and academia. This process is consistent with the "wheel" model of product evolution shown earlier in the chapter (Figure 5-1).

Start-ups form to exploit the challenge of a new product idea that is based on one or more of the following (examples are shown in parentheses):

- Basic or applied research performed at university, government, or industrial laboratories (Valid Logic: simulation, timing verification, and design; Silicon

Compilers: automated chip design; NChip: multichip packaging; and Silicon Graphics: 3-D workstations)

- Applied research directed toward the development of a new product (voice typewriter)

- A new manufacturing process (metal oxide semiconductor [MOS])

- A new component (integrated circuits; microprocessors, including RISCs [reduced instruction set computers])

- A new architecture (parallel processing)

- A new standard (Ethernet, ISDN, UNIX)

- A new de facto standard that fills an early need (Adobe Postscript)

- A new paradigm for computing (Visicalc, HyperCard)

- A new generic application made possible by a new computer (word processing)

- A new professional application (movie making, molecular modeling)

- A new user-specific product or requirement (GM's MAP protocol)

- A new military or government requirement (ADA, Posix, VHDL)

- User-developed software that serves as a demonstration, first prototype, or first release (Nastran, DBASE II)

To explore each of these factors in depth would require hundreds of pages, but a quick review of several of them would be useful. Since the first two items on the list concern research, let's begin there.

The revolutionary and evolutionary changes in technology discussed earlier in the chapter have been the result of research conducted in a number of environments: government-funded research in universities, government laboratory research, corporate research, and individual research. The following subsections briefly examine the technological changes that have resulted from each of these types of research.

Government-Funded University Research

The great new forms of computing have come from government-funded university research. DARPA (Defense Advanced Research Projects Agency) has been the primary funder of large projects, while the NSF (National Science Foundation) has funded smaller projects, university infrastructure, individual researchers, and the training of engineers and scientists through research projects. Table 5-1 shows some of the critical inventions that have been produced by government-funded research.

Government Laboratory Research

Seven hundred national laboratories in the United States and a smaller number in other nations are important sources of research activity and technology training. Occasionally, they also provide prototypes or ideas that stimulate products. For example, a large number of algorithms and programs for scientific computing have come from the Lawrence Laboratories at Berkeley, Livermore, and Los Alamos. NASA's laboratories have pioneered many programs in computational fluid dynamics, and the standard program for finite element analysis (Nastran) is a product of NASA. In the computer-hardware area, NASA stimulated the development of the first integrated circuits because it needed compact, powerful computers. Several of the NASA products were spun off and further developed by private industry. For example, Nastran was transferred to McNeal Schwindler Corporation for continued development and commercialization. Similarly, Ashton-Tate exploited JPLDIS, produced by research at the NASA-funded Jet Propulsion Laboratory, by reimplementing the Fortran version in assembly language and marketed it as DBASE II.

In many cases, laboratories have served as knowledgeable and demanding users, and companies such as Control Data Corporation (CDC) and Cray Research have formed to build computers that would meet the laboratories' needs. These laboratories have been the first users of nearly all innovative computers and hence have supported the industry by acting as risk-taking customers. If government laboratories had not played this role, high-performance computers and many new technologies simply would not exist.

Although success in the 1990s will require being competitive in consumer electronics, small and large computers (including supercomputers), and complex semiconductors, America now faces serious and widespread deficiencies in its manufacturing ability. A concerted industrial-government effort, including a thoughtful industrial policy that looks beyond the strong de facto policies of significant military funding, might galvanize action and help reinvigorate the continually eroding U.S. industrial base.

Corporate Research

In the past, invention has been characterized as proceeding through a well-defined set of stages from basic to applied research, to advanced development, and on to product development, and this is still the case in certain industries. Given the nature of basic

Table 5-1. Inventions Produced by Government-Funded Research.

Date	Funder	Where	What
1946	Army	University of Pennsylvania	ENIAC, the first large-scale, electronic calculator and stored-program computer
1952	ONR[a]	MIT	Whirlwind computer with core memory, first compiler, CAM (computer-aided manufacturing), interactive computing, demo. Air defense, air traffic control
1963	DARPA	University of California,Berkeley; Michigan; MIT	Project MAC and Multics, time-sharing, stimulated AT&T's UNIX
1965–	DARPA	CMU; MIT; Stanford	Artificial intelligence leading to robots, and expert and speech systems
1966	DARPA	University of Utah	Graphics and the training of the key graphics scientists and engineers byDave Evans and Ivan Sutherland, formation of Evans and Sutherland
1967–	DARPA	SRI	Human-interface experiments leading to Xerox PARC's Alto and on to Apple's Lisa and Macintosh
1972–	DARPA	BBN; University of California, Los Angeles; Network Analysis Corp.; etc.	ARPAnet as first packet switch; stimulation of Ethernet and packet radio, the forerunner of cellular phones
1980–	DARPA	University of California, Berkeley	UNIX 4.x to exploit and evolve UNIX
1981–	DARPA	University of California, Berkeley; Cal Tech; CMU, MIT; Stanford; etc.	Computer-aided design for VLSI (very-large-scale integration), including silicon compilers
1985–	DARPA	University of California, Berkeley; CMU; MIT; Stanford	Strategic Computing Initiative. Connection Machine, RISC architecture, Systolic Processing
1985	NSF, DOE	Cal Tech	Hypercubes as the first large multicomputers

[a]The Office of Naval Research, a precursor to DARPA, funded early basic research.

research, products are often an unplanned side effect of industrial accidents. In the case of computing, though, traditional industrial research plays a less significant role than it does in other industries, such as chemicals. Furthermore, since Nobel Prizes are not awarded for computer-science inventions and discoveries, there is no established method for recognizing research accomplishments in this field. However, there have been some noteworthy achievements at industrial labs, including Bell Lab's transistor and UNIX, IBM's work on RISC, and the first development of a distributed workstation environment at Xerox PARC.

Major electronics companies spend an impressive amount of money on research and development. In 1989, *Electronic Business* reported on the top research and development spenders in the United States and Japan (shown in Table 5-2), which spent $13.6 billion and $15.2 billion, respectively.

Occasionally, corporate product development establishes new directions in computing. Some of the more important first developments include disks, printing, relational databases, and the System/360 architecture by IBM; minicomputers, time-sharing, networking, and the VAX architecture and its homogeneous computing environment by Digital Equipment Corporation (DEC); and the Intel 80X86 architecture combined with Microsoft's operating system as a basis for the evolution of the personal computer or, alternatively, the IBM-compatible PC.

Not all "corporate research" takes place in laboratories such as those just mentioned, however. Many technological advances attributable to corporations actually originate with the user base at those companies. The application of computers has been a prime source of new product ideas. Products often progress from a specific program at a firm such as Lucasfilm Ltd. to the formation of a company (Pixar) to exploit the product on a wide-scale basis. The largest software organization (Computer Associates) came from the process of productizing programs encountered by an organization serving IBM customers.

Since computers either supplement or supplant other information-processing systems, including humans, the potential for computing is very large (i.e., as large as the information business itself). Computers will eventually be involved in the creation, storage, or transmission of nearly every bit in the universe. Applications designed to exploit that potential are therefore a major source of ideas for new companies.

Individual Research

Although virtually all the research and development that has resulted in significant products can be traced back to an individual or a project leader, some of the inventions are particularly noteworthy because they led to a new kind of computer or a new way of computing. Most of these advances involved new programming languages or new

Table 5-2. Top U.S. and Japanese Research and Development Spenders.

American Expenditures		Japanese Expenditures	
Company	Amount ($ billions)	Company	Amount ($ billions)
IBM	5.9	NEC	3.7
Digital	1.3	Hitachi	2.8
Hewlett-Packard (HP)	1.0	Matsushita	2.4
Xerox	0.8	Fujitsu	1.9
Unisys	0.7	Toshiba	1.7
Motorola	0.7	Sony	1.1
Hughes	0.6	Sharp	0.5
Texas Instruments (TI)	0.5	Canon	0.5
NCR	0.4	Ricoh	0.4
Control Data Corporation (CDC)	0.3	Omron	0.2
Honeywell	0.3		
Intel	0.3		
National	0.3		
Apple	0.3		
Wang	0.2		

uses for computers. Other advances, such as new architectures or large computers, were team efforts. Table 5-3 lists some outstanding personal contributions to computing.

New Components

In addition to the research organizations mentioned above, the introduction of new components is another important source of inspiration for the formation of start-ups. When a new component (e.g., Motorola 68000) becomes available, many companies will simultaneously form, all of which claim to be unique and ideally positioned to exploit the novelty. For example, when the availability of the Intel 80860 component was

Table 5-3. Outstanding Personal Contributions to Computing.

Who	Where	What
Backus	IBM	Fortran
Bricklin and Franksten	—	Visicalc, the first spreadsheet
Cocke	IBM	RISC
Cray	CDC/Cray	RISC, vector architecture, innovative circuitry, and high-density packaging
Iverson	IBM	APL—A Programming Language
Kemeny and Kurtz	Dartmouth	BASIC
McCarthy	MIT	Lisp
Thompson and Ritchie	Bell Labs	UNIX and the C language

announced in April 1989, I was invited to become the CEO of a company whose stated purpose was:

> developing and marketing a new category of computer system to address a substantial, emerging market opportunity: to bring supercomputing solutions into the mass market of the desktop era . . . with the first line of extremely high performance servers.

Unfortunately, more than a dozen other groups (including a few start-ups) had also formed to build roughly the same product and attempt to enter the same market.

New Architectures

Most recently, the idea of parallel processing has given rise to almost a hundred hardware start-ups aimed at supplying high-performance computing by linking hardware components of various kinds. These new ventures have produced significant advances in the ability to operate a large number of processors, processing elements, or computers together on a single program. But since parallelism is not a market per se, and the difficulty of solving parallelism is so great (including the issue of retraining users), any company that markets parallelism without solving real problems whose solution will produce a significant payoff is certain to fail. Furthermore, given the long lead time required to establish a market, large firms can adopt the concept on an evolutionary basis, after the hard work of developing the technology and markets is done. Despite these drawbacks, all forms of parallel computing will exist by 2001, along with enough users to exploit the various structures.

New Standards

In the case of almost every new standard, new companies form to exploit the time advantage that comes from being first to market with a product that meets the standard. In effect, these start-ups are betting against the long or infinite product-gestation time of large engineering organizations in established firms.

Standards take many forms:

- User group-gropes (a large group of people with varying qualifications groping for a product design) surrounding the standards committees of ANSI (American National Standards Institute), ISO (International Standardization Organization), and the IEEE (Institute of Electrical and Electronics Engineers) that produced languages such as ADA, Algol, and Cobol; interfaces, such as dialects of UNIX; and various communication protocols, including OSI.

- "Industry-compatible," a euphemism for "IBM-compatible."

- De facto, based on a particular part or convention of a dominant supplier. In this case, users and competitive suppliers agree to employ a particular interface, such as the Small Computer Storage Interface (SCSI). Start-ups are likely to create de facto standards.

- Consortia of users and suppliers that posit a standard, which is then processed and formally accepted by national and international standards bodies. Ethernet (IEEE 802.3) was developed in this fashion by Digital, Intel, and Xerox.

- Establishment of a product acquisition and development group that specifies new product standards. The Open Software Foundation (OSF) was formed to evolve UNIX independently of AT&T and Sun Microsystems.

THE ROLE OF START-UPS IN CREATING TECHNOLOGY PROGRESS

The previous subsection discussed the role that technological advances have played in the creation of start-ups. This process has been a two-way street, though, since start-ups have also played a major role in the creation of technological advances. All new classes of computers, from supercomputers to personal computers (but excluding mainframes), originated with start-up companies that used new semiconductor technology. Start-ups have been pivotal to computer development, as proved by a number of substantial innovations, including Microsoft's evolution of MS/DOS as a basis for IBM's Personal Computer evolution; the development of relational databases by Oracle and other start-ups; and the introduction of floppy and small disks using IBM-developed Winchester recording technology. Start-ups have created generic word processing, communications, mail, and spreadsheet programs as well as profession-based application programs such as mechanical and electrical computer-aided design.

TRANSFERRING TECHNOLOGY FROM ITS SOURCES

Successfully securing technology from the sources mentioned above requires an understanding of the laws that govern the flow of technology. These laws deal with the substance of the technology, the transfer process itself, and the inevitable competition to develop products for selected applications. If a new venture is to be viable, it must address all three of these issues.

The following are some common technology-transfer methods, listed in increasing order of effectiveness:

- Papers and conferences at which ideas and algorithms are presented

- Industrial programs for exchanging ideas, people, etc.

- Industrial research consortia

- Direct funding of projects whose mission is to produce a specific result

- Consulting with a high degree of responsibility

- Computer programs that can become industrial-strength

- Transferring trained people, together with a new technology

- Transferring trained people, together with a prototype or an operational product

The best way to transfer technology is to transfer trained people. This method of technology transfer is especially effective if the people can bring a prototype of the new idea with them. Although this is generally not possible if they are coming from a government or commercial laboratory, it may be possible if they are coming from an academic environment. The concreteness of the idea is essential. In the words of MIT's David D. Clark: "One artifact is worth a thousand papers." The prototype not only demonstrates feasibility, it also demonstrates a potential new product in an application context. If the technology embodying the idea cannot be demonstrated at the outset, any company founded to exploit the idea is likely to find itself doing a lot of fundamental research.

Novel concepts or artifacts inspire new product ideas in the minds of every engineer or savvy marketeer, and do so in direct proportion to the media attention devoted to these new developments. Furthermore, at least two redundant east/west firms will be created in response to these concepts or artifacts. The total number of companies formed will be roughly proportional to the amount of investment capital available from all sources. In short, entrepreneurs who think their proposed start-up will be alone in the field are probably mistaken.

ENGINEERING

The two types of engineering done in nearly all companies involve hardware and software. Hardware engineering is the process of designing and building an ultimate physical object, such as a computer component, a computer, or a manufacturing process or plant to produce products. The first stage of hardware engineering is to build a working simulation or model of the product or plant using a computer before any physical construction is undertaken. The final stage is to build and test the physical object itself.

Software engineering is the process of building a program or product that operates wholly within the confines of a computer or computer network. Since all engineering requires an understanding of software, the engineering process described in this section will focus mainly on the formal steps of software engineering.

HARDWARE ENGINEERING

Hardware engineering is the process of utilizing technology to create a new product or, more precisely, a set of documents and specifications from which a manufacturing organization can build the product. A good hardware engineer has vision tempered with judgment, the capacity to deal with endless detail, and the fortitude to stay the course despite setbacks.

During a company's early stages, the founders and hardware engineers must select the right technology to employ in the product. This is a critical judgment call, since the firm's success depends on having the "right tech." Technology cannot be too high (approaching infinity, as in research) or too low (approaching zero, such that anyone can replicate it). Furthermore, it has to be timed right. No other factor in a company's development operates in such a delicate balance. On the one hand, investors want demonstrably unique and proprietary technology, and on the other hand, they are unwilling to invest in any risky research to develop such technology. Thus, really successful start-ups are likely to come directly from the laboratory, where the technology is demonstrable, as in the case of Silicon Graphics and Sun Microsystems, whose founders developed prototypes while at Stanford. The best technology/product, as noted earlier, consists of a prototype together with the people who created it.

As a company develops additional products, the hardware engineers must make this technology decision again and again, knowing that their opposite numbers at competing firms are making similar decisions. Typically, a new technology or new part is "almost available." If the engineers choose to use it and it is delayed in reaching production, their company will have no new product. If they choose to be too conservative, the competition may succeed in offering customers both the new technology and the "bigger bang for the buck" that it represents, leaving the conservative engineers with an uncompetitive product.

In general, the hardware engineers at small companies will be more daring than those at large companies, since they need smaller volumes of the new parts and they must take market share away from established firms by offering more value via high technology. Furthermore, the fact that product cycles are longer at larger companies tends to increase the lead time between the "technology decision point" and product availability. Because of the longer lead time, engineers must forecast technology availability further into the future, increasing the risk and generally resulting in more conservative technology decisions.

In addition to making technology decisions, which many regard as the "fun part" of engineering, hardware engineers must evaluate every aspect of their design for operation at maximum and minimum clock speeds, temperature, component variation, etc. Although many simulation tools now exist to aid in this task, it still involves considerable drudgery.

Finally, in hardware engineering, Ohm's law and Maxwell's equations pale in importance and influence next to Murphy's law. Even with simulation tools, a number of "gotchas" lurk in every design effort. Some are technical; some are personal; some are political. The good engineer will stay the course throughout these setbacks, which is one reason why high-tech ventures like to hire engineers from top universities, where competition is fierce and courses are difficult—the graduates have been "fire-hardened."

SOFTWARE ENGINEERING

In the 1990s, a computer system organization, including one that builds PCs, must understand software. The company is usually responsible for unique programs that are part of the machine (e.g., firmware), plus the software used in the design, manufacturing, and testing of the systems. Furthermore, a great deal of what was formerly hardware design has now become software-oriented. For example, much digital system design is now done in a completely symbolic fashion whereby a "program" is compiled into a chip. Thus, every high-tech company must be intimately involved with the development, use, and maintenance of software whether the firm likes it or not.

Some people regard the development of software products as an unstructurable, unschedulable, unmanageable, and highly creative process that is the province of the last great American inventors. Others see the process as resembling a factory, with thousands of programmers working in one large, open room, all using the same, impersonal bureaucratic process, and turning out thousands of lines of code, as in Japan. The latter model generates almost twice as much code per person as the former model, and at a quality level that is two to three times better. In order to produce at the necessary volume and quality level, start-ups must use methods that are closer to those of the Japanese than to those of the lone inventor.

Since everything about the design and fabrication of a product can be considered in factorylike, or at least job-shop, terms, the idea of developing software on a mass-production basis is indeed tempting. This approach, however, is beyond the means of most new ventures, which must follow the "invention" model rather than the "factory" model in developing their software. Fortunately for those start-ups that must rely on the "invention" model, though, users are interested strictly in the end result (i.e., the unique characteristics, functions, performance, and quality of the product itself), regardless of whether that result was achieved by a creative, inventionlike design process or a standardized, factorylike design process.

PHASES OF A HARDWARE OR SOFTWARE ENGINEERING PROJECT

Every product passes through a series of predictable phases (or stages) from concept to retirement, and most companies eventually develop a phase-review process to track the development of their products. Table 5-4 shows these phases of a product's development, together with the corresponding stages of the start-up's growth.

A product is conceived during the company's concept stage (I), proceeds along until the seed stage (II), is developed in the product development stage (IIIa, IIIb, IIIc, and IIId), and ultimately reaches a phase during the market development and steady-state stages (IV and V) in which it is produced, sold, and maintained. In its final phase, the product may be enhanced and improved for some time before it ultimately passes into a state of retirement at the end of its life. The following paragraphs explore each of these stages in greater detail.

During the concept stage (I), the idea for a product must be explored and demonstrated to some degree. This demonstration can take the form of a feasibility prototype or model, or it can consist of either a demo by a key engineer indicating that such a design is possible or a careful analysis of critical technology.

During the seed stage (II), the requirements are spelled out in a product-requirements specification, a system production definition, and a preliminary user's

Table 5-4. The Phases of an Engineering Project, Company Stages, and Software-Engineering Process.

Bell-Mason Diagnostic Stage	Concept	Seed	Product Development				Market Development and Steady State
			Hiring, Specifications, and Schedule	*Designing and Building*	*Alpha Testing*	*Beta Testing*	
		Preliminary specifications and schedule	Detailed specifications and schedule	Implementation	System testing	Acceptance	
Company stage	I	II	IIIa	IIIb	IIIc	IIId	IV and V
	Formulate technology. Gather market requirements. Outline product. Plan technical feasibility.	Plan product and project based on requirements. Demonstrate technical feasiblity.	Assemble team. Define product. Prepare formal plan.	Build simulation of product, followed by first running system.	Alpha-test product via internal use with internal users.	Beta-test product with real users in their working environment	Produce and sell product by maintaining product and correcting any errors. Maintain product's life with enhancements.
Software Engineering Phase	I	II	IIIa	IIIb	IIIc	IIId	IV and V
	Concept explanation	Planning and definition of requirements	Hiring, designing, and replanning. Preliminary and detailed design	Implementation Unit design, coding, testing	Integration, testing	User acceptance testing	Fixing, adapting, and enhancing
Outputs: product, manual, and specifications	Feasibility prototype or model	Product-requirements specification System production definition Preliminary user's manual	Architectural and detailed design specifications User's manual	First functional product from tested and integrated components	Operational product	Modifications to adapt to user needs User-accepted product	Producible and supportable product with minor release

Table 5-4. *(continued)*

Software Engineering Phase	I	II	IIIa	IIIb	IIIc	IIId	IV and V
Plans		Preliminary project plan Preliminary verification plan	Final project plan Final verification plan	Acceptance-test plan	Product-release plan Installation and training plan	Product-support plan	Enhancement plan for next release
Reviews		Product-requirements review Product-feasibility review	Preliminary and critical design reviews	Source-code review Acceptance-test review	Product-release review Installation and training review	Product-support review	Project postmortem
Resources	Prototypes and first computers		Network	Host computer			
Standards			Program standards and style guide	Configuration management			
People	Architect and product designer	Project leader	Development team				

manual. These are described in the specifications section (page 118), and it may be worthwhile to check the requirements against the actual product definition as part of the process. A seed stage is especially vital to a start-up involving innovative software (i.e., software that is being developed for the first time), because this is the stage during which the planning for the product is done. Without planning, the software schedule will be unpredictable.

During the first portion of the product development stage (IIIa), the main part of the design is carried out, starting with preparation of an architectural design specification, which is subjected to a preliminary design review. This is followed by preparation of a detailed design specification, which is subjected to a critical design review. Successful completion of this latter review is the main exit criterion for this design stage. A user's manual is written and made available. The verification plan is developed, and the project plan is updated.

During the implementation phase (IIIb), the design for each of the software components is prepared, and the coding and testing are completed. Formal design reviews are the best way to evaluate a complex hardware or software project. They are also the cheapest way to debug a program or system. Programs can be assessed by conducting code walk-throughs in which the designer "walks" a team of four to six people through the design. Alternatively, an inspection team can be appointed to go over the code, examining it and comparing it against various criteria. After the design reviews are complete, the programs are tested individually. Hardware implementation consists of two phases: first, an implementation of the design; then, a simulation before physical hardware is constructed and assembled. The exit criterion for substage IIIb is the existence of working subcomponents.

During the alpha-testing phase (IIIc), the subcomponents are integrated into a single system so that system testing can begin. After the system passes the specified internal acceptance tests, it can be released for first use by customers.

During the beta-testing phase (IIId), the system is given to customers for actual use. This phase involves working closely with an appropriate number of customers (e.g., three for computer hardware or large software systems and twenty for mass-produced components or software) to gain an in-depth understanding of how well the system meets the expectations of real users. In this stage, serious errors that result in unreliable operation must be fixed immediately. Critical features that were overlooked for some reason may have to be added. Thus, the product-support organization is first tested during a time when it is building its formal plan for providing support.

Theoretically, the product is announced upon completion of beta testing, when the company has satisfied itself that customers are happy and the product is viable in the marketplace. Actually, nearly all start-ups announce the product during, or even at the beginning of, beta testing. Anything less conservative than announcing at the end of beta testing is a flaw.

Finally, the product is released, and the firm enters the market development stage.

CONCLUSION

Semiconductor and magnetic densities, as measured by the number of bits stored per unit area, are likely to increase at their current exponential rates on into the twenty-first century. These increases will provide opportunities for new hardware systems, which, in turn, will permit the development of new software products (as will be discussed in Chapter 8).

Technology involves the ability to design and build high-tech products. Many developments provide an opportunity for technological progress, including components such as semiconductors, standards, customer application needs, and genuine inventions. Technological advancements come from having trained resources and concentrating those resources on discovery. A significant portion of the world's research and development capabilities are available to entrepreneurs and intrapreneurs in various forms, ranging from papers, demonstrations, and consortia to trained people. Technology transfer is best accomplished by transferring people, as occurs when people leave a laboratory where they have developed an idea and form a separate group or a new company to commercialize the idea by creating a product.

Technological know-how is a necessary prerequisite for a new venture, but it is by no means sufficient. The start-up must also have a mastery of engineering that will enable it to successfully convert its technology into products in a predictable and timely fashion.

Chapter 6 presents the technology balance sheet, which can be used to break a company's technology and engineering abilities down into twelve separate aspects, or dimensions, that are analyzed to determine the status of these two critical areas.

Chapter 6

THE TECHNOLOGY BALANCE SHEET

Just as it is essential to understand an organization's financial health, it is equally necessary to understand and measure its technological health. The first section of the chapter describes the technology balance sheet, a useful approach to measuring a company's technology. The second section presents a number of classic technology-related flaws, ranging from requiring infinite technology (i.e., attempting to develop a product that is predicated on a fundamental discovery or technological breakthrough) to having no sustaining technology. The final section lists the rules for evaluating a new venture's technological position at the end of the concept and seed stages.

THE TECHNOLOGY BALANCE SHEET

The technology balance sheet evaluates each of twelve key dimensions of a start-up's technology. Readers may notice that the dimensions used on the technology balance sheet to assess a firm's technology are very similar to the dimensions used throughout the book to assess a firm's overall status.

Figure 6-1 lists the twelve dimensions to be considered and measured:

- Technology base

- Standards

- Design, quality, and other processes

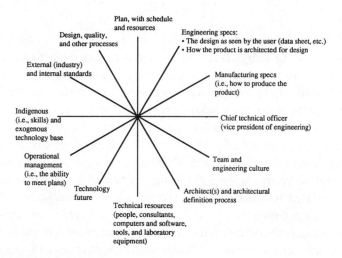

Figure 6-1. Technology Balance Sheet Plotted as a Relational Graph.

- Plan, with schedule and resources

- Engineering specifications

- Manufacturing specifications

- Chief technical officer

- Team and engineering culture

- Architecture

- Technical resources

- Technology future

- Operational management

These dimensions will be discussed in the following subsections.

TECHNOLOGY

The technology dimension includes internal and external sources of components, plus "know-how," as represented by critical personnel, patents, processes, etc. The company must examine every facet of the technology that it needs to build a product and then rank each technology source as objectively as possible.

STANDARDS

Standards should be regarded as a critical aspect of product design. Establishing uniform ways of doing things (such as having an exact dialect of a language for expressing a program and having programming style conventions) permits rapid progress because standardized components can be interconnected and built on one another. Although standards are inherently constraining, Dave Nelson (one of Apollo's founders) believes that constraints are what really breed creativity. In designing a product, it is inherently more difficult to start with a blank slate than to start with some restrictions, because in the absence of established criteria, nearly anything is possible. Effort will therefore be squandered exploring an almost infinite number of options rather than channeled and focused in the most productive directions.

A start-up (or a company of any size, for that matter) must understand and implement both external and internal standards. Major aspects of product design are determined by external (industry) standards covering such areas as inputs, outputs, cost (in memory size), and speed (fifty thousand lines per second). For example, a compiler may be specified as having to accept ANSI (American National Standards Institute) standard C language input, produce code for the Motorola 88000 chipset that is better than the existing compilers, occupy no more than 100 kilobytes of memory, and compile at over fifty thousand lines of code per second.

Internal standards are equally important and range from how logic design or programming is done to line width on printed circuit boards. Internal standards must be specified, published, and enforced in a formal manner. For instance, when Digital Equipment Corporation (DEC) first started, the Engineering Committee took responsibility for creating a set of design standards that covered everything from how a physical environment would be specified and tested (power, temperature, humidity, etc.) to how a copyright statement would be placed in memories and programs. Internal standards also include a list of the components that are permissible in new designs.

Upon seeing such standards and component lists, the first reaction of most engineers is that they are bureaucratic and constrain creativity. However, standards are simply a statement of decisions that have been made regarding good practice, which means the designer doesn't have to think about these more mundane aspects of a design (such as the temperature at which the product should be designed to operate) and is therefore free to concentrate on the truly creative aspects.

DESIGN PROCESS

The design process, which specifies what tools engineers use to create and check each part of their product design, must be documented and managed. The design process is intimately tied to the resources a company has to aid designers. Much has been written about software engineering, and there are any number of valid models for how programming should be done. The important thing is simply to pick a model that is appropriate for the team and operate according to it.

The Software Engineering Institute (Humphrey, 1989; derived from Demming and Juran) has established a five-level ranking to characterize how effectively a team is functioning in terms of its process capability:

1. *Initial:* There is an ad hoc process. Formal procedures may exist, but there is no management mechanism for tracking results against the procedures. The team rarely makes and meets plans.

2. *Repeatable:* A process exists that deals effectively with routine programs but produces unpredictable results with new programs or new tools.

3. *Defined:* A qualitative description of the process exists.

4. *Managed:* The process contains a minimum set of measurements to define quality and cost; a process baseline exists; etc.

5. *Optimizing:* There exist sufficient quantitative measures for each part of the process to allow the process to be completely understood and fine-tuned.

Humphrey describes a method for evaluating a company's process capabilities and also recommends various processes, standards, and methods for attaining software process control. The organization with which he is associated, the Software Engineering Institute, can audit a firm to determine its level of process control, and some members of the institute did so as part of a 1990 trip to Japan sponsored by the Ministry of International Trade and Industry. While there, they found that many large Japanese companies are operating at the highest level in the above ranking (level 5, optimizing), enabling them to achieve quality and productivity levels more than twice that of their U.S. counterparts.

ENGINEERING PLAN

The engineering plan includes the schedule and a list of the resources required. The resources list must cover both the resources for developing the product itself and those for developing any of the manufacturing and design processes that the product requires. The important thing about an engineering plan is that the schedule be realistic. Developing a truly realistic schedule is almost impossible if the product has never before been attempted; it is merely very difficult if the product has been attempted previously but the team has never before worked together. In the latter case, each team member's ability to establish a realistic schedule for his or her portion of the work will probably be untested. In terms of the process-capability levels outlined by Humphrey, it is unlikely that such a software team in a new venture could get above level 2 (repeatable) by the time it ships its first product.

Product-gestation time gets ingrained in the people and the company. Their ideas regarding product-gestation time are often based directly on the lead times at a larger firm, which are guaranteed to be much, much longer. One of the most important aspects of an engineering culture is to establish an accurate but responsive ability to schedule. There are four ways to schedule a project:

- *Optimistically:* Put enormous pressure on the team by preparing an aggressive schedule that the team believes can only be met if everything goes right.

- *Pessimistically:* Build so many delays and contingencies into the schedule that the schedule will certainly be met (an approach unlikely to be used by a start-up).

- *Realistically:* Allow for an appropriate number of contingencies, which will become possible when the team is mature enough and understands the project and each other well enough. However, it often happens that everyone up the chain of command then adds a contingency, and the net result is a bloated, pessimistic schedule (again, not typical of start-ups). With realistic scheduling, the company may end up with two schedules—the optimistic one and the one with the contingencies added.

- *Running blind:* Work on the project until it gets done. The firm that uses this approach had better start with lots of money, be able to raise more money easily, and have plenty of extra resources.

In the final analysis, schedules really don't always work. Any critical schedule milestone must coincide with an immovable deadline such as a demonstration to the board, a trade show, a funding event, or a customer shipment. If customer shipment serves as a deadline, quality must always be used to control shipment.

ENGINEERING AND MANUFACTURING SPECIFICATIONS

The engineering and manufacturing specifications describe the product in several ways. First, they describe its external specification, or the product's function, including performance, as seen by a user. Second, they describe its internal specification, or the product's structure and internal function as seen by the engineering team (i.e., a set of components to be designed). Finally, when the product has been fully specified both externally and internally, manufacturing requires process and product specifications describing how the product will actually be built and tested.

CHIEF TECHNICAL OFFICER

The chief technical officer (CTO), or engineering vice president, is the technical leader in charge of implementing the product. This person is ultimately responsible for all products and is the CEO for the engineering organization. Thus, his or her general qualifications must parallel those of the CEO because the CTO is the "clock" and "standards setter" for engineering.

The company should have selected its CTO by the end of the seed stage, and if it is tackling a technologically difficult product, the CTO must be on board from the start. Funding a high-tech venture without a CTO is extremely risky because he or she is the individual responsible for ensuring that the product is really feasible at the price, quality, schedule, and resource level specified in the business plan.

ENGINEERING TEAM AND CULTURE

The engineering team and culture are just beginning to form by the end of the seed stage, since at this point, a complete team has yet to be hired and the head of engineering may not even be on board. The organizational structure is quite important because the CTO may have positioned himself or herself as a bottleneck by assuming responsibility for all intergroup problem resolution. As with any organization, theory X, Y, and Z will all work. I do not favor highly top-down engineering organizations because they do not bring out the creativity of the people doing the work. Furthermore, top-down structures eliminate critical intraorganization communication. Worst of all, top-down organizations usually do not engender commitment to schedule, resources, and product on the part of the responsible engineers.

ARCHITECTURE

The term *architecture* was coined in 1964 by the IBM System/360 design team to describe a computer's instruction set, or how the computer appeared to a program (or programmer). *Architecture* is now used in a broader sense that encompasses both "external architecture" and "internal architecture." The external architecture describes the general function of any computer component (i.e., what it does)—such as the instruction-set architecture, operating system, compiler, a network protocol, or spreadsheet—and how this component appears to anyone using it. The internal architecture (or "realization") forms the blueprint for how the components that create the external architecture are implemented; it is what a development team designs and builds.

It is therefore vital to have a product architect who can both define the product externally and be able to play a major role in decomposing it for realization and then engineering it. His or her responsibility for product architecture applies equally to all levels of hardware and software. Thus, the product architect is likely to be the most critical person in the engineering group,[1] including the CTO.

The architect's key job is to guide the product's implementation and evolution over its lifetime. The lifetime of a good architecture will be considerable, and the company fortunate enough to have chosen a good architect and architecture will profit immeasurably. Much of DEC's success during its first three decades (1957-1987) was based on constant and evolving architectures for its minis, including the VAX. System/360 hardware and software systems and their successors were the basis of most of IBM's revenues and profits for a similar period. More recently, the Apple II and Macintosh architectures have each prospered for over a decade. In 1990, Sun Microsystems has been attempting to repeat the success of these predecessor architectures by establishing the SPARC architecture as the standard for workstation-class computers.

Although most of the examples cited above involve hardware engineering, the same sort of architectural integrity must also be maintained for software. At Microsoft, every product, such as Word or Excel, has a single architect who maintains the product's integrity (and is usually its chief implementer as well). When responsibility for a product is diffused, as in the case of Fortran or UNIX, by placing it in the hands of some amorphous, committeelike group that is pushed around by numerous standards organizations, the product's efficacy declines and its ability to evolve may be stymied.

In my view, lack of a good architect, or lack of a suitable architecture, is the fatal flaw in many high-tech ventures. Although at first, the product architect may be the CTO or even the CEO, ultimately, someone within the engineering organization must assume responsibility for maintaining the efficacy of the product's external specification, especially with respect to how that product is changed as it is implemented in succeeding product generations. In some cases, as in the example of Ardent's Titan workstation described later in the chapter, several architects may be required as a product is broken into various parts.

Not having an architect is quite risky, because it leaves the product's definition to some nebulous process or to a group that gropes with the product design, as I recently saw in a company building a multimedia system. Not having a way to manage the product's design and delegate it to those who must do the design is almost always fatal. One of the biggest dangers is overcommitment. When a technically difficult project begins, and one person functions as CEO, CTO, and architect, the company, engineering group, and product are all likely to be out of control unless the firm has a sufficiently strong staff, including a chief operating officer. In a start-up, such a project must have a full-time architect who will also play a major role in the product's design.

---

1. My own background and biases as an architect may account for this belief.

In a recent case, the architectural concept for a product was superb, but the architect had four problems that thwarted effective implementation of the architecture. These problems, which are typical of many architects, were as follows:

- The architect lacked an understanding of the specific benchmarks by which the product would be judged in the marketplace.

- He had trouble finishing detailed specifications for the product, leaving the engineering organization with only a fuzzy idea of what it was supposed to be designing.

- He was not knowledgeable about implementation, which meant that the architecture could not be implemented within a reasonable time and at a reasonable product cost.

- His poor interpersonal skills made it hard to keep the actual implementation in synchronization with an ambiguous specification. (This was both his problem and that of the CTO.)

Although not having any architect can be a problem, having too many architects can also be a problem, as illustrated by the following example.

Venus. On Friday, August 13, 1982, I went to a design review for Venus (VAX 8600). The review, attended by several hundred people, focused on the schedule and the risk involved in not getting the chip layouts to the gate array supplier. I asked whether the design had been simulated or thoroughly reviewed. It hadn't, since the group was in such a hurry to meet the schedule that they wanted to skip the checking stage. On Saturday, I visited the project team to talk with its members and found that the management didn't understand the project and that four individuals each regarded himself as the project's sole architect and wanted the credit. The project had about four design styles, because it consisted of four large subsystems.

By Thursday, no one wanted credit. Within six months, the project was brought under control through many management changes and the introduction of a design process that required the use of design reviews and simulation to ensure the correctness of the design prior to building the hardware. The product ultimately shipped two years later than scheduled, whereas, left on its original course, it would probably never have shipped. The project ended up with an organizational structure consisting of four architects and a lead architect to resolve the conflicts among the group and finish the design.

Despite all these dire warnings about architecture, it *is* possible for a talented team of architects to work well together and produce an excellent product. The following story about the architecture and development team for the Ardent workstation (Titan) illustrates this point and shows how an architectural task can successfully be broken up.

The Ardent Titan architecture and development team.   Given the complexity of a graphics supercomputer, Ardent had to break the definition and responsibility for various elements of its design into independent parts and architectures. The entire project worked well when all the roles were defined. The architecture was the basis for three products, including Titan, which could be evolved through three generations over a five-year period.

The company's chief hardware architect, GSM, was responsible both for defining the instruction-set architecture externally and for defining the internal architecture (how the parts of the entire computer fitted together using a core bus). GSM also defined the processor's internal supercomputer architecture and took on many of the difficult processor-design tasks, although he did not lead the hardware project nor was he directly responsible for implementing the processor. After the first version of the machine was introduced, GSM led benchmarking and observed the machine in real applications. This was critical for the design of the next implementation.

JRA was the architect, leader, and key implementer for the development of the parallelizing vectorizing compiler. Having a single individual be responsible both for the architecture and for leading the implementation thereof was an ideal case. The languages architecture and debugger were the responsibility of SCJ.

WT was the architect, leader, and key implementer for the development of UNIX, which supported the Titan hardware and provided a program environment for the compiler and other applications programs.

TD was the architect, leader, and key implementer for the graphics hardware, while WW designed and built the software pipeline to transform and display 3-D objects. MK was the architect and chief implementer for the graphics library.

All architects/implementers had to cooperate on determining each architectural interface and on the entire design.

TECHNICAL RESOURCES

The next dimension on the technology balance sheet is technical resources. This essential category includes people, equipment (both computers and networks), and software to run the engineering enterprise (i.e., operating systems, languages, computer-aided design [CAD] programs, and software licenses). Of all the resources, the technical staff is the most important.

The company's hiring ability determines the quality of the staff. All firms, regardless of how well they may be managed, find that hiring grade-A people takes much longer than anyone had planned. The key to hiring is having the right sources. The most effective approach is to develop a network of contacts with the best people working in each area such that recruiting is by word of mouth. A technical advisory board can be one of the company's greatest hiring assets.

The organization's first hires have to be great because really good engineers like to be involved with other good (or even better) engineers and are intolerant of bozos and turkeys. Great people hire even better people. Poor people hire even poorer people. (This is the pygmy theory of hiring.) Furthermore, because the company can expect to acquire its share of average people merely in the course of making minor hiring errors, it must never deliberately hire average people just to fill slots.

The following stories illustrate some interesting approaches to hiring used by start-ups, along with critical observations on hiring the engineering team.

Ardent and Stellar. Both Ardent and Stellar allowed three months to form their team, but it took six months before the companies were fully staffed. Each firm established a technical advisory board to aid in the product definition, and these boards were the key to finding and recruiting the best people.

WAVETRACER. Richard Fiorintino, CEO of WAVETRACER, recruited engineers by sending a personal mailing to surrounding towns, at a cost of less than $500. Recruiting firms (headhunters) are a last resort, because they will be costly and error-prone. The start-up's leadership team itself is clearly responsible for staffing, no matter what the formal hiring channel may be.

Objectivity. Objectivity, a start-up building an object-oriented database, had a relatively long seed stage, during which it both designed its product and hired its key engineering leaders. When the product development stage started, Objectivity was ready to do full-scale recruiting because it knew what it was going to build and how it was going to build it.

It first created a database of everyone working in the field who had experience in theory, use, and development. It grouped the list according to technology and gave priority to people who had built specialized databases. Using all available sources, Objectivity did a forced ranking of everyone on the list, whether they were available or not. The process was carried out with peers via phone calls and in direct interviews, which were scheduled two nights per week and on weekends.

But the hiring process did not end when the candidates made a commitment and joined the organization. Instead, the process continued for a six-month probationary period, during which each new hire worked with the team and was given an opportunity to discuss his or her design and engineering philosophy at length. Several candidates ultimately left during the probationary period.

Objectivity's scheme had many advantages: the company found a large pool of engineers, got the best people to head the team, formed the team itself, gained an in-depth understanding of its potential competitors, and established links with potential buyers. Objectivity's approach did have one flaw, however: by using the grapevine, the organization risked disclosing basic technology and prompting other firms to start up.

Visix Software.   Visix built a high-quality, high-performance platform for building graphical-interface, networked applications. Its desktop for UNIX, Looking Glass, extends that of the Apple Macintosh to handle networking. Visix achieved product quality by implementing a rigorous hiring process, by managing to keep a small team together over a five-year implementation period, and by having a single product architect. A key step in the hiring process was to review the code of each potential software engineer. Any engineer reluctant to show his or her work to fellow engineers is a likely loser.

GO Corp.   According to Robert Carr, who heads software development at GO Corp. (Carr, 1989), "All good software these days gets done through teamwork." He suggests the following approach:

1. Define the development style. Choices include the collegial model (for people at a more senior level) versus leadership by a chief programmer (where the team has less experience).

2. Hire the best first. Others will be turned off if turkeys are present. Worse yet, the turkeys will want to hire pygmies.

3. Focus on interpersonal skills. Teamwork is number one. Meet with eight to ten other staff members. Don't push lukewarm people. Listen to what your troops are saying.

4. Don't be afraid to rob the cradle. A twenty-two-year-old may have ten years of experience.

5. Hire people who have shipped products and been through the cycle, including support and feedback.

6. Don't skimp on salaries. Staff members should receive stock equal to half their salaries. It is better to hire the best people and pay them well than to hire a greater number of poor people and pay them poorly.

Micrografx.   Paul Grayson, chairman of Micrografx, recommends that a company create a development environment that fosters excellence and specifies three types of reward that can help create such an environment (Grayson, 1989):

1. *Cash:* A royalty can be paid based on 2 percent of sales, with the lead programmer getting 1 percent. Bonuses can be awarded for project completion.

2. *Recognition:* An outstanding team member can be given celebrity status within the company.

3. *Personal growth:* Although team members should have to prove themselves by working on a low-visibility project during their first six months, top achievers can then be rewarded with the opportunity to "do something new."

TECHNOLOGY FUTURE

The technology future dimension measures the new venture's ability to sustain the competitive viability of its technology. This dimension includes such factors as an assessment of the firm's products and architectures relative to the state of the art, morale, process technologies under development, and ability to hire critical people. Like financeability, the technology future dimension represents an overall look at the company's ability to build competitive products in the future.

For example, assume Company N introduces a Motorola 68000 workstation based on a CISC (complex instruction set computer) microprocessor, perhaps with an attached signal processor, while all the other workstation firms are introducing products based on RISC (reduced instruction set computer) microprocessors (such as Sun Microsystem's SPARC, MIPS, Motorola 88000, or Intel 80860). Because the RISC microprocessors deliver higher performance, Company N's product specifications suffer by comparison, at least superficially. Company N's ability to respond to the ensuing performance race by increasing the workstation's functionality with voice and video, for example, and providing a wide range of applications software in the 1990s will determine its technology future.

OPERATIONAL MANAGEMENT

Operational management is the engineering organization's ability to manage itself by meeting its product specification, budget, and schedule commitments. Management includes all the techniques of managing design reviews, management by objectives, staff meetings, team building, conflict resolution, etc. Andy Grove, CEO of Intel, has produced some of the best handbooks on this subject (Grove, 1983, 1987).

As a product reaches the final stages of completion, it will become clear that the team must compromise among the following three indigenous variables:

- The schedule, or when the product will be ready

- The complete set of resources that is applied toward meeting the schedule, including computers, consultants, other software, etc.

- The characteristics of the product itself, including performance, product cost, features, etc.

The best approach is for the company to pick two out of three, manage those, and be happy with the outcome. For a start-up, the schedule and resources are really fixed because of the incredible cost of raising additional funds. Furthermore, it is generally inadvisable to attempt to add critical design resources to a project that is already running late, because the firm is then apt to become subject to Brook's law: "Adding resources to a late project makes it later."

Therefore, the function of the company's first product will inevitably be less than perfect. Faced with the need to cut function in order to meet schedule and resource constraints, it is best to sacrifice some the product's features rather than sacrifice performance. Performance equates to quality in many systems and should not be sacrificed. Likewise, reliability is not a "feature"; it is a quality constraint that must never be sacrificed.

Ardent.   At Ardent, Tom Bentley, a former Hewlett-Packard engineer who headed mechanical design, said it was hard to find contractors who would meet the company's standards. "We expected a designer to meet both schedule and contract cost [goals], while also meeting the product cost, quality, and features constraints. Steve Jobs expects two [of these], and most companies in the valley are happy with just one."

TECHNOLOGY BALANCE SHEET FOR ARDENT

While working at Ardent, I used a technology balance sheet to analyze the company's technology capabilities. Table 6-1 shows the dimensions (and subcategories thereof) that were analyzed.

TECHNOLOGY AND ENGINEERING FLAWS

Some of the technology and engineering flaws presented in this section are similar to various people and business plan flaws that were discussed in earlier chapters. The flaws range from lack of technology, either because extensive research is needed or because the technology is ubiquitous and trivial, to simply having a poor team. As with other types of flaws, predicating a high-tech venture on technology that is flawed in one or more respects could prove to be fatal.

TACKLING A PRODUCT THAT REQUIRES
SIGNIFICANT RESEARCH TO MAKE IT FEASIBLE

A wonderful product that is clearly needed is just waiting to be developed. Designing the product, however, will require an unknown amount of basic and applied research. As of 1990, the estimate of when such a product can be produced ranges from now to

Table 6-1. Technology Balance Sheet for Ardent.

Technology Base

Packaging, mechanical design
(including thermal and acoustic
analysis)

Industrial design

Digital systems design
Signal propagation,
electromagnetic interference,
and radio frequency
interference
General logic design
Gate array design
Testing

Architecture/implementation
Vector multiprocessing
Performance analysis and
simulation
Graphics
Mass storage and input/output
Image processing

Software
Operating and file system
Language and compiler design
Graphical user interface
Database
Quality assurance

Marketing, sales, and product
support
Benchmarking
Mathematics and scientific
progress
Signal and image processing
Visualization
Computational chemistry
Computational fluid dynamics
Mechanical CAD and finite
element modeling
Seismic processing

Technical publication

Engineering Specifications

Reference manuals for all
components

Principles of operation for hardware

Eight-corners test

Manufacturing Specifications

Test vectors and specifications for all
chips and boards

Hardware and software release
specifications

*Chief Technical Officer,
Team/Culture, Architect(s)*

Discussed in an earlier section of the
chapter.

Technical Resources

Computing environment
Multisegment Ethernet and
Appletalk
Macintoshes for documentation
Sun Workstations (local and
windows)
MIPS file and computation
servers

Valid logic for logic design

Verilog for system description/
simulation

Technology Future

Plan outline for next products

Standards

See Chapter 8, Figure 8-5 for product
standards.

Process Definitions

New products introduction

Plan

Embodied in master schedule

Yearly budget with all resources

Operational Management and Control

Schedule fantasy factor = 1.2 after a
major organizational change

Weekly schedule review at each level

Staff meetings at each level of
management, with minutes and
action items

Management by objectives

Products committee to track/
coordinate all products and future
product plans

eighteen months from now to never (although *never* is a word that cannot really be used when it comes to technology). The following example illustrates the slow evolution of a product whose development has required (and will continue to require) a considerable amount of research.

The speech typewriter (speechwriter).   Kurzweil AI was formed in 1982 to build a speech typewriter. Its founder, Ray Kurzweil, has produced an impressive array of inventions, including the first machine to read to the blind (1972), which does optical character recognition of variable fonts and is connected to a speech synthesizer. The company developing the reader was sold to Xerox. A second firm, which was formed in the late 1970s to build keyboard-controlled music synthesizers for the professional and home market, is now for sale in 1990.

The aim of speech research, which has been under way since the 1930s, is to understand speech well enough to permit it to be recognized by a machine. In 1980, at least one market research firm published a report estimating the market for voice-activated typewriters at $3.5 billion in 1990. Kurzweil believed that enough was known about speech understanding to finally build a comparatively elementary but nonetheless useful product that would function within certain limited contexts, such as having the machine run by a single, trained operator who would use a large, but limited vocabulary and speak separated words.

Kurzweil's first task was to advance the art on which to base a product. In order to bring himself up to the state of the art in speech recognition, Kurzweil put together a team from the research community at MIT and Harvard to develop technology for speech understanding. In 1985, the firm introduced its first product and tried to sell a recognizer to a number of software companies (whose products included spreadsheets, word processing, databases, CAD, etc.) as a control mechanism, but the product's capability and accuracy were limited and it worked poorly. Furthermore, users had to "train" the recognizer. The Kurzweil AI product predated a product by Articulate Systems (using Dragon's recognizer) to control the Macintosh.

By 1989, the Kurzweil product had evolved into a unique voice editor that runs on a PC and is capable of recognizing keywords and expanding them using a word processor database and report generator. The voice editor is tailored to a particular application by its vocabulary and phrases and is then further tuned by the user. In 1990, the product is being successfully sold for writing reports in internal medicine, pathology, radiology, and emergency medicine, since these fields all require reports based on distinct, limited vocabularies.

In contrast to speech-research laboratories such as Bell Labs, IBM, and university laboratories, Kurzweil has advanced toward the goal of a typewriter by building and marketing a product. Other companies have also built and marketed speech recognizers for limited use. Unlike other laboratories, NEC has been marketing limited vocabulary recognizers for almost a decade in order to really understand their problems and use.

Thus, for a researcher, a start-up is an interesting alternative to the large company or government-funded laboratory, assuming the firm can find investors willing to wait for their investments to mature. Dragon Systems, Inc. (page 282), provides an alternative role model for how a venture requiring a slow-to-emerge technology may be formed.

No doubt the hottest product—the one that absolutely everyone will have, need, and use *after* 2001—will be the universal speech typewriter! And the next advance will probably be a speech typewriter that does on-the-fly language translation.

REQUIRING A TRILOGY OF BREAKTHROUGHS

It has been observed that a successful start-up cannot be based on more than two breakthroughs in the state of the art. And for each of the areas requiring a breakthrough, an alternative technology should be available as a backup. Clearly, a risk exists when three or more technologies have to be understood (i.e., researched to the point of being usable) and developed. It is almost assuredly fatal for a start-up to engage in research whose result cannot be known or scheduled, because the company's other functions must all be supported in the meantime, and the funding requirements are uncertain and often open-ended. The schedule for such a project contains loops, parallel and redundant exploratory paths, and conditional branches.

The following example discusses Trilogy, Inc., which attempted to develop a product requiring multiple technological breakthroughs. The "trilogy of breakthroughs" flaw is in fact named after Trilogy, since this flaw contributed greatly to the difficulties the firm encountered.

Trilogy, Inc. Trilogy was started to develop an IBM-compatible line of computers with major subsystems packaged on a single semiconductor wafer. Unisys and Digital invested in the technology as codevelopers.[2] The risks included the following:

1. Interconnecting high-density, high-speed semiconductor circuitry on a single wafer

2. Devising a scheme to ensure defect-free parts using redundant parts of a wafer

3. Packaging an entire wafer such that power is input, heat is dissipated, and the wafer is rewired to circumvent inherent wafer defects

4. Developing a CAD system to manage the redundancy-based logic design and interconnect scheme

---

2. I made this recommendation. After Trilogy failed, Digital bought rights to all its technology. The power supply, heat sink, wafer-packaging scheme, and facilities were used as the basis for the VAX 9000.

5. Developing a computer design more complex than previous designs

Some observers felt that Trilogy's pleasant facilities and large staff were fatal flaws. The real culprit, however, was that the requisite technology could not be developed in time to implement a product. The five risks listed above had the following outcomes:

1.   The circuits were slower than specified, increasing the design's complexity while decreasing its competitiveness.

2., 3.   Not enough redundancy was available to cover wafer faults.

4.   The CAD system was quite slow and decreased productivity.

5.   The design was so complex as to increase the design time and adversely affect product competitiveness.

Although the preceding problems occurred during the product development stage, the issues were known at the concept or seed stage. In hindsight, an analysis of the situation should have produced an emphatic "no go" until the required breakthroughs were reduced to a manageable number.

When it became clear that Trilogy's technology was inadequate to build the product, the company acquired Elexsi Computer with its remaining capital and attempted to make it succeed. Unfortunately, minisupers from Alliant and Convex were also being brought to market at that time.

HAVING LITTLE OR NO SUSTAINING TECHNOLOGY

Offering just another commodity product of a particular type (i.e., "brand X") in a crowded field is usually a fatal flaw. Starting a company with commodity technology, such as a new chip, is the opposite of the trilogy-of-breakthroughs flaw. It comes from the belief that the firm has just a slightly better idea about the product or how to sell it. The minicomputer, PC, and workstation industries all began as technology companies to a greater or lesser degree, and the introduction of various components (SSI/MSI, 16-bit microprocessors, and 32-bit microprocessors, respectively) allowed dozens of no-tech companies to enter the market. In early 1990, the smallest PC electronics assembly costs $200, and within five years, just one or two very-high-tech chips (available from Intel and a memory supplier) will form the entire, minimal PC with 2 megabytes to 8 megabytes of memory. Dell Computer is an excellent example of how a company was able to get started and grow with PCs despite the low-tech odds, because Dell considered the whole environment of product, sales, service, and support.

THE NOT-INVENTED-HERE (NIH) SYNDROME

One of the most dangerous flaws is a form of technical arrogance in which a company feels compelled to reengineer every part of a hardware or software system because it believes that it can do a better job than any of its potential suppliers. For a new venture, inventing every possible component in order to make an ultimate product (instead of buying everything possible in order to get to market rapidly with a good product at the lowest development cost) is often fatal.

The other effect of the NIH syndrome is the incompatible-product flaw (page 190). A company designs a new interface, such as a programming language or a feature for an existing language, when an old one would have been just fine. In this case, NIH hurts the buyer, who has to change and adapt to something different. Needless innovations and changes that have the effect of rendering hardware, programs, and data incompatible are extremely costly for the whole computing enterprise.

The NIH syndrome is endemic among most engineers, especially in the United States, the United Kingdom, and France. NIH does not necessarily have anything to do with a team's competence, only its lack of business savvy, although the brightest teams are often the most unhappy about using less-than-perfect components. The NIH syndrome's effects on productivity and on profit and loss are devastating, and this syndrome may account for why Japanese engineers are at least twice as productive as American engineers in a field such as automotive engineering. NIH often triggers the formation of multiple companies in one, a type of business plan flaw that is described on page 50.

Even well-established and well-respected firms have exhibited this flaw. In the early 1960s, IBM found that every computer products group was building a computer based on each group's own logic circuits, requiring redundancy in design, manufacturing, and field spares. Gene Amdahl proposed that any group using components from another group be rewarded and given special recognition. One of his coworkers squelched the idea, claiming that "it's un-American."

THE MISSING COMPONENT

Every day that an organization depends on a risky part or a marginal vendor, it risks its life, because if a critical component (or process) fails to materialize as scheduled, the company may run out of time and, hence, out of money. Selecting poor vendors is a common and hard-to-avoid error. Only through experience will a start-up learn which firms can be trusted to meet their commitments.

Henry Burkhardt, CEO of Kendall Square Research, described the problems of selecting the right vendor by offering what might be called a "tale of three cities." In it, he compared the experience of dealing with vendors in a Texas city, a California city, and a Japanese city:

- *Texas: We have the fastest, biggest, and cheapest parts. If you don't believe it, write me because I'm the president of this new division.* (They don't really have a competitive product. On calling them, the secretary to the president states that you have to write because the letter goes directly to the marketing VP. I wrote to the president and informed them they lie about their parts and even lie about their willingness to listen. The letter does go through the company like wildfire, but the division president is still there, selling the same parts in the same old way.)

- *California: Everyone knows our parts are the fastest and the biggest. We started the industry.* (We ask for a delivery commitment. It reads "We'll make our best effort to deliver." On inspection, the parts fail after a year without special treatment that's not part of the specification. The customers all complain about missed delivery schedules, and manufacturing people scream when they hear the name of the company. Every transaction with the company requires negotiation.)

- *Japan: We have fast, large parts as stated in our specs, and we are committed to high quality.* (Existing customers agree, and no one can identify a part ever failing. We selected them because the contract simply states that they will meet their specs and deliveries. All specs and delivery dates were met.)

The following story illustrates the type of havoc that can ensue when a company deals with a poor vendor.

WAVETRACER. In building a signal-processing computer, WAVETRACER used an unreliable printed circuit board vendor to make its prototype boards. The boards had numerous errors, costing the firm several months over its plan at a critical time when it needed a product and credibility with its first customer. Because of this schedule slip, WAVETRACER was forced to seek additional financing earlier and in a greater amount than would otherwise have been necessary. The valuation was decreased and the external ownership increased.

New microprocessors have historically had bugs. New complex microprocessors from semiconductor companies—including Intel, Motorola, and National—have all had bugs. The more complex the part, the more error-prone it is; hence, another reason for RISC. The first users are able to help find new flaws and often rediscover flaws that manufacturers forget to address. Apollo, Sequent, and several other companies have war stories to tell in this regard.

INABILITY TO HIRE THE ENGINEERS

Hiring is absolutely critical, yet every high-tech venture I know of has had more trouble hiring than it ever planned or imagined. This leads to an additional flaw—lowering the standards. By reducing its standards, the firm risks producing both a downward spiral in quality and a bloated staff that generates no meaningful output. A pygmy heading engineering will proceed to hire even smaller pygmies.

FAILING TO GET RID OF POOR HIRES AS SOON AS POSSIBLE

If a person is found to be a poor hire, he or she must be dismissed at the earliest feasible moment. Negative producers[3] should be terminated immediately, placeholders very rapidly, and marginal producers as soon as possible.

Company X. I know of a firm (let's call it "Company X") that was having trouble staffing a new project with good people and made a borderline hire without proper reference checking. When the team discovered that the borderline individual was in fact a poor hire, they felt they could manage him by close supervision and checking. However, he refused to ask for help, chafed at having his work reviewed, and was late—all sure signs of a bad design(er). Simulation revealed continued bugs with no evidence of progress toward a correct design. In essence, bugs were just being moved around. When Company X finally conducted a design walk-through, the engineer quit and went to a competitor, where he may or may not have greater success. Although Company X did nothing to influence its former engineer's selection of a new employer, outplacing negatively productive people with a potential competitor can do wonders for a firm's competitive lead.

LEAKING TECHNOLOGY AND PRODUCT IDEAS

If a new venture permits its technology and product ideas to leak, it risks giving both established competitors and other start-ups an opportunity to respond. It is therefore important that the staff say no more than is absolutely necessary in order to sell new

---

3. Negative productivity is a principle that I claim is worthy of a Nobel Prize. Normal principles of productivity assume that workers create positive output. Brooks refined the concept of software productivity to express it in terms of the "mythical man-month," and in software engineering, it is understood that different programmers vary in their productivity by several orders of magnitude. According to the principle of negative productivity, it is possible for an individual to produce bad results that others must then redo; hence, someone who is very negatively productive can keep a whole team busy with damage control, preventing the team from producing any output whatsoever.

recruits. They should try to get recruits to tell more about themselves than the company tells about itself and avoid any mention of costs and schedules.

PREANNOUNCING THE PRODUCT

It is absolutely foolhardy to preannounce a product before it has been tested internally and passed its acceptance tests. At the very least, preannouncement is likely to be an embarrassment; at worst, there might be legal repercussions.

In *no* case should a product be officially announced before it is operating well enough to pass formal tests that are comparable to actual customer use. Ideally, the product announcement is made at the end of beta testing at customer sites. Anything less conservative is a flaw.

This is one flaw that is even more painful in large companies than in start-ups. In 1966, IBM preannounced a large computer that would compete with Control Data Corporation's 6600 in an attempt to get customers to wait for the IBM product, which, in this particular case, never came. CDC sued IBM and was awarded $600 million in a consent decree that forbade preannouncement.

TECHNOLOGY BALANCE SHEET RULES

The following is the fundamental rule for evaluating a new venture's technology:

Has the company generated and maintained a complete "technology balance sheet" that is adequate to develop the product and specifies the information listed below?

- **"Buy-out" technology (software and hardware), including semis, etc.**

- **Patentable or unique components that are the basis for the firm's future**

- **Industry and de facto standards that the start-up must "track" or advance**

- **The company's own standards or ways of doing things**

- **Patentable or unique processes, including design**

- **Plan, with schedule and resources**

- **Engineering and manufacturing specifications**

- **Chief technology officer (i.e., the vice president of engineering)**

- Team

- Product architects and architectural processes

- People (including consultants) who embody the technology

- Computer-aided design (CAD) and computer-aided software engineering (CASE) tools, computer resources, and network environment

- Ability to acquire future technology

- Operational management control

The following are some specific rules applicable to the technology balance sheet.

Can the team, at the concept stage, show how all the technology will come together to form a product that will be not only unique but also self-sustaining (i.e., capable of evolving into future generations)?

The technology balance sheet should be used to account for *both* uniqueness and mastery of the technology. Mastering the technology means being able to assemble the "to be acquired" engineering team, consultants, patents, standards, components, design process, CAD tools, etc. This rule tests whether the organization has a way to evolve its product and extend it into future generations or whether it is merely starting on a one-shot basis.

The same rule should be applied again at the seed stage, continually challenging the founders about the uniqueness of their technology. It examines whether the technology remains sufficiently unique, yet implementable, to support a self-sustaining company. The rules in Chapter 8, "The Product," also examine uniqueness.

Can the team, at the concept stage, show how the technology can be developed while requiring fewer than three breakthroughs or significant advancements in the state of the art?

This rule tests whether the technology is too high (sometimes reaching infinity), such that the new venture is engaging in research instead of product development. Applied research or advanced development is being done if a project schedule contains major loops with conditional branches or multiple exploratory paths in its PERT chart. Such a company is likely to be fatally flawed if it has been funded with the goal of developing a product, as opposed to being funded as a research and development partnership. In the latter case, investors are cognizant of the risk, and the goal is to first master the technology before building a product.

Does a simple product development plan, specifying resources and schedule, exist at the concept stage?

This rule tests whether the start-up has a plan outlining the steps and resources that will be required to develop the product.

Does the company have a working product or product prototype and people who understand it?

Ideally, a high-tech venture is based on a working product or product prototype that has been funded by a public institution together with the people who understand and embody the technology, even though such products and people may fail the experience tests required by many financiers.

The next best thing is to base the company on key people who have pioneered in developing technological components. They must have a thorough understanding of the product development process gained through building products for use by others and must be committed to engineering design rather than research.

Probably the worst alternative is to base the firm on the results of military research and development, because it is likely to be fatally flawed, as described in "Augustine's Laws" (Augustine, 1987). Military products are cost- and reliability-insensitive. They don't have to work or are rarely tested to ensure that they work. The development budgets, lead time (measured in decades), and quality of military products are outside commercial bounds.

Has the company's proprietary technology been demonstrated during the seed stage via physical or computer model, breadboard, or some other form of demonstration that would prove its viability, such that the development breakthroughs have been reduced to a level of risk that is acceptable for the product development stage?

This rule verifies that the start-up is in control of its technological destiny by checking whether the seed stage requirements of reducing risk have been satisfied by constructing breadboards, models, or demonstrations of critical technology. Ideally, at this point, the firm has ideas that may result in copyrights and patents in order to protect and enhance its technology.

If the company is depending on a concurrent breakthrough or leading-edge product from another supplier (e.g., a component or system vendor), have the risks been clearly identified and factored into the plan?

This rule determines whether the start-up's risks have been transferred to an outside vendor and then assesses the overall risk in using such a vendor. Information about the vendor's past performance is required, especially evidence of its reliability in meeting delivery schedules. Founding a company predicated on the availability of a component that a manufacturer has never before built is always risky. The new venture gets no points for picking the best technology or engineering the lowest cost if it is then unable to obtain a key part or unable to obtain it on time or in manufacturing quantities.

The evaluation of vendors and components is an excellent position for a seasoned engineer, by the way. Such individuals know which components and suppliers are high-quality and reliable. New engineers, on the other hand, tend to believe specifications.

Does the chief technical officer have the capability and stature to hire, lead, and manage a superb engineering group?

The general qualifications of the CTO must parallel those of the CEO, because he or she is the "clock" and "standards setter" for engineering. The CTO should have a track record of both technical and managerial accomplishment. The CTO's technical background must be solid enough to gain the engineers' respect and confidence in his or her technical decisions. The CTO's managerial skills must be strong enough to deal with conflicting egos, limited resources, and all the other trials and tribulations that a manager faces. This individual should be especially talented at recognizing, selecting, and encouraging top-notch engineers.

Does the product have an architect with proven experience?

As stated previously, the product architect is likely to be the most critical person within the engineering function. His or her key job is to guide the product's introduction and evolution over the course of its lifetime, and a track record of success in past endeavors is the strongest possible recommendation. In some cases, several architects may be required as a product is broken into various parts, but the boundaries of each architect's responsibilities must be clear, and the architects must be capable of functioning as a cohesive team.

Are key technologists, or avenues for hiring them, available?

In one sense, this rule relates to the question of whether the company has the "right tech" (i.e., an appropriate level of technology). If the technology upon which the venture is to be based is so "far-out" that only a handful of technologists skilled in that art are available, the firm is likely to have serious staffing problems. On the other hand, if the start-up is to be based on an ingenious use of a recently introduced or established technology, hiring prospects will be much better. Some innovative ways of finding appropriate personnel were discussed earlier in the chapter.

Does the company have hiring criteria, and is there a systematic recruiting process?

This rule checks whether the firm has established hiring criteria, covering both work habits, management ability, and technical skills. Having specifications for each person to be hired is helpful and perhaps essential. In addition, the company needs a first-rate process for initially identifying potential employees and then bringing them in for an interview, screening them, and finally selling them. A critical part of the process is thorough reference checking of all candidates!

Does the job candidates' prior experience show evidence of operational management ability as well as resources- and schedule-planning ability?

This question examines the planning and management history of the engineer/ management team. History is likely to be the best predictor of a manager's ability to help people enjoy their work and be productive in it. And with regard to scheduling, if the candidates have historically been on time, then they will most likely continue to meet their commitments in the future.

Has engineering outlined a quality design and product-release process together with engineering, manufacturing-engineering, and product-release standards, including, for example, coding practices, design rules, code walk-throughs, and design reviews?

This rule measures the existence and effectiveness of the company's engineering design process. For a software team, it would not be unreasonable to ask whether the process at least satisfies the Software Engineering Institute's process-capability requirements for level 1 and what plans exist to upgrade the process so it will satisfy the requirements of increasingly higher levels (Humphrey, 1989).

It is not uncommon for engineers to react negatively to the establishment of standards and processes. For example, engineers who have just left large firms frequently rebel at anything that might look like bureaucracy or restrictions on their freedom, and engineers coming from a research environment are unlikely to understand the need for any rigor in standards and processes. Object-oriented programming languages and methods promise to make the task of building software substantially easier because they enable modules to be built in a more isolated and independent manner and because more software is likely to be available from other sources and to be reusable.

Is a product development schedule in place, and does it specify gross milestones and resources?

This process question examines whether the start-up has a schedule for the project with enough intermediate milestones. Without such a schedule, it is impossible to make a meaningful business plan. People experienced in high-tech ventures know that it is essential for the company to be operating according to a detailed schedule, even though no schedule can be fully validated until the entire team responsible for the project has been hired and brought on board. An unwillingness to make a detailed schedule at this point is therefore a good early warning indicator that the project will probably be difficult and unpredictable. A start-up can certainly be financed on an open-ended schedule, but this approach can be expected to increase product development spending by at least a factor of 2.

Does the company have a plan for acquiring and operating CAD and CASE tools, computing resources, and its network?

Developing products based on up-to-date technology requires up-to-date engineering tools. Tools represent both a key part of engineering and a large fraction of product development cost. A CAD program for schematic capture or board layout can cost several hundred thousand dollars. A simulator to accelerate the testing of a complex chip may cost half a million dollars. Thus, it is critical for the start-up to prepare a detailed list of all the tools (both computers and the necessary networks) it will require for high-tech hardware and software development. In the early stages, developers often administer their own systems, which may include interfaces with various national and international wide area networks, but as a company grows, the expense of system administrators and network administrators must also be assumed.

CONCLUSION

Chapters 5 and 6 have presented a picture of high information technology and examined how a new venture uses technology to engineer products in a timely and predictable fashion. At each of the development phases described in Chapter 5, the company must have an adequate technology balance sheet covering the following twelve dimensions: its technology base; standards; design, quality, and other processes; plan, with schedule and resources; engineering specifications; manufacturing specifications; chief technical officer; team and engineering culture; architecture; technical resources; technology future; and operational management.

Chapter 7

MANUFACTURING

The manufacturing organization buys materials and converts those materials into products according to the product and process specifications developed by the engineering organization. Manufacturing is measured on its ability to do this in a cost-effective, high-quality, and timely fashion. A major portion of this effort is the management of raw materials and finished goods, which is a balancing act. Enough of each must be on hand to give the company flexibility in dealing with fluctuations in the order rate, but not so much that it feels a financial impact from having excess inventory.

The importance of manufacturing varies with the business in which a particular high-tech venture is engaged. For example, manufacturing operations in a software company primarily involve the reproduction of magnetic storage media and manuals. This process requires little capital investment, and the cash value of the work in progress is low. At the opposite extreme is semiconductor manufacture, especially that involving an advanced process. Here, the capital investment is huge and the work in progress more valuable. The following is a spectrum (in ascending order) of manufacturing complexity and expense for various computer-related products:

- Software—reproduction of magnetic storage media and manuals

- Printed circuit boards and/or assembly of small components

- Small systems (e.g., terminals, printers) involving low technology

- Systems involving a unique or proprietary technology (e.g., print heads, scanners)

- General-purpose computers (collections of boards)

- Complex electromechanical devices (e.g., disks)

- Semiconductor manufacturing involving advanced processes

The essence of manufacturing is being able to plan the output. However, many start-ups go through dramatic changes in their plan during the market development stage. At first, there may be no demand for the product whatsoever; then, demand may suddenly increase beyond manufacturing's production capability. The manufacturing organization is necessarily slow to respond because the typical lead time for materials (semiconductors, disks, printed circuit boards, etc.) is sixteen weeks, followed by four weeks of process time for the product. In other words, a total of five months normally elapse between when the company places orders for materials and when it can deliver its product. The slowness of manufacturing's response time may tempt a new firm to rush headlong into mass production so that it will be able to meet all its orders, but this is often foolish. A few guiding principles for start-up manufacturing are therefore in order.

THE SANDERS GUIDING PRINCIPLES FOR MANUFACTURING

Matt Sanders[1] offers two general principles for manufacturing: emphasize quality, and minimize the use of the start-up's resources (capital, time, and space). These two principles form the basis for eight guidelines, which are examined in detail in the following subsections.

ONLY BUILD PRODUCTS OF THE HIGHEST POSSIBLE QUALITY

The only acceptable engineering, product, and manufacturing strategy is to build products of the highest possible quality. Anything less than the highest quality is likely to prove extremely costly in the long run. At the front end of the manufacturing process, using or accepting poor-quality components is costly in terms of increased inventories and additional work. Likewise, implementing a poor-quality design is costly because redesign and rework will continually be required while the product is being produced. Finally, if the product fails in the field, an expensive service organization will be needed to maintain it. Any product yield of less than 90 percent at customer sites represents a serious product design and quality problem. A 95 percent to 99 percent yield should be the target for the initial products, with 99 percent (or better) the target for steady-state production.

---

1. Matt Sanders is a founder of Convergent Technologies and Ardent and was the principal responsible for establishing the manufacturing organization and operations of both companies.

Quality must be designed in right from the start; it cannot be added on by manufacturing. A start-up should focus on a simple first product, since this approach allows the company to get to market quickly and increases the probability of its having a really well-designed product. Attention should be paid to minimizing components, not only to decrease cost but also to increase reliability (parts that aren't there can't fail). Quality is a discipline that concerns both engineering and manufacturing, and engineers must understand the manufacturing process by which their product is fabricated in order for the firm to produce the best product.

An example of a company that has emphasized the relationship between engineering and manufacturing is Sequent Computer Systems. It has taken a simple step to ensure that manufacturability is a key part of the design—namely, Sequent permits anyone to stop the manufacturing line for any reason. The manufacturing and design engineers responsible for the product can only restart the line after the problem has been remedied. By giving so much power to those building the product, Sequent ensures that engineering delivers perfect specifications, and that if it doesn't, problems are attended to immediately. Under this system, design engineers quickly become expert manufacturing engineers.

ONLY INVEST IN MANUFACTURING IF THE PROCESS IS UNIQUE AND IS THE ESSENCE OF THE START-UP

Today's start-up should invest in manufacturing only when the manufacturing process is an essential and proprietary part of the company. Examples are firms manufacturing complex electromechanical devices, semiconductors, and some proprietary parts of a larger product. In contrast, computer systems ventures should minimize their investment in manufacturing processes and seek high-quality subcontracting sources instead.

It is common for a start-up to want to make everything it can in order to have "control" over its destiny. For most new ventures, however, buying manufacturing capabilities from outside sources not only is a better use of resources but also is likely to yield higher quality and lower costs, because the subcontractors specialize in all the necessary testing and fabrication steps. Since the volume of products is likely to be low at first, the best use of resources is to buy as much as possible from outside sources to avoid investing in new processes.

EXAMINE EVERY MAKE/BUY DECISION

In addition to the decision regarding in-house manufacturing versus subcontracting, additional make/buy decisions must be made with respect to all parts of the enterprise, including product design, design processes, sales, service, and support. The start-up may find it cost-effective to buy one or more of these capabilities from an external organization.

GET TO MARKET FAST

If the company plans effectively from the outset, it can get to market rapidly and minimize its investment in manufacturing, whether that be in-house manufacturing or subcontracted manufacturing. The key to time-to-market and product quality is for engineering and manufacturing to function well together from the beginning. Oftentimes, engineering will build the first product prototypes and then (when the engineers have learned how to build the product) turn the process over to manufacturing. This approach leads to delays and keeps the manufacturing organization from hitting the ground running. It is wiser to give manufacturing responsibility for building *all* the products, including the prototypes.

USE MINIMAL CASH

A good way to leverage the firm's cash is to minimize inventory through design and by using outside suppliers. The start-up should get a subassembly supplier that will fund the inventory and give favorable payment terms. By making inventory part of the product cost, the company can convert what would otherwise have been a fixed manufacturing cost to a variable cost. It can also negotiate flexible terms for varying quantities in order to reduce the cost due to unpredictably fluctuating volumes.

HAVE ONLY A MINIMAL STAFF, BUT HIRE THE CRITICAL PEOPLE

Farming out everything that it can will save the new venture not only on capital equipment and inventory costs but also on personnel expense. Once a company hires someone, it has a commitment to that person. Indirect manufacturing personnel are a fixed expense, not a variable cost, and the goal of start-up manufacturing must be to push manufacturing spending into the variable-cost category as much as possible. Therefore, instead of hiring a staff of specialists and training them from scratch, the firm should use subcontractor personnel who have already passed through the learning curve. This approach is likely to be cheaper and result in the production of better products. Using a range of subcontractors does require the company to have the appropriate logistical systems and personnel to handle coordination, however.

Although most of the advice given so far has been to minimize cost and hire as few people as possible, when people *are* hired, it is important to hire the right ones. The head of manufacturing is one such critical hire. A materials person who understands the procurement of top-quality components is likely to produce the highest payoff. A person assigned solely to work on quality will produce the next highest payoff. The final members of the team should be responsible for testing and for developing unique processes (if either of these will be done in-house).

MAKE SURE PRODUCT COST IS PREDICTABLE AND LOW

Predictability comes from understanding product cost. As stated above, the start-up should make its costs variable rather than fixed, insofar as possible. This means religiously tracking the parts list during the design process and making sure that product cost and quality are major design constraints, not afterthoughts. Paying strict attention to quality and establishing a cooperative relationship with subcontractors and vendors will help ensure that costs are predictable.

The cost of manufacturing a typical computer product, once the assembly process reaches steady state, is:

80-85 percent	Materials
10 percent	Indirect labor (fixed) for salaried personnel and supervision
2-3 percent	Direct labor
2-3 percent	Depreciation of facilities and equipment (for simple products)

Readers should note the importance of the cost of materials and indirect labor.

AVOID THE EVIL OF INVENTORY

As stated earlier, material control is a balancing act. Having too much material means that all the start-up's capital may be tied up in inventory. On the other hand, having too little material means lost sales opportunities. The balancing act is complicated by the long built-in delay (typically five months) between the time materials are ordered and the time finished goods are ready to be shipped. Inventory is a very important area on which to focus management attention, because it is the biggest cash sink for a high-growth venture—and the place where the company can be lost.

OFFSHORE MANUFACTURING

Offshore manufacturing has enabled numerous U.S. start-ups to follow many of the guidelines given in the preceding section. The relationship between Stardent and Kubota is an especially good example of the merits of subcontracting manufacturing and paying careful attention to quality. In the Stardent/Kubota relationship, Stardent is responsible for designing basic hardware and software for its Titan workstation as well as acquiring software in each market area (e.g., chemistry and imaging). Kubota is responsible for all manufacturing.

Partnership with a Japanese firm has had an especially significant impact on product quality. In the late 1940s, American manufacturing expert Edward Demming visited Japan and told the Japanese the importance of making quality the number one priority. He emphasized that a faulty part had to be either reworked, thrown out, or (worst of all) used in the product. He proved all three of these alternatives to be more expensive than making the part correctly the first time. Being a statistician by training, he also showed the Japanese the evils of "tolerance buildup"—the cumulative effect of using a number of parts that are each barely in-specification, which can result in a faulty final product unless the tolerance specifications are tightened to prevent this.

Japanese manufacturers such as Kubota have learned this lesson well. Kubota is a century-old firm that manufactures mechanical equipment and also designs mechanical engineering software and integrates MCAD (mechanical computer-aided design) and CAM (computer-aided manufacturing) software. Since the fabrication of computers fundamentally involves mechanical assembly, Kubota is able to use its manufacturing skills to produce a high-quality product. Its plant is run by engineers who understand the fundamentals of the materials and processes required to form the parts and know how to combine them into a high-quality product. American computer manufacturers, in contrast, are often headed by either MBAs or individuals who have worked their way up through the ranks without coming to understand the total picture of their operation.

Kubota's dedication to quality is reflected in the failure rates of the two products built by Stardent's predecessor companies, Ardent and Stellar. The failure rate of the Ardent workstation (built by Kubota) was half that predicted by the parts count, while the Stellar failure rate was equal to that predicted by the parts count. Once Ardent and Stellar merged, and Kubota began manufacturing both products, the failure rate of the original Stellar product improved toward that of the Ardent product.

It would be unfair to give all the credit to the Japanese, however. In addition to the excellence of Kubota's manufacturing, several other factors contributed to the reliability of Ardent's Titan workstation. First, Ardent's mechanical and electrical designers were Hewlett-Packard alumni, and HP is an ideal training ground for engineers who build reliable products (albeit expensively). Second, Ardent had stringent standards for design quality. Third, the engineers tested the design rigorously at all eight corners of operation (all permutations of high and low values of voltage, temperature, and speed). Fourth, Kubota insisted on a "perfect" design in order that the product be manufacturable.

MANUFACTURING FLAWS

Nearly all of the flaws discussed in this section result from having a poor plan. Some of them result from failing to adhere to commonsense rules of good practice to reduce risk. Many of them affect quality, clearly a critical factor in the case of manufacturing output. The first flaw involves a quality problem that manifests itself in manufacturing, although its root cause may lie in either manufacturing or some other part of the organization.

A PRODUCT MANUFACTURING LINE WITH A HIGHLY ERRATIC FLOW

A manufacturing line may flow extremely erratically for a number of reasons:

- The line may be poorly designed and may run only rarely.

- Its yields may be inadequate because of poor materials or poor training.

- The vendors may be unreliable.

- The sales forecasts may be erratic.

It is unusual to see a new venture with a really fine manufacturing facility unless manufacturing is the company's dominant focus. The assembly line often runs poorly for one or more of the above-listed reasons. Thus, right from the start, the firm is likely to get a reputation for unpredictable product quality.

POOR MAKE/BUY DECISIONS

A company I know of that started to build a system to eliminate paper in a very large office provides a good example of the problems that can arise when a firm's make/buy decisions are poorly thought out. The system was supposed to scan every piece of paper entering the building and convert it to image format. From then on, all storage, transmission, and viewing would be via computer. The company began by building every component of the system: a jukebox to manage the optical disks on which the information would be stored, scanners and viewing computers, all the computers to be used throughout the network, and all the applications software. Although the firm could have bought virtually all the computers and workstations needed for the system, it designed every component itself to get the lowest manufacturing cost, even though the entire system cost several million dollars.

The firm ultimately had to be downsized to supply only the large file systems using the optical storage jukebox that it manufactured. It never got around to building the software to manage the elimination of paper because it had spent all its resources attempting to reduce the cost of components that it could have bought off the shelf.

HAVING A MANUFACTURING FACILITY THAT IS TOO BIG

A high-tech venture courts trouble if it builds an extensive manufacturing facility in anticipation of high volumes before the product has even been introduced to, or accepted by, the marketplace. Some companies, such as NeXT, have survived this flaw, but it is nevertheless dangerous. As stated above, most start-ups find it best to conserve their cash and use subcontractors.

USING A CRITICAL, BUT MARGINAL, COMPONENT OR PROCESS

If the product is based on a critical, but marginal, component or process, the net result is a product that is poor (e.g., unreliable, very costly due to work-in-progress delays, or not producible in adequate volumes). Successful technology follows only one or two well-worn paths, not many. Technology progresses rapidly when everyone goes down the same paths and develops all the understanding required to make the process work.

By its nature, a start-up must strike out in a direction other than that in which larger or existing companies are going. The trick is to distinguish between potentially productive directions and foolhardy ones. The greatest temptation is to use a new semiconductor component even though, at present, it doesn't quite exist. At the beginning stage of any new technology, a number of false starts will be made, and only a few of the paths taken will lead toward success.

ATTEMPTING A PROCESS
THAT REQUIRES SIGNIFICANT BREAKTHROUGHS

A start-up may be predicated on a new process requiring significant breakthroughs in manufacturing and yet not be staffed with a leader or the critical process-engineering design skills needed to achieve those breakthroughs. During the past twenty-five years, the humble printed circuit board has made new computer classes possible, given birth to new companies, and caused great grief to others. How these events have come to pass provides an excellent illustration of the importance of selecting the right process technology.

Printed circuit board technology is measured by yield (hence, cost), size, and interconnection density, the latter being a combination of line width and number of layers. Organizations with large and bureaucratic manufacturing and field-service organizations, such as Digital Equipment Corporation (DEC) and IBM, have traditionally taken a very conservative approach and favored small printed circuit boards. Manufacturing wants tiny boards in order to get perfect yields and to make testers small, cheap, and simple. Field service wants small boards in order to have compact and economical units that will facilitate field replacement. In contrast to manufacturing and field service, system designers want very large boards in order to be able to get the entire system (e.g., the PC), or at least one major component (e.g., a processor), on a board. High-tech ventures tend to be founded by system designers, not manufacturing and field-service people, so start-ups have pushed the size limits upward to build new computers and new computer classes.

In 1968, examples of the small-board approach included DEC, which was using small boards suitable for packaging circuits with discrete components and automated assembly, a technology borrowed from IBM. When ex-DEC personnel founded Data General and built that company's first mini (the NOVA), they packaged one major component (central processing unit, memory, and input/output) per board, ending up with a three-board computer. DEC increased its board size markedly in the next few years.

Another manufacturer using small boards was Computer Controls Corporation, which built the first 16-bit integrated circuit minicomputer using very small boards that had only one or two integrated circuits per board. Had it packaged the computer on larger boards, resulting in lower cost, it might have survived without the Honeywell merger, making it a competitor today.

In the 1990s, it is very difficult to build a large or cost-effective multiprocessor system using small boards because the shape of an ideal system is a cube, or simply a single printed circuit board as in the case of a PC. By using small boards, one cannot build a very large cube (or a very large computer).

So far, this discussion has made a case for "large is better," but it is possible to try manufacturing printed circuit boards that are too large. An example was Elexsi, which, in 1982, built a large supermini as a multiprocessor, using boards that were beyond the limits of the standard manufacturing process (photolithography, plating tanks, solder machines, component inserters, and testers). Elexsi was driven by its engineers to build very large boards so that it could get its ECL processor on one board. Pressuring the manufacturing organization to do something completely contrary to the infrastructure cost the firm at least a year and a half in entering the market—and probably its life.

HIRING PERSONNEL WITH A BACKGROUND IN MANUFACTURING AT LARGE COMPANIES

The new venture may be tempted to hire as its manufacturing head an individual who has had responsibility for setting up and operating a manufacturing plant within a large organization. This is highly risky, since the large-company person will probably be unable to function without a big staff. The skills required to succeed in a large corporation, such as negotiation or managing a big staff, are not especially useful for a start-up, which, by its nature, is small and focused.

MANUFACTURING RULES

Unless the company is breaking new ground in manufacturing processes, as would be the case with disks or semiconductors, manufacturing is not stressed as a critical dimension. In fact, by the completion of the seed stage, the head of manufacturing may not even have been hired. In the case of software, manufacturing is almost trivial. Nevertheless, the start-up should keep the following rules in mind in order to avoid rude surprises.

Does the company have a well-defined organization and processes that will enable it to produce products at the cost, quality, and schedules required by its customers?

This is the basic test for whether the firm is disciplined and will be able to survive. The organization that fails to satisfy any of these fundamental requirements is doomed.

Does the company have initial ideas and an outline for a manufacturing strategy, including the degree of integration (i.e., which components or assemblies it will buy and which it will build), plant location, critical processes, specialized components, and quality control?

This rule tests whether the organization has given any real thought to manufacturing its product. In the case of software, manufacturing is straightforward and is usually done externally; and in the case of systems that require no new processes, the plan may be quite simple. If the start-up is building a computer component, such as a disk or semiconductor, in contrast, then manufacturing is its principal reason for existing, and thus, the firm must have a detailed outline for an extensive plan. For other systems requiring high volume, such as a terminal or PC, an extensive plan is needed to demonstrate that the organization can meet cost and quality requirements. This plan may involve a partnership for offshore or automated manufacturing.

If a strategic manufacturing partner is required, have candidates and contacts been identified?

This rule tests whether the company is approaching its manufacturing needs by looking for a partner to share in financing the manufacturing operation or by building the required expertise from the outset.

Will contract and/or offshore manufacturing capability be required in order for the start-up to produce effectively in terms of quality and cost?

In 1990, finding an offshore partner is a straightforward process because all governments (except that of the United States) understand that manufacturing is vital to their economy. Manufacturing high-definition computing television and pocket/wallet computers calls for collaboration with offshore manufacturers because of the capital and skilled labor needed to satisfy volume, cost, and quality demands. For complex components requiring skilled assembly (semiconductors and disks), manufacturing has moved to the Pacific Rim, where a higher level of skills is available from a better-trained work force. A study by International Data Corporation (IDC) shows that between 1982 and 1989, the manufacturing of nearly all hard disks, floppy disks, and tape drives moved out of the United States.

By the end of the seed stage, does the start-up have a plan in place (complete with costs) that identifies critical processes, suppliers, and an approach to running the manufacturing operation?

By the end of the seed stage, the company should have a good idea about potential suppliers of parts and processes, including special devices such as test equipment. A new venture that starts up without even a rudimentary manufacturing plan is quite likely to require additional funding once it faces equipment "sticker shock."

If the company intends to do its own manufacturing, have the plant size and factory location been figured into the plan?

The manufacturing plan is more than a spreadsheet exercise that relates space, people, and product output. It must include an initial attempt to define the plant design in order that the requirements for space and people, including those with special skills, may be understood. Unlike many of the other resources, acquiring manufacturing capacity calls for a great deal of careful advance planning. If the start-up is predicated on a novel manufacturing process or will need highly trained individuals who can evolve the process, the plan must take into account the location and availability of a work force.

If achieving the planned unit cost and schedule goals is predicated on essential breakthroughs in the manufacturing process, are the necessary resources (manufacturing vice president, specialists, time, and money) available?

If the firm's product technology is embodied in its manufacturing process, as opposed to its product design, then the manufacturing process must be treated as an engineering design and managed and measured as such. High-tech ventures are often predicated on the development of new processes for the manufacture of disks, tapes, semiconductors, printers, and various display devices. In these cases, starting up without a seasoned vice president of manufacturing is a flawed approach.

One firm based its business plan on having a highly automated plant. Although no fundamentally new processes were required to build the plant itself, a total system did have to be developed to ensure proper coordination of all the process steps in order to produce the product.

Is the product design planning process predicated on producing a design that ensures manufacturability and the highest quality?

This rule tests whether manufacturability and quality have been designed into the product from the outset. Manufacturability is not always regarded as a critical aspect of product design. More typically, the product is "thrown over the wall to be built" after the design is done because its manufacturing is thought to require simple and well-proven processes. However, such an approach is unlikely to yield the lowest cost or the highest quality. Unless the firm plans to produce a manufacturing-intensive product, it will probably not have a manufacturing person on board at start-up. The best way to ensure both manufacturability and quality is to hire people who have manufactured high-quality products before.

Does the company manage its raw materials and finished goods inventories in an optimal fashion?

As I observed at the start of the chapter, managing raw materials and finished goods is a balancing act. The start-up must have enough of each on hand to enable it to respond flexibly to fluctuations in the order rate but not so much that it feels a financial impact from having excess inventory.

Does the company introduce products into manufacturing rapidly, accompanied by clear product and process specifications?

The best guarantee of a speedy time-to-market is for engineering and manufacturing to function well together from the beginning. Although engineers must understand exactly how their product is built, manufacturing should be responsible for building all the products, including the prototypes.

CONCLUSION

In the case of manufacturing (as with every other dimension of an organization), achieving the highest quality is the most important operating principle. Without quality in every part of the operation, costs will be high, predictability will be nil, and customers will be unhappy.

The health of a start-up's manufacturing dimension will be assured if it follows these eight guiding principles suggested by Matt Sanders:

1. Only build products of the highest possible quality.

2. Only invest in manufacturing if the process is unique and is the essence of the start-up.

3. Examine every make/buy decision.

4. Get to market fast.

5. Use minimal cash.

6. Have only a minimal staff, but hire the critical people.

7. Make sure product cost is predictable and low.

8. Avoid the evil of inventory.

Chapter 8

THE PRODUCT

People, product, plan.
—Venture capital adage

The venture capital adage "people, product, plan" clearly emphasizes the product as one of the crucial elements of a start-up. The product, together with various services the company sells, is the organization's output; it is what customers buy and use. Customer purchase orders convert the product to revenue, and the quantity of those orders determines whether the firm is viable.

During the concept stage, the product is represented by a few sketches and perhaps a prototype demonstration in a laboratory. After that stage, the product progresses through various design phases as a series of specifications and demonstrations until it can be realized and replicated through a manufacturing process, as described in chapter 7. As the company enters the market development stage, the actual product is produced by the manufacturing organization and shipped to customers for revenue.

A product can be viewed in three ways:

- *The product specification:* Instructions or information (the bit pattern in the case of software) developed by engineering to describe the product so that a manufacturing organization can replicate it.

- *The product itself, or reality:* The physical product coming from a production line or replicated from a master software tape; this is what customers ultimately buy.

- *A market, or the buyer's image:* Specifications, pictures, and brochures that describe what a product is or how it appears, explain why someone would want it, or cause prospective customers to believe it can do something significant for them.

In this chapter, we will look at the product in many different ways, starting with the buying rationale. Products are placed within a product space, ranging from sand (silicon) and iron (magnetics) to organization-specific use, with training, learning, and service. A historical view of how the computer evolved into classes and gave birth to the associated applications software provides a background for the product development cycle. Important product-design issues, such as evolvability, and common flaws in developing products are also explored to show readers what to watch out for in product design and product positioning.

UNDERSTANDING WHY CUSTOMERS BUY

Many factors affect whether a customer will buy a product from a particular manufacturer. In the case of an established product class, the most obvious rationale is the product's relationship to other products in its class in terms of performance and price. New products, in contrast, may be purchased on a sole-source basis. As the industry matures and a commodity, high-technology market forms, then more factors, including appearance and prestige, become important. No matter what product or service the new venture intends to supply, its staff must understand why the customer will buy that product. The following subsections examine the most significant determinants of the customer's purchasing decision.

PERFORMANCE AND PRICE

In the early days of computing, computer pioneer Herb Grosch posited the following relationship between performance and price for computers introduced at the same time:

$$\text{performance}_{time} = k \times \text{price}^2$$

This relationship argues that an economy of scale exists, i.e., for twice the price you get four times the performance. With the introduction of new classes of computers, however, it has been shown (Bell, Mudge, and McNamara,1978; Mendelson, 1987) that this relationship is flawed, and if it ever was valid, it holds no longer. Today, a strong diseconomy of scale exists, such that:

$$\text{performance}_{time} = k \times \text{price}^{0.8}$$

We can observe this phenomenon by looking at various machine classes in the price versus performance plane of the sketch[1] in Figure 8-1, in which different classes of

1. This sketch was used to "position" Titan, Ardent's first graphics supercomputer against other potential competitive computers.

scientific and engineering computers are characterized, from supercomputers and mainframes to personal supercomputers. The diagonal lines are constant performance/price lines. If there is no economy of scale, all computers built at a given time should lie on the same line. If there is economy of scale, higher-priced computers should lie above the line. If there is diseconomy of scale, lower-priced computers should lie above the line. Since there is no economy of scale for any of the constituent parts of a computer, the lower-priced machines offer the best performance for the price.

To understand why someone will buy a particular system or software package requires a deep understanding of the product application and the buyer. Drucker (1985) devotes much of his book *Innovation and Entrepreneurship* to understanding the buying decision in an abstract fashion. The two most obvious purchasing rationales include:

- Better performance for the same price

- Better performance for the price at another price level

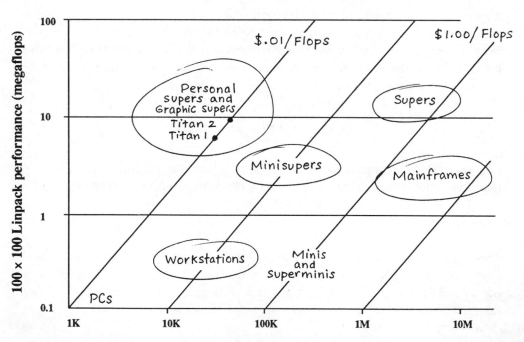

Figure 8-1. Sketch used in 1986 to "Position" Titan, Ardent's First Graphics Supercomputer, in the Performance Versus Price Space.

In the high-performance computing world, where performance is one of the main measures of comparison, having a system five to ten times faster than any other competing product simplifies decision making for the buyer. However, performance will fail to be a sufficiently convincing selling point if the user cannot program the computer or cannot obtain critical software to make the product useful. Furthermore, in the future, performance is unlikely to be enough to differentiate a product for very long, since computers evolve so rapidly. Established vendors will evolve their hardware quickly in order to hold their customers. If product evolution still isn't fast enough to hold customers, vendors may even sell futures—promises of machines that aren't quite ready yet.

The second buying rationale listed above, better performance for the price at another price level, causes inherently new usage and creates new markets, such as the computer in the home. Because performance and price are relatively easy to measure, they are employed in this book as simple, straightforward criteria for segmenting computer classes and uses.

ECONOMICS, PERSONAL POWER, AND APPEARANCE

Ultimately (in the five- to ten-year time frame), buying decisions are based on economics, including personal economics. Decision criteria also include such unusual attributes as the feeling of personal power associated with having the largest and most prestigious machine. Even appearance can be used to segment a computer market. Some early buyers were attracted to NeXT's first black-and-white workstations because of their attractive packaging, even though they lacked software and offered only incremental gains in functionality over the Macintosh or existing workstations. After the first few buyers, NeXT had to compete on the basis of true functionality and applications.

NEW CAPABILITIES

Yet another rationale for purchasing is that the product offers the user completely new capabilities. The potential market for new products is often impossible to predict, except by producing the product and building the market for it. For example, as "multimedia" becomes available, it's difficult to understand exactly who will use it or to make a compelling argument for why such capability is needed. However, many who have seen these programs say that comparing them to current products is like comparing color TV to black-and-white TV or comparing a Macintosh to an IBM PC running MS/DOS without Windows. "Multimedia" products reaching the market in 1990 (such as

MACROMIND) are great, and almost everyone would prefer a dynamic, color presentation to dull, black-and-white overheads. On the other hand, Steve Jobs has described multimedia as "the AI [artificial intelligence] of the 1990s"—i.e., a great promise that may not be fulfilled. The market is probably limited by a lack of low-cost playback units. Readers are invited to start a company to build these, if they think they can beat Sony and other consumer electronics firms to the market and then survive there.

Some of the factors influencing computer-equipment purchase decisions are shown in Figure 8-2. In order to determine why someone would buy a hardware component or system (or a new software package or system), weights must be assigned to these factors for each of the potential customers. Although the figure has a decided hardware and manufacturing orientation and flavor, it applies equally to software.

The final test of the product is whether it can meet the cost and quality goals set by the company and (most important) by the customer. Many of the criteria listed in Figure 8-2 can be quantified, either as operational or as one-time costs, permitting users to truly "value" their purchase. Although quality is often synonymous with performance, reliability, and ease of use, quality cannot be measured as quantitatively as cost. For example, quality can run the gamut from a poorly performing program that "feels" bad to a program that has a look and feel that exceeds the user's expectations. Understanding and measuring the product is the task of everyone in the firm, but marketing (the product-management organization) is responsible for the critical accounting function that measures the company's competitive product position.

When it comes to product planning, the start-up should keep in mind the following three important observations about the behavior and motivations of buyers in the computer market:

- If cost is a significant factor in buying a computer, such as when the individual will be paying for it, he or she should: (1) wait as long as possible to buy, because computers evolve rapidly, and (2) always buy the lowest-priced machine that can perform the task.

- If the requirements for the computer are unknown, as they are with a central service, or if the buying institution is not the paying institution, as happens with a service center that is paid for by the government or when charges are billed to someone else, then the customer should buy the largest, most general, and most expensive computer that can perform the greatest number of tasks.

- Readers should always remember that performance and price are not necessarily the main determinants of a product's success. Products must be differentiated by additional characteristics, including the way the buying organization, such as a company, functions (e.g., conducts its business).

- Purchase price, cost of ownership, return on the investment, and apparent lifetime based on the rate of technological change (obsolescence)

- Peak performance or response time, and work throughput

- Unique features or functions that differentiate the product from competitive and potentially competitive products

- Availability of the appropriate applications software or other parts of the infrastructure needed to carry out the buyer's mission

- Adherence to former and future standards, past compatibility (knowledge of how to use the product), future compatibility (or growth path), and cost of converting any data or software from a current standard or system

- Level of comfort with the vendor and individual sales/service person, including support; ease of purchase, installation, and use; machine appearance; brand prestige (e.g., "Cray aura," "IBM feel," or "Macintosh cult"); and ability to associate with other users

- Need for specialized programming, knowledge, and training

- Personal control over the allocation and management of the buyer's resources

Figure 8-2. Buying Criteria for Computer Systems (Including Software).

MARKET CONSIDERATIONS FOR A NEW PRODUCT

A key part of understanding the buying rationale for a product is to precisely understand the overall market considerations, including the dynamics of introducing a new or existing product into a new or existing market and the issue of nichemanship.

NEW OR EXISTING PRODUCT IN NEW OR EXISTING MARKET

Table 8-1 shows four quadrants (existing product into existing market, existing product into new market, etc.). Each quadrant presents a unique set of problems and opportunities and raises some fundamental questions that must be answered before the start-up attempts to introduce a product into that product/market quadrant.

Table 8-1. Example of Market/Product Opportunities and Key Problems.

Product	Market	
	Existing	*New Customers and/or Use*
Existing	High-tech commodity (e.g., disk) *Can you achieve the level of cost and quality required to beat the established suppliers?*	Distribution or application pioneering (e.g., mail order or home PC) *Can you establish infrastructure?*
New	Substitution (e.g., work-stations replacing minis or mainframes), applications software (e.g., derived from users) *Can you find the customers?*	Pioneering to an *emerging market* (e.g., first spreadsheet, voice or handwritten control of PC) *Are you first and right?*

Introducing a new product into a new market (the lower-right quadrant of Table 8-1) is a very difficult task, since the start-up essentially has to "make the market." The difficulty of making a market is usually proportional to the distance between the new product and other known products and markets, because the more unfamiliar a product is, the harder it is to establish a market for it. At the other end of the spectrum, introducing a new version of an established product (the upper-left quadrant) poses a different set of problems. Established products (such as disks) are high-tech commodities that are usually differentiated by cost and quality. If a company starts up to enter a well-established market with a well-established product, it is fundamentally betting that it has a unique approach to the product design or a special method of manufacture or a lock-in feature.

In the case of software, where all products cost virtually nothing to produce, the organization is betting that it has a unique way to distribute its product so as to address a fundamentally new set of users, thereby creating a new market. If patent and copyright laws continue to support "look and feel," then software products will continue to be high-priced. However, if it becomes legal to clone software so that it looks exactly the same to a user and carries out operations on exactly the same data, then software prices will fall to near zero, since software cloning is almost always possible, given enough time.

Introducing a new product into an existing market (the lower-left quadrant of Table 8-1) involves the process of substitution—getting buyers to switch from the product they are currently using to the new product. Chapter 12, "Technical Workstations," includes a description of how Apollo successfully replaced time-shared minicomputers by introducing a new product into an existing market. Building on this initial impetus, Apollo enjoyed a second, significantly larger gain with fulfillment of new applications that only became possible through better user interaction and larger, multiple-windowed screens. Among the applications were software engineering, office automation, and electrical and mechanical computer-aided design (CAD). Stellar was subsequently formed to do it again in a similar way, only this time by building a graphics supercomputer to replace fast workstations, including those connected to a shared supercomputer.

The real key to introducing a new product is to develop one whose obvious superiority to existing products justifies a high margin. The following rule applies:

A new venture must maintain high operating margins to fuel its growth. In order to justify the higher margins, its product must be significantly better than products from established suppliers. Predicating a start-up on a product that is only slightly better than existing products is an approach doomed from the start!

Although the phrase "significantly better" usually implies a clear advantage in performance, price, or quality, another attribute, uniqueness (discussed below), can also serve to differentiate a product and thereby become the basis for profitable sales.

MARKET NICHEMANSHIP: UNIQUENESS AS A MEANS OF JUSTIFYING HIGHER MARGINS

Nichemanship is the art of introducing a new product or service that will serve a well-defined segment (a "niche") of an existing, larger market that is being poorly served by current suppliers. Niches are created by developing a product with unique features that appeal to a select segment of buyers. Niche products are distinct from newly invented products that create entirely new markets, such as a new computer price class or the first spreadsheet. Successful niches include:

- The minisupercomputers from Alliant and Convex, created to meet the needs of scientific and engineering users who were working with superminicomputers and who required power for computation

- Military computers or components, such as those available from Performance Semiconductors

- Fault-tolerant transaction-processing computers from Stratus Computer that attacked a small segment of Tandem Computer's market

- High-performance and high-feature word processors targeted toward the document-preparation and typesetting users who formed the basis of desktop publishing

- More powerful spreadsheets able to display more complex data for technical users

Nichemanship is one way that a small company can play on the same field as the giants of the computer industry without getting trampled to death. Jeff Tarter, editor of *Soft•letter* (1989), offered the following advice to a firm that had just entered the desktop-publishing market with no way to differentiate itself:

> Be a Goliath; Davids rarely win. In the software business small market shares are rarely profitable. One or two companies get 80–90% of profit dollars. Davids get fringe customers that the large companies cannot serve through normal sales channels or make extravagant demands for hand holding, advanced features and pricing concessions. Some alternatives: 1. become a mini-Goliath in a niche e.g. home, academe or 2. get an alternative channel through a mass merchandiser or a private label e.g. Tandy.

VIEWING THE NEW PRODUCT AS PART OF THE BIG PICTURE

A new product in the computer field—be it hardware, software, or a combination thereof—should be examined from a number of different perspectives as objectively as possible. Although this is difficult for the product's inventors or investors to do, the rewards of such a multifaceted examination are great, because it can reveal the product's weak points, if any, and predict the likelihood of its market success. In the following subsections, readers are asked to contemplate the functional use of computers, consider where a new product falls within the "computer product space," understand the basic nature of computer classes, decide whether the product creates a new computer class or application, and view the new product from a historical perspective.

COMPUTER FUNCTIONS

Figure 8-3 shows a taxonomy of computer use within various organizations. Note that the need for, and resulting economics of, computer use vary considerably from one organization to another. To a great extent, the functional use determines the configurations, software, and performance/price requirements.

COMPUTER PRODUCT SPACE

A new computer product will be part of a system that is the sum of all its hardware and software components, including the highest-level programs required to perform a

Commercial organizations
- Financial accounting and control, with record storage and batch processing for the firm
- Billing, inventory, accounts receivable/payable, payroll
- Transaction processing for sales and intrafirm/interfirm transactions
- Business analysis

Technical organizations (science and engineering)
- Numbers, algorithms, text, graphs, storage, and processing
- Data acquisition and real-time experimentation
- Interactive problem solving using computer simulation rather than experiments to model for science, engineering, and product and process design, including computer-aided manufacturing (CAM)
- Communication, databases (notebooks)

Manufacturing
- Record storage and batch processing
- Continuous and discrete real-time control
- Plant scheduling and process optimization

Communication
- Message switching and organizationwide electronic mail
- Computer networking, including all local area networks (LANs)
- Voice and speech, teleconferencing

Office automation, electronic (desktop) publishing, and word processing
- Image processing for the transduction, storage, and transmission of documents

Education
- Reading, writing, communication
- Mathematics
- Computer-assisted instruction via simulation models
- Database and network access

Home
- Entertainment (e.g., games), instruction (including simulation), database, network access

Figure 8-3. Taxonomy of Computer Use Within Several Major Organizational Categories.

given application. The system and its component parts can be characterized in terms of the three dimensions of the computer product space shown in Figure 8-4:

- *Class:* The class dimension is characterized by price (and the dependent variable, performance).

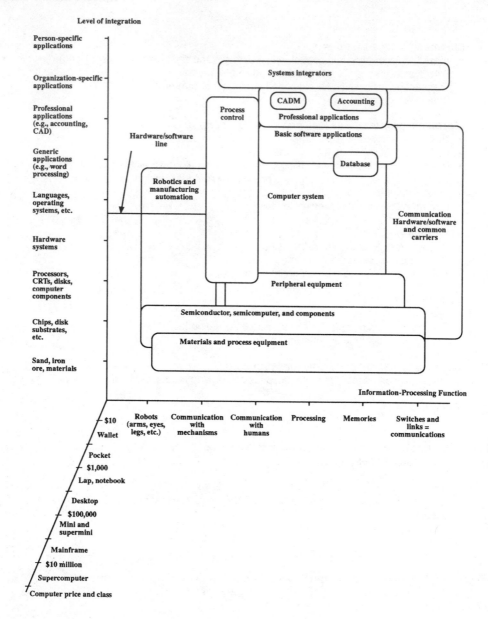

Figure 8-4. The Information-Processing Product Space Formed by the Level-of-Integration, Function, and Price/Class Dimensions.

- *Function:* The function dimension involves processing or control, memory (e.g., database), switching (communications), transduction (interfacing to humans), and other information processes (such as robots).

- *Level of integration:* In the level-of-integration dimension, each level carries out a particular function, building on a lower level and producing a function for use by the next higher level.

Figure 8-4 shows a plane within the three-dimensional space and characterizes some of the products within the computer and communications industries. The computer product space can be used in various ways to plot historical trends; a component product (point or line), such as a disk or spreadsheet within a given level of integration; a system product or product line covering a volume of price and function in the space and based on a set of levels of integration; all the products of a given firm or industry segment; and trajectories of products and companies.

Figure 8-5 shows the standards that define the interface at each level of integration for a particular system in the workstation computer class, the Stardent 3000 graphics supercomputer. Each computer class has a particular set of standards that define the interface at each level of integration.

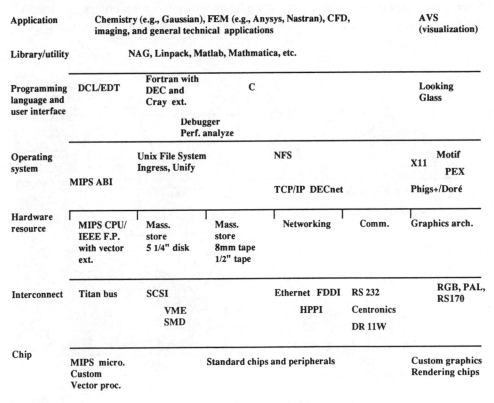

Figure 8-5. Standards Used for the Stardent 3000 Graphics Supercomputer at Each Level of Integration.

COMPUTER CLASSES

Computers can be classified in a number of different ways. The following subsections show how they can be classified in terms of evolutionary stage, price, both price and weight, and according to several other criteria.

Classes by Evolution

Figure 8-6 shows the evolution of computing styles, applications (whether commercial or technical), and operating systems.

Classes by Price

A simple view of the computer classes is given in Figure 8-7, which lists what buyers believe to be almost twenty distinct kinds of computers, ranging in price from $10 toys to $20 million supercomputers. Given the plethora of computers, together with the consolidation taking place through corporate acquisitions and mergers, one might be skeptical of a start-up aimed at building yet another general-purpose computer.

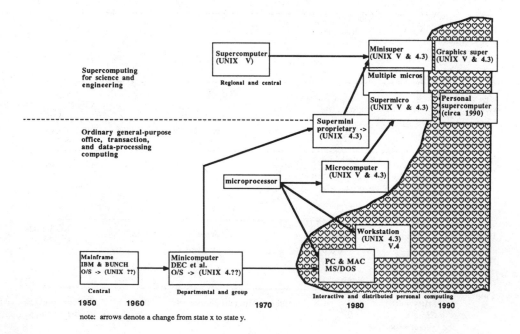

Figure 8-6. Evolution of Computing Styles with Time.

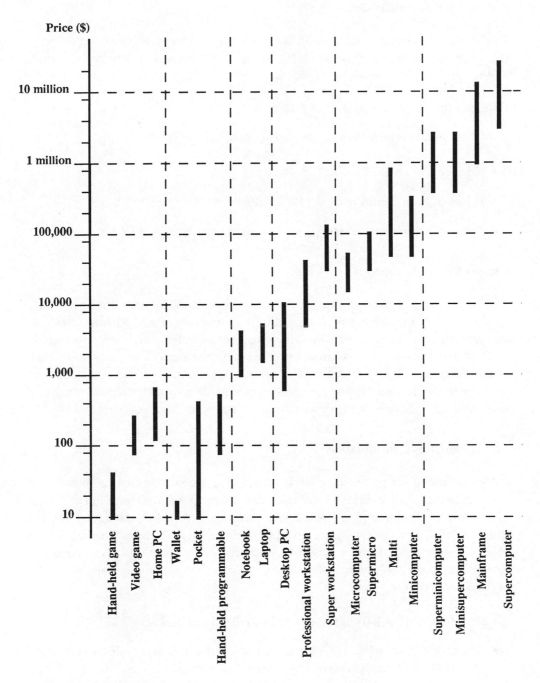

Figure 8-7. Computer Classes/Prices in 1990.

Classes by Price and Weight

Dave Nelson (an Apollo founder) and I posited an interesting model for characterizing computer classes, which is given in Table 8-2. Note that the relationship between price and weight is:

price = $10 \times 10^{class \#}$ weight = $0.05 \times 10^{class \#}$

Other products and services can also be characterized by classes:

- Prices of cars = $6,000 \times 1.5^{class\#}$

- Prices of transportation devices = $k \times 10^{type \text{ (shoes, cars, trains, ICBMs, etc.)}}$

- Prices of French restaurants$_{t=1985}$ = F (ambiance, location) $\times \$15 \times 1.5^{\# stars}$

Classes by Application

Class is determined quite subjectively by the buyers who regard one or more products as equivalent. In a similar fashion, computing is a commodity for which other products and services can be substituted. For example, users could employ a service to get a result, or they may lease or purchase any number of computers from different classes—such as a collection of PCs, a shared microcomputer, or a variety of minicomputers—to produce the same result. Figure 8-8 plots the size of the computer market, in terms of computer size (i.e., class) and application, at several points between 1960 and 1987.

Computer-Class Consolidation

After examining the preceding charts, readers might conclude that the number of computers and computing styles within a class always grows with time, but this is not necessarily the case. It is quite possible for a computer class to be consolidated when a company makes a single architecture available for a large market range. That firm is thus able to dominate a single market and become the leader. As a result, all other firms must then become compatible with this form of computing. The following are some examples of class dominations:

- Mainframes: IBM 360 (circa 1964) for centralized computing.

- Minis: DEC VAX (circa 1978) for a wide range of computing styles and the IBM AS/400 series, which evolved from earlier business minis.

Table 8-2. Nelson-Bell Computer Classes.

Class No.	Where Used	Class	Price ($) [a]	Weight (Lbs.)
0	Wallet	Calculator, personal data card[b]	10	0.05
1	Pocket/palm	Calculator, personal database	100	0.50
2	Briefcase	Notebook and laptop portable	1,000	5.00
3	Office	PC and workstation	10,000	50.00
		Personal supercomputer	50,000	150.00
4	Project, group	Micro, graphics super, mini	100,000	500.00
		Department minisuper, supermini	500,000	1,500.00
5	Center	Mainframe	1 million	5,000.00
6	Center, region	Supercomputer	10 million	50,000.00

[a]As of 1990, the price of each class may extend upward to encompass the price of the next class and downward by a factor of 2 or 3.
[b]"Smart card" with on-board micro storing thousands of characters to a million characters.

- PCs: IBM-compatible PCs controlled by Intel's 80X86 architecture and Microsoft's DOS operating system.

- Workstations: Sun Microsystems, UNIX, or an evolution of MS/DOS and OS/2. By 1995, it should be possible to determine whether workstations will remain a distinct computer class or merge and become competitive with PCs.

Some Closing Thoughts on Computer Classes

Only computer classes that are available on a ubiquitous basis from competitive sources will survive and thrive. All proprietary systems, though not competitive, will continue to be available to serve a declining installed base at premium prices in 2001. These suppliers will not be significant.

As noted above, the range of computer classes extends from the few-dollar card computer to the $20 million supercomputer. It is unlikely that a company can be formed to exploit the over-$50-million computer market.

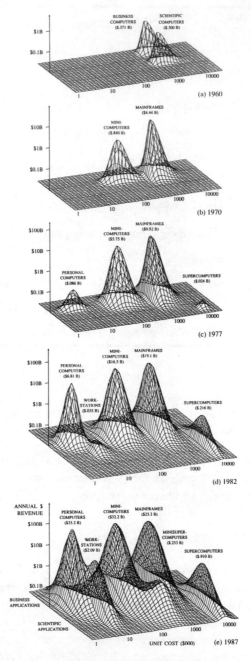

Figure 8-8. Market Size for Various Computer Classes and Applications with Time. (Courtesy of the IEEE Scientific Supercomputer Subcommittee, from "The Computer Spectrum: A Perspective on the Evolution of Computing.")

There are ample opportunities for new computer products that do not fit into the computer-class taxonomy given above. For example, there exists a potential market for a variety of stationary and mobile robots to move things and carry out tasks remotely (e.g., surveillance).

CREATING NEW COMPUTER CLASSES AND APPLICATIONS

As semiconductor and magnetic density evolve to offer greater performance and greater functionality, as discussed in Chapter 5, there are several approaches that a high-tech venture can use and several forms that new products can take:

1. *Creation of a new class:* The start-up can use the increase in density made possible by the new technology to build a less costly version of the previous generation.

   This strategy creates a new, lower price class. A new company will be required to exploit this new product form. Once the class forms, new firms will also be required to build appropriate software.

2. *Evolution:* The start-up can use the increase in density to build a system with increased performance having roughly the same price as the previous generation.

   The result is the next, evolutionary model of a computer in the same price class, but with the power of a previous generation's higher-class model. For example, every three years, such a system provides four times the memory, requiring two more bits of addressing.

3. *Invention:* The start-up can push the new technology to the limit in an unorthodox fashion to gain performance, although at an increased cost.

   This strategy allows a given manufacturer to enter the next higher price class. It is also the strategy required when pushing technology to build the next supercomputer. As noted above, however, it is unlikely that a company can be formed to exploit the over-$50-million computer market.

Figure 8-9 shows how new classes form and how old classes are reimplemented with new technology as a function of time. A company that has a fixed organization, existing user base, and established cost structure always tends to adopt the second strategy in the preceding list, evolution. This satisfies the firm's current users and the marketing and sales departments, as well as those engineers who feel safer with evolution than with setting out on a new path. A new organization is required if the first or third strategies are to be adopted.

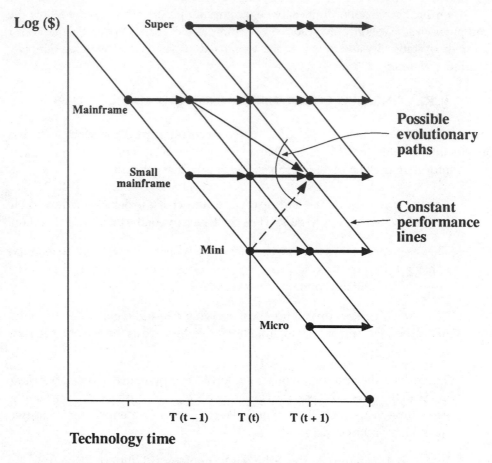

Figure 8-9. Computer Price Versus Time for Each of the Computer Classes.

The process of evolution in software is almost identical to the process of evolution in hardware classes, whereby a new release or version of a program can:

- Become smaller and simpler, thereby addressing a new market that doesn't require the advanced features of the old product

- Increase functionality by using a more powerful platform that has more processing and memory with which to operate

- Be recast to employ another computing style (e.g., graphics) so as to permit a new type of use and address a larger base of users

VIEWING NEW PRODUCTS FROM A HISTORICAL PERSPECTIVE

The brief history of the computer industry presented in this subsection will enable readers to appreciate the industry's dynamics and gain insight into the opportunities for future products. Two observations are critical:

- All new forms of computing (from supercomputers to pocket calculators) and constituent software (from computer-aided design of molecules to databases and human user-interface paradigms) require new companies to introduce the new computer class or invent the new way of computing.

- IBM has dominated the entire history of computing, beginning in 1950. It is incredibly robust and dynamic and has been able to retain its leadership during the whole period. While rarely being the first to introduce a new product or leading in a given area (except disk memories), IBM ultimately leads in market share.

Although the following overview characterizes computer generations in terms of hardware technologies, it should be realized that with changes in hardware (for example, the Macintosh), a new industrial structure forms around the new computing paradigm. Just as the old-line hardware suppliers are irrelevant to advancing modern computing, the traditional suppliers of software for mainframes are irrelevant to the new distributed and interactive workstation computing environments. Several orders of magnitude more software companies form to exploit each new computer class than there are firms actually producing computers within the class. Similarly, for each new computer class, the number of component suppliers that form to support the computers in that class is at least equal to the number of computer-producing firms within the class. For example, twenty-nine companies started up during the period 1977–1987 to build Winchester-technology disk drives, with a combined investment from private and public sources of nearly $1 billion.

In the beginning, when Eckert and Mauchly established UNIVAC and built the first commercial computer, they designed and built every part of the computer (except for the vacuum tubes), including its power supplies, logic and memories, and tapes. They also wrote all the software. Today, a high-tech venture can simply assemble a computer, complete with software, from component suppliers. Table 8-3 shows how the structure of the industry, including the use of manufactured components from other industries (e.g., semiconductors, disks, cathode-ray tubes [CRTs], and all software components), has evolved.

Table 8-4 shows the top circuit component suppliers ranked by revenue at various times. It is interesting to note that the suppliers of circuits rarely make many of the technology transitions from generation to generation. On the other hand, old computer

Table 8-3. Sources of Computer Components in Each Generation.

	Generation			
Component	1st & 2d	3d	4th	5th
Technology	Vacuum tubes, transistors	SSI, MSI[a]	LSI, VLSI[a]	ULSI[a]
Power supply	mfg.	mfg., cs	mfg., cs, std.	cs
Logic	mfg.	semico.	semico.	std., semico. std., mfg.-custom
Memory	mfg.	mfg., cs, semico.	semico., std.	semico., std.
Packaging	mfg.	mfg.	mfg., std., cs	mfg., std., cs
Mass storage	mfg.	cs	cs, std.	cs
Terminal	mfg.	cs, std.	cs	cs
Communications/ LAN	mfg.	semico.	semico. std.	semico. std
Operating system	mfg.	mfg.	mfg., AT&T, Microsoft	AT&T, OSF, Microsoft, IBM
Databases	—	mfg.	cs, std.	cs, std.
Languages	mfg.	cs	cs, std.	cs
Generic applications	mfg.	mfg.	3d, std.	cs
Professional applications	user	3d	3d	cs

Abbreviations:

mfg.	=	manufactured by the computer manufacturer
cs	=	obtained from a component supplier
semico.	=	a general product of the semiconductor industry
std.	=	a standard product available as a commodity from numerous sources
3d	=	software written by a third-party software house

[a]Integrated circuit sizes measured in transistors per chip:

SSI	2–64	Small-scale integration—circuits suitable for logic
MSI	64–2K	Medium-scale integration—circuits suitable for arithmetic units and register arrays
LSI	2K–64K	Large-scale integration—circuits suitable for small microprocessors and memories
VLSI	64K–2M	Very-large-scale integration—circuits suitable for all processors and large memories
ULSI	2M–64M	Ultra-large-scale integration—circuits suitable for complete systems on a chip

Table 8-4. Leading Tube, Transistor, and Integrated Circuit Manufacturers at Various Times.

Tube	Transistor 1955	Transistor 1960	Integrated Circuit 1978	1989
RCA	Hughes	Texas Instruments	Texas Instruments	NEC
Sylvania	Transitron	Transitron	Motorola	Toshiba
GE	Philco	Philco	Fairchild[a]	Hitachi
Raytheon	Sylvania	GE	National	Motorola
Westinghouse	Texas Instruments	RCA	Intel	Fujitsu
Amperex	GE	Motorola	RCA[b]	Texas Instruments
Tungsol	RCA	Clevite	Signetics[c]	Mitsubishi
Ranland	Westinghouse	Fairchild	General Instruments	Intel
Eimac	Motorola	Hughes	AMD	Matsushita
Philco	Clevite	Sylvania	Mostek[c]	Philips
				SGS-Thom
				Samsung
				Sharp
				Siemens
				Sanyo
				Oki
				AMD
				Sony
				AT&T

[a] >National   [b] >GE   [c] >Philips
note: >went to or was acquired by

companies tend to continue existing because of their established base of customers that have installed their computers and have software to use on them. These customers are buying "code museums."

Products of the First Generation: 1950–1959

In the first generation, large computers operating in batch mode were the dominant form of computing. They typically cost between $250,000 and $10 million. Using vacuum-tube technology, the major vendors, IBM and Remington Rand Univac, had a combined market share of about 90 percent. The total market was small, however, since primary memories were small (less than 64 kilobytes) and costly, disk memories did not yet exist, and programming was very difficult. Matters improved near the end of the decade, however, as IBM introduced its first disk, the RAMAC, in 1957. Fortran (1959) and Cobol (1960) became available to assist programmers and to aid in transporting programs between different manufacturers' machines. In addition, a few desk-size computers, costing about $50,000, were introduced.

Products of the Second Generation: 1960–1968

The second generation was based on transistor circuitry, and the cost of computers was reduced enough that large organizations could afford computing for routine commercial applications. Smaller computers became possible, and new companies formed to build them, including Digital Equipment Corporation (DEC; 1957), which introduced its first true minicomputer (the PDP-8) in 1965. Computers began to take on a broader role in control and communications outside of computation and data processing.

Products of the Third Generation: 1969–1977

With Kilby's and Noyce's invention of the integrated circuit (1958), the evolutionary basis of all subsequent computing classes was established. Whereas in the first two generations, only a few companies started up, the integrated circuit allowed nearly a hundred companies to form to build minicomputers, because the cost and difficulty of designing circuitry was almost eliminated. Computer-component industries emerged to supply peripherals, memory subsystems, and various types of software, ranging from languages to applications.

Minicomputers costing $10,000 to $100,000 were developed and embedded into larger systems—such as process controllers, telephone systems, and mainframes for small organizations and groups—establishing the notion of departmental computing. The mini made a particularly strong impact in technical applications, including factories, engineering, and scientific applications. Out of necessity, the mini had to communicate with other systems, because it was accessible and affordable. The result was that it pioneered distributed processing. In 1978, DEC introduced the VAX 11/780 as an extension of the earlier PDP-11 series and established the superminicomputer class ($250,000–$1 million), which had the power and capability of mainframes.

Figure 8-10, which summarizes the outcome of the ninety-two minicomputer companies founded during the 1970s (Bell, 1984), illustrates the odds of establishing a viable business in a new product class.

Fifty companies started up and retained autonomy for a while.
- Prime continued to grow by acquiring Computervision and in 1989 was in significant debt through a leveraged buyout.
- Data General continues, practicing the UNIX religion.
- Tandem started in 1975 and has remained successful.
- Nine stalled or found niches to support their customer base.
- Thirty-eight ceased to exist.

Nine companies merged with larger firms.
- Concurrent (formerly Perkin Elmer, formerly Interdata) acquired Masscomp.
- Two continued with niche products.
- Six ceased to exist.

Eight existing companies built minis.
- DEC and IBM continued to build aggressive products.
- Control Data Corporation continued as a distributor.
- Five ceased manufacturing.

Twenty-five existing noncomputer firms built minis for special use.
- Hewlett-Packard (HP) acquired a company and became successful.
- Hughes, Raytheon, and Texas Instruments (TI) still build special computers.
- Twenty-one ceased manufacturing

Note: This figure does not include struggling Wang Laboratories or the plethora of companies that started up in the 1980s to make minis using multiple microprocessors.

Figure 8-10. Outcome of Ninety-two 1970s U.S. Minicomputer Start-ups.

Figure 8-10 gives rise to the following related observations:

- IBM always has a large market share, no matter when or what part of the market it enters, provided that it enters the market.

- Few companies can enter fundamentally new businesses. Only one firm, HP, was able to survive the transition from its instrument business into computing.

- Only four companies can be considered leaders after twenty-five years: DEC, HP, IBM, and Tandem.

- Seven winners in 1980 became struggling companies against microprocessors and distributed workstations.

- Of all the organizations, about 25 percent were successful, in that they survived as an operational entity at a site.

- Entering a well-defined niche is a way of surviving, but not of leading.

- The probability of survival for even a few years after a merger was about fifty-fifty.

Products of the Fourth Generation: 1978–1990

The fourth generation could be called "the age of microprocessors and the dawn of distributed computing." Although the dates shown for each generation in the subsection headings imply a clear-cut boundary between generations, this is not in fact the case, because each generation includes the maturing products of the previous generation and the seeds of the next generation. In particular, the seeds for the fourth generation were sown during the third generation, with the production of the Intel 4004, the first and widely used microprocessor.

Although the computers of preceding generations spawned very few computer classes, the 4004 and its successors gave rise to many different computer classes, as shown in Table 8-5. By 1978, single-user personal computers were being configured around micros with CRTs, keyboards, and floppy and large hard disks (circa 1982) produced by a high-technology component industry. These personal computers appeared in every form, from the home computer, which sold for a few hundred dollars; to personal computers; to powerful workstations, which initially sold for $50,000.

One of the most important standard components to evolve was the operating system. Once UNIX and MS/DOS became available by 1981, the problem of developing an operating system was reduced to licensing a fully developed product, including all documentation for reproduction, from AT&T and Microsoft, respectively.

Table 8-5. Computer Classes Formed from New Microprocessor Introductions.

Year	Class	Components	Companies (Year Product Introduced)
1971	Calculator	Intel 4004	Busicom (1971)
1973	Business terminal	Intel 8008	Datapoint (1973)
1973–1977	Personal computer	8080, 6502	Micral (1973), SCELBI (1974), Altair (1975), Commodore (1977), Radio Shack (1977), Apple (1977)
1981	IBM PC	8088; MS/DOS	IBM (1981)
1981	Workstation	68000; UNIX	Apollo (1981), Sun (1982)
1981	Micro[a]	68000; UNIX	Onyx (1980), Altos (1982), NCR (1982), Plexus (1983)
1982	FT multi[a, b]	68000	Stratus (1982)
1982–1985	Multi[a, b]	68000; 32x32	Synapse (1983), Arix (1984), Sequent (1985), Encore (1986)

[a]Substitution for minicomputer-technology-based computers.
[b]Multi = multiple-microprocessor computer; FT = fault-tolerant multiprocessor.

New companies using microprocessor technology formed to establish the personal computer, workstation, micro, multi, and other computer classes. As each of the new classes began to capture a noticeable proportion of an established firm's revenue, that firm was forced to respond to the new mode of computing. Usually, the new classes proved unsuccessful, and sales started to decline. IBM is the exception; the IBM PC (1981) was designed and built in reaction to Apple's success. In 1989, DEC and IBM entered the workstation market with RISC-based products designed to compete with the market leader, Sun Microsystems.

The following observations can be made about the introduction of new computers:

- Established computer companies—driven externally by their existing customers and internally by their marketing and engineering groups, organization, and cost structures—tend to build computers a certain way with a previous design (architecture) to service an established customer base. In effect, computer firms usually build code museums to hold programs created on earlier machines and to serve their present customers.

- New computer classes must be created by new ventures that are neither bound by traditional use nor locked into providing compatible code-museum environments. Early in the development of the class, traditional suppliers tend to aid the new firm's formation by buying computers to serve their company.

- When a computer start-up begins to take a noticeable portion of potential revenue (e.g., about $1 billion) from large, established vendors, they respond by designing products appropriate to the new style of computing. Thus, the new firm begins to be limited by competition rather than being assisted by it through distribution agreements.

Products of the Fifth Generation: 1988–2001[2]

Products of the fifth generation are characterized by a ubiquitous network, ultra-large-scale integration (ULSI), reduced instruction set computers (RISCs), and parallelism. Personal computers and their workstation cousins, which many feel characterized the fourth generation, were interconnected via local area networks. In the fifth generation, all computers are interconnected locally and globally to form a distributed computing environment. All of the local area networks are finally interconnected via a hierarchy of fast networks, including metropolitan networks, wide area networks, and the integrated services digital network (ISDN), provided that it ever exists.

If the connection is very tight and a group of individuals can carry out their work together by operating on the same problems and share the same information, on an instantaneous basis, then the fifth generation will have arrived. Steve Jobs calls this "interpersonal computing." At this point, the facility will be as capable and robust as the original time-sharing systems introduced in 1970!

The fifth generation is also characterized by the use of RISC, which has enabled performance to evolve at the rate of 60 percent per year (or a factor of 2 every eighteen months) since 1985. RISC uses a somewhat simpler architecture that permits a single processor and the important supporting circuitry to be placed on a single chip. The supporting circuitry includes floating point arithmetic, virtual memory translation hardware, and fast cache memories. As with previous generations, the fifth generation will have fully arrived when the RISC architecture has replaced virtually all other computer classes.

---

2. It is especially difficult to tell when one generation ends and another begins when writing a book near a boundary line. Therefore, the dates for the fourth and fifth generations have been shown with a two-year overlap.

(It is important to keep in mind that the start of a new generation can only be identified after the fact, when history shows that a new technology has replaced virtually all other forms of computing that characterized the earlier generation.)

The RISC notion dates back to Cocke at IBM Research in the late 1970s. The chronology of companies adopting RISC for computer products includes:

1983   Introduction of RISC-based computers by Ridge and Pyramid

1986   MIPS Computer Systems (based on Hennesey, Stanford)

1987   IBM's RT Workstation, based on the original 801 project

        HP's Precision (IBM alumni Joel Birnbaum and Bill Worley)

        Sun's SPARC (based on Patterson, University of California at Berkeley)

1988   Apollo's Prism

1989   Motorola's 88000 microprocessor

        Intel's i860, a numeric accelerating processor for the 80386/80486

The significance of the various technology factors can be seen in Figure 8-11. The two bipolar technologies that formed the basis of supercomputers, mainframes, and minicomputers evolved at a constant rate of 14 percent per year, doubling in performance every five years. The CMOS microprocessor, based on traditional architectural ideas, evolved at roughly 40 percent per year. These micros began to overtake the ECL-based technology in the late 1980s.

However, just as the crossover in performance began to happen, the RISC microprocessor was introduced by MIPS Computer Systems and created a discontinuity in performance by a factor of 2 to 4 over traditional architectures, such as the Intel 80X86 and Motorola 68000. The shift to a RISC architecture, which is inherently easier to build, provided an additional stimulus that accelerated the evolution. With RISC, the first chip to be implemented in a new semiconductor process, such as VLSI ECL (circa 1989) and eventually VLSI gallium arsenide (circa 1995), becomes the newest-generation microprocessor.

Unlike previous processor evolution, which averaged product-gestation times of three to six years, the microprocessor "tracks" the semiconductor process with a new design *at double the performance* approximately every eighteen months, as shown in Table 8-6.

Parallel computing, an equally important idea whose time has come, will mark the fifth generation as clearly as distributed processing and RISC. With parallel processing, performance can be increased almost infinitely by interconnecting a number of

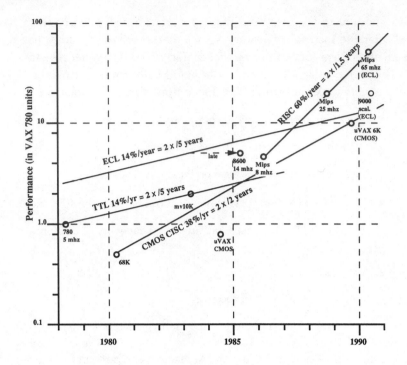

Notes:
Circuit Technologies
ECL   =   emitter coupled logic (bipolar semiconductor)
TTL   =   transistor-transistor logic (bipolar semiconductor)
CMOS   =   complementary metal oxide semiconductor (field effect)

Computer Architectures
CISC   =   complex (or complete) instructor-set computer
RISC   =   reduced instruction-set computer

Figure 8-11. Performance Versus Time for Various Computer Architectures.

microprocessors. As with all other concepts that mark a generation, nearly every computer will be built with some form of parallel processing beyond concurrent compute and input/output. The alternative computer structures of the 1990s, based on parallel processing, are shown in Table 8-7.

In effect, the monoprogrammed, massively parallel computers become the 1990s counterpart of the attached array processors that were introduced in the 1970s.

HINTS FOR DESIGNING GREAT PRODUCTS

Designing a great product means more than just having a great idea for the product's architecture. It also means doing everything right and not committing irreparable flaws.

Table 8-6. Performance Measures for Leading-Edge, RISC, One-Chip Microprocessors.

Year	Clock (Mhz)	PkMips[a]	Mflops[b]	Mflops[b] with Vector Unit
1986	8	5	1	—
1987	16	10	2	16
1988	25	16	5	25
1989	40	25	—	—
ECL Shift Permits:				
1990	80	50	10	100
1992	160	100	20	200

[a]PkMips = millions of instructions per second (peak).
[b]Mflops = millions of floating point operations per second for the linear algebra package, Linpack, solving a 100 X 100 matrix.

With shorter design cycles, it is of paramount importance to design products (i.e., have an architecture) that can be evolved over several generations, each of which may last only eighteen to twenty-four months. The following subsections explore how a high-tech venture can achieve these goals.

MAKING COST AND QUALITY PART OF THE START-UP PLAN BY DESIGNING THEM IN

As indicated in Chapter 7, quality plays a critical role in the start-up manufacturing process. If the level of quality is inadequate, few sales will be made in today's quality-conscious marketplace, and the product will be doomed. Without incorporating cost and quality goals into the product design, it is impossible to create an accurate business plan and model for the company, because quality affects sales volumes and product support costs as well as warranty and staffing costs. The worst thing about making a poor product is that engineers must fly all over the world in a chaotic fashion to diagnose and repair it.

I believe the best way for a start-up to address the quality issue is simply to sell its products with a money-back guarantee. This approach dramatically simplifies the contracting process, because it avoids customer acceptance tests, performance guarantees, and all the legal mumbo jumbo of the contracts that customers formerly used to protect themselves against nonoperational systems. Here's how two firms successfully employed such guarantees to promote the sale of their products.

Table 8-7. Parallel Computer Types, Style of Use, and Application (in Increasing Order of Specificity).

Computer Type	Form	Application
General-Purpose		
Simple uniprocessor	A processor and its memory	Simplest PC, workstation, microprocessor
Multiprocessor	All processors sharing memory	All mainframes, minis, workstations, large-transaction processing
Multivector processor	Multi, using vector processors	All types of supercomputers
Monoprogrammed for a Single Task at a Given Time, Multiple Uses		
Multicomputer	Interconnected computers	Large area networks, high reliability, technical high performance, distributed database
SIMD (single instruction multiple data)	Massive (1M) data parallelism	Supercomputing, signal processing
Bound to a Single Application by Hardware and Software		
Array processor	4-8 processing elements	Digital signal processing
Special SIMD	Graphics and image processors	CAD, visualization
Neural net	Pattern recognition	Speech, signal processing
Systolic processor	Pipelined processing	Specialized signal processing
Data-flow processor	Research phase	Unlikely multicomputer

Silicon Compilers' and Ardent's guarantees. The chip CAD software sold by Silicon Compilers was first offered with the guarantee that any chip produced by the compiler would operate according to the specifications. This eliminated the fear of buying the compiler and still not being able to get a working chip.

At Ardent, we offered a thirty-day money-back guarantee that allowed buyers to return computers in the event they were unsatisfied with their purchase.

Both these firms found that the contracting process was considerably simplified. In Ardent's case, there was no need for lengthy and complex acceptance criteria. Customers simply tried the product, with any and all programs they chose, and decided whether or not to keep it. Out of a thousand computers delivered, only two were returned.

THE BUILDER-IS-THE-USER PRODUCTS

The easiest and best kind of products to build are those originally intended for use by the engineer or his or her close friends. In this situation, the designer knows the users and gets immediate feedback about the product. The ultimate developer-is-the-user product is a C language compiler, which is written in its own C language that the product developer must constantly use and enhance. This approach has been employed to develop operating systems (especially UNIX); most computer languages, from Algol to Zeta-LISP; generic programs such as word-processing systems; and operating environments, including windows and desktops. Computer languages inherently originate with a user who needs to perform operations (the verbs that form the syntax of the language) on special data structures.

Nearly all computers—including minis, the first time-shared computers, PCs, and workstations—were developed by people who needed them for an application. Sun Microsystems claimed that a major factor in its success was hardware engineers selling to *software* engineers, and HP called this the "next bench" syndrome (i.e., the product will be used by the person at the bench next to the developer). Declared Jobs at Apple: "Never build a computer you wouldn't want to own."

The minicomputer, Cray, and spreadsheets. Nearly all the computers with which I've been involved were first designed for a particular and personal use. Digital's PDP-5, progenitor of the first minicomputer, was developed in 1965. It originated with a need to build a special-purpose data-acquisition device for an Atomic Energy of Canada reactor. Instead of creating a one-shot front end, we took the opportunity to build a component (tool) that could be used to build this and many other applications. Ted Hoff credits the PDP-5's successor, the PDP-8, as being the design model for developing Intel's first microprocessor. In effect, the first mini was the model for using embedded computers for control.

Seymour Cray claims that he is merely building computers for his friends who do numerical simulation. And Dan Bricklin has described conceptualizing the first spreadsheet, Visicalc, as a student at Harvard Business School and personally working with financial spreadsheets.

When a company designs products according to the "builder-is-the-user" paradigm, it will have no trouble identifying the users and their needs. However, it is less clear whether a very large body of customers will respond the same way as the initial designer/user group and buy these products. Thus, even a well-designed product may only appeal to a select market, which, when satisfied, is saturated. As an example, Gold Hills made a LISP operating environment for the PC and grew very rapidly to satisfy its market. Unfortunately, the market (in 1990) consisted of a slowly growing population of about ten thousand programmers who were LISP users and evangelists. Once that market was satisfied, sales dropped sharply, and the firm had to downsize itself to fit the true market. The advantages and dangers of forming a company this way—i.e., by picking atypical users to satisfy—should be obvious.

EVOLVABILITY AS A REQUIREMENT

As the new venture starts up, it should be clear about whether its technology position will enable it to develop subsequent products based on the first, core product. With shorter product-gestation times for hardware, it is crucial to build systems that can be evolved easily and over a range of products using the same basic technology or components. Without evolvability, the company won't be able to get large enough, fast enough to become self-sustaining, since each new product will be disjointed from the preceding ones. Software evolvability implies building a product that can be either modified to include new features with every release or, alternatively, downsized and simplified in order to address markets that do not require all the features of the initial version.

An excellent way to meet the need for computer-system evolvability is to design the product as a "multi." The multi is a type of computer introduced in the early 1980s when the first powerful microprocessors became available. It is built by connecting a number of processors, memories, and input/output modules to a single bus whereby any module can communicate with any other. Although the use of a universal bus to support multiple processors is a relatively new idea, the concept of a universal bus to support a processor, memories, and input/output devices dates back to DEC's PDP-11 Unibus,[3] introduced in 1970. Multis "work" because each processor has local cache memory, reducing the bus traffic.

The multi offers a number of advantages over computers built as discrete projects (see Figure 8-12), including lower product and development costs, greater reliability, and improved interconnections to other systems. Furthermore, a multi can be evolved as new processor and memory components become available. Only a few mainframes and supercomputers deliver comparable performance, and none equals the performance per dollar, performance, and price range or is able to be evolved automatically.

Figure 8-12 shows the Encore Multimax product line (computer family A in the figure) and contrasts it with computers built as a series of discrete projects. The Multimax evolved over time in two ways: (1) the processor module was simply replaced with the next-generation microprocessor, and (2) a version was developed that could only grow to half the maximum size of the original model (ten modules versus twenty modules). Table 8-8 summarizes this evolution.

---

3. The Unibus operated at 2 megabytes per second and was the principal method of interconnecting options to the PDP-11 and VAX computers for almost fifteen years. The VME bus (operating at 20 megabytes per second) is an industry-standard bus related to the Unibus, but it may not have as long a life due to rapid technological change.

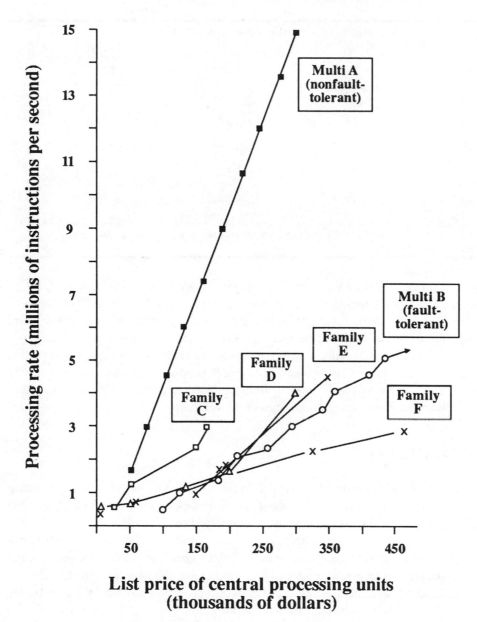

Figure 8-12. Performance Plotted Against Price for Two "Multis" and Four Conventional Computer Families Available in 1985.

Because of the compelling advantages, all but the most trivial and largest computers are built in this fashion as multiprocessors, including those made by Apollo, Arete

Table 8-8. Evolution of Encore Multimax Performance Versus Time.

Model	Date	Cache	Performance Range (VAX 780 Units)
120	1985	32K	1.5[a]-15
310	1987	64K	4.0-20
320	1987	64K	4.0-40
510	1989	256K	17.0-85
500	1989	256K	17.0-170

[a]The processing module has two processors. Up to twenty processors can exist in one system. The bus that interconnects processors and memory transfers 64-bit words at a 12.5 megahertz rate (100 megabytes per second).

(Arix), Compaq, DEC, Data General, Encore, Masscomp, MIPS, Motorola, NCR, Sequent, Silicon Graphics, Solborne, Stardent, and Stratus. PCs of the 1990s will evolve this way, and by 2001, many microprocessors will be packaged on a single chip. Designing and building computers as multis dramatically changes the industry and work force, since a team of fifty engineers can produce a better product than three or four teams of five hundred building a range of "point" products. Similarly, a factory needs to produce only a few board types, resulting in drastically reduced product costs due to manufacturing economies and design improvements.

PRODUCT FLAWS

It is often difficult to separate flaws involving the product per se from those involving flawed technology or a flawed business plan. The lack of a concrete and producible product that can be delivered for a customer application is clearly a product flaw. In a world of standards, an incompatible product that requires a whole new infrastructure of support is almost certainly doomed. Failing to get all the details of the product specification correct when a company is attempting to establish a new product class or new product niche can also be fatal. The following subsections examine these and other product flaws that can derail the unwary start-up.

BUILDING A SPECIALIZED PRODUCT
WHEN A PLAIN OLD COMPUTER WILL DO

An ordinary computer, with appropriate software, will usually fill a buyer's need better than a specialized product. Thus, any company building a special system is likely to be a software supplier or a value-added reseller (VAR) with a computer application.

Often, as a new application is discovered, the temptation is to respond to that need by making a special product or even a unique computer. Obviously, if the product is trivial or intended for another function, a general-purpose computer won't be able to compete. For example, all clocks and watches have a specially programmed computer as their basis, and a general-purpose computer cannot perform this function because of cost and packaging. Clocks and watches ultimately take on many of the functions of on-board human information-processing devices like calculators, calendars, and phone books. Furthermore, these timekeeping devices can communicate by display and by voice. In the very long run, when computers will cost virtually nothing and occupy virtually no volume, all computers will perform the same infinite number of functions.

Table 8-9 lists firms that all started building unique computers but subsequently discovered that they were concentrating on what they bought, not what they planned to sell, and eventually had to focus on their application. The scenario is invariably the same:

A high-tech venture starts by building its own proprietary computer in order to sell hardware and get higher list prices and margins. The firm's first fallback is to resell another supplier's product in order to keep its revenue high. Finally, the company has to resort to selling only software, since customers already have a computer or a channel through which to buy one and merely want another applications program.

HAVING TECHNOLOGY BUT NO PRODUCT

Some start-ups fail to define an actual product concept and have only a set of techniques or technology (e.g., artificial intelligence [AI] or rule-based programming) for building products. In the case of products such as those built using the emerging multimedia technology, it is difficult to distinguish between a flashy demo and a complete system that more than a few users might buy. Thus, testing for the existence of a product versus a technology can be quite difficult.

Artificial intelligence product companies of the early 1980s clearly illustrate the difference between having technology and having a product. In 1980, the Japanese issued a challenge to the world by initiating a fifth-generation computer research program based on nonprocedural programming, whereby highly parallel computers would perform functions in a "humanlike" fashion based on artificial intelligence research. This stimulated the birth of a number of "AI and rule-based" systems companies as well as increased funding for computer-science research, including the formation of research consortia such as Microelectronics and Computer Technology Corporation (MCC) and Semiconductor Research Corporation (SRC). The case of BREIT International illustrates the problem of focusing on technology as opposed to a product.

Table 8-9. Products Unable to Compete with General-Purpose Computers.

Era	Product	Company Examples
1960s	Process control	Foxboro, Leads and Northrup, Honeywell
1965	Nuclear instrumentation	Chicago Nuclear
1970s	Industrial controller	DEC, Gould
	Mechanical design stations	Computervision
	Typesetting stations	Compugraphic
1980s	ECAD (electronic computer-aided design) stations	Daisy, Valid Logic
	Electronic typewriters	Brother, Smith Corona
	Word Processor	Wang
1985	Document processing	Cygnet, Filenet
1990s	Handy pocket minders	Casio, Sharp
All	Military computers	All military vendors

BREIT International.   In August 1984, BREIT's CEO, a former computer salesperson, came together with a Martin-Marietta programmer working on military AI programs. BREIT started with eight people (six of them programmers), riding the AI wave. The productive and creative programmers were versed in AI and system programming, including natural language recognition, rudimentary databases and knowledge bases, and graphical interface design. A hardware person with knowledge of videodisk technology also joined. BREIT defined "knowledge transfer" as its product area, thus separating itself from the unsuccessful computer-aided instruction product area.

BREIT's staff—which had grown to include the president, a marketing person and a consultant, two salespeople, two administrators, two secretaries, and ten software engineers—worked together for twenty-two months. After the first fifteen months, they alpha-tested an intelligent computer-aided instruction program with a superb graphical interface. Based on the alpha tests, the firm concluded that the product was too general and couldn't solve a real need. The last seven months were aimed at further generalization and, hence, less emphasis on a specific user.

BREIT received two rounds of financing (spending about $1.5 million), which resulted in the production of interesting demonstrations of what might ultimately have become a product. Had the company been funded for a seed stage, instead of being directly formed, time and money could have been saved. Alternatively, given that BREIT had invested a small amount in developing a technology, additional funding might have produced a product that users would buy, if the firm had had sufficient maturity and savvy to direct the conversion of its technology into a useful product. BREIT may simply have quit too early and had the wrong product target.

FALLING IN LOVE WITH AN IMAGE OR MOCK-UP OF A PRODUCT

An attractive, but superficial, mock-up of a product concept or demo may be built to sell investors and future employees. Although the product might be flawed in some way (e.g., a commodity, unbuildable, too expensive), the model can override rationality.

Being able to see or touch a product concept means an almost certain sale to product or company funders. At DEC, practically any physical model was a key to selling the development of a product. Many notable firms got their start with a beautifully designed mock-up. As the following examples illustrate, however, countless ill-founded ventures and bad product ideas got their start the same way.

Viatron, Zilog, DEC, and "Company X".   In 1970, Viatron had working models of its MOS (metal oxide semiconductor)-based desktop computers, which it offered at $49 per month. Although the models played a key role in the marketing to investors and prospective customers, they were driven by real, working computers. The company couldn't build the MOS chips. Before it went bankrupt, Viatron, which had gone public, set a 1970s record for start-up losses. The president indicated that the key to his fund-raising success was promising incredible returns based on ambitious technology claims.

In 1981, Zilog built a wonderful wooden model of one of its first UNIX systems, the S8000. A female reporter took one of Zilog's executives to dinner and began querying him on the computer and when it would be ready to ship. Wanting to seem powerful and important, he replied, "What do you mean *ship*? It's a *+#@*! wooden model!" The quote was printed verbatim. The company eventually left the systems business.

One of the best and most creative industrial designers I know is Ken Olsen. Although customers rarely saw his prototypes, the engineering model shops at DEC could turn out models of a design in metal or plastic in one to three days, depending on the complexity and material. Unfortunately, the boxes' appeal often oversold Ken, especially if the general concept was his idea, and going from proto to product often cost the firm tens of millions of dollars. What went into the boxes was often less than useful to a customer. An example of this occurred in the early 1980s, when DEC's disastrous foray into PCs cost the company nearly a billion dollars.

The worst case of the model's being the product occurred at a firm I'll call Company X, which built a box with blinking lights to satisfy government tests so that it could receive a progress payment on its contract. The people involved went to jail.

Despite these horror stories, models do have their place. Convergent Technologies found out that AT&T wanted a UNIX PC and built a cardboard and plastic model of such a device. AT&T bought a hundred thousand computers. When it sold Megaframes to computer companies as a brand relabeler, it could color, logo, and repackage a model for a new box even before a firm asked. The model became the salespeople's tool kit.

BUILDING AN INCOMPATIBLE PRODUCT

Engineers are especially prone to ill-directed creativity when it comes to inventing new and incompatible, but not necessarily better, systems.

A high-tech venture must either create the standards or follow them. If the company fails to make its new product a standard, then it gets to build the product twice—the first time its way and the second time according to the market's requirements.

One of the most serious flaws is for a firm to (re)invent a new architecture, protocol, language, human interface, file format, etc., when an existing one is just fine or could be evolved to do the job. Incompatibility is the most costly form of the not-invented-here syndrome. An excellent case in point is the first computer I designed at DEC, the PDP-4, which was incompatible with its predecessor. Fortunately, DEC survived. Today, no start-up making such a dumb mistake on such a grand scale would survive. Yet almost every start-up invents some new interface that should in fact have been compatible with an established or de facto standard. The following examples illustrate the dangers of blazing a new trail—especially if that trail parallels an existing super-highway.

DEC's first 18-bit computer.   DEC's first computer, the PDP-1, was introduced in 1960 and had an 18-bit word. Three years later, I designed a second 18-bit computer, the PDP-4, which cost roughly half as much and used different components, including a new input/output scheme oriented toward process control. The PDP-4 was somewhat simpler to build and solved a few problems better than the PDP-1, but as noted above, it was incompatible with the earlier model, and all its software had to be redesigned from scratch. We made no attempt to have the two use the same languages. All subsequent 18-bit computers were PDP-4-compatible. It was a tremendous and silly waste of resources for a small company. At the time, none of us had an understanding of the costs and importance of software, both to DEC and to its customers. The right solution would have been to have evolved the PDP-1, using the new ideas.

Ardent, Stellar, and Stardent architectures.   Titan, Ardent's graphics supercomputer, used multiple MIPS chips as the basic computing engine. Ardent bought the manu-facturing rights to Raster Technologies chips for coloring 3-D polygons. The team started by extending the MIPS scalar architecture to connect a fast vector processor according to the Cray supercomputer design formula. In the process, it dropped compatibility with the MIPS system. This meant that system software, including UNIX and compilers, was unique. Programs such as third-party databases, compilers, and other applications running on the MIPS system could not be used on Titan without being recompiled and retested. A year later, Ardent realized its mistake as customers demanded software, much of which was available from MIPS, and a MIPS-compatible interface was built. Because of Ardent's failure to design a compatible product in the first place, the Titan project required more work than would otherwise have been necessary, the product got to market later, and the company was jeopardized.

Stellar started at an even lower level by inventing a unique architecture for both computation and graphics and had to do even more design work. When Ardent and Stellar merged to form Stardent, the company settled on an architecture that is upward-compatible with MIPS yet exploits the Ardent multiple-processor technology of supercomputing (architecture and compilers that understand parallelization).

Amdahl Corporation.   In the early 1970s, Amdahl was created to build very-high-end IBM 360-compatible products. Just as Amdahl's first product was being designed, IBM modified the architecture to provide a significant virtual memory function, necessitating a major redesign. The resulting delay in the product essentially cost Amdahl its ownership by forcing it to obtain additional funds from its Japanese partner, Fujitsu.

It is essential for a start-up to understand, and have a rational policy about, the standardization or proprietariness of various interfaces that it maintains. When an existing standard is adequate, then it should be followed exactly. The decision becomes more difficult when a new standard is needed and is in the process of being developed, either on a de facto basis by a large supplier or by a committee.

Stardent's Doré graphics library and AVS visualization architectures.   Stardent attempted to establish two standards for 3-D graphics and for visualization—Doré and AVS. Doré was created during the time when a standards body from various manufacturers was working on Phigs+. Phigs+ became the standard, although Doré was superior by almost all measures. Doré was freely licensed to all comers, and it runs as a second standard on many different computing platforms. Stardent must support both Doré and Phigs+ on its platforms.

AVS (Application Visualization System) is a high-level programming environment that enables the user to take scientific data and view it in a flexible and interactive fashion. Stardent salespeople regard AVS as providing a significant competitive advantage. AVS is licensed to other companies, but not to firms that Stardent views as competitors, such as Silicon Graphics. However, Silicon Graphics now employs AVS's inventor and architect and may build a more competitive product, which it would then license to other companies, but not to firms that it views as competitors, such as Stardent.

If this occurs, the small but growing community of users who require visualization will have to learn, and choose between, two similar but incompatible systems. Stay tuned.

STRATEGIC PARTNERING THAT
GIVES AWAY PRODUCT AND TECHNOLOGY

In this age of strategic partnerships, it is not uncommon for a start-up to be working hand in hand with a partner that produces, resells, builds on, or otherwise significantly contributes to the start-up's product. In such cases, it is very easy for the fledgling company to end up giving away its product and/or the technology on which the product is built.

Lockheed and Dessault; Design Power and Intellicorp.   Lockheed developed a mechanical design package, CADAM, that was based on the standard 2-D representational structure of traditional blueprints. It gave the source code to the French aircraft maker Dessault, which turned the package into a 3-D design program, called CATIA. Today, CATIA is one of the dominant CAD/CAM programs.

When Design Power started up, it developed a design program called D++ that was written in KEE, a language created by Intellicorp. Soon, Design Power had an opportunity to raise quick cash by selling D++ to Intellicorp. The sale looked too easy and too good to be true. Fortunately, Design Power wrote a very strong nondisclosure statement into the agreement to protect D++, making it very difficult for anyone seeing the source code to write a design program. What Design Power was attempting to do was to get Intellicorp to become its VAR and service provider for the program. However, if no strings had been attached to the sale, Intellicorp would have received a direct infusion of technology and product, thereby enabling it to take D++ and sell it in exactly the same fashion as Design Power. Without the restrictions, in short, selling D++ would have been equivalent to selling Design Power itself.

DEVELOPING A PRODUCT SPECIFICATION THAT
IGNORES A CRITICAL APPLICATION REQUIREMENT

Ignoring the details often dooms a high-tech venture, as a host of firms building technical computers have discovered (Chopp, Culler Scientific, Cydrome, E&S, Elexsi, ETA, etc.). The Ardent story below points out how focusing on just one or two attributes and neglecting the really important ones can spell disaster. The start-up must have a detailed understanding of the requirements when it begins the project; otherwise, the resulting product may be fatally deficient.

Positioning the first graphics supercomputer at Ardent.   In 1986, Ardent's goal at start-up was to produce a new class of computer, the graphics supercomputer, to solve the following computing-visualization paradox:

> Supercomputers provide excellent computational capability but have no graphics capability. Graphics workstations provide the ability to visualize 3-D objects (e.g., molecules, mechanical structures, physical system modeling) but have little computational ability. A high-performance graphics workstation cannot be achieved through networking because both local and national networks are inadequate to connect the workstations to supercomputers.

When Ardent began, visualization was just starting to be recognized as a critical need for supercomputing. Visualization simply means displaying the results of a computation graphically in order to provide users with insight. *Interactive* visualization extends this notion to let users interact with the computation by visualizing its state in order to guide future computation and thereby enable them to participate in analysis or design. Figure 8-13 shows how Ardent positioned its product as the supercomputing equivalent of a workstation.

Ardent decided to use a Cray-style supercomputer architecture with a vector multiprocessor and high-performance 3-D graphics hardware. Supercomputers obtain their very high speeds by operating on a string or set of numbers (a vector) all at once. Vector-processing rates are measured in millions or billions (and eventually trillions) of floating point numbers per second. Linpack, for solving a set of linear equations, is one benchmark for measuring this. I sketched the performance (in Linpack megaflops) versus price curve, as shown in Figure 8-1, to initially position Ardent's first product, Titan.

Unfortunately, no single dimension can be used to characterize a computer. The other performance dimensions for the product that we recognize in hindsight (shown in Table 8-10) include integers, measured in millions of instructions per second (mips), which is typical of system programs; scalars or operations on single numbers, measured by the Whetstones benchmark; vectors, measured in floating point operations per second; graphics, measured by shaded polygons and lines per second; images, measured by pixels per second; and input/output, measured as a data rate to disk and network. The requirements for each of these performance dimensions for various markets and attributes of the computer range from nonexistent or very low to very high.

Titan was originally designed to achieve high performance by using a RISC chip set manufactured by MIPS Computer Systems. One chip was a high-speed microprocessor, and the other was a coprocessor to accelerate floating point operations. As the design progressed, Ardent focused almost exclusively on vector processing and radically

The Vector Equivalent of Technical Workstations

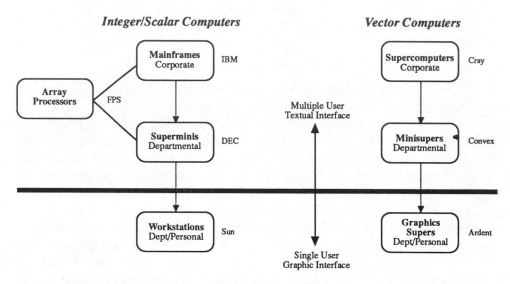

Figure 8-13. Ardent's Graphics Supercomputer Positioned as a New Computer Class Formed as the Vector Equivalent of Technical Workstations.

reduced the scalar performance by removing the MIPS floating point chip to cut product cost and simplify development. Unfortunately, almost half the market (general purpose and chemistry) used extensive scalar operations, since their computations weren't suitable for vectors. The problem posed by the questionable scalar performance became apparent in the middle of the product development stage but was not remedied.

When the Titan ran the first customer benchmarks, it barely beat a lowly workstation, since the scalar performance was low and a few other features (such as a fast divide instruction) were not as fast as the market required. The price, targeted to be comparable to that of other workstations ($50,000), ended up closer to twice as much. Titan's strength and weakness were the same: it was a supercomputer with excellent performance for its price, but its price was higher than that of a standard workstation. For ordinary programs, it performed similarly to $50,000 high-performance workstations, but for programs written to be used on a supercomputer, it performed better than $300,000 minisupercomputers.

Table 8-10. Requirements for Performance Dimensions and Markets[a].

Performance Dimension				Market			
	Chemistry	Fluid Dynamics	MCAD	Petroleum	Image Processing	Animation	General Purpose
Integers	m	s	m	m	s	m	l
Scalars	l[b]	s	m	s	s	m	l[b]
Vectors	l	v	l	v	v	l	m
Graphics	v	s	l	m	m	v	—
Images	—	s	—	v	v	m	—
Input/ output	m	m	l	l	v	l	m

[a]v=very large, l=large, m=medium, s=small, —=negligible
[b]Failure to provide good scalar performance cost the chemistry and general purpose markets.

Thus, depending on the user, Titan looked either like: (1) a fast, but very expensive, workstation or (2) a bargain-priced minisupercomputer. Workstation buyers felt that the price was too high, and price has a tremendous effect on volume. (I believe that demand increases by five to ten times every time the price is halved.) At a price of $100,000, demand was estimated to be one thousand units, whereas at $50,000, the volume would have been at least ten thousand units. Minisupercomputer buyers found Titan's price very attractive, but these customers buy only one unit at a time and put vendors through a rigorous benchmark screening process, which meant that the cost of each sale was roughly half the price of the machine.

Furthermore, an extraordinary sales and marketing effort was required to select pretrained users. Ardent's sales force failed in this regard, especially since Ardent never had a head of sales for very long. An excellent benchmarking group was ultimately put in place to identify prospects until the next product came out, remedying the problem by having very fast scalar speeds.

Ardent was able to produce two next models—one that was cheaper and one that was more expensive. This allowed a higher average selling price, since the company could more fully satisfy the users' needs. The low-priced model performed more like a personal supercomputer and could compete with ordinary workstations across the board and still offer supercomputing capability. The more expensive model was sold both as the original and rarefied low-volume graphics supercomputer and as a higher-margin, larger, and more expensive minisupercomputer. Having a faultless first product would clearly have changed the course of the firm, but virtually all supercomputer builders have made errors on their first machine, including Alliant, CDC, Convex, ETA, NEC, and Stellar.

PRODUCT RULES

At the concept stage, no attempt is made to determine a product's efficacy, only that there exists a product or service concept that a customer could evaluate and decide to buy. The product rules in this section test the rationale for why customers will buy the product, the market size, and how the product will be sold.

At the concept stage, has the company translated its technology uniqueness into a relatively concrete product concept (what) that is also self-sustaining— i.e., that provides for the evolution of future generations of the product?

This rule requires that all aspects of the product design be traceable to technological roots. Before the new venture proceeds into the seed stage, it must have an outline for a possible product architecture capable of sustaining itself over several product generations. The product concept (i.e., what) can be tested by looking at its specification or a product mock-up or an operating breadboard that a potential user can examine and react to. Product mock-ups are invariably key props for selling potential customers and, hence, investors. In the case of a hardware or software system that is similar to existing products, a user, buyer, or buyer surrogate (marketing person) can simply look at specifications of the product's features and functions.

Have rough goals been formulated for product cost as well as quality and compatibility?

For hardware, the most important goal is manufacturing cost; for software, the most important goals are size, performance, and operating-environment compatibility. This rule emphasizes reality by forcing the company to attempt to put a cost on its product right from the concept stage. Only in this way is there any hope of sketching a financial model for the firm and, hence, testing its financial viability. By the seed stage, the start-up must have a good cost estimate in order to be able to create a realistic business plan.

By the seed stage, does a product definition or functional specification exist for the product being designed?

Having a detailed understanding of the specific customers and their requirements is essential in order for a start-up to focus on the product design. The functional specification should include goals and constraints for the product and project, functions to be performed, user characteristics and operating environments, a proposed solution, design trade-offs, and acceptance criteria.

Does there exist a data sheet that spells out the planned features, functions, and benefits?

By the time the seed stage is finished, the start-up should have a pretty firm idea of what it will be building. The simplest way to test for this is to examine the product's preliminary specifications in the form of a data sheet or brochure. In its "test marketing," the company usually uses the data sheet to prepare a set of overheads describing the product. This presentation should enable prospective buyers to understand and react favorably to the product (their response should include pinpointing missing features and describing their own buying requirements). The product should be receiving favorable reactions from all prospective customers at this point, since it's unlikely that a product will ever get any better than this initial conceptual view.

If the company is producing a software product, does a preliminary user's manual exist?

In the case of software, the start-up must make the product quite specific by developing a user's manual that fully describes the program and how to use it.

By the end of the seed stage, does the product continue to show a minimum of a one-year product lead?

In order for a lasting company to be formed, the product must still be viable at the time the venture starts up. During the seed stage, new technology and products will have become available, and the competitive picture may be entirely different from what it was during the concept stage. The company should ask itself whether its original idea really remains viable in view of the current competitive scene. Whether the organization continues to maintain a comfortable lead in product development at the beginning of the product development stage should almost be the determining factor in deciding to proceed with the start-up.

Is the product architecture capable of evolving into multiple products or lines rather than yielding only a single, "point" product?

This rule examines whether the product is based on a lasting architecture or is merely a one-shot phenomenon. A lasting technology and a lasting product base are required in order to produce a lasting company. In the process of examining the market, other alternatives may come to light. The start-up's goal should be to use either hardware or software technology as aggressively as possible, while not risking the schedule.

When positioning a product in a multidimensional space, does the company understand and attend to all the dimensions, not just the most glamorous?

As an example, I wrote the following eleven rules of supercomputer design based on the Stardent experience. Many of these rules apply to other products as well.

1. Performance, performance, and performance are the top three objective criteria for a supercomputer.

2. Amdahl's law,[4] generalized, implies that everything matters—a variant of the proposition that "no chain is stronger than its weakest link." Or as the architect Mies van der Rohe stated: "God is in the details."

3. The scalar speed matters most, and a new super must be the fastest of comparable computers in its class. If it cannot do all the mundane calculations fast enough, a computer is doomed to a niche and is likely to be unsuccessful. Furthermore, it will not be able to replace its earlier predecessors.[5]

4. The vector speed—i.e., the computer's advertised speed—can be as arbitrarily high as costs allow. The past rule of thumb was to have a vector unit that would produce two results per clock tick. Large increases (i.e., of more than one hundred) over the scalar speed provide only a small benefit except for selected applications, making the computer special-purpose (such as the Connection Machine). The NEC SX-3 has a peak speed of sixteen times the clock. The vector (peak), or advertised, speed is the speed that the manufacturer guarantees the computer will not exceed on any application.

---

4. Amdahl's law for building high-performance computers states that every computation is composed of a serial part that must be run sequentially and a part that can be run in parallel at the highest speed using multiple processing elements. The overall speed of the computation is controlled by the slow, or serial, part.

5. This is the CDC Star rule. Star was designed in the late 1960s, and two machines were installed at Livermore. Neither of them worked well, nor were they able to take on a significant workload because the new computer could not compute as fast as the CDC 7600, its predecessor, for scalar problems. Users weren't able to optimize the computer for vector applications quickly enough, since the compilers were inadequate. Star was the basis of the CDC 205 and later ETA architectures. None of these computers ran fast enough on a broad set of applications to be commercially viable.

5. Allow no holes in the performance space (e.g., arithmetic function, input/output, mass storage) into which a benchmark can step, resulting in large performance losses.

6. Provide peaks in the performance space in order to produce extraordinary performance for a benchmark. Use this single number to advertise (characterize) the machine and to challenge other machines.

7. Obey computer-design law number one: provide enough address bits for a decade of constant architecture implementation.

8. Build at least two generations of the architecture. No supercomputer designed by a team has ever been perfect the first time around. Do it again after the first generation has been used and is really understood.

9. Build on the work of others. Designing a super is hard, so understand exactly why and how every existing machine works and move forward using this knowledge. Make sure the machine can run as much existing software as possible.

10. Make the machine easy to use. Have a great compiler and diagnostic tools to aid users in vectorization and parallelization. Training for supers is nonexistent in academe, since computer-science departments are not oriented toward training people to use computers or to operate computers that produce numbers. No computer-science texts exist, or are likely to exist, dealing with how to program a parallel, vector processor (i.e., supercomputer).

11. Have an abundance of resources when embarking on the design of a supercomputer. The fatality rate for companies making machines is at least 50 percent, even though the design may be good. Building a new super costs a minimum of $200 million in 1990 (or $50 million for a minisuper) just to produce a breadboard or simulation of the machine.

CONCLUSION

At the root of having a great product is first conceptualizing a product that is complete and unique and then understanding the rationale for why customers will buy the product. Since the introduction of the first commercial mainframe in 1950, computers have evolved, based on the evolution of semiconductor and magnetic density increases (Chapter 5), to form established price classes: supercomputers, mainframes, minicomputers (also superminicomputers and minisupercomputers), workstations, and various other personal computers, including notebook-size computers. By 2001, there will emerge powerful, useful, and ubiquitous pocket- and wallet-size computers that everyone will carry on their person. Each of these computer classes requires and attracts unique application software products. In the fifth generation of computing, beginning in 1988, products are based on networks, standards, and distributed, personal computing, which Steve Jobs calls "interpersonal computing."

Chapter 9

MARKETING AND SALES

We look for market first when deciding to invest.
—Don Valentine, Sequoia Capital

Marketing and sales are so interdependent that sales personnel often walk around with titles like "marketing representative." When the product is ready to be sold, marketing is responsible for clearly segmenting the market, providing initial sales leads, and supplying the right product information for the sales personnel and customers. Sales is responsible for identifying specific buyers, closing sales, and when the product has been delivered, ensuring that the customers are happy.

MARKETING

In the past, I have argued that marketing organizations provide little in the way of value. From an engineer's perspective, marketing facilitates the birthing of a product by initially establishing the requirements that help define the product and by creating a wonderful image of the product in the minds of potential buyers, making them want it. Finally, when the actual product becomes available, marketing helps a sales organization sell it. In the 1970s and 1980s, I believed that obtaining market input during the formation of a product was usually a waste of time, based on my own experience at Digital in driving system and generic computer products.[1]

---

1. For example, when I led the team that defined the VAX architecture and when the VAX computing environments were put in place, the only input we sought was from Ken Thompson, one of the UNIX developers. One marketing person attended biweekly status meetings, at which he was assigned data-gathering tasks.

I took this stand because most engineers like to hide behind the cloak of "marketing says" instead of really understanding what a product must do and who will use it.

In the 1990s, however, I have come to believe that it is critical for marketing to be involved in the formation of a product from the very beginning in order to increase the probability of success in the marketplace. In today's market, competition is guaranteed to be greater than in the past, products are steadily becoming more complex, and any new product must be both right and substantially better than average from the outset. All these factors argue in favor of a strong marketing effort. I still firmly believe, however, that *engineers must define the product and take responsibility for its efficacy.*

The preceding definition of the engineering function's responsibility almost completely overlaps Davidow's (1986) definition of the strategic principle of marketing: "Marketing must invent complete products and drive them to commanding positions in defensible market segments." If the engineering organization lacks an understanding of the product and its applications and fails to make a commitment to meeting the requirements of real users, the product is almost certain to grow in an unlimited fashion in response to "marketing input."

The CEO is responsible for resolving the inevitable conflict between what engineering can build in the small amount of time available and what marketing believes will sell.

In reality, the product's goodness (i.e., its effectiveness, uniqueness, and quality) is probably the determining factor in a high-tech venture's success. A company with a really poor product is most likely doomed, regardless of how great its marketing and sales efforts might be. Given a better-than-average product, a firm with an outstanding sales force may do well despite a lack of marketing. Having a great product, a driven sales force, and wonderful marketing is the ideal and should be strived for, although new ventures almost never live up to the ideal, in my experience. Unfortunately, most start-ups don't come out with great products at first, and it takes them longer than anticipated to build a sales organization and learn to sell the product. To put marketing into proper perspective, it could be said that poor marketing can be the number two company killer.[2]

It is often difficult to separate the concept of the product from other equally important views of the market, including:

- The product itself that is often characterized as the market—e.g., the disk or spreadsheet markets

- Customers who use and/or buy the product—e.g., the government, academic, home, small-business, and large-company markets

---

2. I believe that a poor CEO is the number one killer of start-up companies. Venture capitalist John Shoch rates lack of team as the number one killer.

- Various ways of distributing the product, called the channels of distribution—e.g., the distributor, OEM (original equipment manufacturer), and VAR (value-added reseller) markets

It is critical to understand that if a product is to be useful for a professional or other information-processing system, it must be complete. That is, it must include every level of integration between a computing platform (hardware) and any necessary "application" software—in short, all the levels of integration that are required for the product's final application in the target markets. In order to achieve completeness, the channel of distribution must often participate "actively" in the product development process by supplying application software. In many cases, the application software is so important that a program such as Autocad may, by definition, be the complete product from the user's perspective. The hardware platform on which it runs is regarded as a mere component!

The creation and distribution of generic computers with generic software and profession-specific applications programs must be clearly understood by all companies involved in the distribution chain.

THE SIX BIG QUESTIONS THAT GUIDE MARKETING

This subsection of the chapter focuses on the mechanics of marketing and is organized around the following six questions that the start-up must answer:

1. What is the product, and is it complete and ready for use by the potential customers?

2. Who will buy the product?

3. How will the product be used—i.e., for what application?

4. Why will customers buy the product, in terms of its features, functions, and benefits?

5. Where will the product be sold—i.e., through what distribution channels?

6. When will orders be received and filled—i.e., how long will the process take?

The product itself (question 1) is primarily the domain of engineering, as discussed in Chapter 8, but marketing shares the responsibility for the answer. Identifying the customer groups initially (question 2) is a marketing responsibility of paramount importance for successfully designing the product and then selling it. How the product will be used and why customers are likely to buy it (questions 3 and 4) are really fundamental and lie at the heart of market planning. Where the product will be sold (question 5) is the responsibility of both sales and marketing, and how long it will take to get orders (question 6) is the domain of the selling organization, but with strong marketing involvement.

Question 1: What Is the Product?

Chapter 8 was devoted to an extensive discussion of the product. However, a few additional comments about the marketing-related aspects of this topic will be found in the following subsections.

Question 2: Who Will Buy the Product?

More than half the U.S. population is engaged in service industries that have information technology as their base. The Computer and Business Equipment Manufacturers Association projects that, by the year 2000, the worldwide revenue of the U.S. computer and business-equipment industry will almost triple from 1990's level, to reach over $700 billion. The computer industry consists of roughly one-half equipment, one-third software and services, and one-sixth business equipment and forms. In addition, the telecommunications industry is becoming closely related to the computer industry and is about half its size. Thus, the combined industries are projected at over $1 trillion.

Harvard University's Program on Information Resources Policy has mapped the more than eighty service and product industries that compose the information business (Figure 9-1). The computer industry includes computers, software, modems, terminals, time-sharing, and service bureaus. Other industries that make up the information business include telecommunications, communication (radio, TV, newspapers), and almost all consumer electronics. Although it does not appear on the map, computers also play a key supporting role in many large service industries, including financial (e.g., banking, stock markets, and insurance) and travel, where information represents token transactions involving money, stocks, future risk, and future transportation, respectively.

The map was designed to show the historical evolution of the industry and its companies, the effect of government regulation, strategic positioning of companies, and the ability of companies to migrate from products to services. Since the computer is the enabling technology for virtually every product and service in the information business, the map's purpose in the present context is to show the diversity of products and services within this business and, hence, the scope of opportunities for new high-tech ventures.

Figure 9-2 shows International Data Corporation's estimate of the number of worldwide information-technology users versus time. Note that the time periods are in

PROFESSIONAL SVCS
FINANCIAL SVCS
ADVERTISING SVCS

DATABASES AND VIDEOTEX NEWS SVCS
ON-LINE DIRECTORIES
DIRECTORIES
NEWSPAPERS
NEWSLETTERS
MAGAZINES
SHOPPERS
AUDIO RECORDS AND TAPES
FILMS AND VIDEO PROGRAMS
BOOKS

LOOSE-LEAF SVCS

SERVICE BUREAUS
SOFTWARE SVCS
SYNDICATORS AND PROGRAM PACKAGERS
SOFTWARE PACKAGES

TELETEXT
TIME-SHARING

GOVT MAIL
PARCEL SVCS
COURIER SVCS
OTHER DELIVERY SVCS

MAILGRAM
TELEX
EMS

INTERNATL TEL SVCS
LONG DIST TEL SVCS
LOCAL TEL SVCS

VANs
DBS

BROADCAST NETWORKS
BROADCAST STATIONS
CABLE NETWORKS
CABLE OPERATORS

MULTIPOINT DISTRIBUTION SVCS
DIGITAL TERMINATION SVCS
MOBILE SVCS
FM SUBCARRIERS

PRINTING COS
LIBRARIES

PAGING SVCS
BILLING AND METERING SVCS
MULTIPLEXING SVCS

RETAILERS
NEWSSTANDS

BULK TRANSMISSION SVCS
INDUSTRY NETWORKS

DEFENSE TELECOM SYSTEMS

SECURITY SVCS

CSS SVCS

PABXs

COMPUTERS

TELEPHONE SWITCHING EQUIP

RADIOS
TV SETS
TELEPHONES
TERMINALS
PRINTERS
FACSIMILE
ATMs

MODEMS
CONCENTRATORS
MULTIPLEXERS

PRINTING AND GRAPHICS EQUIP
COPIERS

POS EQUIP
BROADCAST AND TRANSMISSION EQUIP
WORD PROCESSORS
VIDEO TAPE RECORDERS
PHONOS, VIDEO DISC PLAYERS

CASH REGISTERS

INSTRUMENTS
TYPEWRITERS
DICTATION EQUIP
BLANK TAPE AND FILM

CALCULATORS

GREETING CARDS

FILE CABINETS
PAPER

MICROFILM, MICROFICHE
BUSINESS FORMS

FORM → ← SUBSTANCE

SERVICES
PRODUCTS

ATM - Automatic teller machine
COS - Companies
CSS - Carrier "smart" switch
DBS - Direct broadcast satellite
EMS - Electronic message service
PABX - Private automatic branch exchange
POS - Point-of-sale
SVCS - Services
VAN - Value-added network

Figure 9-1. A Map of the Information Business. (Courtesy of the Program on Information Resources Policy, Harvard University. John F. McLaughlin and Ann Louise Antonoff, *Mapping the Information Business.* Reprinted with Permission.)

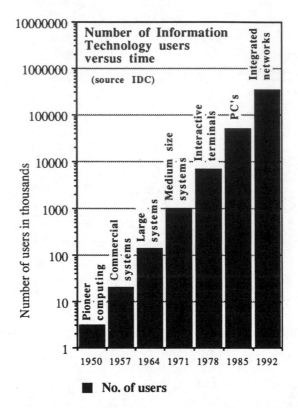

Figure 9-2. Estimate of the Number of Information-Technology Users Versus Time. (Courtesy of International Data Corporation. Reprinted with permission.)

seven-year increments, whereas the computer generations have occurred roughly each decade. By the late 1970s, terminal-based, centralized computing was limited to less than 10 million users. With the advent of PCs, the number increased about an order of magnitude. The 1992 estimate is that there will exist a ubiquitous network with over 300 million users. This is probably slightly optimistic, due to the lack of good internetworking, but may occur by the year 2000.

Market Segmentation—The Key to Determining Who Will Buy.   The most important part of market segmentation begins with the identification of potential customers who might buy and use a particular product. Ideally, in performing this segmentation, the company comes to understand precisely who the buyers/users are—including their educational background, demographics, buying motivation and patterns, etc.—so that a product can be designed to really meet their needs.

Three different segmentation schemes are helpful in pinpointing the users:

1. The buying organization—e.g., a collection of companies, a governmental group, a household, an educational institution

2. The function of the user's department or organization—e.g., finance, engineering, manufacturing—including its physical environment

3. The user's profession—e.g., secretary, VLSI (very-large-scale integration) design engineer, actuary

The first segmentation scheme simply identifies which doors to knock on; the second identifies the relevant departments within the specified organizations that are potential buyers; and the third identifies the characteristics of the final and actual users.

The variety of alternative product solutions, from centralized mainframes to fully distributed personal computers, makes customer segmentation quite subtle, because oftentimes, the user is not necessarily the buyer. The only thing that is clear about buyer segmentation is that, for a particular profession-based application, it is usually possible to identify the individual(s) within an organization who will ultimately use a given product. This person (or group), which is referred to as a customer or user performing a given application, is the only place to start in constructing a market.

What's unclear is whether such individuals have any influence over the purchase of what they use. Frequently, a strong central service determines the computing environment for an entire corporation. In more enlightened large organizations, this absolute power is moderated to take into account the needs of the actual users. For example, with GM's purchase of EDS to be the computing czar for the corporation, it is difficult to find anyone, including GM Research (where maximum freedom should exist), who claims responsibility for how computers are purchased or used. Thus, a buyer may be an individual engineer or financial analyst who needs the product or a group entrusted with the responsibility for finding and acquiring tools for others.

In short, it is essential to keep in mind that computer use and computer users are often segmented from the purchase and operation of computing. Hence, all facets of buying, using, and operation must be understood in order for marketing to be successful in any organization, including governments, industry, academe, and the home.

Segmentation by the Buying Organization—The SIC Code.   The simplest segmentation is by Standard Industrial Classification (SIC) code—that is, how the organization is classified. (Figure 9-3 shows the categories employed in the SIC coding system.) The SIC code can be employed to identify companies and general trends that may be helpful in marketing, but it does not begin to identify specific users of

- Agriculture, forestry, and fishing

- Mining, including petroleum

- Construction

- Manufacturing (discrete, continuous, drug, etc.)

- Transportation (air, rail, highway, pipeline, communication, radio, TV)

- Wholesale trade

- Retail trade

- Finance (banks and brokerages), insurance, and real estate

- Service, including medical institutions and universities

- Public administration—i.e., all levels of government, including the military

Figure 9-3. Standard Industrial Classification Code Groups.

a computing product because the application of computers is more closely related to profession (e.g., cost accountant, computational fluid dynamicist) than to organization.

Segmentation by the User's Organization. A taxonomy of corporate users is given in Figure 9-4. Although identifying the tasks of various departments may be only marginally useful in segmenting the market, it does help the start-up determine the size and importance of each department within a larger organization.

Segmentation by the User's Profession. The best segmentation, by the profession of the individual who will be using the computer, can be obtained by examining the structure of academic disciplines within a modern university that aligns itself to solve technological problems. Figure 9-5 shows a partial list of academic disciplines, together with the applications that each one often requires. Since many of the disciplines have mathematics as their base language, generic programs that understand mathematics are often used across many of the disciplines. Similarly, word processing for text and spreadsheets for numbers, along with electronic mail, are the tools for all communication within an organization.

The balance of this subsection contains several important observations about how computer applications form in response both to generic tasks, such as preparing

- *Commercial department:* Includes users who do financial accounting and control, billing, inventory, accounts receivable/payable, payroll, transaction processing, and business analysis.

- *Technical department (science and engineering):* Includes users who deal with numbers; algorithms; text; graphs; data acquisition; real-time control; simulation; product and process design, including CAM (computer-aided manufacturing); and communication.

- *Manufacturing department:* Includes users who do record storage and processing for inventory, continuous and discrete real-time control, and plant scheduling and process optimization.

- *Communications and computation (management information systems):* Includes users who manage or use message switching, electronic mail, voice-messaging systems, teleconferencing, centralized computers, and computer networking.

- *Office automation, electronic (desktop) publishing, and word processing:* Includes anyone involved in image processing for the transduction, storage, and transmission of documents.

- *Education:* Includes teachers, students, course planners, administrators, and others involved in training and computer-assisted instruction.

Figure 9-4. Market Segmentation by Department.

documents, and to those tasks required by users in specific professions, such as petroleum engineers or actuaries.

Given the large number of quite big software companies (e.g., Computer Associates, Lotus, Microsoft, and Oracle) that supply generic application programs for word processing, spreadsheets, databases, etc., there exists only a relatively small opportunity for new generic programs except for programs predicated on a new, broad-based programming paradigm, such as the fundamental understanding of mathematics.[3]

In terms of the professional disciplines, the largest opportunity for start-ups is for enumerated applications based on a potential market of at least every person (or other information-processing system) who would use computers to supplement or supplant his or her own activities in information processing.

Computer manufacturers exist to design, build, and sell computers. Applying computers to the innumerable generic and profession-specific applications requires an

---

3. This market, created in the 1980s, is well on its way to becoming established.

Arts and humanities:
Animation
Computer-assisted art, including sculpture
Music

Business, economics, and finance:
See Figure 9-4, "Market Segmentation by Department."

Computer and computational science

Engineering:
Aeronautical and astronautical
Biotechnology of all kinds
Chemical
Civil and structural
Computer
Electric power
Electronic, including digital systems, signal, and image processing
Environmental
Manufacturing associated with various industries and/or technologies
Mechanical
Nuclear
Petroleum

Mathematics:
Linear and nonlinear analysis
Numerical analysis
Statistics
Linear, nonlinear, dynamic programming, operations research

Medical and biological science (and biotechnology, shared with engineering)

Science:
Astronomy
Atmospheric
Astrophysics
Chemistry
Geology and geophysics
Oceanography
Physics
    Acoustics
    Computational fluid dynamics
    High-energy physics
Psychology and social science

Figure 9-5. Academic (Intellectual) Disciplines and the Applications They Require.

equally large number of professionals who understand both computers and the particular professions. Generic and profession-based applications lie outside the purview of computer manufacturers simply because the plethora of skilled professionals who might use computers usually have nothing in common with those who manufacture computers.

In the unlikely event that an applications program is developed within a computer-manufacturing organization, the likelihood of successful exploitation of the program is very small, unless the applications organization can be separated from the manufacturing organization. That is, producing hardware and developing applications software is virtually impossible under the same corporate "roof." If a hardware company has a significant software product that could be a potential "standard," the best way to exploit that standard is to spin it off into another firm.

The emergence of new computer classes has created opportunities for start-ups to form in order to develop applications programs based on the new computing paradigms. Because existing firms operate within the parameters of their established corporate cultures, costs, and customers, manufacturers in one computer class have usually been unsuccessful in entering a new class. Similarly, suppliers of applications have usually been unsuccessful in adapting existing programs to a new computing environment (e.g., translating batch-oriented mainframes to interactive visualizing workstations). Autodesk is an example of a high-tech venture that grew to dominate a large mechanical designer market using the PC, despite the existence of decade-old companies such as Computervision that used the minicomputer. In electrical computer-aided design (CAD), Daisy, Mentor, and Valid started up based on the workstation. As PCs evolved, new firms entered the market as challengers.

The Industry X Profession Table(s)—Locating the Customers. Given that most products serve professionals by making them more productive in some way, the start-up must locate these potential users precisely within their organizations. If the start-up has a broad range of products, then a good strategy to minimize its marketing, selling, and support costs is to build products designed for use within the same organization but by other, related professionals. For example, selling programs to cost accountants in a manufacturing organization might lead the company into materials-requirements-planning programs.

Constructing a basic, but exhaustive table of the professions (and subprofessions) within each relevant industry segment is the best starting point for identifying all the potential customers for a product. Many different tables can then be generated to analyze and address all the aspects of the potential market, segmented by customer groups. A sample of this format, giving the industry and prospective customers (by

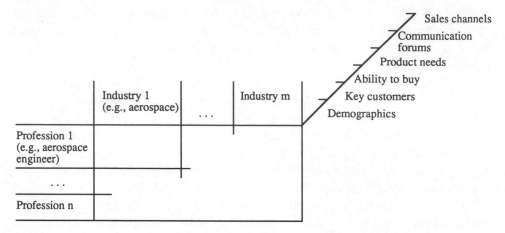

Figure 9-6. Industry X Profession Tables to Describe the Characteristics of Potential Buyers/Users of a Company's Products.

profession and subprofession), is shown in Figure 9-6. Some common tables of data that must be prepared in order to fully understand the characteristics of each market segment include:

- *Demographics:* Number of professionals within each industry (SIC) group

- *Key customers:* For product introduction, feedback, and setting priorities

- *Ability to buy:* Budgets and resources for computing

- *Product needs:* Product (e.g., software) that is relevant for each group

- *Communication forums:* Shows, magazines, and professional societies

- *Sales channels:* How each group buys—e.g., VAR, manufacturer, ISV (independent software vendor), system integrator

Note that alternative tables using this format (e.g., location X profession) are helpful for segmenting customers within a geographic region instead of by the SIC code.

Question 3: How Will the Product Be Used?

In addition to defining the product itself, ensuring that it is complete for use by the intended customers, and identifying potential buyers/users, the start-up must determine the actual application for the product. In the case of most professionals, the product is used to enhance their ability to process information. Thus, implicit in the product is an underlying assumption about its application. For example, let's look at the evolution of features in a generic word-processing program and see some of the different ways in which various users might apply such a program:

- *Text only:* Letters, memos, office communication

- *Tables:* Simple reports—e.g., for expenses

- *List processing:* Forms and mailing-list processing

- *Indexes, etc.:* Producing reports, manuals, books

- *Scientific and math notation:* Technical documents

- *High-quality text layout:* Desktop publishing for brochures

It is also important to note that spreadsheet programs like Excel or Lotus 1-2-3 are used for innumerable applications beyond their intended function, such as making slides or generating relational databases and reports. In addition, of course, there exists a plethora of templates to transform a spreadsheet into a generic business-planning document, for doing profit and loss statements and performing other accounting functions.

The concept of the level of integration plays an important role in a product. It might be expected that, as the product's level of integration decreases, the number of products sold would increase. However, the number of buyers/users is not at all correlated with the level of integration. The following levels of integration and the customers who buy products at each level illustrate the point:

- *Platform—e.g., language, operating system:* systems programmers and builders

- *Mail, word processing:* every user

- *Application program X:* professionals needing X

At the lowest level, systems programmers use the platform to build their own applications, but this is a relatively small class of users. At the application level for a series of professions, the size of the professions and the functionality of the product (i.e., what it can do for the user) determine the market size. Thus, although a given application program used by a particular set of professionals may be sold in very low volume, the collection of all the professional applications that share a common platform is usually quite large.

Customer/Application Profile Table.   The main tool for understanding how the product is to be used is a detailed customer/application profile (CAP) for a set of possible products. This takes the form of a table of all the customers (derived from the organization table) versus the applications for the products. Table 9-1 provides a qualitative view of the size of the overall chemistry market for application programs (the rows) broken down into four markets: pharmaceutical chemicals (e.g., medicinal and agricultural), biotechnology (e.g., protein engineering), polymers (e.g., films and plastics), and materials (e.g., surfaces and composites). Within each industry, theoretical, synthetic, and analytic chemists constitute three kinds of professional users. There are different classes of application program categories. If we proceed further, each application domain must list the programs that are critical for each of the professionals. In some cases, the same program might be used by a given professional in each industry, whereas other programs are specific to a particular industry. Eventually, the table has to be filled in with guesses about the actual market sizes.

The Role of Influential Users and Early Adopters.   Selecting the earliest users, and especially the beta-site customers, is one of the most important decisions that a start-up can make. Ideally, the company is able to persuade the most influential members of an intellectual community to test and embrace its product. Once this elite is won over, then early adopters in large corporations start to buy, followed by the beginnings of a "mass market."

In the earliest days of computing, IBM gave its largest computers to prestigious universities are the most important customers that a high-technology venture can have. Putting computers into academe guarantees that the brightest, hardest-working, and most motivated people will fearlessly test the product and give an honest, no-holds-barred opinion. Therefore, *universities should be the first beta-test sites for all new computers and applications.*

In the earliest days of computing, IBM gave its largest computers to prestigious universities to stimulate early computer use. It slacked off in the 1960s, 1970s, and 1980s because it did not feel the need for or forgot the value of university interaction and training of next generation users . By going back to academic users, IBM gets a true competitive picture of its products. Apple has a very strong university gifts program, and the whole NeXT venture was predicated on serving the university market.

DEC and universities: When DEC was just founded and barely profitable, it gave one of its first PDP-1s to MIT. The researchers (i.e., the faculty and graduate students) used the machine to generate much of the early software, such as editors, compilers, debuggers, operating systems, and applications programs.

In 1978, when the VAX 11/780 was introduced, John Pople, who has been a leader in computational chemistry, got serial number 1 in order to test VAX's efficacy for

Table 9-1. A Computational Chemistry Customer/Application Profile.

Application	Industry			
	Pharmaceutical 36%	*Biotechnology* 18%	*Polymers* 22%	*Materials* 24%
Modeling	s l m	l s s	m m s	m m s
Molecular static	l l l	m s s	l s s	l m s
Molecular dynamics 48%	v m s	m s s	l s s	m m s
Semiempirical	v m s	m s s	v s s	v l s
Ab initio 36%	v m s	— — —	v s s	v m s
X ray	s s l	m m v	s m v	s m l
Nuclear magnetic resonance (NMR)	s m l	s l v	s m v	s s m
Instrument control	— m v	— l v	— m l	— s m
Sequence analysis	— — —	l m l	— — —	— — —
Database 16%	s l l	v l v	s m s	— s s

Notes: v = very large; l = large; s = small; m = medium; — = nonexistent. For each application, a group of three estimated values is shown within each industry. The first value in each group is for the theoretical chemists in that industry; the second is for the synthetic chemists; and the third for the analytic chemists.

chemistry codes. After he found that the machine worked better than all the IBM and Univac mainframes he was then using, Pople told his friends, and VAX became the standard for departmental and project-level technical computing until 1985. Furthermore, even in 1990, the VAX 11/780 is the unity benchmark against which all technical computers are compared. About ten thousand 11/780s were delivered into this technical community.

Through the years, DEC provided much hardware for research, including the VAX 11/750s used by Bill Joy to do the UNIX Berkeley extensions that were the basis of both DEC's and Sun's versions of UNIX. Collaboration with Carnegie-Mellon University generated some of the earliest multiprocessors. In the late 1980s, DEC and IBM provided hardware to MIT as part of Project Athena, which was the co-originator (with DEC) of the X Window standard.

Question 4: Why Will Customers Buy the Product?

The start-up must fundamentally understand the buying rationale; otherwise, it is unlikely to be successful in convincing users to buy its product. Chapter 8 described various categories of product-buying criteria, and this chapter will develop some of those criteria further.

Features, Functions, and Benefits (FFB) Lists and Competitive Tables.   The best way to understand the buying criteria is to start by creating an exhaustive list of the product's features, functions, and benefits, including its price and performance characteristics. Independent of whether the product is completely novel, the FFB list is the fundamental basis for all product and market analysis.

The most common use for the FFB list is in creating a table that compares the start-up's product with the nearest competitor's products or collection of products. Often, a simplified version of such a table is the basis for an advertisement for the product. For example, IBM once ran an un-IBM-style ad showing a table that compared its laser printer with that of the market leader, Hewlett-Packard, in terms of price, performance (speed), and features (number of fonts, ability to feed envelopes, etc.). Of course, the IBM printer won in every category shown in the table. I love these ads.

The Applications Versus FFB Table.   The second use for the FFB list is in comparing the requirements for the product with the applications or customer needs. Table 9-2 shows the basic functions required on a hardware platform: scalar processing, vector processing, computer graphics, and image processing. The first row of the table, labeled "Product," is an honest analysis of how well the proposed product does on each of these functions.

The applications listed serve as a "filter" when testing the product's suitability to carry out the application. Regular typeface has been used in the body of the table to indicate a good fit between an application and the base product. Underlining indicates a product weakness, and boldface type indicates a competitive advantage. For example, not having very high graphics performance may make a product deficient for modeling. The comparative weakness of not having the highest scalar speed is offset by vector performance in two of the application classes. Having high vector performance is useful in five of the application classes.

Table 9-2. Base Product Requirements for Each Applications Area.

	Scalar	Vectors	Graphics	Image
Product	l	v	l	l
Applications				
Modeling	m	s	<u>v</u>	s
Molecular static	l	m	l	s
Molecular dynamic	l	v	m	s
Semiempirical	l	**l**	m	l
Ab initio	<u>v</u>	v	m	l
X ray	<u>v</u>	v	l	l
NMR	l	m	l	s
Instrument control	m	m	l	s
Sequence analysis	l	v	m	s
Database	l	v	s	s

Notes: v = very large; l = large (or high); m = medium; s = small (or low). Underlining indicates weakness, and bold indicates significant strength.

Question 5: Where Will the Product Be Sold?

In the early days of computing, the computer manufacturer supplied broad-based application programs or programming templates for an organization, such as the corporate-accounting and general-ledger programs. In other cases, large companies (such as GM) wrote many of their own programs for specific profession-based applications, ranging from accounting to computer-aided design.

With time, computer manufacturers have produced fewer programs for generic and profession-specific applications, principally because the manufacturers are oriented toward building various classes of computers for as large an audience as possible. It would take an enormous staff, in addition to computer engineers and marketers, to produce the range of necessary applications. Since, as noted earlier, a single company is unlikely to be able to do more than one thing well, applications programs had to be produced outside of computer-manufacturing firms.

Thus, creating a "complete" product requires a large collection of application programs (i.e., more component products). In this respect, the distribution channels for high-tech products are unlike the channels for other products because they are "active," providing added value (including service) so that the final buyer/user can perform the intended function. Of course, the last stage in any distribution channel is the buyer/user, who ultimately integrates all the components and becomes knowledgeable about the system.

Figure 9-7, which shows the channels of product development and/or distribution, can be used to characterize the very broad industrial structure of building products within the component and system framework and delivering a useful product to the end user. One of the least understood and most underappreciated aspects of marketing is the "active-channels" concept, which produces applications programs and, in effect, "finishes" the product, making it suitable for use by an actual buyer. Without this finishing, which is accomplished by adding an applications program (a program that is in fact often more complex than the underlying base system), the product is entirely useless to a buyer. The levels-of-integration dimension of the computer product space (discussed in Chapter 8) provides a map of the various levels required to form the complete product.

In some cases, products require specialization beyond that of the professional target, such as the logic designer or tax accountant, and the user may require consultants. Specialization is usually done by the distributing organization or user's organization. Although users do customize certain products, it is becoming a rarity (in terms of both percentages and actual numbers) for users to write their own applications programs, because the existence of massive quantities of PCs provides a common programming environment and a very large target market for a relatively small team of professionals (sometimes consisting of no more than one person) to write a successful profession-specific application. For instance, if software written by a single programmer can be priced at $50 per copy, selling only a hundred thousand copies per year will generate $5 million in revenue.

Figure 9-7 shows various alternatives for distribution and applications-development channels, according to whether each channel is passive (involving distribution only) or active (providing added value). Passive distribution implies that a single manufacturer takes responsibility for a complete product, with all the levels of integration required for successful use.

In the direct-sales and distributor-based channels, pricing and product responsibility rest solely with the start-up. In cases where another company is actively involved in the product's development, pricing and product responsibility are less clear. Similarly, the distribution of costs and profit is often unclear when two firms share

Direct sales: Passive development in the distribution channel.
- Direct sales: The manufacturer[a] sells the product with its own sales force or through company stores
- Direct sales, with resale of application products from other suppliers.

Mail order and telemarketing: End users buy without salesperson contact.
- Users buy direct from the manufacturer.
- Mail-order house buys the product from the manufacturer for sale/distribution.

Distributors: The link between hardware/software manufacturers and end users.
- Component distributors: Direct or mail-order component sales to companies or individuals for use in building larger systems.
- Resellers (dealers), including leasing and installation: A form of distribution whereby another, usually "geographically local," company buys equipment from one or more manufacturers for resale. Such a form is potentially unstable because the manufacturer is likely to take over the distribution.
- Wholesalers: A stage for distributing goods to retail stores.
- Warehouse sales: Distribution that eliminates one stage in the wholesale/retail chain by having customers go to more central locations rather than to local retail stores.
- Retail sales (dealers): A final stage of distribution to reach an end user with a combination of product, training, and service.

Brand relabeling for resale by another company: Often, a traditional computer company distributes under its own label a product that has been manufactured in whole or in part by another organization. This is also erroneously called an OEM (original equipment manufacturer) relationship. For example, in this relationship, either firm may assemble and test the hardware and software components that form the system.

Value-added channel with "active product development" and distribution: A third party performs a major portion of the development or support to form a complete product that is ready for the end user.
- Third-party developer or independent software vendor: A company with an application program for a particular application market segment to be distributed either via the equipment manufacturer or as an OEM, VAR, system integrator, jointly with the manufacturer, or as a manufacturer.
- Original equipment manufacturer: Basic equipment is supplied to another manufacturer, which adds hardware and software to form a complete application for a particular, usually narrower, use. The purchased component is generally a small fraction of the complete system.
- Value-added reseller: A reseller that adds something of value (e.g., advice and training, customization of particular software, or unique software for a profession) and resells the completed system. Typically, a VAR designs and produces unique application software such as CAD/CAM (computer-aided design/computer-aided manufacturing).
- System integrator: A company that builds products, using any necessary hardware

(continued)

(continued)

and software systems, to meet a particular buyer's requirements. System integrators usually serve special government and military computing needs. In some cases, the system integrators simply supply the product and its required paperwork to satisfy the government user in a completely parasitic fashion, thereby increasing the price with little or no attendant benefit, except full employment.

Joint marketing of equipment and applications products: For highly technical or complex software, the seller of a hardware system and the developer of a critical application product (an ISV) jointly market and sell the resulting product.

[a]The term *manufacturer* refers to the producer of a hardware component, a computer system, or a software product.

Figure 9-7. Channels of Product Development and/or Distribution.

responsibility (cost) for product efficacy, sales, and product support. Joint relationships in which two organizations share such responsibilities are inherently unstable, unless they are managed very skillfully by both parties.

In the case of an "active" distribution channel, the principal activity is that of application development, producing either a generic or profession-specific system that utilizes one or more basic hardware platforms. Thus, what at first glance appears to be a channel of distribution is really the dominant system supplier for a product. In effect, an application-development company, or third-party application developer, could use any hardware, but the product that it produces is unique and based on the firm's knowledge of a specific application field that aids a professional in a given discipline. To the user, the application is the product, and the hardware platform is irrelevant.

The DEC Market Map—The Many Paths from Product to Customers.   The challenge in creating a product is to invent and assemble a collection of components that, used together, will solve a particular customer problem. Figure 9-8 is a flow graph that illustrates the many paths by which a large hardware company's product can find its way to the end user. The example shown is from Digital Equipment Corporation (DEC), as it was organized circa 1982 to address a large number of different and varied markets, products, and channels of distribution. In order for a product to reach the market in a "complete" form, it must make a full circuit through all the levels of the graph. For example, a simple path is user-written, tailored applications, using base hardware and software from DEC. The computer could be operated or serviced by any of three alternative organizations: DEC, the buyer, or a third party.

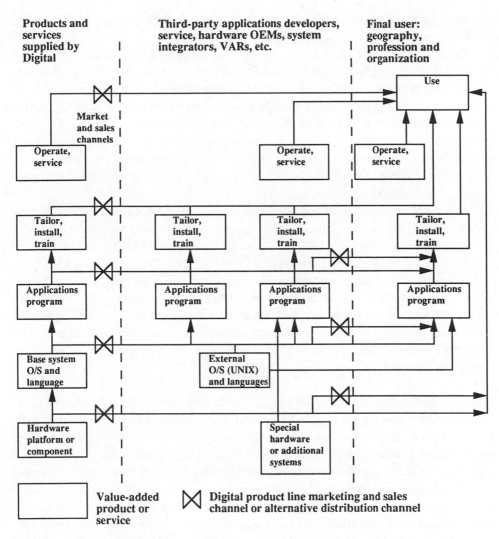

Figure 9-8. Product-Distribution and Final Development Paths for Digital Equipment
Corporation (Circa 1982).

In the 1980s, it was common for applications products to be developed by a
company and then resold as a system using DEC's hardware. In this fashion, the
reselling firm was able to charge a percentage on the hardware system as well as charge
for its software. Of course, customers, the software company, and DEC were all
unhappy with the situation because responsibility was unclear and there were too many
markups in the chain. By the end of the 1980s, when no single hardware vendor

appeared to be competitive for all time, application-specific product organizations stopped being involved in the distribution of hardware.

The DEC map is useful, and even essential, in identifying the multiplicity of paths by which a complete product may be sold. Due to this multiplicity of paths, a "channels conflict" can occur when two or more sellers appear on a customer's doorstep with the identical product but with different deals. Usually, one seller is the original manufacturer, and the other is a VAR reselling the same manufacturer's product to take advantage of a quantity discount, but with an applications software program that it bought from a software supplier. A large user is often able to purchase the hardware more cheaply directly from DEC and buy the applications software from the same supplier that the VAR uses.

Although the map is complex, DEC was most successful because it maximized the number of distribution channels, even though doing so made life more difficult for the selling organization. In 1983, DEC reorganized and began to eliminate some of the channel conflict by eliminating various distributors that it thought did not add value. In the process, it no doubt eliminated some channels that *were* adding value. By the late 1980s, DEC's revenue began to decline, and in 1990, DEC was unprofitable for the first time in its history. Meanwhile, IBM and Sun Microsystems adopted the DEC-pioneered multiple-channels approach to obtain applications software and to resell computers. In 1990, both IBM and Sun have grown. DEC is currently reinstalling a market structure not unlike the one it had destroyed by 1985.

Knowledge-Engineering Market Map.   In order to examine the "expert-system" or "knowledge-engineering" product world, it is necessary to start with the hardware platform and work all the way up through generic and profession-based applications to arrive at a product that can be used by a professional to carry out a particular task. Figure 9-9 shows the various levels of integration, beginning with a basic hardware platform such as a mainframe, workstation, or personal computer that uses traditional operating systems and programming languages. More modern systems, such as workstations, have a human-interface layer for controlling multiple processes via windows. The LISP language environment hosts generic knowledge-engineering tools, such as ART or KEE. In the early 1990s, dozens of "expert-system shells" based on unique and proprietary languages, or based on extensions to the LISP language, allow users to write a specific expert system. A database environment usually exists to hold the knowledge and database for the application.

The following are examples of some of the functions that expert systems can be structured to perform:

- *Advice:* A system that helps determine whether a particular customer should be given credit is in use at American Express.

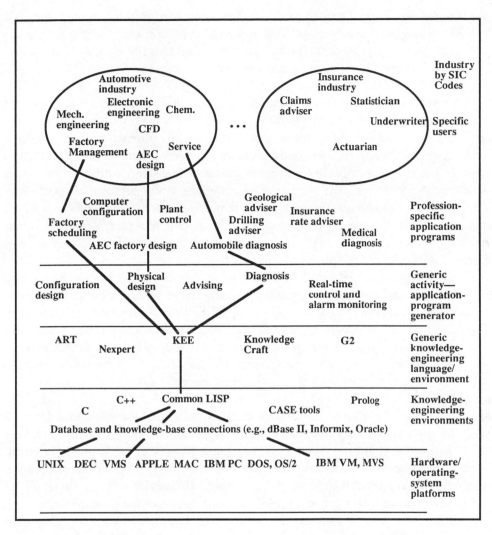

Figure 9-9. Market-Map Template for Knowledge-Engineering Products.

- *Diagnosis:* A diagnostic system used by GM aids in pinpointing faults in a car that result in various noises. Medical-diagnosis systems help determine whether a patient has a disease, given his or her history, observations, and test results.

- *Configuration design:* The DEC configuration programs enable sales and manufacturing personnel to put together a plan for building a particular model of a computer, such as a VAX/9010, to meet various customer requirements.

- *True system design:* Design Power sells a program for designing steam plants that includes electrical, structural, and mechanical equipment. The program takes customer requirements and produces a physical plant design, which is represented as specifications of equipment and 3-D drawings.

A program can be constructed based on certain needs to look ahead or to work with imprecise data. Such a program can often be employed by users who work in different portions of an industry but have similar application requirements. For example, a drilling-adviser program may advise petroleum engineers about the geologic subtleties found while drilling for oil. These engineers and/or geologists are within the petroleum industry segment. Similarly, within the consulting or service segment are petroleum engineers who would also use such a program. However, in a case such as this, the buying patterns, use, and SIC codes of the various groups of professionals are often radically different. It is critical for the start-up to build and understand the market map before fully designing the product.

In 1990, the infant (less than $100 million) "knowledge industry" supplies proprietary shells, application tool kits, and consulting to companies that need to build special tools to tackle problems that can only be solved using the knowledge-engineering approach. By 2001, this industry will be completely absorbed by a new and traditional software industry that uses "expert-systems" technology to provide tools for structural engineers, tax and investment advisers, and other professionals. The "expert-system-shell" business will become commoditylike compilers that implement a few standard language shells.

Being Global.   Perhaps the most important decision a new venture faces in distributing its product is whether to attempt a global marketing strategy or simply find foreign distributors as the firm evolves. Jim Morgan, CEO of Applied Materials, argues that a high-tech company must start up with the idea of being a worldwide enterprise. If the organization does not compete globally, it will remain small, be unable to grow and prosper, and rapidly lose market share to offshore competitors that dominate the worldwide market. In Applied Material's case, its largest market is outside the United States because other suppliers dominate the U.S. market. Morgan believes that Japan is the best place to train a company to be a global, high-quality manufacturer. The Japanese culture teaches a firm the importance of relationships, including being close and open with your customers and understanding them. It also teaches patience and a concern for the long term.

Question 6: When Will Orders Be Received and Filled?

As was indicated earlier in the chapter, how long it will take for orders to be received and filled is basically a sales question rather than a marketing question. Practically every new venture is overly optimistic about the time that will be required to get orders. In the beginning, all selling is "missionary selling" and takes a lot longer than a start-up would initially estimate.

THE MARKETING ORGANIZATION AND ITS FUNCTION

Both engineering and marketing employ models as part of their work in building the company. Engineering begins by creating some sort of model that describes the product's structure and behavior. It then creates a working product that a manufacturing organization can replicate. Marketing begins by creating a model of a marketplace for the "model product" in terms of specific buyers and ways in which the product can be sold. When the final product is ready, the model is tested by a sales channel that offers the real product for sale. The validity of the market model can only be tested once the actual product is available.

Marketing is first responsible for defining the complete product for the user, including securing any components, such as applications software, from outside the company. A market map is drawn to depict the myriad paths for completing and selling the product. Finally, marketing must ensure that product-revenue projections are met by producing information that a sales organization can use in convincing customers to buy the product. Marketing is the collective mouthpiece for the firm and the guidance system for the sales organization; it accomplishes this latter task by outlining which customers to visit. It must create leads. Furthermore, marketing must arm the sales force with various selling tools. Marketing's job, in essence, is to make selling easy.

Marketing designs and implements the tactical plan (i.e., the T-shirts, testimonials, trade shows, seminars, news events, and advertising), in accordance with an evolving market model, which it creates, tests, and recalibrates. Recalibration is done each time the product is presented. It begins with the concept, proceeds through product introduction, and ends when the product is retired.

The Marketing Balance Sheet

The marketing balance sheet plays the same role in evaluating a start-up's marketing as the technology balance sheet plays for engineering. The dimensions to be evaluated include:

- The marketing processes

- The marketing plan

- The marketing-support output (e.g., literature, public relations)

- Tactical sales support, including lists of targeted customers

- The head of marketing

- The top-level marketing team

- A customer and/or technical advisory board

- The marketing resources, tools, and people

- A system for control, with MBOs and output measured against the marketing plan

Three of the more important dimensions that characterize marketing—the head of marketing, the marketing plan, and marketing processes—are discussed in the following subsections.

The Head of Marketing.   The head of marketing for any high-tech venture needs to be an artist and an inventor. He or she is part wizard, part technologist, part street fighter, and part strategist. This key individual possesses a powerful imagination but is able to balance a checkbook, and goes through life with head continually in the clouds but with feet planted firmly on the ground. His or her charter is to invent a product in the minds of buyers, produce both the strategic and tactical marketing plans, build an organization, and behave in a professional, organized fashion from day one. The head of marketing is an idea-driven artisan who feeds on creative opportunity and tends to think in terms of trade shows, testimonials, T-shirts, ads, and news releases that will attract attention to the company and its product.

Marketeers with extensive experience in large, established firms in a well-established marketplace (e.g., minicomputer, mainframe) are generally not especially useful in a high-information-technology start-up that plans to enter an emerging marketplace. Marketing in large organizations is concerned with the creation of slowly evolving products to support a bureaucratic, arcane company and its existing customer base. The process is institutional and is executed through a fill-in-the-blanks process, using tactics designed to satisfy all the various marketing-support organizations and functions, such as competitive analysis, pricing, sales training, advertising, public relations, product testing, and product support. Marketing people with this type of background tend to be bureaucratic and lack both imagination and fundamental marketing skills. With luck, they are capable of budgeting and managing expenses, and possess good supervisory skills.

The greatest drawback in working with marketing personnel experienced in timeworn markets is not that they are likely to produce negligible output, though, but that they tend to prevent the development of anything new or creative. At best, these people bring a textbook, conservative approach to new products that invariably squashes innovation and ensures that no new kinds of products reach the market. In sharp contrast to high-information-technology marketeers, traditional marketeers filter out product innovation through a series of testing phases taken directly from textbooks that deal with marketing toothpaste and soft drinks. It is ironic that many regard the Japanese as the world's best marketeers, because they do not have MBA programs or formal marketing training. Instead, they spend a great deal of time living with the potential users of a product, more time building products for the users to try, and the most time refining the next-generation products.

What are the ideal requirements for the marketing head? At one extreme, creativity is essential if he or she is to grasp the myriad ideas for applications that are expressed during presentations to customers. Analytical ability is equally important. Thus, the head of marketing must have a rare blend of intuitive and analytical skills. As if this weren't hard enough, a high-tech venture also needs someone who can develop a marketing plan, lead a department and team, and manage according to the plan.

Although, as noted above, marketing people with extensive experience in large organizations have probably been corrupted beyond hope, people who have been in a large-company environment only long enough for initial training may make a contribution to a start-up. Two kinds of technicians who come from large firms could be useful: the supervisor who can hire, plan, and manage a staff and the product manager who can gather and synthesize product requirements and carry out the functions associated with a successful product introduction.

A marketing person who is product-oriented may come from an engineering background. However, this type of person may be overly bureaucratic and less creative than candidates from other backgrounds. Lee Iacocca—an individual with an engineering background who cannot, or will not, deal with the detail and rigor of engineering but wants to be part of the creative process of defining and building products—is a case in point. Alternatively, a candidate coming from sales may focus strictly on sales-organization support and never raise questions about the product or whether sales representatives are calling on the right customers. A sales representative, having to deal with customer requests, becomes quite creative and is highly tactical, concentrating almost exclusively on the sales process rather than the product.

Kvamme. One of the most creative and perceptive marketers in Silicon Valley, Floyd Kvamme, entered marketing with an engineering background at Fairchild Semiconductor. The head of sales at Fairchild, Don Valentine, required all marketing personnel—including Floyd, Jerry Sanders (founder of AMD), Mike Scott, Mike Markula, and Gene Carter (key executives in the Apple start-up)—to spend at least a year selling before progressing up the marketing ladder. Floyd led National Semiconductor's marketing when it started up, ran its plug-compatible business, went on to head marketing at Apple, and is a venture capitalist at Kleiner, Perkins, Caufield, and Byers.

The Marketing Plan. Davidow (1986) differentiates three types of marketing plans: for a new business, for a fundamentally new product within an existing business, and for a new device (or the next product release with minor enhancements). By definition, all start-up marketing plans are plans for a new business. At a later stage, when new products or enhancements are added to the existing business, the initial plan is updated accordingly. These subsequent marketing plans usually do not require or receive the rigor of the initial plan, created when the company first begins operating.

Insofar as the scope of this book is concerned, the key activity for a start-up marketing person is constructing a marketing plan. Later, in the product and market development stages, the company's focus is tactical, with the administration of marketing processes to support selling. But in the beginning, there must be a solid marketing plan based on the organization's view of the marketplace. The marketing plan has three parts: a market map, which describes the entire marketplace of interest; the tactics (i.e., the expenses) for supporting the selling of the product; and the financial cost models for addressing various market segments.

The basis of the strategic part of the marketing plan is the market map, which segments the market into identifiable customers. Each segment must indicate the size of the market, barriers to entry, competitors, market-share goals, and the total cost to enter the market (including, for example, any companies that must supply critical software or other components). As stated at the beginning of the chapter, the plan should describe what the product is, who will buy it, how the product will be sold, and why it can be sold. The plan should also specify where or through which distribution channels the product will be sold and when it will be sold, in terms of order-gestation time and effort.

The plan should indicate the identities and quantities of customers, which can be derived using a competitive market filter that starts with the profile for each customer and is matched to the product's features, functions, and benefits (see Table 9-2) The tactical part of the plan includes the detailed support literature and educational aspects taken from the relevant key marketing processes.

Finally, and most important, the plan includes a forecast of units and revenue for each of the market segments versus expenses that will be incurred in obtaining the projected revenue (in essence, a pro forma profit and loss statement for each market segment). In order to make such a detailed plan, the start-up must have a sales model, which is created by the person responsible for selling.

The Marketing Processes.   Figure 9-10 describes the processes that are necessary to support the selling of the product. Each of these processes yields a measurable output, such as a manual; a news release and the resulting news article; a sales brochure; a seminar; an application note; a new application that is, in itself, a product; the training of sales personnel; the plethora of information returning to the company in the form of customer feedback; and finally, support for high-level selling when customers visit the home office. When the marketing effort is in full swing, the head of marketing must be concerned about maintaining the integrity of the department's output, in terms of quality and productivity. This may take the form of independent reviews by an outside advisory board. However, responsibility for the integrity of the output must be fully delegated within the department.

- Product user information (e.g., manuals).

- Public relations information: news releases, advertising, and technical or other authoritative papers that support the company's initial concept and products as they are released and attain significant positions.

- Sales-support literature—i.e., collateral material: brochures, data sheets, price lists, reports, overheads, and slides and videotape presentations.

- Direct-mail programs with telemarketing support.

- Trade shows, regional seminars, and technical presentations.

- Sample application notes and/or new application products from engineering, an applications product development organization within marketing, or third parties.

- Competitive analysis and product pricing.

- Benchmarking, including the distribution of results based on tests conducted during actual use.

- The training of sales and product-support personnel.

- Focus groups, consisting of eight to ten potential users with similar backgrounds, that are run by a very knowledgeable moderator to initially validate the product concept and provide timely feedback on the product's features and specifications. This is not a sales situation. Rather, the purpose is to listen to feedback, and the aim should be to elicit actual feelings as opposed to polite comments.

- Customer and product-testing visits to the home office (or factory), with high-level selling of the company and its products.

Figure 9-10. Marketing-Process Outputs.

The Press

It is essential for a high-tech venture to have a really good relationship with the technical press from the day the company first opens its doors. If it had to rely strictly on advertising, no firm could afford to generate the amount of exposure it needs in order to attract customers, so getting as much free press as possible can be very beneficial. Ronna Alintuck, formerly of Gateway and a Regis McKenna alumna, offers the following advice about dealing with the press:

1. Limit access of the press to your best spokespersons. Top analysts are likely to be very bright but have short attention spans. You rarely recover from putting the wrong person in front of the press.

2. Don't try to impress the media. They've probably met more successful and more famous people already. Be genuine.

3. Don't waste their (and your) time. Don't call them if you have nothing to say.

4. Once you know them well, ask their opinion and take their insights into account. Respect the guidance they give to you.

My own recommendation is for the start-up's spokespersons to be incredibly direct, honest, and open. This even means being frank about stiff competition and difficulties that the new venture may face. If spokespersons avoid discussing problems, or try to gloss them over, the press is very likely to search out other views of the firm at its competitors. When the spokespersons are not in a position to be candid about a certain topic, they shouldn't be coy about answering but instead should simply declare the subject area off limits.

MARKETING FLAWS

As was the case with technology flaws, marketing flaws overlap with flaws in other dimensions, such as technology, product, business plan, and sales. At the heart of a high-tech venture's business plan is the following question: "Will customers buy the product at a given price and rate?" Many of the flaws involve not understanding this question. Other flaws involve trying to attack markets already held by strong competitors. As with all of the organizational dimensions, not having the right people can cost the company a great deal of time—and maybe its life.

Being Too Early with a Pioneer Product

The first product of a new class is inherently more expensive because of new technology, the learning curve, and lack of competition. Most entrepreneurs argue for fast introduction, followed by evolution in order to get the product finished and introduced into the marketplace. Thus, the first product may be barely usable. A pioneering product usually attracts only a small number of users unless the need for the product is extraordinarily obvious. In cases where the market is fueled only by early adopters, it's critical for the start-up to have the right price and cost. However, a small market is unlikely to support a high price. The only real solution is simply to wait until the technology has advanced to the point where it becomes feasible to offer the product.

Pocket PCs are an interesting case in point. One might logically expect that a large company such as IBM *should* be producing pocket-PC prototypes, complete with cellular radios and fax, and having the devices tested by its work force in order to explore truly personal computing (let's call it "intimate computing") for the twenty-first century. However, to be really effective, such a device may have to understand voice and/or handwriting. The following story will shed some light on why large firms such as IBM have not yet tried to market pocket PCs.

Workslate, the first pocket PC. In December 1983, Convergent Technologies introduced Workslate at a price of $895. First presented in the American Express Christmas catalog, Workslate was sold almost as a high-tech novelty product through several different distribution channels instead of being marketed as a compatible and integral part of Convergent's office computer line. The device's small, hard-to-use keyboard was a significant drawback, since it made text entry difficult. On the one hand, Workslate was an expensive phone book, memo pad, and calculator; but on the other hand, it was a forerunner of palm-top helpers such as dictionaries, bibles, and the phone directory, calculator, calendar, and memo pad from Casio and Sharp. In short, Workslate was about six years ahead of its time.

Anyone connected with Workslate's development, marketing, or purchasing could have asked two questions: Who would buy the product for any application that could be named? Who would buy it at the specified price? The answer to both questions was "almost no one." Ultimately, only five thousand units were sold rather than the two hundred thousand units that had been planned for in the materials purchase. The product was discontinued in July 1984, and the company wrote off $15 million.

In 1990, Atari and Poquet introduced IBM-compatible pocket PCs for $500 and $2000, with a small and full screen, respectively. Since both have small keyboards, the utility (and hence, the market) is likely to be somewhat limited unless it can be shown that the keyboard doesn't hamper input or until a use niche can be established.

Failing to Realize That Emerging Markets Take Time, Patience, and Capital

Emerging markets take time. If the start-up is predicated on putting a new product into a new and undeveloped market, the process is likely to take longer than planned. It is practically impossible to construct a model that can tell how long it will take, or how expensive it will be, to develop an emerging market.

Several high-tech ventures started up in the mid-1980s using rule-based systems technology developed by computer science's artificial intelligence (AI) community. These firms have evolved rather slowly and together have annual sales of less than $50 million. The technology-to-product transition has been slow to occur, with a relatively small number of applications using the rule-based programming approach. The organizations that have remained small and operated in a controlled fashion have been successful.

The first AI companies.   Teknowledge was founded in 1981, along with three other firms—AI Corp., Intellicorp, and the Carnegie Group (based on Carnegie-Mellon's work in AI). Teknowledge's mission was to become known as the premier AI company. Its strategy was to hire all the best people so that no one else could start up. It rented expensive space in Palo Alto, hiring AI researchers from Stanford's AI laboratory who had little or no product experience.

Teknowledge made "strategic alliances" with several large U.S. and European companies, including GM, by selling stock in exchange for a close working relationship on applications. It initially trained other organizations in rule-based programming, built special systems, and did government research in order to develop its next-generation technology. All three of these activities were potentially profitable, and the firm could have run profitably from the outset. Since such a venture was service- and labor-intense, Teknowledge attempted to build a high-standard product in order to obtain higher operating margins and higher valuation.

New, small, low-overhead competitors, such as Neuron Data, began to introduce standard rule-based products for a small fraction of Teknowledge's price. They had small staffs and equally bright people, but unlike Teknowledge, their people had product development and start-up experience.

Teknowledge raised tens of millions of dollars through private and public funding. In 1988, with money still in the bank and sales of its expensive product rapidly declining, Teknowledge merged with ailing Cimflex, a Pittsburgh-based company building custom programs for manufacturing. The Teknowledge portion of the organization was reduced to a small operating division doing contract research. Those at Teknowledge who were responsible for the merger (and who were also founding shareholders) did not suffer financially.

In contrast, Intellicorp (which began as IntelliGenetics) started from the same Stanford core technology to do gene sequencing. After the firm went public, the gene-sequencing business turned out to be less robust than it had originally thought. Intellicorp went on to develop and market its proprietary language, KEE, for building rule-based systems.

Chapter 11 includes the story of Gensym, which succeeded by understanding and focusing exclusively on process-control applications.

Trying to Establish a Technology Monopoly

The case of Teknowledge also demonstrates the flawed approach of starting up with the intention of creating a technology monopoly by cornering the market on all the bright people. It is impossible to achieve a technology monopoly. Attempting to hire all the "smartest" people in a new area in order to prevent the formation of competitive companies is a dream derived from biotechnology start-up strategies. The supply of top-quality individuals, albeit finite, is large, and all the ones who weren't asked to join the new venture are natural, highly motivated candidates for starting competitive firms.

Attempting to Establish an Always-Emerging Market

An emerging market is unable to support a very long, slow market development with accompanying incremental product tuning. As such, taken over a decade or longer, the market is still emerging. Market development may be limited by the need to change basic institutions or processes or to create a generation of potential users. The ultimate product cannot be built; instead, over time, partial products are introduced that chip away, niche by niche, at what is perceived to be the true market.

One of the greatest temptations is to attempt to define an obvious, previously untapped market that the availability of compelling new technology (e.g., multimedia for computers) would appear to make possible. Computer-aided instruction (CAI) epitomizes a market that has been emerging for a quarter of a century. Computers have made incredible progress in aiding learning. One of the simplest, yet least obvious, uses is a "help" menu that enables a user to learn about a system. Other forms of training include industrial simulators for power plants, aircraft, military-game simulation, computer simulation of industrial firms and cities, educational games, industrial courses, and computerized instruction in the classroom. However, a general program to provide ordinary classroom instruction (or even replace the instructor) at all elementary, high-school, and college levels still remains elusive, even though the need for such assistance would appear evident, in view of American students' poor ability to learn such subjects as mathematics.

Plato and computer-aided instruction.   In 1965, Professor Don Bitzer at the University of Illinois and Control Data Corporation built a system, Plato, for supplying computer-aided instruction. Bill Norris, the president of CDC, was its chief proponent and salesman. CDC invested several hundred million dollars to build an instruction network using Plato and its large 6600 computers. The Plato system used the first multimedia terminals, with computer interaction, slides, voice, and audio output. Although Plato has been successful with thousands of courses and millions of course hours in university training and applications, including teaching basic skills to prisoners, it and newer PC-based CAI programs have yet to deliver the promised revolution. Clearly, improving education is an important goal of all countries. Perhaps the CAI revolution awaits the revolution in ubiquitous, zero-cost, multimedia capability foreseen by some for the 1990s.

If Plato were located in Silicon Valley, some company would no doubt start up to develop a low-cost computer platform to utilize the vast array of courses. Corvus, located in the valley, is still waiting for the market surge. Apple serves the market, albeit in an ad hoc fashion. By making computers fun-and-game-oriented, Nintendo may have found the true pathway into the market.

Attacking Walled Cities

A classic marketing flaw is to attack a large company's customer base with a competitive replacement product. Rarely is this approach successful, since customers would prefer to buy from a few suppliers that are also the leaders. The new product typically attacks a strongly held market by using a different or incrementally improved next-generation technology. Existing suppliers, particularly start-ups, are unwilling to give up their market position and can hold their share of the market by enhancing their products through evolution. Attacking the customer base (e.g., IBM, Lotus 1-2-3 clone) of a supplier that is unwilling to accept the loss of revenue (e.g., add-on disk memories) or loss of control (e.g., database) is a flawed approach. It will succeed only if the new technology is compelling and the competitor cannot move prices rapidly (e.g., plug-compatible IBM mainframes).

Autodesk successfully attacked the mechanical computer-aided design (MCAD) market by building a product that ran on a PC as opposed to the older minicomputer (e.g., Computervision). It succeeded because the established companies neither saw a threat nor were able to lower their margins, since they had fixed costs and fixed ways of operating based on selling a few, expensive software packages.

Two major industries have formed through efforts to attack a large company's customer base: plug-compatible computers (pioneered by Amdahl) and disks (pioneered by IBM alumni). Both industries originated at a time when IBM had extraordinarily high profit margins on computers and peripherals. Al Shugart, disk pioneer and IBM alumnus, described the opportunity as follows: "IBM's high profit was immoral. Any self-respecting engineer would start a company just to bring lower-cost products to the mass market."

However, by aggressive pricing and by increasing the complexity of the disk subsystems, the established firms have decreased the significance of the plug-compatible peripheral business. The 1980s saw failures by Information Storage Systems, Memorex, Storage Technology, Telex, etc. In place of the plug-compatible peripheral industry, a substantially larger disk-component industry has formed, based on IBM's Winchester technology, to serve the high-volume PC and workstation markets. Given the cost difference (as measured in cost per byte) between large and small disks, a strong disk add-on industry could reemerge in the 1990s to attack the high-margin part of the minicomputer and mainframe industries.

Cullinet.   Cullinet was founded in the late 1970s by John Cullinane, an IBM salesman who started the firm to sell a distributed-database product created by one of his large customers. The company evolved to build products on a totally opportunistic basis to fill the niche in IBM's product line. It succeeded for a while selling its standards-oriented database before IBM's relational database became popular. Because a database system constitutes a predominant portion of a computer's operating system, IBM found it unacceptable to have such a key piece of its system built by another vendor. In 1989, Cullinet became part of Computer Associates, a large and successful company based on developing general-purpose software that it derived from specific solutions it had encountered in consulting for IBM users.

Amdahl Corp.   Amdahl Corp. was founded in the early 1970s by Gene Amdahl to make high-performance IBM System/360s. Amdahl was formerly the head of an IBM laboratory that built a high-performance computer, but the laboratory was closed because IBM felt that the demand for, and profitability of, large systems was low and the development cost too high. During Amdahl's start-up, the technology took longer to develop than anticipated, requiring more funding. Fujitsu funded Amdahl in return for 49 percent of the company and for technology transfer in the form of training, CAD, gate arrays (derived from IBM-pioneered master slice), packaging, software, and manufacturing rights. When Amdahl entered the market, the cost of mainframe computing dropped by 40 percent and continued to decline at a rate of 15 percent per year. Previously, the cost had remained nearly constant.

Andor—Amdahl could do it again in the 1990s.   In 1987, Gene Amdahl started a new company to build an IBM-compatible computer using complementary metal oxide semiconductor (CMOS) gate arrays. Andor's first deliveries are scheduled for 1991. The firm could be successful, unless IBM and the Japanese plug-compatibles (Fujitsu and Hitachi) switch to CMOS[4] and sell lower-priced computers. A custom CMOS computer (microprocessor) would be significantly faster and cost significantly less than a gate-array version. When or whether such a chip could be built is anyone's guess.

---

4. Chapter 13 describes why the ECL-based products are doomed, except at the very highest performance.

Building a "Just Another Product" of an Existing Type

Predicating a company on capturing a small part of a newly established market with a product that is "just another X" (JAX) when a new technology becomes available is a flawed approach. Virtually all new computer classes initially attracted hundreds of entrants (see Chapters 8 and 12). Only a few of those ventures were successful in the beginning, and only two or three survived for as long as ten years.

Failing to Find an Adequate Market Niche

A company may attempt to carve out a suitable market niche with a product whose cost is either too high (not enough buyers are available) or too low (selling expenses cannot be covered). In either case, it will be unable to develop a business.

As indicated in the previous chapter, niches provide a protected space in which a new venture can conduct its business, free of competition, until it becomes established. A niche is often the only way a fledgling company can develop a product that will return high margins and, hence, be profitable enough to fuel growth. However, if the niche is too tiny, the firm won't be able to find buyers and will therefore have no market. If the niche is too large, there will probably be many competitors, and prices will be too low to obtain adequate margins. A strategy whose objective is to claim a niche from other niche players or from newly established, aggressive start-ups is almost certain to be fatal.

The elusive graphics supercomputer and the risks of nichemanship.   Ardent and Stellar attempted to define a new niche that they believed would be profitable and unique. It was to be carved from two nearby niches: minisupercomputers and high-performance 3-D workstations used for visualization. However, these niches were owned by aggressive competitors (Silicon Graphics and Convex), which fought to maintain their market positions. Trying to carve a niche from the Silicon Graphics market position was essentially an attack on a "walled city," a flaw just discussed. Trying to carve a niche from the Convex market position was essentially an attack over a desert. The desert existed because the cost of the graphics supercomputer was so low as to make it infeasible to sell a low-priced minisupercomputer. In addition to the time-consuming problem of defining a new niche for a visualization supercomputer, the selling costs were higher than anticipated, resulting in an impracticable business plan.

Relying on a Single Customer to Distribute the Product

Virtually all the systems companies that have experienced sudden death have done so because they depended on a single customer that would relabel and sell their product and the customer then decided not to continue the relationship and funding. For example, Cydrome teamed with Prime, ETA was part of CDC, and Multiflow had an agreement with Digital.

The problem stems from the relabeler's changing its mind or not being fully committed to the supplier. A start-up that is considering doing business with only one customer should think again. Even with the best relationship, the firm is still at the mercy of the reselling organization.

Rob Peglar, an engineer with ETA, commented on the CDC relationship:

> Many people in the computer industry assume that most computer-company failures must be a result of poor product, design, or manufacture of some kind. Not so. Computer companies fail because of poor management and erroneous, ill-timed decisions—or the lack of coherent, timely decisions.

Having an Incomplete Product

A new venture may attempt to sell an incomplete, and therefore useless, product if it mistakenly assumes that there exists a very broad market for a general-purpose computing tool when the product is in fact differentiated only by having the "right" application software. Specific customers for a system have to be identified in the beginning, and then the appropriate application software must be secured to address the markets. The product must be complete!

A common oversight in building a new hardware system or platform, or a generic software tool, is for a start-up to ignore the particular applications programs that must be generated by either the user or independent software vendors until the product is introduced. As a result, the company finds itself with a product that cannot immediately be used by the intended buyers. By the time the firm discovers the dilemma, it is in a significant budget crunch as it scurries to persuade software vendors to "port" their applications to another platform.

Software vendors are generally very enthusiastic about porting the software necessary to make a product complete, because they find it an effective method of financing their companies. Larry Ellison, CEO of Oracle, described this as "laundered venture financing." Oracle was able to charge various newly financed platform start-ups as much as $1 million for porting its database. The optimum strategy for a software vendor is to demand up-front financing and hope the platform venture goes under before the port is done.

Failing to Identify Who Will Buy the Product and Why

The customer/application profile must be used to pinpoint the customers. The buying rationale is then examined once the customers/applications have been identified.

Product developers are often tempted to simply develop products that, on the surface, appear to be major leaps forward from an existing product. Both Analytica (described in Chapter 11) and Javelin, its Boston-area counterpart, were founded to develop a product that would extend and take market share from Lotus's 1-2-3. Javelin attacked 1-2-3 head on and was repelled by the loyal user base that wasn't interested in switching to a new product, no matter how powerful. Although neither of the new products was successful as a mainline replacement, when Analytica's product was repositioned as a database and Javelin's product was repositioned as a high-performance analytical tool, both were able to find a niche at lower and higher price levels, respectively.

Assuming That Universities Are a Market unto Themselves

All too often, high-tech ventures focus on the university market segment. Universities apply computers in a broad range of academic disciplines and really represent only the leading edge and early adopters for the application of many products. University users are demanding, critical, and provide user feedback. In addition to locating beta tests at universities, as suggested previously, it is wise to sell the first few products of a given application to universities and get their feedback and imprimatur. Unfortunately, universities demand high discounts. Thus, unless a start-up has a completely unique product (i.e., a monopoly, such as Xerox had with the first photocopier), it is hard to maintain adequate margins by predicating an entire applications market on extensive university sales.

Having a Poorly Thought Out Cost Plan

Very high, fixed market-entry cost (e.g., advertising, support) can make the sale and distribution of a new product infeasible. Various products appear to suffer from this flaw. The Ardent computer, for example, was limited because of its early pricing as a workstation. It was simply priced too low to be sold in an established minisupercomputer market at high enough volumes to cover the market-entry costs. Similarly, the Analytica story, described in Chapter 11, involves poor marketing and the wrong price.

Preannouncing a Product and Having It Stolen

Calling on potential customers, or hyping a nonexistent product to verify the product specifications, signals what a new venture is doing. This gives competitors a chance to respond before the company can get off the ground. If the product is being sold to a buyer that could develop such a product itself, the buyer is likely to either be working on a similar product already or be prompted to begin working on one. In some cases, the outright theft of trade secrets occurs.

The risk of giving away the store by calling on customers and potential competitors during the seed and product development stages is very high. The Stardent story is a wonderful example of the importance of security in developing the first product. Allen Michels, founder of Convergent Technologies and Ardent, described Ardent and Stellar, prior to their first product shipment, as "the battle of the big mouths." The winners in the battle were competitors and users that obtained more competitive products.

Visix Software. Visix was founded in 1987 to build a graphical user interface and system manager for UNIX. Visix representatives called on several hardware platform companies while the start-up was working on its first product, Looking Glass. In two cases, established hardware firms began building competitive products using ideas that had been discussed under nondisclosure agreements with Visix. In one case, a recruiting company was employed to go after Visix employees to help in implementing what the engineer in charge described as "a product we stole from Visix." Visix did not file suit, choosing to concentrate on making money through the sale of its products rather than through litigation.

Having the Start-up's Product Announced Prematurely by Universities

The task of universities (faculty and graduate students) is the discovery, production, and distribution of knowledge. Nondisclosure contracts signed by the university community virtually guarantee instant, wide-scale disclosure of a product or company. Conversely, if a start-up wants to gather intelligence cheaply, it should be networked and simply ask the university community what potential competitors are doing.

Hiring the Wrong People, Especially the Head of Marketing

Flawed hiring practices are common among high-tech ventures. As was the case with the head of sales, locating the right head of marketing is unlikely. In my experience, the probability of finding an appropriately qualified individual when the company starts up is about one in four. Although the head of sales can finally be tested with quantitative measures in the marketing development stage, it is very difficult to measure the head of marketing. The full Bell-Mason Diagnostic provides one such measure, but if a company is in trouble from a marketing standpoint, this will probably become evident by the end of the seed stage when it fails to satisfy the marketing rules for that stage.

According to Ronna Alintuck, some common flaws among marketing candidates hired for start-ups are that they:

- Have MBA degrees and believe their degrees make them better marketeers

- Believe they can precisely predict the outcome of a marketing program

- Were not personally responsible for at least one marketing success, yet have never failed with a marketing program

- Are not passionate, emotional, and controversial

- Are too easygoing or stop thinking about work the minute they leave work

- Are afraid to say "I don't know"

- Are process-oriented, committee people and make decisions based on consensus

- Are not both creative and technically adept [as evidenced by their ability] to understand and enjoy the technology and product for which they are responsible

MARKETING RULES

In the concept stage, the efficacy and uniqueness of the product or service is the major determinant of market success. Thus, the product and technology dimensions are emphasized more strongly. At one end of a product-demand-curve spectrum, no market exists at the current price level. At the other end of the spectrum, the company may predicate its business on capturing a small fraction of a very large market with a marginally better, niche product or technology. Either strategy is almost certain to fail. During the concept stage, the organization must focus on really understanding whether there exists a market that is large enough or manageable enough to enable the company to get the toehold it needs in order to develop.

Have the sets of customers (i.e., who) been identified for the product?

In order to begin working on a marketing plan, it is essential for a new venture to start by clearly understanding which customers will buy the product, by profession and by use, including their organizational affiliations. This first step is carried out during the concept stage.

Does the marketing plan at the concept stage contain a list of the customer/ application profiles (i.e., who/what) to be developed during the seed stage?

This rule, distinct from the rules for the product, focuses on whether the start-up understands who the buyers of its product are and how they will use or apply the product. This testing takes the form of a series of customer/application profiles, which describe representative individuals in specific use segments. These profiles include the users, the operational environment, specific unmet needs, the ability to buy, etc. If the organization does not have this type of detailed image of the user, together with an understanding of the intended use, it lacks the information required to design an effective product and reach customers through an effective marketing and selling effort.

Has the start-up identified a compelling buying rationale (i.e., why) for each of the customer groups to purchase the product?

In the case of a totally unique product, the company must construct a compelling buying rationale to attract new customers. Ideally, the utility of such a product (e.g., the first spreadsheet) will be self-evident. In the case of a more conventional product, the new product must add a feature or dimension that no competing product has. At all stages, the firm must continue to be able to answer this question affirmatively.

Has a simple estimate of the market size been developed, supported by articles and extrapolated market numbers as well as other public information?

The market size must be quantified in terms of the aforementioned customers and their applications in order that a business plan with numbers can be made. It is useful to be able to size the market in various ways, including starting with basic demographic data. Most libraries can provide a plethora of "free" data that characterize the world-wide information-product markets. And for nearly any product idea, regardless of its merit, at least one or more market surveys can be purchased at $1,000 per kilogram that proclaim the existence of a viable billion-dollar market at some future time.

Has the start-up created a simple market map showing the paths the company will use to reach each of the sets of users (i.e., how)?

This rule diagnoses whether the firm knows how, or by what channels, to reach the customers. Although sales is responsible for supplying the specific numbers, marketing has to identify the alternatives and recommend the best routes. The principal role of the marketing map, however, is to ensure that the company is aware of the need for "active" distribution channels. A flaw in many marketing plans is to forget about all the other vendors in the distribution chain. In many cases, however, the start-up's product will not be "complete" (i.e., ready for use by the final buyer) without one or more products that must be supplied by these vendors. Nearly all hardware and software products depend on additional products in order to form a complete product and, hence, a successful market.

At the end of the concept stage, does the start-up have a simple outline of a market plan, which can be expanded during the seed stage?

This rule examines whether, at the end of the concept stage, the company knows how to make a market plan so that, given a product, it can help salespeople identify and reach the customers. A finalized, detailed plan is not required at this point, only an outline for such a plan.

By the end of the seed stage, has a product requirements specification been written?

Defining the product is a key activity of the seed stage. Marketing is responsible for defining the product requirements so that engineering can make the product specification for designing the product.

At the end of the seed stage, are the preliminary customer/application profiles (with needs analyses), initial product concept, and projected unit cost roughly in line with the hypothesis developed at the beginning of the seed stage, and have any changes been factored into the business plan?

During the seed stage, the marketing person is finding users who understand the product and may be influential in specifying its details. This is an excellent time to form and recruit a technical or customer advisory board (TAB or CAB), which will help godfather/godmother the product into existence by advising the company on critical features and functions as well as how to build the product. The customer/application profiles (CAPs) describe who is going to buy and what they require by way of product.

As the company begins to build the CAPs, it must understand what information it needs from the data-gathering process, including a ranking of what it believes are the critical features, functions, and benefits (i.e., why) in the buying decision.

A focus group is an effective technique for really hammering out product functions. A small, select group of eight to ten potential users come together to give a product and market critique. The idea is for the start-up to listen to direct, but not necessarily polite, feedback and to refrain from selling. The group must be moderated by someone who really understands it all.

In determining system configurations, for example, one of the requirements for a new system may be the ability to communicate with existing systems. At the lowest levels, communication takes place according to certain industry and de facto standards and protocols and dialects, such as IBM's System Network Architecture or the Department of Defense's Transport Control Protocol and Internet Protocol (TCP/IP). Other communication is via file and database formats and standard languages. The start-up comes to fully understand all these detailed requirements by building the customer/application profiles, reviewing customer inputs, and listening to a focus group. Each of these activities will help the company understand how the product will be applied.

By the end of the seed stage, have the sets of customers and their applications (i.e., who) been identified for use during the product development stage?

Once the organization reaches the end of the seed stage, it must have a pretty clear understanding of who is expected to buy its product, by profession and by use, including their organizational affiliations.

By the end of the seed stage, has the concept stage market map been updated and refined based on initial explorations and field research performed during the seed stage?

By the end of the seed stage, a really complete market map is required in order for the start-up to enumerate and understand all the ways in which the product can be delivered to the market, although the specific route remains to be chosen. The map should start with the SIC code/customer/application groups, then look at various distribution and product-finishing channels, including VARs, independent software vendors, retailers, dealers, distributors, OEMs, and brand relabelers. The final stages of the map end up within the company as a supplier of a component or a system. Some testing of the market map should have occurred in the process of understanding the CAPs and determining the availability of other software to work in conjunction with the firm's hardware or software product.

Does the person responsible for marketing have experience in successfully marketing high-tech products in the start-up's market and product space? Can he or she attract, lead, and manage a "grade-A" marketing staff?

"Grade-A" marketing people are those who have been responsible for high-tech market successes, working collaboratively with engineers, and can function with minimal resources under severe schedule pressure and changing plans.

Can the head of marketing bring to the company a vision of how the product will be used to establish a unique and lasting market?

The responsible marketing person or the vice president or director of marketing plays one of the key roles in a high-tech venture. Although the head of marketing is not necessarily on board at the concept stage, having a leader is essential during the seed stage and as the company starts up. Marketing must be a strong partner in the product-definition and planning process.

A marketing person coming from a sales background can be highly creative but may only deal in tactics, ignoring product and market planning and management. An engineer may focus excessively on planning and management and not attend to tactics (i.e., helping salespeople sell). An ideal background is an engineer who has spent enough time selling successfully to understand the requirements for marketing.

Is the preliminary market plan outline (i.e., what the company has to do in order to deliver the product) in place, based on potential product position and competitive analysis? Does it include a tactical plan for programs, with costs and resources as a function of time?

As the company enters the product development stage, it must have a plan for a market plan in order to establish goals for output, guide spending, and determine resource requirements.

Does the market plan outline include the following components?

- **Preliminary corporate and product-positioning platform or statement with competitive market environment**

- **Simple product specification (features and functions), which has been translated into potential benefits for users**

- **Simple descriptive customer/application profiles of key market areas**

- **Global targets of opportunity**

- **Market map refined with a preliminary outline of requirements for selected paths**

- **Global tactics to reach the market, including advertising, PR, trade shows and seminars, etc.**

The start-up's market plan outline must contain substantive detail regarding the key topics listed above.

SALES

Sales must produce orders so that manufacturing can ship the company's products for revenue. Since so much has been written about selling, I will provide only a brief overview of this dimension. White (1977) offers a fine description of the sales organization and the motivation of sales personnel, including enumerating all the ways in which a sale can be closed.

During the concept and seed stages, only a model for the sales organization exists. If the company's product is to be marketed within twelve months, the head of sales may be hired by the end of the seed stage.

Often, sales is so closely related to marketing, particularly during the early stages of a start-up, that it is hard to diagnose the two as separate entities. Once the product begins to be sold, however, the sales organization can be measured quite easily in terms of the booking of products to be delivered, with the company being rewarded according to the amount actually sold. Unfortunately, it takes at least six months to fully implement any changes in the sales organization—e.g., a new head, regional managers, individual account representatives, or a commission plan.

THE CONSTITUENT DIMENSIONS OF SALES

The sales function, like marketing and engineering, can be decomposed into its constituent dimensions to form the sales balance sheet. The dimensions of the balance sheet are:

- *Formal processes for running the sales organization:* These processes include formal training and periodic sales meetings; order processing, revenue recognition, product shipment, and revenue collection; sales forecasting; customer visits and presentations; field seminars; field marketing program development; etc.

- *Selling plan and model:* These form the basis for controlling sales and sales productivity.

- *Presales-support and sales-support outputs and quality levels.*

- *Customer-support quality level.*

- *Head of sales.*

- *Regional sales heads.*

- *Sales resources:* This dimension includes the field sales personnel, offices, and infrastructure.

- *Operational control of the organization:* This dimension includes MBOs and the ability to meet the selling plan.

In the start-up's later stages, rules test each of the preceding dimensions.

At the seed stage the only relevant factor for sales is a realistic sales plan outline and model for selling.

The Selling Plan and Selling Model

Because sales costs determine whether the product is feasible at the price level, they therefore directly determine whether the venture itself is really feasible. Thus, sales is responsible for providing a realistic sales model for each of the customer groups identified by the marketing organization. The following parameters must be determined in order to make both a sales plan and the business plan for the company:

- Time and cost to hire and train sales and sales-support personnel

- Sales-cost profile, including the complete cost of making a sale versus time

- Order-gestation time, from first contact to final sale

- Sales productivity (sales/year), including the learning curve of the company's salespeople

SALES FLAWS

As was the case with all the other functional areas—including engineering, manufacturing, and marketing—the sales effort is subject to numerous flaws that can limit a new venture or even cause it to fail. Several of the most common of these flaws are described below. Sales management is simply an "art form," like other areas of management, that demands understanding and experience. Nearly all new ventures are plagued by a combination of marketing and selling start-up problems that cause them to miss their revenue plan and require additional funding. When this happens, the sales organization points to the marketing organization as the cause of the problems, and marketing, in turn, accuses sales of being untrained and incompetent. Both point to engineering for product deficiencies.

Having an Overly Optimistic Order-Gestation-Time Model

New ventures are almost always too optimistic about how long it will take to get orders. In the case of products entering emerging markets, all the selling in the beginning is "missionary selling," which follows the time-honored model of first selling to a research community, then to early adopters, and ultimately (it is hoped), to a large market. In order to compensate for this tendency to underestimate the order-gestation time, market calibration is included as a normal stage of a start-up's development.

Having Sales Costs That Are Too High to Support a Viable Business Plan

When the selling costs begin to be tallied in the market development stage, it may become apparent that the start-up is in dire trouble because of high selling costs. The trouble may stem from the company's failure to understand where, on an economic basis, the product will be sold at the price levels that are assumed in the business plan and required by the marketplace. The nonexistent-niche market flaw is directly related to the characteristics of selling a product (price, sales-gestation time and cost, and support cost).

Lack of an Effective Sales Leader

The head of sales is the critical person for the marketing calibration stage. He or she must hire and lead the sales team and assist in closing sales. The probability of getting the right sales leader is less than fifty-fifty, in my experience. All sales heads can sell themselves for a while, but ultimately, the numbers tell the story. Unfortunately, the company will be operating at its highest expense rate by the time the sales leader's shortcomings manifest themselves.

Having an Overly Optimistic Hiring Plan

The sales plan may make rosy assumptions about the availability of job candidates who are already skilled salespeople or who can be trained to sell the product in a relatively short time. The sales plan may also neglect to provide for adequate sales-support personnel. Although these individuals are called "sales support," they are often the ones who actually do the selling when a complex product's content is the basis for the sale.

This common flaw comes from not understanding the support needs (costs) and results in doubling the cost of sales. All of the systems companies with which I've been associated over the last decade consistently overestimated the salespeople's ability to be trained to understand and sell technical products. Invariably, successful salespeople either completely understand the product themselves (which only happens in a minority of cases) or have someone who might be termed a "technically knowledgeable alter ego" accompany them on sales calls when the product is discussed in detail. Depending on the energy and competitiveness of the sales representatives, between one-half and two sales-support people are required for each salesperson.

Having an Incorrect Product-Support Cost Model

After the product's introduction, it may become apparent that the product is much harder to use than was originally anticipated. Thus, a field organization is required to support the product, including training customers and helping them apply the product. Often, the difficulty in using the product is attributable to some type of product flaw that results in a need for significant and inordinate "hand-holding." Sometimes, users are simply unable to cope with the product's complexity within a reasonable time. In either case, more time and costs are incurred before the product can be sold in quantity.

SALES RULES

It is highly unlikely that a new venture can bring a head of sales aboard at either the concept or seed stage. However, having a model of the "sale," including all the costs and the time frame, is critical. The only way a realistic model of selling costs can be made is by using a similar product as an example. Even the "worst-case model" will probably turn out to be optimistic, however. In most instances, this occurs because the start-up has prepared its model by comparing its product with a steady-state product from an established company.

At the concept stage, does the start-up have an initial outline of channel-of-distribution alternatives, their typical requirements (e.g., selling cycle[s]), cost of sale, and a first model of the sale?

A selling model is required for each distribution channel, including sales-gestation time and effort, geographical distribution of customers, etc. At this early stage of the company's development, the sales organization is not a large component of the plan. Thus, a requirement right from the start is a model of the sale that includes selling cost and time. Without this model, the firm is likely to be flawed because its product will be economically infeasible to sell and support.

By the end of the seed stage, has the start-up developed a sketch for a preliminary sales plan—including distribution channels, organization, and "model" cost—and verified it against similar products?

The sales organization is usually formed after the product is well along, since it's usually inappropriate to hire salespeople at start-up time. However, a person who understands the sales process in the specific market area is required in order to build a credible sales model. In many cases, the head of marketing assumes this role in the venture's initial stages, especially if he or she has experience in selling.

Vital details that are often overlooked in the sales-planning process include the need and time for sales training, the requirements for a salesperson, and the need for technical sales-support personnel.

By the end of the seed stage, has the company identified sales-management candidates with the appropriate experience who will sign up to meet the sales-cost and sales-productivity model contained in the business plan?

The start-up must identify a potential sales leader who will check the efficacy of the business plan. Although the person may not actually be hired at this time, identifying likely candidates is critical.

CONCLUSION

Six questions determine the success of a product or service and, hence, of a company that is started to produce that product or service:

1. What is the product, and is it complete and ready for use by the potential customers?

2. Who will buy the product?

3. How will the product be used—i.e., for what application?

4. Why will customers buy the product, in terms of its features, functions, and benefits?

5. Where will the product be sold—i.e., through what distribution channels?

6. When will orders be received and filled—i.e., how long will the process take?

Marketing is responsible for answering all of the above questions. It shares the responsibility for question 1 with the engineering organization and for questions 5 and 6 with the sales organization.

The start-up can employ a variety of techniques to answer these questions and evaluate the marketing organization. For example, a customer/application profile addresses question 3. A market map is required to enumerate all the paths the company can use to distribute its product (question 5). And the firm must have a sales model in place by the end of the seed stage to guide the selling process (question 6).

Nine dimensions characterize the marketing balance sheet: the marketing processes; the marketing plan; the marketing-support output (e.g., literature, public relations); tactical sales support, including targeted customer lists; the head of marketing; the top-level marketing team; a customer and/or technical advisory board; the marketing resources, tools, and people; and a control system, with MBOs and output measured against the marketing plan.

Eight dimensions are important for sales: processes; a selling plan and model; sales support; customer support; the head of sales; his or her regional sales managers; the field sales resources; and operational control. The need for quality pervades all these dimensions. At the seed stage, the Sales Dimension is concerned only with a realistic model for sales costs, productivity, and order-gestation time.

Chapter 10

THE BELL-MASON DIAGNOSTIC

When you can measure what you are speaking about, and express it in numbers, you know something about it: but when you cannot express it in numbers, your knowledge is of a meager and unsatisfactory kind: it may be the beginning of knowledge, but you have scarcely, in your thoughts, advanced to the stage of science.

> —William Thompson, Lord Kelvin (1824-1907)
> *Popular Lectures and Addresses, 1891-94*

Everything should be as simple as possible, but no simpler.

> —Einstein

The Bell-Mason Diagnostic and Prescriptive Method is a rule-based tool that is applied manually to characterize and plot the status of a high-information-technology venture at each stage of its growth. The start-up is compared to the diagnostic's definition of an "ideal" company by testing it against a set of rules, which are applied by answering a series of questions for each of twelve evaluation dimensions. The answers are tallied and plotted on a relational graph, which is then compared to the ideal for that stage of development. The graph highlights the firm's potential deficiencies and pinpoints areas that are in or out of balance.

THE FOUR ELEMENTS OF THE BELL-MASON DIAGNOSTIC

The four major elements of the Bell-Mason Diagnostic include:

1. The five stages of company growth

2. The twelve dimensions that are measured to assess a start-up

3. The rules used to evaluate each dimension

4. A relational graph plotted against the ideal model for success

These elements are described briefly in the following subsections.

ELEMENT 1: THE FIVE STAGES OF COMPANY GROWTH

The range of computer- and communications-technology-based companies is large and will reach the trillion-dollar level before the year 2000. Hardware components start-ups produce and sell such items as integrated circuits and disks. Software components start-ups serve all computing power levels and deal in dozens of software segments. A few of the offerings in systems programming include languages, operating systems, utility programs, network management, and general software-engineering tools. Complete computer systems manufacturers may create anything from voice-controlled, pocket-size PCs to supercomputers. End-user applications software ventures bring us games as well as programs for inventory control, word processing, and mechanical design. Distribution, service, customization, training, and operations also constitute a major segment of the industry.

But despite their variety, all healthy companies starting up in the information-technology field must pass through the following four predictable, measurable, sequential growth stages in a roughly identical fashion:

Stage I: Concept

Stage II: Seed

Stage III: Product development

Stage IV: Market development

These four stages correspond to key product, market, and corporate development milestones and are intentionally distinct from a definition based on the infusion of capital (i.e., the rounds of funding).

Assuming they have successfully maneuvered through the preceding four stages, companies then reach a fifth stage, known as steady state—a mature but still growing stage at which they are considered to be stable, solidly established, and sustainable organizations.

This book has focused on the definition and analysis of the first two stages of growth, concept and seed, when both the product and the market approach are hypothetical but are undergoing detailed planning and development. Decisions made during these stages are excellent predictors of the company's performance in later stages. In fact, the success of the entire venture is most often determined wholly at the concept stage.

ELEMENT 2: THE TWELVE DIMENSIONS
THAT ARE MEASURED TO ASSESS A START-UP

The Bell-Mason Diagnostic enables the user to make a complete assessment of a high-information-technology start-up by measuring twelve principal and relatively independent dimensions. (Although the diagnostic is, as noted, geared toward high-information-technology ventures, it might, if modified, be useful in evaluating other types of companies, including retailing. For example, "location" could be substituted for "technology" as one of the dimensions.)

The twelve dimensions are organized in four groups, each containing three dimensions:

- Technology/engineering (Chapters 5 and 6), manufacturing, (Chapter 7), and product (Chapter 8)

- Business plan (Chapter 3) and marketing and sales (Chapter 9)

- CEO, top-level team, and board of directors (Chapter 2)

- Cash, financeability, and operations/control (Chapter 4)

Thus, it should now be clear that each of the preceding chapters has discussed either one, two, or three of the dimensions. The dimensions are designed to cover every aspect of a start-up in a complete, independent, and nonoverlapping fashion, including input (people, cash, financeability, and technology), output (product and service, and the ability to produce and deliver products), balance sheets, the organization and people who run the company, and finally, key processes.

ELEMENT 3: THE RULES USED TO EVALUATE EACH DIMENSION

Each of the twelve dimensions is evaluated at each of the four stages of a company's growth by comparing the start-up with an ideal for that stage. This comparison is performed by having key participants in the venture answer a series of questions, which, in effect, constitute a checklist. The questions themselves are the rules that define the "ideal." Thus, the company is on track across all dimensions if it answers "yes" to all the questions.

Fully (or at least nearly) achieving the ideal values at one stage is a necessary prerequisite for the firm to advance successfully to the next stage. If a company fails to satisfy the requirements of a rule (i.e., by answering "no" to any question at a given stage), it will probably have to correct the situation at a subsequent stage. Thus, those managing the start-up can choose to "pay now or pay later."

ELEMENT 4: A RELATIONAL GRAPH PLOTTED AGAINST AN IDEAL MODEL FOR SUCCESS

Figure 10-1 shows each of the twelve dimensions as a spoke in a polar graph, with the spokes separated by 30 degrees. Plotting the scores for the answers to the twelve sets of questions produces the "value" for each dimension. The dimensions grow in value from the center of the circle to its circumference as the company progresses through the stages of growth.

The figure shows two of the four elements of the diagnostic: the stages of growth and the dimensions that are measured. And as will be discussed below, this type of graph can also be used to show the ideal model for success at each of the stages. This enables the user to see at a glance how a start-up's current status compares with the ideal values for all of the dimensions at a particular stage. The fourth element of the diagnostic—the questions, or rules—does not appear on the graph but operates in the background, permitting the evaluation of each dimension at a given stage.

Figure 10-2 shows how the ideal grows with each stage, as the company begins at the concept stage with technology, a plan, a leader, and enough resources to get to the seed stage and then progresses from there to the product development stage. The graph reveals hot spots requiring attention by graphically portraying the organization's strengths, weaknesses, and overall balance at each stage.

APPLYING THE DIAGNOSTIC

The Bell-Mason Diagnostic can be employed in several ways, as described in the Preface. The three most common uses are:

- As a template, or reference, for planning a high-tech venture

- As a tool for performing a diagnostic "outside review" or "self-assessment" of a company

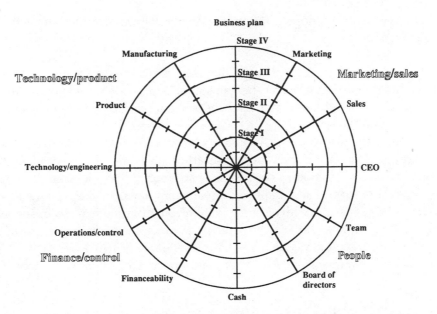

Figure 10-1. Relational Graph Used to Measure the Twelve Dimensions of a Start-up at Each Stage of Its Growth.

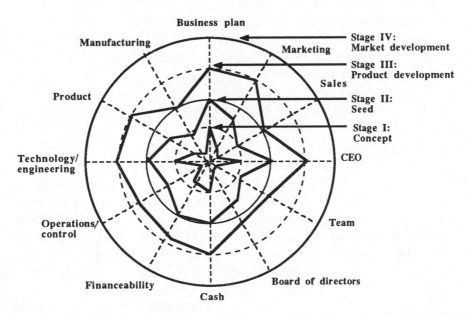

Figure 10-2. Relational Graph Showing the Status of an Ideal Start-up at the End of Each of Its Four Stages of Growth.

- As a means of developing a prescription for change to achieve a more ideal organization

Whatever the ultimate application, if the user becomes adept with the concepts underlying the Bell-Mason Diagnostic, gains sufficient experience or knowledge of the industry, and then applies common sense, he or she is likely to significantly strengthen the start-up's position.

Although the diagnostic attempts to be resistant to the destructive effects of ignorance and denial, which pervade many start-ups, readers should keep in mind that the method is only as good as the people answering the questions and the people evaluating the answers. For example, a company may have a business plan that meets the diagnostic's standards with respect to content, but that content may nonetheless be fatally flawed because the analytic work is poor or the staff has an insufficient understanding of some key issue. Thus, it is possible for a firm to obey all the rules but still fail because the quality level of the organization and/or its product is too low.

THE FIVE STAGES OF COMPANY GROWTH

The accompanying flowchart (Figure 10-3) illustrates the stages of growth for high-information-technology ventures, together with the possible outcomes for each stage. These are the same stages that were shown in a computer-program format in Chapter 1. Note that three of the substages of market development also appear in the figure. This section examines each of the five stages in detail and closes with a discussion of the different ways in which a start-up may transition from stage to stage.

STAGE I: CONCEPT (0–? MONTHS)

The concept stage is the company's starting point. It takes nothing to enter this stage except a kitchen or dining-room table at which to sit and begin exploring and planning the proposed venture. Participants at this stage usually include one or two players who want to develop an idea they have for converting some technology into a product.

The product might be targeted for a market that did not previously exist, as in the case of a newly emerged market. Or it might simply be aimed at a niche of an existing market, such as a performance- or cost-oriented segment of that market. If the product represents a significant improvement in performance or price, the start-up may target it as a replacement in an established, growing, main-line market.

The concept stage can be initiated from any viewpoint—such as market, technology, or product—but it requires the drive of a core group who have been infected with entrepreneurial fever. Ideally, the founding team includes a CEO who is capable of carrying the team through to stage V, steady state.

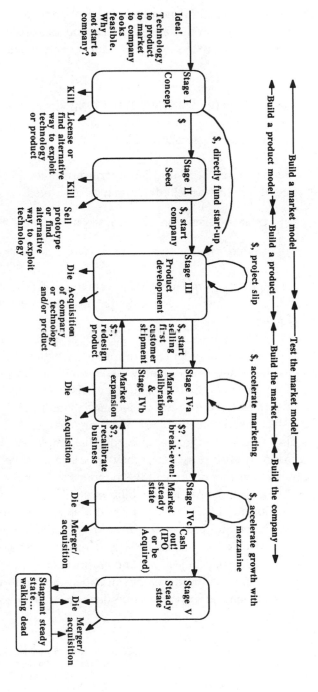

Figure 10-3. Flowchart of the Stages of Growth for a Start-up, Including the Criteria for Moving Among the Stages.

The players remain in the concept stage for a few days to as long as a year. They are "self-funded" until they develop a skeletal plan and secure the funding to move either to stage II (seed) or directly to stage III (product development) and begin staffing the organization.

STAGE II: SEED (PLANNING THE COMPANY) (3–[6]–12 MONTHS)

The purpose of the seed stage is threefold:

- The entrepreneurs must ensure that any critical technology is under control in order that stage III (product development) can be scheduled.

- They must create a cursory product definition so that the market can be assessed.

- They must produce a realistic business plan, which ties costs and revenues together.

The seed stage lasts six months on the average. It can take over a year, however, to prove technology/product efficacy if the proposed company utilizes a particularly difficult technology.

Although not all high-tech ventures go through a seed stage, it is strongly recommended[1] that they do so in order to allow for the formation of a first-rate team and the development of a detailed, high-quality plan for the company (as described in Chapter 3). If the founders receive a large infusion of cash with which to start the firm more rapidly, they tend to skip the rigors of this critical planning and technology-solidifying stage and instead redirect their attention to hiring people. Although the seed stage is vital, it is also a difficult stage because potential employees want to know that an organization is properly funded before they agree to join and because an extra round of financing means a further dilution of the founders' stake in the enterprise.

The technology and product feasibility are validated during the seed stage by creating a breadboard of the product or a critical part of the product, together with a product specification and a model of the corresponding target market(s). A formal business plan is prepared, as is a plan for stage III (product development), with the latter plan detailing resources, specifications, and product development schedules. Funding is secured for the entire product development stage, in accordance with the advice given in Chapter 4 and the answers to the key questions about financeability presented there.

---

1. January 5, 1990, I examined a well-written plan for $5 million that would have taken the proposed company from stage I (concept) directly to stage III (product development). I urged against it. The next day, I found a critical technological breakthrough on which the entire product was predicated. Although the necessary technological issues could have been examined by one or two people during a three-month seed stage, attempting to assess those same issues with a large staff at the product development stage would have been hopeless and would have led to compromising the product.

STAGE III: PRODUCT DEVELOPMENT (6–[23]–37 MONTHS)

The goals of the product development stage are to hire the staff, specify and plan the product, and design and produce the actual working product. During this stage, the product must be tested for several months under actual operating conditions by a reasonable number of real users. (The actual number of beta-test users depends on the product's cost and volume.)

The entire product development stage takes an average of just under two years, with entry into the stage being marked by securing funds and exit from the stage being marked by the existence of a working and user-tested product. This stage consists of the following four substages, which correspond to the four main product development phases (described in Chapter 5, Table 5-4):

- *Substage IIIa: hiring and planning (0–[3]–6 months):* The development team is hired and then generates a detailed plan and product specification.

- *Substage IIIb: designing and building (4–[14]–24 months):* The product is designed and built.

- *Substage IIIc: alpha testing (1–[3]–5 months):* The product is formally tested in-house, under conditions as stringent as those of actual use.

- *Substage IIId: beta testing (1–[3]–5 months):* Since it is highly unlikely that any product will be flawless enough to be shipped without extensive testing and acceptance by the intended users, the product must be delivered to a number of actual users for testing. (Product testing by relatives and friends does not count.) Although initial beta testing can be facilitated by bringing the first users into the company to evaluate the product on-site, the product must also be shown to work in the users' environment. The product will then have to be modified as necessary in light of the test results.

Following beta testing, the detailed plans for producing and marketing the product are created, and funding is secured, if necessary, for introducing the product into the market.

STAGE IV: MARKET DEVELOPMENT (2–[3]–4 YEARS)

The market development stage is the culmination of all the work done in the preceding stages. It is the period during which the planning performed in stages I–III is tested and then tried out in the marketplace. Although the firm's ultimate fate often becomes apparent during this stage, the seeds of success or failure have already been sown in the earlier stages, when the product was designed and the marketing plans were made.

Entry into this stage is marked by the first customer shipment, and exit is usually marked by company acquisition or IPO (initial public offering). Once the product has proved itself with internal (alpha) and external (beta) testing in stage III, the start-up must begin spending significantly more money to produce, market, and sell the product. The rate of expenditure typically triples when the firm enters the market development stage, provided that inventory costs can be kept to a minimum. The three substages of market development (discussed further below) include calibration of the existing market model, expansion of the market to reach a break-even point, and operation of the company at a profit for a minimum of six quarters. Just as product development is the stage at which the technology-to-product transition (i.e., the product plan) is tested, market development is the stage at which the product-to-market (use) transition (i.e., the market plan) is tested.

During the first three stages of a company's existence, the size of its staff is limited, which tends to minimize expenses. It is therefore relatively easy for the firm to appear "in control" even though no output is being produced. In the market development stage, however, the profit and loss statement has lines that directly relate to producing revenue at a planned level at some future time. These items include product cost and all the fixed and variable sales and marketing expenses, such as advertising, salespeople, support, installation, and service. The first sign of failure to meet the plan's "bottom line" often shows up right away in the "top line"—i.e., the revenue is not present. When this happens, a number of the intervening expense lines must be cut instantly in order to meet the bottom line. Otherwise, the organization gets significantly "off plan," with the inevitable need for "another round" of financing and the resulting dilution of ownership. The bottom-line failures that affect most start-ups are actually a direct consequence of failure to meet the top line—i.e., the sales plan. Most high-tech ventures suffer from a top-line problem at some point.

The three substages of the market development stage, mentioned briefly above, include:

- *Substage IVa: market calibration (3–[6]–9 months):* This substage is entered with the initial shipment of the product to customers and is the first time every line item of the business plan is finally tested. During this product/market calibration, or market-beta-testing, phase, which lasts an average of six months, the product is introduced into the market and the product, market, pricing, and sales plans are modified as needed until a refined plan for profitability is arrived at. The company adjusts its fixed spending in engineering, marketing, manufacturing, and administration to meet the unit variable product and sales costs, so it can move toward the "break-even" point. The major purpose of the market calibration phase is to determine the product's average selling price and its cost of sales, together with the order-gestation time.

- *Substage IVb: market expansion (6–[9]–12 months):* In this substage, which lasts an average of nine months, the firm continues to calibrate itself and moves, under its refined plan, to achieve its first break-even quarter, the exit criterion for this substage.

- *Substage IVc: steady-state operation (18 months):* During the final substage of market development, the start-up demonstrates that it can run profitably by sustaining steady-state profitable operations for six quarters.

Sustaining profitability implies that a successful company has been formed. At this point, the firm has a number of options. It could remain in its current state while it continues to build stature. Alternatively, it could "cash out" in some form, with its founders and investors achieving financial liquidity by selling a portion of the organization to someone. Virtually all start-ups aim toward the final funding round's being the initial public offering, which keeps the company independent while enabling founders, funders, friends, and key employees who have invested in the firm to finally receive value for their efforts. Although, ideally, the company reaches the steady-state stage by going public and remaining independent, most high-tech ventures in fact end up being acquired by another firm. For example, in 1989, 18 personal-computer-related companies went public at a valuation of $300 million, while 149 companies were acquired at a valuation of $2.1 billion.

Although "cashing out" is a declaration of having entered the steady-state stage, a healthy company may choose to remain private and profitable, thereby entering steady state surreptitiously. In the case of a privately held firm, the main investor issue is the ability to provide a return on the investment.

STAGE V: STEADY (SUSTAINING) STATE

Although in substages IVb and IVc, the company sustained steady-state operations for a period of approximately two years, it lived a relatively sheltered existence, beyond public scrutiny. In stage V (steady state), however, the goal is to develop the organization in such a way as to ensure its "immortality." This stage requires continual strategic maneuvering, whereby the firm attempts to retain and consolidate its niche in every aspect of its operations, including technology, product, market, service, business plan, finance, operational style, and culture.

There is a chilling alternative to a healthy, dynamic, and fully mature steady state—namely, the company may "go public," only to settle into a stagnant steady state (known perversely as "the state of the walking dead"). In this condition, the venture cannot attract additional funding and is not viable for more than a few years, since it is unable either to maneuver into permanent and sustaining product and market niches or to find an alternative way of operating in the long term. Single-product firms are likely to end at this point, unable to evolve a next product or create a unique and permanent way of doing business. Even when such a company has a plan for permanency, the public may perceive it as "stuck," with no way to finance itself, and therefore not worth investment or speculation. In this situation, the only recourse to death is some form of merger.

Hence, when I speak of a company's having successfully arrived at the steady-state stage, I am not referring to the creation of a stagnating organization that endures merely through momentum but to the creation of a healthy and enduring organization that operates in such a manner that indefinite growth and profitability may reasonably be anticipated.

TRANSITIONING FROM STAGE TO STAGE

The transition from stage to stage is usually linked to the requirement that additional funds be obtained to carry the start-up to the next stage of growth. Funds are also required when the firm misses its product or market development plans and has to remain in and loop within a particular stage. Thus, any company, within any given stage, may choose, or be forced to choose, one of the following options, listed in order of severity of consequences:

- *Move to the next stage:* The firm progresses to the following stage in its ideal growth pattern, but with some inevitable dilution of ownership as stock in the company is traded for funding to achieve the next stage of growth.

- *Loop within the current stage:* The venture must receive more funds (i.e., obtain another round of financing) and remain at the current stage until it gets back on plan. Increased funding usually means increased investment and therefore greater (possibly complete) dilution of ownership for all the current investors.

- *License the technology/product to another company:* The firm uses licensing as a means of funding the current stage and thereby getting on the road to success.

- *Return to an earlier stage:* The start-up backtracks without achieving the objectives of the current stage. For example, a product recently introduced into the market may be found to be fatally flawed and must then be redesigned from scratch.

- *Have its assets acquired by, or merge with, another company:* The firm turns over its assets (including technology, capital, people, products, equipment, and buildings) to another organization and ceases operating as an independent entity.

- *Cease operation:* The firm sells any assets.

THE TWELVE DIMENSIONS THAT ARE MEASURED TO ASSESS A START-UP

Innumerable factors, large and small, indigenous and exogenous, influence the course of a high-tech venture. These can be distilled and categorized into only twelve key elements, or dimensions (shown in Table 10-1), which determine the firm's ultimate fate in the marketplace. By using the Bell-Mason Diagnostic's rules to evaluate the strength of each of these dimensions at each stage of growth, the start-up's health can be assessed and its future outcome predicted and managed. In effect, the organization is compared against an ideal. Of course, the very process of conducting the assessment (i.e., identifying and carefully scrutinizing critical issues) is likely to have a significant positive impact on the start-up's outcome.

Because all twelve dimensions are important, they are all given equal weighting on the relational graph (shown earlier in Figure 10-1). Achieving superiority in only one area, such as having the best people or producing the best design or even reaching the market with the best overall product, is simply not enough in the competitive era of the nineties.

Many catchy formulas have been offered for how to start a successful high-tech business. One of the earliest venture capitalists, Arthur Rock, characterizes the entrepreneur's traits as follows: "a burning desire to start a company. . . . A person has to be very, very honest . . . recognize problems, foresee problems, recognize shortcomings, and admit and learn from mistakes." Rock reduces the whole issue to "People, people, people," while others advocate a more balanced, but still simplistic, maxim: "People, product, plan." Poduska, who believes that great people will rapidly adapt to any situation, states his belief in people over product or plan like this: " 'A' people with a 'B' plan beat 'B' people with an 'A' plan." In contrast, Don Valentine, the head of Sequoia Capital, has no fears about recruiting or replacing key people in a start-up because he looks for "markets first, products next, and then people." Bob Keeley, a Stanford professor who has studied start-ups, believes that without a very good first product, the company is likely to fail because it will run out of time.

Whenever stories of business success or failure are told, almost invariably, a simplistic formula like one of the aforementioned will be cited as the moral of the tale. The modern entrepreneur must avoid such maxims, no matter how clever they are or how reliable their source or how true they may once have been, since none of them even begins to capture the challenge of the contemporary high-tech venture. Such over-simplifications deemphasize all sorts of critical factors, including the need for cash, the ability to control the organization during a period of rapid growth, having the right product before the start-up becomes just another company producing a commodity product, and the complexities and challenges of competing with a plethora of firms that are being founded to produce what will become a high-tech commodity.

Table 10-1. The Twelve Dimensions of the Bell-Mason Diagnostic.

Technology/Product	Marketing/Sales	People	Finance/Control
Technology/ engineering	Business plan and vision	CEO	Cash
		Team	Financeability
Product	Marketing		
Manufacturing/ product delivery	Sales and product support	Board of directors	Operational control

THE RULES USED TO EVALUATE (SCORE) EACH DIMENSION

Organizations are not subject to universal physical laws like those that govern much technology. Instead, start-ups have to conform to the laws of moral and ethical behavior and of governments. None of these "contractual" laws determines whether a company will be successful, although violating any of them will almost certainly spell its doom at some future time.

"Laws of good practice" come from observation and result in "heuristics," used herein to define the ideal start-up. Each of the twelve dimensions is evaluated against these laws of good practice at the firm's point of transition from one stage of growth to the next. The evaluation is performed by applying a series of rules to each dimension, with the rules taking the form of a set of specific questions. In the diagnostic, all the rules are weighted equally to "score" a dimension. In practice, however, the rules will be given varying weights to reflect the difficulty and criticality of each issue (such as the existence of a plan).

The relationship among the laws of good practice (i.e., the heuristics based on observation), the rules or requirements of behavior that an ideal start-up should satisfy, and a question to which the organization can answer "yes" or "no" is illustrated in the following example, which shows the development of a diagnostic question that can be asked in the course of evaluating a company's technology:

- *Heuristic based on observation:* Software-engineering experimentation has shown that if a firm uses an inspection process in which one or more engineers examine, or "walk through," another engineer's programs, the resulting product will have fewer errors. Although this law applies to "average" software engineers, a few exceptional programmers may produce correct codes by themselves without such a formal review process.

- *Rule:* The engineering organization must have a design-review process that includes code walk-throughs, inspections, or some other rigorous method of verifying a design.

- *Diagnostic question* (the preceding rule, rephrased as a question): Does the engineering organization have a design-review process that includes walk-throughs, inspections, or some other rigorous method of verifying designs before they are integrated and become part of the final system?

Each "rule" is stated in the form of a question, phrased so that a simple "yes" or "no" represents a "pass" or "fail" with respect to a particular issue when a dimension is evaluated at the start-up's point of transition from one stage of its growth to the next. For example, in order for the engineering organization to begin designing the product in detail, the company must be able to answer the following question affirmatively: "Is there agreement between engineering and marketing on the product (performance, feature set, function, and cost) and schedule?"

Ideally, all rules must be adhered to (i.e., all questions must be answered in the affirmative) before the start-up proceeds to the next stage. Failing to adhere to a rule (i.e., answering a question in the negative) at a given stage can have different implications, however, depending on which rule is involved and why it cannot be satisfied:

- If the rule is critical and the question cannot be answered affirmatively, the venture is likely to fail. (E.g., at stage III: "Does the product work according to market expectations?")

- If the rule is critical and the next stage in the growth process hinges upon adhering to the rule, the company is likely to remain in limbo until the question can be answered affirmatively. (E.g., at stage IIIc: "Does the product work satisfactorily during in-house testing so that it can be tested by real users?")

- If the rule is so hard that virtually no start-up achieves the ideal, the company can safely proceed to the next stage if it is doing at least as well as could be expected from the average firm.

- If the rule is irrelevant for some reason and can therefore be disregarded in the scoring, the organization can safely proceed to the next stage. (E.g., at a software company, manufacturing, though important, is low-tech and almost inconsequential.)

- If the firm does not adhere to the letter of the rule but has found a better way of adhering to the spirit of the rule, it can safely proceed to the next stage. (E.g., it hires only "perfect" people.)

Each question should be answered with care. If time permits, the evaluation could also measure the quality of the work, moving beyond simple "yes" or "no" answers and assigning grades. The transitional diagnostic questions are designed to elicit information about each dimension at the level of detail required to effectively bring the product to market and the firm to steady-state operations. These are sharply focused, hard questions—precisely the sort of questions that a CEO or board should want the organization to address honestly. Such questions as "Does the company have a market plan?" or "Is the product sound?" are too vague to bring the critical concerns facing the start-up into clear focus so they can be properly addressed. In contrast, the diagnostic focuses the issues sharply by using more detailed rules (i.e., by asking more detailed questions), which permit a more meaningful assessment of the critical issues. Here's an example of an effective, sufficiently detailed diagnostic question: "Have design reviews for each critical milestone of the project been included in the schedule and adhered to?"

The rules for each dimension become more stringent with each stage in a start-up's growth. Note how the product development rules (questions) evolve as the company progresses through the following stages:

- *At stage I (concept):* "Does the company have evidence of product concept possibilities, given the technology, that customers are likely to buy?"

- *At stage II (seed):* "Does there exist a simple product development specification with features and functions that can be presented to potential users?"

- *At stage III (product development):* "Are an appropriate number of beta-stage systems (at least three for large systems and at least twenty for mass-user software) operating in real user environments and demonstrating unique capabilities or providing users with significant performance/price benefits?"

Notice that several of these questions have multiple parts. In such cases, each part must be answered affirmatively according to the logic of the question in order to determine the start-up's readiness to progress to the following stage.

THE OUTPUT:
THE RELATIONAL GRAPH AND MODEL FOR SUCCESS

The relational graph, a type of polar coordinate graph shown earlier in the chapter (see Figure 10-1), is also known as a Kiviat graph.[2] Since the graph displays both the four stages of growth and the twelve evaluation dimensions, it enables the user to quickly assess a company by examining all twelve dimensions simultaneously at a given stage. When the relational graph is employed as a management tool, it permits areas of concern to be pinpointed so that problems can be corrected.

---

2. The Kiviat graph was first used to plot various dimensions of computer-systems performance. The polar graph is commonly used in Japan, where it is taught in secondary school.

The graph is formed by plotting in the area between the four concentric circles to denote the state of a given dimension at each of the four stages of growth. At every stage, the value for each dimension should lie in the range between the circles for the previous and current stages. Since a company may not have completed all the requirements for a particular stage, it is possible that the value for one or more dimensions may lie somewhere within a previous stage. Such a discrepancy simply indicates that the firm is underdeveloped in some dimensions for the stage in which it purports to be.

Once the twelve dimensions are plotted for a particular growth stage, they can be compared against the ideal relational graph for that stage. Figure 10-2, presented earlier, shows the ideal state for each of the four growth stages, as a requirement for each dimension, and illustrates how the dimensions grow as the stages progress. The three outlines plotted on the figure represent the state of evolution of each of the dimensions that is required at the concept, seed and product development stages. Ideally, as the company grows, each dimension evolves to meet the target standard for the current stage.

In Figure 10-2, points plotted at the circumference of the circle for a given stage represent the dimensions of greatest importance at that stage. For instance, at the concept stage, the four dimensions that form the axes—the business plan, CEO, cash, and technology—are the most critical. Other dimensions, such as sales and product, are less important at this stage. All dimensions should be fully evolved and lie on the outer circle by the time the company reaches steady (sustaining) state (i.e., becomes an established firm) at the end of stage IV.

To cite another example, the emphasis during the product development stage is on growth in the engineering organization and development of the manufacturing organization. These changes are in preparation for the market development stage. Although, during this stage, the marketing plan is also being developed and other activities are taking place, they are not receiving the same attention as engineering (product development), which is critical to the current stage. The product development stage is only concluded when the product has been successfully beta-tested, such that it can be introduced into the market for sale, which will occur at the beginning of the market development stage.

THE BASIC RULES FOR DIAGNOSING A COMPANY

Each of the dimensions is, in effect, defined by the rules, or questions, that form the diagnostic. That is, an ideal start-up will satisfy all the rules that define all the dimensions. Figure 10-4 gives twenty-five rules (in the form of evaluation questions) that will help the reader better understand each dimension. These rules can be used to evaluate a company broadly and superficially, but quite easily, at any time.

Technology/Engineering

Does the company have a fundamental, defensible, and measurably superior technology, as indicated in its "technology balance sheet," that enables the sustained conversion to products by an engineering group of proven capability? Does the "technology balance sheet" include the following dimensions?

Technology base

Standards

Design, quality, and other processes

Plan, with schedule and resources

Engineering specifications

Manufacturing specifications

Chief technical officer

Team and engineering culture

Architecture

Technical resources

Technology future

Operational management

Product

Does the product have well-defined and unique features, functions, and benefits to support the price and match the competitive market requirements? Can the company build the next generation of follow-on products?

Manufacturing

Does the company have a well-defined organization and processes to produce products at the cost, quality, and schedules required by its customers?

Does it manage its raw materials and finished goods inventories in an optimal fashion according to just-in-time principles?

Does it introduce products into manufacturing rapidly, accompanied by clear product and process specifications?

Business Plan and Vision

Does the company have a written five-year plan that is *working and realistic* and that emphasizes (i.e., spells out in particular detail) the plan's first two years? Does the plan provide an integrated overview of all aspects of the firm and specifically identify the following: corporate vision and mission, lasting technological advantage in terms of a "technology balance sheet," product strategy, market segmentation and competitive market position, people and the reward structure, and the financial and financing requirements?

Are resources and milestones spelled out in the plan, and does the plan balance costs and customers to give a realistic forecast of returns, as noted in the financial portion of the plan? That is, quite simply, does the plan make sense?

Marketing

Does the company have a complete strategic and tactical market plan (both of which are defined below), together with the leader and organization to implement it?

Does the strategic market plan cover the following topics?

What (the complete product)

Who (the buyers) and how they are reached via a "market map"

How (the manner in which the product will be applied, along with any missing components needed to deliver a complete product to a buyer)

Why (the buying/using rationale, in terms of features, functions, and benefits)

Where the product will be sold—i.e., distribution channels

When (the time frame and cost model for selling and receiving the product)

Does the tactical market plan contain detailed information to support the marketing of the product, including a definition of the programs, resource requirements, and schedule?

Sales

Does the company have a driven sales group headed by a proven leader, and do the group and its leader have the understanding of and experience with the product class, price, and customers that will enable them to realize the selling cost and time model?

CEO

Does the CEO possess the level of intelligence, energy, ethics, and quality required to establish the clock and culture for the proposed company?

Does the CEO recruit (help select and sell) great, critical hires?

Has the CEO demonstrated management, team-building, and leadership abilities involving product development, in a resource-constrained environment, and on a "do-it-from-scratch" (i.e., start-up) basis, and is he or she likely to be able to manage the company throughout all the stages of its growth?

Does the CEO attract capital, board members, key customers, and strategic corporate partners?

Team

Is the top-level team composed of high-quality individuals with measurable experience and expertise in the various areas? Are they capable of attracting grade-A personnel as well as leading and managing their respective functions?

Is the team "do"-oriented rather than "management"-oriented—i.e., can each of the members "play" several positions on his or her team as opposed to just managing a team of players?

Do the members function collectively as a team in an integrated fashion, as opposed to operating as a collection of egocentric or warring individuals?

(continued)

(continued)

Board of Directors

Is the board composed of individuals whose experience and expertise enhance the company's competence at its current *and* subsequent stages of growth?

Do board members act as reviewers, counselors, and company missionaries for sales and finance rather than behaving like corporate decision makers?

Is the board reviewing the firm's strategic plans and direction as well as providing the CEO with advice about current operations?

Cash

Does the company have enough cash to complete the current stage according to plan and carry it into the following stage while it secures the next round of financing in concert with its investors?

If the cash is below a three-month supply at the current rate of expenditures, can the organization either obtain adequate cash from operations or seek extra cash through a relatively predictable financing channel within that three-month period?

Financeability

Are multiple investors willing to contribute to the next stage of the company's growth, based on the corporate, product, and market outlook for the firm, in the context of their feelings about the economy, high technology, and the market sector?

Control

Is the company operating according to an overall plan, and are only a minimal number of changes being made to that plan? (Have missed milestones, if any, been minor and explainable?)

Does everyone in the organization operate according to a formal schedule and management by objectives? Is everyone informed about the firm via effective staff meetings during which review, direction setting, and problem identification/resolution take place? The control dimension is verified by reviewing the archives of the team and of each department!

Are critical processes in place to govern spending and hiring so as to assure progress against the plan in a controlled fashion that will produce high-quality output?

Figure 10-4. The Basic Rules for Diagnosing a Start-up.

CONCLUSION

High-tech start-ups are characterized by the growth of twelve dimensions throughout four stages until the company reaches the fifth stage, steady-state. The preceding chapter has described the 12 dimensions and the rules to evaluate each dimension for a company in the concept and seed stages.

The Bell-Mason Diagnostic is designed to evaluate the dimensions and plot them against an ideal at each stage using a twelve-dimensional relational graph. Diagnosis is carried out by answering questions that come from heuristics or rules that define an ideal company. The heuristics come from experience and understanding. The entire diagnostic consists of over 600 rules, and the evaluation at a substage of product or market development may embody 100 questions.

Twenty-five questions (rules), which will help you understand each dimension, are asked in the diagnostic process. These rules can be used to evaluate a company broadly and sufficiently, but quite easily, at any time.

Chapter 11

CASE STUDIES

This chapter provides a glimpse of how a number of actual high-information-technology ventures have formed. The Bell-Mason Diagnostic is used, after the fact, to assess the health of several of these companies at various points in their growth.

The first two examples come from software start-ups of the early 1980s:

- *Ovation:* a now-bankrupt software firm that conducted an aggressive sales and marketing effort but was unable to produce a product.

- *Analytica:* a decision-support software company that had a good product but conducted a poor marketing effort.

The next six examples involve firms that appear to be healthy and whose products are representative of the types of products that a start-up might be founded to build:

- *Dragon Systems:* a manufacturer of speech-recognition systems that used product sales to fund the development of its technology and its understanding of the market as computers with sufficient processing power for speech recognition evolved. Dragon's story provides an example of how a company can start up in a self-funding fashion and evolve slowly with and develop a very complex technology.

- *Cirrus Logic:* a $100 million, public "semicomputer company"[1] in Silicon Valley that builds complex chips for the PC industry.

---

1. A semicomputer company is a firm that supplies microprocessors or microprocessor peripherals in the form of semiconductors.

- *Gateway Design:* an organization that began as a self-funded company and is now a division of Cadence, located in Lowell, Massachusetts. Gateway builds software products to describe, simulate, and test complex digital systems.

- *Gensym:* a small, privately held, profitable firm, located in Cambridge, Massachusetts, that builds G2, a real-time, expert system for process control.

- *MasPar:* a Silicon Valley company in the market development stage that is building a massively parallel computing system for highly parallel applications.

- *Thinking Machines Corporation:* a Cambridge, Massachusetts, firm that produced a forerunner of the MasPar computer. Thinking Machines' story serves to illustrate how government funding, through research and product purchasing, can be used to create, evolve, and understand the use of an innovative computer based on massive parallelism.

The start-ups discussed in this chapter span hardware, software, and systems in both the Boston and Silicon Valley areas. I am on the board of directors of Cirrus Logic, a user of Gateway's Verilog product, an investor in Gensym and Thinking Machines, and a friend of MasPar's founders.

OVATION: THE CASE OF THE MISSING PRODUCT

Ovation was a company founded in 1982 to build "the next generation of integrated microcomputer software," a development that many were saying was upon us at that time. Ovation's product was defined as a package that would seamlessly integrate word processing, spreadsheet, database-management, and communications functions. It was to have been marketed in volume to *Fortune* 1,000 companies at a price of $695, which was comparable to the price of the most popular spreadsheet, Lotus's 1-2-3. Healthy funding was secured from choice venture capital firms.

Despite having gotten off to a strong start, Ovation stalled and ultimately failed in stage III (product development). It declared Chapter 11 bankruptcy about two years after its founding, having spent approximately $7 million without producing a product. Since Ovation took a high-profile position in starting up, its failure attracted press coverage. The question is, what went wrong?

PRODUCT DEVELOPMENT STAGE

The relational graph in Figure 11-1 plots Ovation's actual accomplishments against the model of success for stage III (product development) at the time when the company was perceived to be at the end of that stage. The graph tells the whole story practically at a

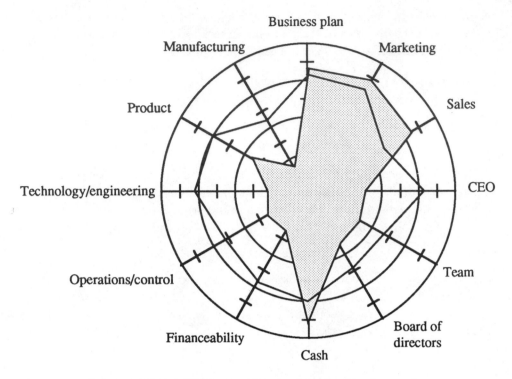

Figure 11-1. Relational Graph for Ovation Showing a Lack of Product and an Overemphasis on Marketing and Sales at the End of the Product Development Stage.

glance, clearly indicating that the dimensions were out of balance with one another. The product, as indicated by its definition, had just reached the seed stage, but no technology or development team was in place to build a product of inherent and protectable value. Ovation's prolonged inability to produce any tangible output eventually prompted analysts to coin the word "vaporware" for such products.

PLAN

The business plan was clearly not a dynamic control document. It was stuck at the seed stage and reflected the realities of product schedule slips and rescaled forecasts.

MARKETING AND SALES

In sharp contrast to the understaffing evident in the technology and product development areas, however, the marketing and sales departments were completely staffed and running at full tilt, producing all the sales collateral, demos, sales materials, and communications programs. (In Figure 11-1, note that sales is substantially overstaffed for the product development stage.) The group spent at a high rate, in hopes of generating indeterminate future revenues on a product that didn't exist and ultimately never would. The marketing and sales effort was impressive, as indicated by the fact that Ovation had already won an award for having the most important and innovative new product, and the approach should have proved effective—if the actual product could have been built.

PEOPLE

The CEO receives bad marks for his inability to get Ovation back on track once the imbalance in its growth pattern became evident. The top-level group clearly was not operating as a coordinated and unified team, with complementary functions making steady progress. The board, in its capacity as primary reviewer and counselor to the company, also failed to identify and rectify the problems before they turned into fatal errors. This latter point is not surprising, since the board had virtually no outside representation and was composed entirely of the marketing and sales staff that the CEO had drafted from his previous company, a Digital Equipment Corporation (DEC) reseller. The head of engineering was not on the board and, by some accounts, may have been treated as an outsider rather than as a team member.

CASH, FINANCEABILITY, AND CONTROL

Ovation's substantial cash, more than what a normal start-up might have been able to obtain, was spent aggressively at a time when the chances for future financing were diminishing. The company's poor track record for achieving any externally measurable results (such as alpha testing, beta testing, bookings, or sales) negatively impacted further funding. Control and operations were primitive in relation to where Ovation was supposed to be in the product development stage; hence, the firm was out of control, and had been all along.

POSTMORTEM

Even with twenty-twenty hindsight, it is not certain that prompt intervention would have saved Ovation or made it viable. However, careful and constant monitoring, using a method such as the Bell-Mason Diagnostic, would have served as an "early warning system," guarding against the expensive eventuality of failure. In Ovation's case, the results of the diagnostic would have sounded an alarm almost at the very outset.

At the first signs of failure, Ovation had two viable options:

- Cease operations and return any remaining funds to the investors because the technology was inadequate to support the product. (However, I am unable to cite a precedent for this course of action.)

- Reduce the company to a minimal marketing effort until a product could be built, which might have enabled Ovation to achieve an improved balance between its technology (i.e., its ability to produce a product), its product definition, and its future funding scenario.

Thus, Ovation is simply another case of Ken Olsen's wallpaper remover (described in Chapter 5)—all concept and no product, which is too often a fatal flaw in start-ups.

ANALYTICA: FAILING WITH A GOOD PRODUCT

Analytica was formed by Eric Michelman and Adam Bosworth to build a decision-support software product for the PC with an easy-to-use graphical interface. Adam and Eric had already worked together in 1982, when they explored a project-scheduling program with Andrew Lehman, who ultimately built the program as Time Line. Since Eric had been interested in decision support from his student days at MIT, he and Adam (who had designed eighteen successful banking applications) decided to develop such a product.

CONCEPT AND SEED STAGES

In March 1983, the company was funded with $1.3 million based on a plan for a revenue growth of $60,000, $4 million, $15 million, and $34 million and an Apple II product demonstration that Adam had built. The business plan was based on the wildly successful Lotus model: take nine months to build and introduce a product; spend lots on marketing and sales; and charge a high price. Although everyone knew what spreadsheets were, no one knew what a decision-support program was, why one was needed, or how to build one. The product, ultimately called Reflex, was initially nicknamed "What If and Why."

Founding consisted of merging with a stalled company, Taurus, which was selling a user-friendly interface shell for CP/M and DOS. At its inception, the plan of the combined company (eventually named Analytica) was to milk the existing Taurus product and develop Reflex.

Taurus had a staff of about twenty, and its president became the CEO of the new firm. The merged board consisted of four venture capitalists and the president; the founders attended the board meetings. Some of the board members had operational experience but no experience with software products. Taurus had to relocate to be with the six-member Analytica team that was building the company's future product. The head of engineering, Brad Silverberg, an engineer on Lisa, came from Apple with Eric. The CEO, two engineers, and three members of the support staff from Taurus remained with the company after a year.

Figure 11-2 shows the relational graphs for the Analytica start-up at the concept and seed stages. Notice that at the concept stage, the diagnostic is able to pinpoint the flawed business plan, given the newness of the product concept, the lack of specification, and poor market understanding. The lack of a CEO also shows up right at the concept stage.

By the end of the seed stage, when the venture capitalists created the merged company, the firm was already in serious trouble. Clearly, there was no vision and plan for the company as a whole, since Analytica was nothing like what the founders had originally proposed and the new president did not prepare a new plan for the combined organization. Whereas marketing was behind in planning, sales was ahead, in view of the fact that it was assembling a sales staff. The board at this point was OK, even though its members lacked software experience and did not act conservatively with respect to control. There was as yet no indication that the firm was out of control, except that the merger with a failing company, by definition, meant that the new organization was unable to meet its plans. The lack of a clear product specification at the seed stage was a sign that both the technology/engineering and the product had problems right from the start.

PRODUCT DEVELOPMENT STAGE

With the company in full swing, everyone had ideas for the product, including the fully staffed marketing and sales groups; the new, strong engineering team; and the board. The product specification for Reflex advanced the state of the art in the graphical user interface; in database design, including implicit data typing; and in the ability to add and subtract fields within the database. The product also had a variety of analytic powers, with the ability to do charting. For example, it could make a chart by extrapolating from a historical database.

However, for a product with such a plethora of features, Reflex had a weak underpinning because of the decision to run the program "in core" instead of working with a virtual memory environment. The fact that the program had to reside in memory at all times significantly limited the size of the applications and the underlying database. This was almost, by definition, a fatal flaw from the standpoint of potential corporate users (particularly since Analytica planned to market the product according to the Lotus model) and was therefore a misinterpretation of the market. After a year, Eric and Brad were finally granted explicit control over the product specification.

Given the program's size and complexity, the fact that it constantly grew in functionality, its lack of definition, its complex but undefined graphical user interface, and the naïveté of everyone concerned with the schedule, it was inevitable that Reflex

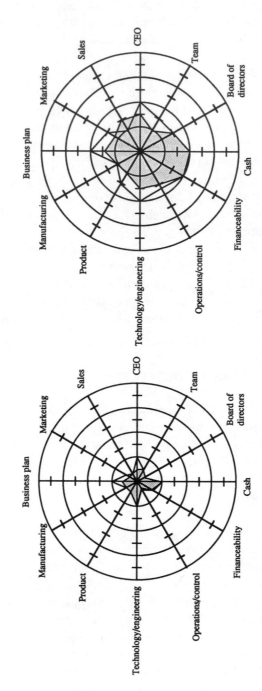

Figure 11-2. Relational Graphs for Analytica Showing the Concept and Seed Stages.

would be late and could not be accurately scheduled. At least one of the developers became so frustrated by the uncertainty that he left the company. Adam later estimated that Reflex could have shipped six months earlier if charting had been omitted from the first release.

In view of the product slips, the board regarded the team as grossly incompetent and put incredible pressure on its members. Eric made the following observations about the schedule:

> We really didn't know it was a two-year project. It was easier to deliver the bad schedule news in six two-month slips rather than a year. In retrospect, the development team did an amazing job by getting the product out in two years.

> Two years is the standard gestation time[2] for complex software products, especially if they've never been done before.

Adam offered the following comments about a company's first software product and its evolution:

> The first product doesn't need to do everything; it only needs to do something that a user needs. It has to be incredibly focused, and the development team must understand it won't solve all the problems of the world. For example, Paradox's first release was poor, its second release was good, and the third one, great. Paradox is a $50-million-a-year product. Like Analytica and Reflex, ANSA sold Paradox to Borland.

In April 1984, the CEO was replaced with a former divisional general manager of Data General who had no experience in developing or selling software products. At this point, the company required its second round of financing. Despite the fact that the product was behind schedule (it had not yet started internal [alpha] testing), the firm continued to grow until it reached forty-four people. The head of sales, who came from Lotus, was hired to introduce Reflex using the 1-2-3 model. Reflex's product position was changed by Dan Rosenthal, a marketeer, who redefined the product as an analytic database instead of a new class of decision-support tool. This repositioning made Reflex comprehensible to potential users and gave them a basis for comparing it with other products.

In 1985, the protracted third round of financing occurred, bringing the total financing to about $7 million. Marketing, training, support, and sales personnel were now being let go, because it was costing the company about $400,000 per month to stay

---

2. Ashton Tate's Dbase IV version 4.0 was shipped in October 1988 with bugs and was unusable. Version 4.1 was finally shipped in the summer of 1990. In the process, the company's president lost his job. Lotus 1-2-3 version 3.0 was almost two years late from its announced availability date, and Windows 3.0 from Microsoft, which was introduced in the spring of 1990, was over a year late.

in business while the seven developers continued working on the product. In March 1985, Reflex shipped and attained a level of two hundred units per month, which was far short of the plan. However, Analytica was clearly running out of money, and the venture capitalists were fatigued. Adam approached Borland, and the firm was sold in exchange for a few million dollars worth of Borland stock. The common stockholders and first-round investors received nothing. In October, the engineering team moved to Borland and were given Borland stock options.

Adam left the company in 1989 for Microsoft and Brad did likewise in 1990, while some of the team still remained at Borland. When Analytica closed, Eric became an independent software developer, operating with independent but highly experienced software developers in a "distributed garage-shop fashion" to develop Silverado, an add-in database for Lotus 1-2-3 that was sold to Computer Associates, and Budget Express, which was sold to Symantec. In 1990, he built and tested a work-group product to sell to a software publisher.

Figure 11-3 shows the obvious shortcomings of Analytica's position at the end of the product development stage. When the product was first introduced, the engineering group had a schedule fantasy factor (SFF) of over 2. The product wasn't what was promised, but it was still interesting and clearly salable. The business plan was at risk because there had been no market calibration for an enormous PR machine, nor did the company have the financing to proceed with a high-visibility, Lotuslike marketing plan. Sales expenses were always running ahead of plan. By now, there was clearly enough blame to go around: two CEOs had failed in every respect, and the board had allowed the organization to operate for almost two years in an out-of-control fashion. Although Analytica had cash when Reflex was introduced, it was clear that the venture capitalists were tapped out and would close the firm down if the product failed to take off.

POSTMORTEM

Once Reflex was in Borland's hands, the picture changed dramatically. Borland immediately dropped Reflex's price to $100 at a gross margin of 40 percent, and during the first year, about 200,000 units were sold.

Adam and Eric believe that, in hindsight, the $1.3 million first-round funding was more than adequate to develop and introduce Reflex. They both give similar advice to programmers who want to produce a product that can be developed by a small team:

> Don't use venture capital. Start small, build from your own equity, ship ASAP, and evolve the product. Don't believe your own b.s. Don't fight for elegance because you are paying for it yourself.

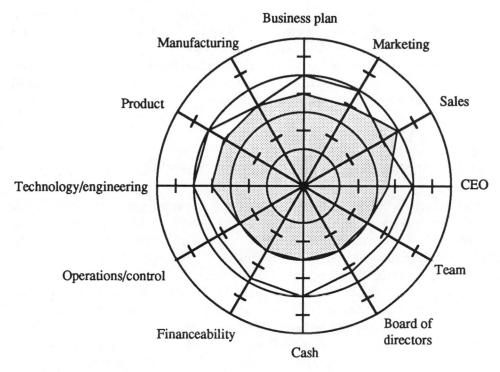

Figure 11-3. Relational Graph for Analytica Showing the Product Development Stage.

Furthermore, the company was constantly out of control. Since the board must insist on control, and control is ultimately the responsibility of the CEO, both failed in Analytica's case. Across the board, spending must follow the development schedule and not lead it (as had happened in the case of the founding) or be independent of it. And it is pointless to hire a sales department until product testing begins.

A company must constantly revise its plans whenever it fails to meet any milestone. In the product development stage, spending and control must be locked to the availability of the product, not to an abstract plan.

Although Analytica's business plan was flawed, the fact that what emerged as the product ultimately was able to be marketed successfully using a different approach proved that the initial marketing effort was similarly flawed and that sales, which should have performed a check on marketing, also failed. With better communication among the entire team, Analytica might have been able to understand and market Reflex properly.

The bottom line: Analytica is a classic case of an out-of-control company in which expenses were running ahead of product availability. The development team built a very good product, but it was a serious mistake to have tried marketing it according to the Lotus formula. In view of the fact that Reflex was ultimately successful after being correctly marketed, the product really can't be faulted—only everyone associated with marketing and selling the product and managing the firm.

DRAGON SYSTEMS, INC.: SELF-FUNDING RESEARCH WITH PRODUCT DEVELOPMENT

Jim and Janet Baker met at Rockefeller University and, as graduate students, had already earned reputations in the speech-research community. In 1972, they switched to Carnegie-Mellon University (CMU), which had more equipment to support research. Three years later, they received their Ph.D.'s from CMU's Computer Science Department, where they worked in the speech-research laboratory.

After leaving CMU, the Bakers worked at IBM Research, in Yorktown, New York, for three years. They then spent the next several years working in the Exxon Office Systems group, doing speech research. When Exxon decided to switch all its effort to development, they resigned in protest because they felt that research was essential for future products. Left without an employer, they made a completely spur-of-the moment decision to start their own company.

In 1982, the Bakers founded Dragon Systems, Inc., which became a leader in speech-recognition-technology products. They had saved enough money to fund a team of four for a year and a half while the product was being developed. Since speech products represent a slowly emerging market that is limited by the state of the technology, the Bakers planned to operate at a low level of funding, extending their technology and developing a product and market. They ruled out the "big bang" start-up approach as inappropriate in the case of speech products, since the product development process would be so tedious.

Dragon, while funding itself from product revenue, has consistently advanced the state of the art. The basic idea of its product is to permit speech input to be substituted for keyboard input in a completely transparent fashion, so that any application can be operated via speech input. Dragon sells its product directly to users and through original equipment manufacturers (OEMs) and value-added resellers (VARs), which incorporate it into more specific applications. For example, another start-up, Articulate Systems, uses Dragon's speech recognizer as a front-end control device for the Apple Macintosh.

Dragon operated with conservative goals and delivered its first product, capable of recognizing a sixty-four-word vocabulary in real time on an 8088 (the PC), in 1984. In

1990, the Dragon recognizer is capable of recognizing thirty thousand words when spoken in isolation, with only minimal speaker training, and sells for $9,000 as a PC option.

Having bootstrapped its start-up without outside investment, the company is employee-owned, wholly supported by customer revenues, and profitable.

CIRRUS LOGIC: GOING FROM RESEARCH TO FIRST PRODUCTS IN ELEVEN YEARS ON SHEER TENACITY

The history of Cirrus Logic encompasses several phases, beginning with a 1974 invention, which was further developed by a 1981 start-up company in Utah, which then moved to Silicon Valley and became Cirrus Logic in 1984. The following subsections trace the development of this firm, which went public in 1989, and examine the factors that contributed to its success.

RESEARCH STAGE: THE INVENTION AND ITS DEVELOPMENT

In May 1974, Suhas Patil, an assistant professor at MIT, invented the concept for storage/ logic array (S/LA), a method for designing digital systems. S/LA represents the logic of a design, along with the associated physical layout for complex VLSI (very-large-scale integration) chips, in a structured fashion. Both the logic view of the design and the physical structure are visible and part of the design. Use of S/LA has resulted in quick design turnaround, with density and performance comparable to handcrafted VLSI circuit implementations. Suhas described the development of S/LA as follows:

> S/LA came from a recognition that my techniques for asynchronous logic design for correctness by construction had to have a flat, 2-D implementation *to match the topology of* VLSI to be of any value. . . . I was bothered by the gap between how a design was conceptualized and how it had to be physically realized.

> The S/LA idea occurred as a "flash recognition," just like most inventions. By June, the research team I headed had built a breadboard that worked the first time. We packaged it in a 29-inch suitcase and toured Europe and the United States with it.

> Next came the hard part. No one in the computer or semiconductor industries cared. They were quite content with the status quo. I tried to work with MIT's Lincoln Laboratory, which had a semiconductor laboratory to do chips, but they had their own agenda.

> In December 1975, I went to the University of Utah, where General Instruments (GI) had set up a semiconductor laboratory. The decision to leave MIT after ten years was hard, but as a married assistant professor, I was dipping into savings I had made as a graduate student and was headed for debt. Utah was a wonderful opportunity to test the invention. NSF [the National Science Foundation] let me carry my $250,000 research grant to Utah, and Larry Hill, senior vice president of GI, supported the effort with a $330,000 grant.

At the University of Utah, Suhas continued to develop S/LAs and spent the summer of 1977 at Sperry Research showing how the technique could be applied to mainframe design. An eight-channel communications chip was designed in 1978 to demonstrate the efficacy of the technique and its applicability to LSI (large-scale integration), but again, traditional designers, including the semiconductor design group at Digital, ignored S/LA.

In June 1980, a decision was made to look for real problems to which Suhas's method could be applied. Jerrold, a division of GI, had just farmed out a chip design for a TV encoder to Motorola, and Suhas was able to carry out a design in parallel so his method could be compared with traditional design.

PATIL SYSTEMS INCORPORATED: A START-UP TO DEVELOP TECHNOLOGY

In January 1981, Patil Systems Incorporated (PSI) was formed. (In naming the firm, Suhas had followed the advice of friends: "If you're serious about a company, put your name on it.") Suhas described PSI's strategy as "up-front, customer financing." PSI would develop components (not designs for a client company), would not be a design-automation software company, and would not have a semiconductor fabrication facility.

PSI contracted with General Instruments to develop the software for S/LA and to develop chips using the compiler, in exchange for exclusive rights to the compiler after two years. By the winter of 1981, PSI's first chip was completed, beating Motorola in time. This was the first demonstration that S/LA actually worked, since twenty thousand parts were made and installed in a Jerrold product. Three other chips, including a clone of a difficult Intel communications chip, were designed using the software, but none was fabricated. By the end of 1982, with eight employees, the company was profitable and retained earnings of $70,000.

Unfortunately, Hill retired from General Instruments, and the GI semiconductor facility used for the work was dismantled. Suhas had lost his internal advocate and was cut loose from what had been a synergistic relationship. Suhas described Hill's management principles as follows:

1. Assume something will always go wrong. Always have enough cash to cover and withstand mistakes.

2. Controlling costs in a small company is done by controlling head count.

3. Always have a statement of work that everyone understands. This can be changed as necessary, but always know where you're going.

4. Every month, write a technical report to describe what you've done. [In 1990, Suhas expanded this rule to include a weekly one- to two-page report on what happened last week and what's supposed to happen next week.]

In March 1983, PSI began its first private offering, selling 9 percent of the company for $380,000. Suhas's completed business plan did not attract much interest, perhaps because Utah was simply off the beaten path. Suhas's father, a retired executive from India, was on the board and helped with the financing and control.

In June 1983, PSI got a letter of intent from Jerrold for three hundred thousand parts for a new design at a price of $4 per part and a nonrecurring engineering charge of $100,000. The design was started in August, with Suhas as the architect and two of his students/employees carrying out the detailed design of the cells and the chip. By October, the president of GI summoned Suhas and the heads of Jerrold and the semiconductor division to New York to ask why the company had to go to PSI for chips when it already had designers. Fortunately, the team was able to demonstrate that the design was nearly complete, and PSI was allowed to continue the contract, although it had to turn over fabrication rights to the semiconductor division. The chip worked and proved to be critical for future funding.

By the end of the year, Suhas concluded that it was pointless to continue operations in Utah without access to capital, foundries, trained people, and customers and therefore decided to move to Silicon Valley. Four team members went with him, and one entered academe but eventually rejoined the company.

CIRRUS LOGIC: A SILICON VALLEY SEMICOMPUTER START-UP

In January 1984, Kamran Elahian, a Silicon Valley start-up veteran, was hired as a consultant to help write a business plan and raise capital for PSI. By February, the team moved to California, and in March, Nazem and Associates had invested $200,000 to seed the California company. The firm continued to design and manufacture custom chips for GI using several Silicon Valley foundries.

In May 1984, Suhas met Mike Hackworth, a senior vice president of Philips' Signetics semiconductor company responsible for MOS (metal oxide semiconductor) and linear products. Mike joined PSI in January 1985. Suhas's advice on recruiting: "If you really want someone, go after them hard. Never take 'no' for an answer. A 'no' doesn't necessarily mean 'no' forever."

By September 1984, a plan to raise $5 million was complete. The company's revenue plan (see Table 11-1) showed profitability in the fourth year. The plan called for designing and supplying custom chips from customer specifications. A chip-fabrication facility would be built in the second year. The firm would convert digital systems designs that used older technologies to S/LA-based CMOS (complementary metal oxide semiconductor) designs, with regional sales and satellite design centers. In the third year, the company would begin selling its design tools.

The California firm, named Cirrus Logic, began operating in November 1984 with $1.5 million. Kamran served as the interim president. The first round of financing was completed in May 1985, when $6 million arrived from venture capital companies. Suhas was in charge of technology and served as chairman of the board.

For the first two years, Cirrus designed and sold custom chips. However, this did not produce the desired revenue growth or product family, as shown in Table 11-1. According to everyone in the semiconductor industry, the only way to ship large volumes was to manufacture standard parts. This "common knowledge" about high-volume standard parts tended to impede the formation of companies to manufacture and sell custom-designed parts, including gate arrays. In 1986, the decision was made to concentrate on standard parts and to find "godfathers" for whom general-purpose chips would be designed. The first of these was a mass storage controller for Seagate. By 1987, Cirrus had three standard parts and was on its way to becoming a semicomputer company.

TECHNOLOGY, ENGINEERING, AND PRODUCT

Cirrus Logic and its technology evolved through the following classic stages:

1974	The basic idea for S/LA came with an "Aha!" during *research* at MIT.
1975	The idea was evolved.
1977	The idea was then tested in several stages of *applied research* at the University of Utah and rejected by all the companies to which it was offered.
1981	Patil Systems, Inc., was formed with *seed* funding and contracts to develop computer-aided design (CAD) software to support S/LA and to test the software on a first production chip.
1983	The first private placement of stock in PSI took place.

Table 11-1. Cirrus Logic's Plan Versus Actual Revenue and Products.

	1985	1986	1987	1988	1989	1990
1985 plan revenue[a]	1.00	6.30	23.0	52.0	95.0	—
1985 plan net profit[a]	-3.90	-5.30	-0.8	1.7	18.9	—
Actual revenue[a]	0.13	0.35	5.0	9.2	36.9	87.0
Actual net income[a]	-0.76	-4.40	-6.4	-8.4	4.1	15.4
Products (custom)	1	3	—	—	—	—
Products (standard)	—	—	3	13	28	—

[a]In millions of dollars.

1985	Cirrus Logic began *product development* as a custom semiconductor supplier using the technology developed by PSI.
1987	Cirrus evolved a standard semicomputer product line for PC disk controllers, communications, graphics, etc., and entered the *market development and calibration* stage.
1988	Cirrus became profitable during the *market expansion* substage of market development and expanded their product line.
1989	The firm went public (*steady state*), with revenues of $37 million.

Because technology is the basis for any new venture in the computer field, maintaining the best technology balance sheet is the key to long-term success. The technology balance sheet shows that Cirrus Logic has three principal strengths: S/LA with automated tools to support quick turnaround of designs (a CAD process) and trained engineers to use the tools; semiconductor process independence, which enables the company to use a wide variety of fabrication facilities; and expertise in designing microprocessor peripherals. With these strengths in technology, Cirrus is able to build its state-of-the-art products. Future options include moving to other hardware besides the IBM PC (e.g., Intel 80X86) and to other peripheral areas, such as speech and image processing.

Given Cirrus's dependence on complex design skills, it might be natural for the firm to locate design facilities in other parts of the world to take advantage of the availability of highly skilled talent, such as Gateway (discussed in the following section) has done by locating a software-engineering laboratory in India. This approach would be especially easy in Cirrus's case, since a large fraction of Cirrus employees are foreign-born engineers.

PLAN

From the beginning, both PSI and Cirrus Logic had a clear plan based on technology and products. PSI was founded to develop technology for designing chips and, in a second phase, to test that technology by designing real chips. Cirrus's first business plan was to design complex custom parts for specific customers and to start by using Silicon Valley fabrication facilities. By the third year, it had become clear that a custom business would not enable Cirrus to attain its planned revenues, nor was a foundry necessary. Although, as shown in Table 11-1, Cirrus's actual results turned out to be relatively close to the plan, the company deviated by getting out of the custom design business and into the semicomputer part business. Cirrus neither built a fabrication facility nor established satellite design facilities.

MARKETING AND SALES

Mike Hackworth's background at Signetics was oriented toward marketing. Cirrus's technological strength was thus complemented with Mike's ability to select the product areas (e.g., disk controllers) and to sell the right "godfather" relationships (e.g., Conner Peripherals, Seagate) in order to achieve production volume.

PEOPLE

Throughout the development of the company, Suhas concentrated on building relationships and finding key people who could advise and help him and who would join the firm. His advisers and mentors included a businessman in Weston, Massachusetts, who served as his host family in the United States; various entrepreneurial MIT professors (Amar Bose, Ed Fredkin, and Francis Lee); Larry Hill of GI; Dean Brown, who headed the University of Utah Innovation Center; Ted Bonn of Sperry Research; and entrepreneur Vahan Gabusian. For example, Suhas, a most persuasive recruiter, hired Mark Singer, a graduate fresh out of Berkeley Business School whom he met on an airplane, to help with the business operation while PSI was in transition to California.

PSI had a good probability of succeeding in its CAD development because the inventor led the original research team. The firm was profitable and might have continued operating as a designer or supplier of custom chips in Utah, with the implicit assumption that it might someday be acquired by GI. However, Suhas wanted more.

Suhas led the company in its second phase and, as mentioned earlier, recruited Mike Hackworth. Mike, who had done it before, understood the semiconductor industry and had the confidence of the team.

Cirrus regarded recruiting as its number one concern. Although an advanced degree is not a requirement for promotion in the technical area, the firm is staffed with an unusually high number of Ph.D.'s who have made the transition from research to product development.

The number of board members increased with the multiple rounds of financing and in 1990 included Mike, Suhas, and six outside members with a broad range of experience.

CASH, FINANCEABILITY, AND CONTROL

PSI operated in control as a contracting business. It was very careful about spending and taking financial risks. Suhas also offered the following advice with regard to salaries: "Never be the highest-paid employee in your organization, even though you may head it. This sets an excellent example and helps keep salaries from running away." Hardly any CEO follows this advice.

Cirrus Logic started out less in control than PSI had been, because it was operating on a much larger scale than PSI and was subject to greater contract fluctuations. As a result, Cirrus required five rounds of funding before the IPO (see Table 11-2).

GATEWAY DESIGN: TECHNOLOGY AND PRODUCT, INTUITION, AND LEARNING FAST

Prabhu Goel, who founded Gateway Design, was born in India in 1949, the son of a civil engineer. After receiving his bachelor's degree from the Indian Institute of Technology in Kanpur in 1970, Prabhu came to the United States to study, obtaining his Ph.D. in electrical engineering in 1974 from Carnegie-Mellon University. His dissertation dealt with testing digital circuits. He then took a job with IBM, where he contributed to testability. In 1977, he began working on electronic computer-aided design (ECAD) programs, which were used within IBM. In 1981, he went to Wang Labs to head its CAD development.

In 1982 Prabhu founded Gateway, planning to fund the company through his consulting revenues while he developed and sold high-technology products. During its first four years, Gateway operated with no written plan, board, chief financial officer (CFO), sales or marketing personnel, customer service department, or head of engineering. From the first year, Gateway was profitable and controlled itself by never spending in advance of its shippable backlog. Gateway's story illustrates the importance of achieving and maintaining a lead in product development and of having technologists in control

Table 11-2. Funding and Valuation of Cirrus Logic.

Round	Price/Share	No. of Shares[b]		$/Round[a]	Raised[a]	Valuation[a]
		Round	Total			
3/83 (common stock)	0.001	1.000	—	0.001	0.001	—
3-12/83	3.000	0.127	1.27	0.380	0.380	3.8
Company is restarted, with first-round investors' stock taken as series A of PSI seed.						
3/84 (A)	0.950	0.200	—	0.200	0.576	—
5/85 (B)	1.800	4.150	—	7.500	8.100	—
3/86 (C)	2.500	2.000	—	5.000	13.100	—
11/86 (D)	3.750	1.200	—	4.400	17.500	—
4/87 (E)	5.410	1.960	—	11.000	28.500	—
6/89 (IPO)	10.000	3.340	11.97	31.000	59.500	120.0
6/90	22.000	—	—	—	—	316.0

[a]In millions of dollars.
[b]In millions.

at the top. Although the company broke nearly all the conventional rules, it still scored high in the Bell-Mason Diagnostic.

CONCEPT AND SEED STAGES

In 1982, Prabhu visited Cirrus (not to be confused with Cirrus Logic, discussed in the preceding section), a small, successful British CAD company that was selling a logic-simulation program called HILO. In July of that year, he resigned from Wang and started Gateway as a new CAD company. His unwritten business plan called for using consulting and lecturing income to fund his product development. Because of Prabhu's strong reputation in logic design for testability, he could command high consulting fees, enabling him to spend most of his time developing the product.

The proposed product would be an automated test generation program for circuits with scan paths. Having known and contacted many of the potential users for such a program, Prabhu was confident that there existed a reasonable market for it. He built the product using a terminal connected to a VAX. Figure 11-4 shows the company's position at the concept stage (about March 1982) and at start-up (August 1982)—i.e., at the end of what is normally the seed stage.

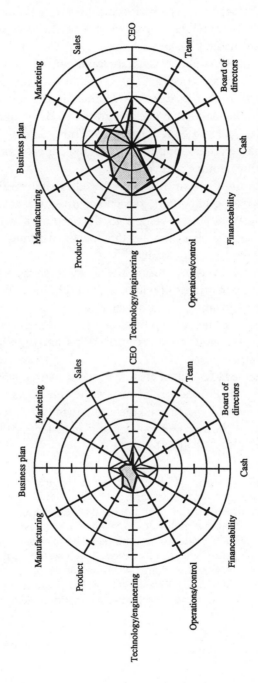

Figure 11-4. Relational Graphs for Gateway Showing the Concept Stage (March 1982) and Seed Stage (August 1982).

PRODUCT DEVELOPMENT STAGE

In August 1982, Prabhu used a mail-order firm to help him incorporate Gateway in Delaware, with an initial capitalization of $500. In December of that year, Prabhu successfully ran the first customer benchmark program for Texas Instruments. The second successful benchmark was run for Raytheon in February 1983. The alpha testing of the product, TestScan, priced at $150,000 for a VAX, was complete. The final product was then ported to IBM mainframes. In making the transition from VAX to IBM, platform independence (i.e., having a program be independent of what platform it uses) became a goal for all subsequent products. Thus, Gateway's products would all be rapidly portable to other computers. Charging for the porting of software to other platforms became a source of revenue.

In July 1983, after Gateway had experienced a year of profitability and had a product in hand with two expected orders, a second engineer was hired to maintain and extend TestScan. While TestScan was being sold, the need for a second product with a much larger market became clear. Prabhu thus began working on TestGrade, for testing conventional, nonscan logic circuits.

A critical period ensued during which contract negotiations with the first two customers took up hundreds of hours, with Prabhu usually being outnumbered by a factor of ten. In negotiating a contract, he took special care about operational commitments and liability while holding firm on price. Raytheon finally signed in December 1983. TestScan was then shipped, accepted, billed, and the revenue collected during the first quarter of 1984.

Prabhu decided to build on his first product's success by recruiting a world-class simulator designer, Phil Moorby, one of the developers of HILO. Phil's charter, beginning in June 1984, was to build the ultimate mixed-mode simulator for specifying digital systems at the register transfer and gate levels. Phil offered the following comments on why he joined Gateway:

> Knowing Prabhu, I had a gut feeling that he would be successful. While at Wang, he grilled us on HILO and really worked us hard, but he also didn't expect utopia. He didn't ask for ridiculous enhancements that didn't make business sense. He had a technical sense, a business sense, and the ability to negotiate with people. He was unique and had tremendous talent and made me feel confident. The day I joined I felt successful. There was always the sense that if you don't succeed, then it's your own fault. We just went after everything we were capable of doing. We never relaxed on an account. Prabhu's style was such that you felt like you could never get anything by him so you always were trying to do your best and cover all angles, because if you didn't, he would.

Figure 11-5 shows the status of the Gateway start-up at the end of the product development stage.

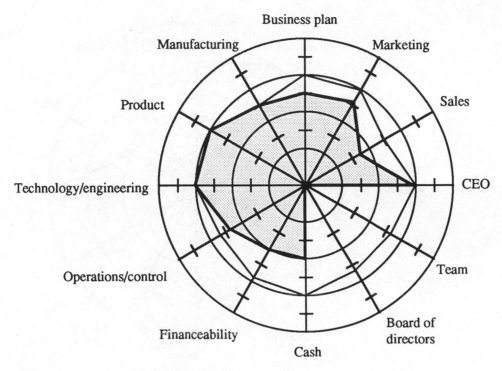

Figure 11-5. Relational Graph for Gateway Showing the Product Development Stage
                 (December 1982).

MARKET DEVELOPMENT STAGE

With one product on the market, another product under development, and three
employees on the staff, Gateway moved to commercial office space and entered the
market development stage of its growth. Gateway's products were promoted solely by
word of mouth, and sales were made by the existing employees. For control purposes,
shippable bookings were used to manage the cash flow and eliminate the payment of
income tax. The diagnostic (Figure 11-6) shows Gateway to be a tiny company at this
point, but very well rounded and in control.

Phil's product, Verilog, was capable of describing digital systems at multiple levels
of abstraction for simulation. It was ready for demonstration by the first quarter of 1985.
A road show during which the product was demonstrated to thirty potential customers
in Silicon Valley and Los Angeles yielded an order from Sun Microsystems (the main
host for the simulator). In fiscal year 1985, Gateway had revenues of $1 million with
bookings of $1.1 million. A vice president of marketing was then hired. Before leaving

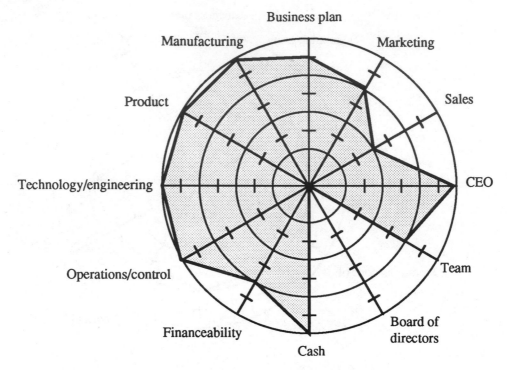

Figure 11-6. Relational Graph for Gateway Showing the Market Calibration Stage (June 1984).

a year later, he was instrumental in hiring Craig Robbins as the vice president of sales. Craig resided on the West Coast, where the bulk of Gateway's customers were located.

In December 1985, Prabhu was contacted by three venture capital groups. In May 1986, an agreement was concluded whereby Greylock and Fidelity Ventures would receive one-third ownership of Gateway for $2 million, with the financing being completed in July. Henry McCance of Greylock and Gordon Kingsley of Fidelity Ventures joined the board of directors. Clearly, Gateway was not in need of the cash. Instead, like Microsoft, it sold part of the company to get expertise in hiring and financing along with the financial community's imprimatur on the firm so it could advance rapidly within the high-tech business community. Prabhu believed a financial partner was needed for future financing.

During the four years beginning in 1986, revenues went from $1.5 million to $12 million, with a backlog of orders worth $17 million (much of which had been shipped but not billed). The first CFO, Dan Keshian, arrived in 1987. The usually high level of bookings in the later years was used to manage the company's cash flow, reduce its tax liability to zero, and fund its growth during the following year.

In October 1989, Gateway and Cadence, the fastest-growing company in the electronic CAD market, announced their merger. Cadence was challenging Mentor Graphics, the leader in ECAD. Gateway's value was $80 million in December, at the time of the merger; in July 1990, the Gateway portion of the combined organization was valued at $135 million. This gave the venture capital investors a return of more than twenty times their investment after only four years. Although it might be argued that Greylock reaped an exceptionally high rate of return on its initial investment and ongoing advice, Prabhu stated: "Greylock joining me gave me the insight to hire a CFO and put the financials in place early on so we would be prepared to manage the growth we anticipated."

By 1990, Prabhu was managing a substantial division of Cadence, with personnel on both coasts of the United States and in India. Phil Moorby, who became the first Gateway Fellow in 1988, started work on a completely new kind of design-automation software. This approach allowed the technologist to continue working productively in a way that was most beneficial to Gateway and most rewarding for him, without his having to become a manager.

TECHNOLOGY AND PRODUCT

The Gateway story shows how technology developed by two individual contributors was capable of generating lasting product families. TestGrade, enhanced in 1985, remains on the market in 1990. Verilog, the logic simulator, was introduced in 1985, and a faster version, Verilog XL, was introduced in 1987. A simulator for the Department of Defense-specified language VHDL, incorporating Moorby's algorithm from XL, was introduced at the Design Automation Conference (DAC) in June 1990. This algorithm enabled Gateway to introduce software-only simulators that could compete with specialized hardware accelerators. Bill Kaiser of Greylock commented:

> From a product/feature comparison, we almost always won based on performance, so there was a bit of an open field, which made it easier to do business.

Prabhu incorporated logic scan test methodology, a technology that he had learned at IBM. By having superb technology and technical leadership, Gateway was able to attract the talent that was needed in order to keep the firm at the forefront. In 1988, when Gateway had four evolving products, Gary Leive was hired as vice president of engineering.

Quality was the cornerstone of product development. Prabhu and Phil established a culture in which products were designed to require minimal technical support, because a product would not be released if it had bugs. A substantial amount of software testing was automated through the use of test scripts. A customer service department was added in the first quarter of 1986, to provide customer training and answer questions.

In late 1986, Gateway established a development subsidiary in India. By 1990, the twenty-eight engineers there were producing new, high-quality products at a small fraction of the per-person cost of U.S. engineers. This subsidiary is scheduled to grow to over a hundred engineers and, in the early 1990s, represents a major asset of the company.

PLAN

A plan for developing a premium-priced, advanced line of products and marketing them can be quite simple and need not be written down, provided the founder can self-fund the venture. Self-funding is an ideal approach to starting a company that others in a comparable situation should use. The plan, similar to Autodesk's, was to write a variety of programs and then select the winning product(s) for growth. Autodesk developed and evolved a simple drawing program, AutoCAD, for a mass market of architects and structural and mechanical engineers. Prabhu and Phil were the world's experts in a small but growing technical product area, and they understood their customers' needs. Gateway's strategy, like Autodesk's, was to use the emerging powerful workstations in order to provide a design and simulation facility for every engineer. Gateway's third product, Verilog, became the cornerstone for market growth, and the company bet its future on it.

MARKETING AND SALES (AND SUPPORT)

Right from the start, Prabhu and Phil understood the market because they were the key developers of the technology and products that defined the market. Prabhu, the chief marketeer, had an uncanny ability to relate to users and their problems because he had served as product developer and manager of CAD systems within IBM and Wang.

In the beginning, the responsibility for documentation, including the sales collateral literature (documentation describing the product), rested with the product developers because of their knowledge of the product, market, and customers. In late 1986, a product-marketing person was hired to help the engineers describe their products and to prepare product information for the sales team.

Bill Kaiser of Greylock offered the following observation:

> Gateway had an outstanding product that was adopted quickly by some blue-chip customers. Early on, companies like Motorola provided word-of-mouth reference accounts to help the sales process.

In the spring of 1987, Ronna Alintuck was hired to handle public relations, corporate marketing, and market positioning. Ronna was given a free hand but only a small budget. Her philosophy, like Gateway's, was based on doing only a few things well and in a way that would communicate effectively with the company's engineering market. Prabhu acted as sponsor and coach for her nontraditional marketing.

Gateway decided to attend only two out of a possible eight trade shows, regarding the remaining six as redundant. At the DAC (Design Automation Conference) and the more prestigious academic conference, ICCAD (Integrated Circuit CAD), it often gave away promotional items.

Gateway's brochures were initially limited to informative product-description literature. Only in 1989 did the firm produce a glossy, corporate-type brochure. It was filled with data about the company and its philosophy, people, and products and also included puzzles designed to be intriguing to engineers.

In 1988, Gateway ran a series of space ads with testimonials and photographs of Gene Amdahl; Forest Baskett of Silicon Graphics; Tom West of Data General; and me, for Ardent. Gateway's ads were run in only one trade publication, *EE Times*, which was read by the potential buyers. The ads used a quote from Einstein—"Imagination is more important than knowledge"—as a recurring theme to position Gateway as a company whose products inspire the creativity of their users. By 1990, most CAD companies had switched to testimonial-style ads.

Gateway's first users' group meeting was held to coincide with the 1987 DAC. Some of the more important milestones that the company achieved in marketing included:

- *May 1988:* Gateway was named the "hottest CAE [computer-aided engineering] growth company" by *Electronics* magazine.

- *February 1989:* A CAE analyst described Verilog as "the clear-cut winner in mixed-level simulation."

- *June 1989:* Prabhu was named "entrepreneur of the year" by *Inc.* magazine.

- *July 1989: Electronics* magazine claimed that Gateway had become Mentor's main rival, despite the fact that Mentor was over twenty times larger than Gateway.

PEOPLE AND CULTURE

As noted earlier, Gateway operated during its formative years without a board, CFO, sales or marketing personnel, a customer service department, or a head of engineering. Responsibility for these functions initially rested with one person and, as the company grew, was distributed among the developers. Thus, Gateway gave its employees enormous responsibility. Occasionally, that trust was misplaced, and Prabhu had to learn the difficult lesson that it is unwise to wait too long to make personnel changes when someone gets in over his or her head. Prabhu summed up his feelings about employees as follows:

Other than our focus on product and financial control, there was persistence, hard work, and recruiting the right people. We let people run with their mission rather than trying to control things too closely. We may not have always hired people on paper that had the experience for the job, but as they exercised their positions, they flowered. I also think that having a technologist at the top helped. In the beginning, when we were out there with the customers, I was able to relate to their product needs in the marketplace.

Clearly, Prabhu set the product, technology, quality, and teamwork standards for the company—i.e., he established its culture. The following story told by Prabhu illustrates the important role that commitment and teamwork played in Gateway's success. It describes an event that not only generated business for Gateway but incidentally turned out to be an excellent team-building project as well.

On [the] Friday before Memorial Day weekend in 1986, Prabhu was on the West Coast and learned that the company was third in a race for a Hughes benchmark of mixed-level simulation that the whole industry was watching. The leading contender had a capability, stochastic analysis, that Hughes felt they needed. Prabhu called a friend, who explained stochastic analysis. Prabhu called back to the company and outlined a plan to add the capability to Verilog. All eight engineers in the company canceled their weekend plans.

On the plane back, Prabhu worked on the benchmark and a demo to exploit the new capability. The demo, which relied on having extended graphics monitoring of queues (the company called these dancing bar charts), turned out to provide a dramatic demonstration of the product that also helped sell it. Gateway had listened to the Hughes requirement (because they would have otherwise lost the sale), and by winning the benchmark, Gateway got the business and a number of other contracts.

Henry McCance observed:

Gateway was such a joy because Prabhu operated openly and was a great listener and fast learner.... We said, "Why don't you look at Hale and Dorr as counsel?" Within the month, they were signed up. . . . The board suggested [creating] a technical advisory board, and by the next board meeting, the company had a first-rate TAB.

Ronna describes the company like this:

[Gateway's] ability to market itself to itself was very important. At the first Annual Gateway End of Fiscal Year Party in 1987, as he [Prabhu] was introduced as not being affected by success in light of all the publicity, he shed his normally conservative business attire and came out in a sequin-covered suit to the *Saturday Night Fever* sound track. Next year, he was dressed as Batman. The company wanted to reflect its goal of having innovation and fun.

CASH, FINANCEABILITY, AND CONTROL (AND PROFITABILITY)

A key part of Gateway's culture involved being in control, not spending money before it was earned, having adequate cash, and being profitable every year. In Prabhu's words:

> We never allowed ourselves to believe that we could spend more than we had. From the beginning, there just wasn't a huge cash reserve, and I felt the time I'd spend getting the extra money would take longer than it would to get the product out the door. As we grew, we also had the independence to focus on the fundamentals but not constrain ourselves to a quarter-to-quarter focus.

Henry McCance described several elements of the Gateway culture that were instrumental in the firm's success:

> Prabhu went to auctions and bought supplies from companies we had funded that were going under. . . . Prabhu did it differently. Most software companies book products they can't ship and then start spending against the soft bookings. Prabhu only booked products he could ship and then shipped products against this backlog. He just forgot to bill until the next fiscal year and was able to save on taxes.

Similarly, when Gateway went to its first trade show in Las Vegas, it hired a demo van (which doubled as a hotel room and moving billboard) because the company might not have been able to demonstrate its products in a hotel suite. In this regard, it is unclear how much Gateway's culture will change now that Gateway has become part of Cadence and Prabhu has stopped staying in inexpensive motels.

GENSYM: OUT OF THE ASHES

In September 1983, Bob Moore came to Lisp Machines, Inc. (LMI), to head a division developing expert systems for process control. Bob had a Ph.D. from MIT in electrical engineering and had been in the process-control industry for more than a decade, with experience in managing marketing, sales, and engineering. Lowell Hawkinson, an alumnus of MIT's Artificial Intelligence (AI) Laboratory, led the development effort. Over the next three years, LMI spent about $3 million to develop Picon, a rule-based process-control program, the first product of its type. Picon was demonstrated in 1984 and in 1985 was put on-line at Exxon and Texaco. The division, with about ten professionals, had roughly a dozen major customers, and its sales exceeded half a million dollars.

At the AAAI (American Association of Artificial Intelligence) Conference in August 1986, the Picon team came to the realization that LMI had no future. The team's members reasoned that unless they formed themselves into a separate company, it was likely that little would ever come of their product and their work.

Two LMI vice presidents had just been dismissed, and the firm was headed for a painful restructuring. However, strong forces on the board supported Picon. LMI was in the process of getting yet another round of financing. Its president, Ward McKenzie, had come from Digital over a year earlier as part of an aggressive expansion of LMI based on building its second-generation LISP machine, which it and Symbolics had originally licensed from MIT. Ward raised $25 million and built a large, full-fledged computer company to manufacture, sell, and service products for the minuscule and slowly emerging AI market. LMI had wanted to compete with Symbolics, which was successfully building and selling essentially the same product. Symbolics was subsequently forced out of the LISP machine business as general-purpose workstations became faster.

CONCEPT AND SEED STAGES

Ed Fredkin—an entrepreneur, inventor, Boston University physics professor, computer pioneer, and venture capitalist—agreed in August 1986 to cofound and seed-fund the Picon development team. The concept stage was completed in two weeks, with a plan created by the six key team members. Their intention was to license Picon from LMI or build a next-generation version of a Piconlike product from scratch if LMI refused to license Picon. They stopped communication with LMI, and the team resigned (taking no proprietary material with them). Gensym was incorporated two days later, with the aid of $300,000 from Fredkin. The team began looking for office space and computers.

Figure 11-7 shows the status of the Gensym start-up at the concept and seed stages.

PRODUCT DEVELOPMENT STAGE

The product development stage began in late September 1986. Host computers were provided by Symbolics and Texas Instruments (TI). The team started developing a product that would have substantially more capability than Picon. Gensym's president, Bob Moore (using the Finis Conner model of product development: "Sell, design, build"), began talking to customers to survey their needs.

Gensym's five-year business plan, written in the fall of 1986 and revised in January 1987, called for $93 million in sales in 1991. The plan showed $1 million in revenue in 1987

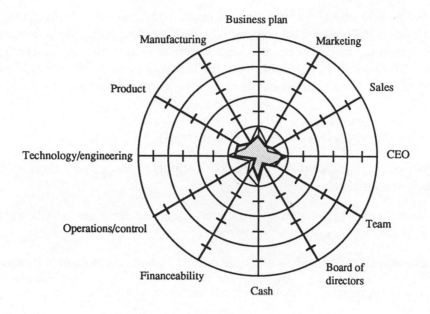

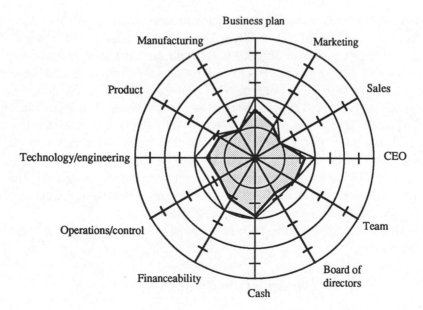

Figure 11-7. Relational Graphs for Gensym Showing the Concept Stage (Labor Day 1986) and Seed Stage (Late September 1986).

and an 11 percent after-tax profit based on sales of $6 million in 1988. In April 1987, the firm's product, G2, entered beta testing. The basic funding plan was to keep a low profile, minimize funding from the venture capital community, and make a few strategic alliances. In March 1987, Gensym had contact with about fifty venture capitalists. Bob Moore believed that the following factors accounted for their lack of interest:

- AI and expert-systems software were out of favor.

- The venture capitalists didn't believe the overly optimistic business plan for selling process-control systems.

- The company's valuation was considered excessive, since it was unwilling to give up controlling interest.

- Gensym's estimate that it would need only $2 million was thought to be naive.

- The development schedule was regarded as overly optimistic.

- The company would not send out business plans except on a strict nondisclosure basis.

In May 1987, $1 million of stock was sold to private investors and Palmer Associates, providing capitalization of $1.6 million. The founders retained 70 percent of the company for their investment of $50,000. Gensym demonstrated its first product in August. Beginning in September, it sold and installed the early version of the product at several sites, including Du Pont, in what Gensym's chief scientist described as a combined alpha/beta test. G2 was also used as part of a more complex product being developed by Reliable Water, a company founded by Fredkin to build desalinization plants. In September 1987, Gigamos, the firm that had bought rights to the LMI technology after LMI's bankruptcy, sued Gensym for damages; in June 1988, the case was settled out of court for an undisclosed amount, with the parties agreeing that both were free to pursue their own interests. During the period when the product was being finished, alpha/beta-stage sales were about $250,000.

The relational graph in Figure 11-8 shows Gensym's status at the end of the product development stage.

MARKET DEVELOPMENT STAGE

In April 1988, just nineteen months after Gensym started up, G2 version 1.0 was introduced, marking the beginning of the market development stage. Another $1.1

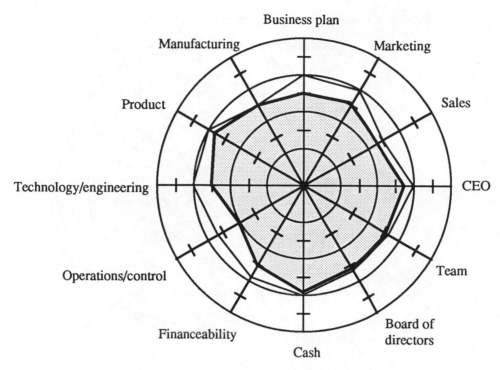

Figure 11-8. Relational Graph for Gensym Showing the Product Development Stage (April 1988).

million of financing was raised at $1.60 per share, to give Gensym a valuation of $6.4 million. The company had its first profitable quarter ending September 1988. By the end of 1989, Gensym had operated profitably for six consecutive quarters. Its after-tax profit was very nearly 15 percent on revenues of approximately $5 million, and Gensym entered the steady-state stage. The relational graph in Figure 11-9 shows Gensym's status at this point.

Although the market calibration and market expansion stages, which are marked by the first profitable quarter, usually take a total of between one and two years, these stages actually took six months in Gensym's case. The fact that the product was first delivered in September 1987 accounts for the shortened time frame. In effect, the company overlapped the last stage of product development with the first stage of market calibration. Market development really started when Gensym delivered G2 beta units to the first customers, even though the final product wasn't announced for wide-scale sale until seven months later, in April. The second major version of the product, 1.11, shipped in March 1989, and version 2.0 shipped in August 1990.

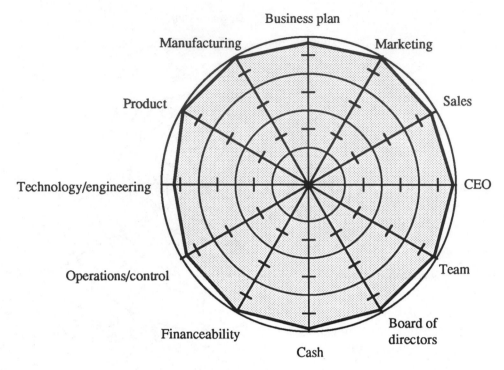

Figure 11-9. Relational Graph for Gensym Showing the Market Development Stage (January 1990).

TECHNOLOGY, ENGINEERING, AND PRODUCT

Gensym's technology was developed over a ten-year period, with ideas coming from Moore's process-control experience as well as the experience of Lowell and Michael Levine (the chief scientist) at MIT's Artificial Intelligence Laboratory. Clearly, the bulk of the firm's technological understanding came from building Picon at LMI.

Gensym's engineering style was characteristic of the MIT AI Lab's tradition of attracting bright people, giving them lots of computing resources, and generally leaving them alone. Several companies emerged from this environment, including Gold Hill, LMI, Symbolics, and Thinking Machines Corporation.

The January 1987 plan called for a beta release in April of that year (three months later), but this did not occur until August (seven months later), giving a schedule fantasy factor of 2.3. The chief scientist described the development project as mildly chaotic, since the group did not work according to any classic software-development-process model, nor did it start with a rigorous schedule or specification. A cursory product description came into existence in the spring of 1988. According to the usual definition and metrics of software control, the software-engineering process was out of control from the beginning until the completion of product development. The development project simply proceeded on the faith that the individuals involved could "do it again." After all, given G2's relationship to Picon, it was the team's second system.

In 1990, Gensym's ability to complete software engineering according to its schedule has improved considerably. Both the SFF and the quality level of its releases, measured in faults per one thousand lines of LISP code, have also improved.

Gensym epitomizes the software product company whose engineers were trained to be creative and then rewarded for their creativity. As Gensym grows, its challenge will be to keep ahead of competitors who build knockoff products by the software-engineering book.

PLAN

Gensym's initial plans are shown in Table 11-3.

Bob Moore's 1983 business plan prior to coming to LMI was to produce revenues of $25 million by the end of the fifth year on an investment of $2 million. This plan turned out to be more accurate and realistic than the January 1987 and December 1987 plans.

All three of these plans were highly optimistic and tended to focus on what was possible rather than what was likely to happen. For example, the entire distributed process-control market was projected by one market survey company to grow from $200 million in 1980 to $3 billion in 1990! However, all the plans were difficult to validate in terms of the time it would take for the conservative process-control market to develop. Quite probably, each plan was oriented toward the "greedy" investor who wanted to see a $100 million business in five years. None of the plans was calibrated or modeled as to likelihood or according to market development and order-gestation times.

MARKETING AND SALES

From the start, Gensym tried to interest various hardware platform and process-control companies in becoming strategic partners in order to help with funding. Symbolics and TI saw this need and responded with hardware. A number of early users helped with the development, including Du Pont and Reliable Water.

The president of Gensym also headed marketing and sales, where his experience in all phases of the business, including development, proved especially valuable. Because its president wore several corporate "hats," Gensym knew the critical applications and customers intuitively and quantitatively and was also able to maintain a direct link with customers at the highest level.

Table 11-3. Gensym's First Plans Versus Actual Revenue.

	1987	1988	1989	1990	1991
1/87 plan revenue[a]	0.98	6.10	21.10	54.2	92.8
1/87 plan profit[a]	-0.60	0.60	2.80	10.2	19.7
12/87 plan revenue[a]	0.60	2.30	4.80	14.2	42.9
12/87 plan profit[a]	-1.00	-0.47	-0.50	2.2	7.8
Actual revenue	[a]0.52	1.87	4.50	8.0	—
Actual profit[a]	-0.90	-0.50[b]	0.70	N.A.	—
G2's product-release cycle	beta	1.0	1.11	2.0	—

[a]In millions of dollars.
[b]Includes third-quarter profit of $80,000 and fourth-quarter profit of $80,000.

PEOPLE

All of Gensym's founders had worked together on Picon as a team at LMI and were technically oriented toward the product and the market area. Lowell, the chairman of the board and CEO, and Bob run the company as a team and focus on the inside (product development and operations) as well as the outside (marketing and sales).

After the first round of investment, the board consisted of the three founders (Lowell, Bob, and Ed), together with one of the venture capitalists and Ted Johnson, former vice president of sales at DEC. Ed claimed that the board played a critical role by insisting on early profitability, which Lowell felt may have been achieved at the expense of a potentially higher growth rate.

CASH, FINANCEABILITY, AND CONTROL

By one measure of control, Gensym didn't make its top line. Faced with this problem, a typical start-up would begin to decline, entering a stage of "hoping for a better top line" as it ran out of money. The keys to Gensym's success were financial control, not spending ahead of its reduced revenue, and being able to meet the bottom line. The fact that the founders own a large fraction of the company perhaps helped with control, even though they had only invested a relatively small amount of cash. Bob Moore contrasts the plan with the actual outcome:

> As far as the early business plan is concerned, we have actually followed the plan, except with the "time axis" stretched out. . . . [T]he investment to start Gensym was projected at

$2 million, and this was almost exactly what it took. Basically, everything happened slower, including product development, hiring, sales, etc. But we kept in balance and built the company "according to plan" at a slower pace.

Gensym became profitable in its eighth quarter. Financing took a minimum amount of time away from running the firm.

With a healthy balance sheet, Gensym has lots of options if it needs cash for growth, provided it remains profitable. Going public would force the team to spend more time dealing with the externalities of finance, and this would hardly be worth the risk until the company is substantially larger. A merger might be possible, but this would jeopardize Gensym's culture and growth potential. Clearly, the firm is in an ideal position until it becomes visible enough to attract significant competitors.

EPILOGUE

In July 1990, Gensym bought Picon for slightly over $50,000 at an auction conducted by a judge selling the assets of Gigamos.

MASPAR:
A MASSIVELY PARALLEL, COMPUTER SYSTEMS COMPANY

In the late 1960s, Westinghouse built the first computer with a single instruction stream controlling multiple data streams (referred to as an SIMD-type computer). Other SIMDs were constructed in the 1970s, including ILLIAC IV, built by the University of Illinois with Burroughs; the MPP, built by Goodyear; and the DAP, built by ICL. In 1990, the basic DAP architecture is still being sold. In 1985, Thinking Machines Corporation (TMC) introduced a massively parallel SIMD computer called the Connection Machine. Based on a 1981 Ph.D. dissertation by TMC founder Danny Hillis, the computer has sixteen thousand to sixty-four thousand processing elements. In 1982, Tom Blank wrote a Stanford Ph.D. dissertation on an SIMD computer to be used for simulating digital systems. During a 1987 semiconductor conference, a team from Jeff Kalb's group at DEC reported on the design of VLSI chips for an SIMD computer. Each chip had thirty-two processing elements.

CONCEPT AND SEED STAGES

In July 1987, Kalb—a technologist and manager with fifteen years' experience at National Semiconductors, Data General, and DEC—moved to California to explore new opportunities, including the possibility of exploiting DEC's SIMD architecture with its blessing. In September, at the offices of the venture capital firm Merrill, Pickard,

Anderson, and Eyre (MPA&E), he began writing the MasPar business plan to develop a massively parallel computer based on DEC's VLSI chips and architecture. In October, MasPar was founded, and the second employee, Jim Peachy, a Hewlett-Packard manufacturing alumnus and former chief operating officer (COO) of Pyramid, joined. In November, negotiations with DEC broke down, and Kalb sought out Tom Blank, who had become a Stanford professor, to help write the business plan based on an alternative architecture.

On January 6, 1988, the business plan was complete, and Blank signed on as architect and head of computer applications. MasPar began the search for start-up funds. The plan called for raising $24 million, in three installments, for the firm to go public. MasPar's product, priced at less than half a million dollars, would deliver computing power equal to roughly half that of a $22 million Cray YMP supercomputer. Specifically, the MasPar product was a scalable, massively parallel computer that could deliver a peak of 1.2 gigaflops or 30 gigaops on 32-bit integers using up to sixteen thousand processors in steps of one thousand processors. The price range was $60,000 to $350,000 for 128 megabytes of memory, excluding the front-end workstation. The first shipments to universities and laboratories were scheduled for the fourth quarter of 1988. For the first four years, beginning in 1989, MasPar projected revenues of $1.8 million, $11 million, $26 million, and $93 million.

The market sizes were derived from Dataquest's segmentation into price bands and application. MasPar targeted the two largest Dataquest segments, design automation and scientific (a very general market). The "why buy" marketing question was answered as follows: one to two orders of magnitude in performance and/or price/performance, software libraries to handle the parallel operations, a VAR and OEM strategy for applications, high reliability through engineering, and a full systems capability with a well-funded field sales and support organization.

In February 1988, John Nikolls and Peter Christy arrived to head hardware and software development and to complete the core development team.

The relational graph in Figure 11-10 shows the status of the MasPar start-up upon completion of the concept and seed stages.

PRODUCT DEVELOPMENT STAGE

By March 1988, the first venture financing was complete, with $6.5 million in the bank at $0.67 per share. The company valued itself at $10.8 million. Jim Anderson of MPA&E and Floyd Kvamme of Kleiner, Perkins, Caufield, and Byers joined Jeff to form the board of directors. Anderson and Kvamme also helped with the early marketing and planning work.

Since MasPar did not conduct a seed stage during which the product and development project could be planned in great detail, all the detailed planning was pushed

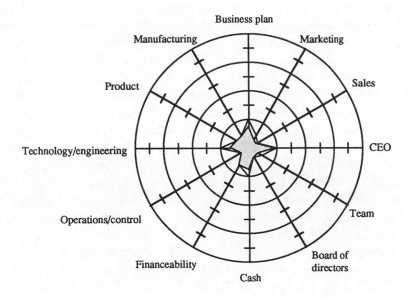

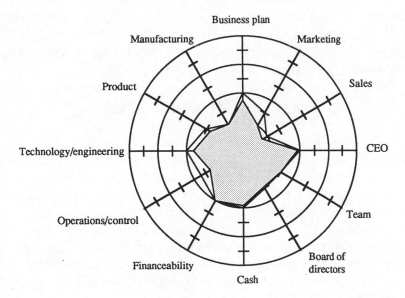

Figure 11-10. Relational Graphs for MasPar Showing the Concept Stage (October 1987) and Seed Stage (March 1988).

into the first part of the product development stage, during which the product specifications and schedule were being prepared and hiring was taking place. By September 1988, the product was specified, a seventeen-member engineering staff was on board, and a detailed development schedule had been prepared. At this point, detailed design was started, and by November, a simulation of the architecture was completed. The custom chips operated in April 1989, and in July, the logic was completely simulated using a hardware simulator. The product-design stage ended in October, when the fabricated product prototype entered the debugging stage (IIIc) to begin alpha testing. On October 18, during the northern California earthquake, a logic analyzer fell on the system, disrupting the schedule. Another six-week slip occurred because certain components failed to meet their specifications.

In June 1989, MasPar acquired its second round of financing, raising $11 million at $1.15 per share, giving it a valuation of $30.8 million. Daniel Tompkins, a former CFO and a partner in DSC Ventures, was added to the board.

In December 1989, the product operated. On January 9, 1990, alpha testing was completed, and MasPar announced its MP-1 family of products. Five computers were operational. With the announcement, the first computer was also delivered to a customer to begin beta testing. Two basic models were introduced, with from one thousand to four thousand and from one thousand to sixteen thousand processing elements, delivering a peak of 1.3 gigaflops or 26 gigaops and priced from $170,000 to $810,000 for systems with 256 megabytes of memory and the front-end workstation. The targeted markets included computational fluid dynamics, computational chemistry, image and signal processing, and VLSI design.

The relational graph in Figure 11-11 shows the status of the MasPar start-up at the end of the product development stage.

MARKET DEVELOPMENT STAGE

Although beta testing was not completed until May 1990, with the shipment of six units, production-unit shipment had begun in March of that year. Stage IVa (market calibration) began with the product announcement. By May, the order-gestation time was six to nine months, versus a planed three to six months. Critical applications programs in each targeted market area began being ported to start a vertical marketing approach. Distribution relationships were established to provide multiple market segments.

In late June 1990, the third round of financing was completed, based on a private placement memorandum issued in late March. The five-year plan, beginning in 1990, projects revenues of $3.1 million, $19 million, $52 million, $106 million, and $177 million, with profitability in 1992. Another $15.5 million (for a total of $32.6 million) was raised at $1.85 per share, bringing the valuation to $66.5 million. Although only $10 million had been sought, the oversubscription was high enough to increase the financing. As Jeff

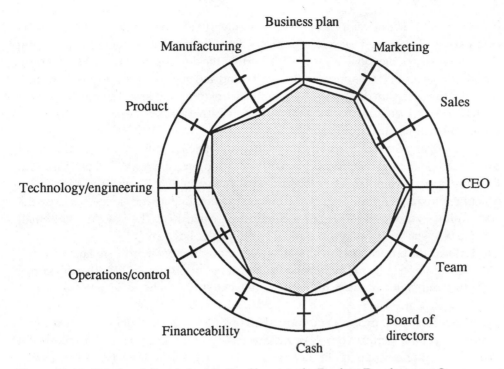

Figure 11-11. Relational Graph for MasPar Showing the Product Development Stage
(January 1990).

Kalb remarked, given the enormous investment in raising the capital, MasPar followed
Kleiner's law: "When the hors d'oeuvres are passed, take two."

After the introduction, MasPar was shipping at a rate of almost one machine per
week at an average selling price of over $200,000. Demand in Europe was the highest for
large machines. Small machines were shipped in the United States, Japan, and Australia
to early adopters and to seed OEMs for product development.

Dave Cane, a founder of MassComp, lists three necessary conditions for a successful
start-up: "[having] a very good product, keeping the customers happy, and not running
out of money. In order to do this, the team must find the work relatively easy to do
because everything else about starting up is so hard." The MasPar story seems to
embody these three principles.

TECHNOLOGY, PRODUCT, AND MANUFACTURING

Product development actually took twenty-four months, in contrast to the originally
planned nineteen months, which translates into a schedule fantasy factor of 1.26 (i.e., 24

divided by 19). The development cost of roughly $10 million was about 1.5 times the original plan. However, in absolute terms, the development time was short, considering the complexity of the MasPar product, including the development of two VLSI chips. Although the product was one of the first of its kind and involved breaking new ground, the entire project team did have experience in developing successful products, and the design process, including the design of the two chips that formed the product's core, was within the team's capabilities.

In 1990, any team that is building its first custom chip of four hundred thousand transistors can expect the process to take at least two years before a final product with the chip can be shipped. Dave Nelson—a founder of Apollo and CEO of Fluent Machines, a company building a workstation incorporating digital video—sums up the conventional wisdom regarding custom chip design like this: "The way to make a small fortune is to start with a large one and do custom VLSI design."

Kalb ran the project, coordinating architecture, applications, hardware, and software. He was able to handle all these responsibilities because some of his other functions including managing manufacturing were delegated to Peachy, who acted as a chief operating officer.

The first MasPar products performed according to plan and delivered their rated performance and performance/price characteristics on highly parallel applications. Provided that a particular application requires parallelism, the MasPar computer often outperforms the Cray YMP supercomputer.

The situation in massively parallel computing is highly competitive. MasPar is providing a lower-cost alternative to the Connection Machine using the SIMD approach. Alliant, Intel, and NCUBE use the multicomputer approach by interconnecting a large number of ordinary microprocessors. Both approaches are programmed in a similar fashion.

PLAN

The plans used to secure funding were very crisp, clear, and basically correct. The original plan for starting the company consisted of seventy-six pages, whose breakdown is shown in Table 11-4.

Had MasPar gone through a seed stage for planning, its plan would have been more accurate with respect to the project schedule and resources, but it's unlikely that all of the team would have signed on to write a seed stage business plan.

The private placement memorandum consisted of forty-two pages, not counting an additional twenty-five pages of financial and stockholder information and product literature.

Table 11-4. Elements of MasPar's Original Plan.

Element	No. of Pages
Summary and short form	8
Parallel-processing tutorial	8
Product and implementation	13
Potential applications	3
Business strategy, including market size, development schedule, and manufacturing	20
Competition	7
Risks and future product directions	3
Financial plan with detailed product cost	12
People	2

MARKETING AND SALES

When MasPar first started, the board served as marketing advisers. In October 1988, a vice president of marketing was hired from Convex and became responsible for industry applications marketing. In April 1989, the head of sales joined from Silicon Graphics, where he had headed North American field operations. The strategy of selling computational-intense, parallelizable applications programs for customers buying minicomputer-priced products is based on a highly segmented and niche market.

Although MasPar achieved its product-design goal, the company's success will depend first of all on how well the marketing and sales organizations are able to segment the applications (e.g., logic simulation, computational fluid dynamics) that can fit the architecture. This challenge is identical to the one that Ardent faced when it introduced the graphics supercomputer. Next, MasPar must find the right customers, including developing the channels of distribution with VARs, OEMs, system integrators, and independent software vendors that develop applications to exploit the SIMD architecture. No small part of the problem will be to educate potential users about the nontrivial nature of parallel programming. Alternatively, given the computer's input/output structure, it can be configured for a variety of tasks, including databases, communications switching, and display.

Kalb sees Blank's role as head of both architecture and applications as critical: "Unless the architect understands how the computer does on real problems, we have no way to exploit and eventually improve the architecture."

As noted above, MasPar's future will depend solely on how effectively the marketing organization first segments the market and then develops the critical segments. Given the finicky and difficult nature of parallelism, MasPar's success will be achieved on an application-by-application basis. The Stardent product and market-positioning flaw (discussed in Chapter 8) should serve as a useful guide.

PEOPLE

MasPar started as a product development-centered team and was led by a technologist and manager. The top team members all had the right experience and backgrounds. Having a COO was critical because Kalb played such a key role in engineering the product. In later stages, a vice president of engineering may be required to take some of the load off of Kalb. Overall, it is hard to believe that the people dimension could have been improved. However, until the product is successful, the marketing and sales strategy and personnel remain untested.

CASH, FINANCEABILITY, AND CONTROL

MasPar performed in an almost textbook fashion with regard to the cash, financeability, and control dimensions, despite the product-schedule and cost overruns. The fact that the original plan overestimated general and administrative costs helped to offset the increase in research and development costs. Hiring the original team took longer than expected, thereby decreasing spending and lengthening the development schedule. However, by taking more time and operating with fewer people, MasPar probably developed a better product and plan.

MasPar used management by objectives, staff meetings, and weekly reviews to manage and track progress.

THINKING MACHINES CORPORATION: THE FIRST MASSIVELY PARALLEL COMPUTER COMPANY— GOVERNMENT AND VENTURE FINANCING

Massively parallel computing is no exception to Silver's start-up rule: "Anything worth doing is worth duplicating." In 1990, AMT (derived from ICL's DAP), MasPar, Thinking Machines Corporation (TMC), and Wavetracer offer SIMD computers, segmented by price and application. About twenty computer companies offer multicomputers based on interconnected microprocessors. All are aimed at providing large amounts of computation for highly parallel applications, generally in the technical computing market.

In the spring of 1983, TMC started up in Cambridge, Massachusetts, to build a large, massively parallel SIMD computer. The company was initially financed by a number of private investors, including William Paley and Frank Stanton of CBS. By 1990, over $40 million was raised to finance the firm, which has a valuation of nearly $200 million.

TMC's first Connection Machine was delivered in 1985. Unlike nearly all its SIMD competitors, TMC sells high-end computers in the $1 million to $10 million range, which it defines as supercomputers. As is the case with Cray and IBM products, the cost of TMC's machines includes support personnel who help with customer applications. As a by-product, these support personnel become experts in applications and help sell additional computers. In 1989, TMC's first profitable year, the company's product revenues reached almost $40 million.

TMC is backed by the Defense Advanced Research Projects Agency (DARPA) Strategic Computing Initiative, whose goal is to develop a teraflop computer by the mid-1990s. A substantial amount of the product development funding comes from DARPA. For example, in 1989, TMC was awarded a three-year, $12 million contract aimed at building a 1-teraflop computer. The SIMD and the multicomputer, unlike traditional supercomputers, can be built in a scalable fashion to provide the most peak computing power. Government agencies and universities either buy or are given DARPA-purchased machines in order to encourage, understand, and develop the use of such machines. By 1990, TMC had sold about fifty computers for large database retrieval, petroleum exploration, and computational fluid dynamics.

CONCLUSION

This chapter has presented the stories of eight high-tech ventures to give readers some insight into how it should—and shouldn't—be done. The first two examples illustrated two classic failure modes for a start-up: no product but excellent marketing (Ovation), and good product but wrong approach to the market (Analytica). The last six examples illustrated how to create healthy component, system, and software firms. The Bell-Mason Diagnostic (Chapter 10) was used as an overall framework for discussing and evaluating the companies.

Chapter 12

TECHNICAL WORKSTATIONS: HEURISTICS FROM HISTORY

The first decade of scientific and engineering workstation development provides useful lessons for information-technology start-ups. Many of the observations presented in this chapter have been used as heuristics to develop the rules that form the "ideal" model for the Bell-Mason Diagnostic.

In the mainframe and time-shared systems of the 1970s, Teletypes and simple alphanumeric cathode-ray-tube (CRT) terminals provided the primary user interface. High-priced, high-performance terminals were employed for scientific and engineering applications that required the display of graphical and image information.

In the 1980s, distributed workstations interconnected via a local area network (LAN) were developed. These featured high-performance graphics combined with computation and were dedicated to a single user. This powerful tool enabled new applications in computer-aided analysis, design, engineering, and visualization that had previously been economically infeasible or impossible.

In 1981 and 1982, Apollo Computer and Sun Microsystems came out with the first low-cost and practical workstations, followed by Hewlett-Packard (HP). These machines were based on the Motorola 68000 and its successor microprocessors. During the first five years after the 68000 was introduced, over twenty-five new companies were started. Products were introduced so fast and furiously that they were nicknamed JAWS, for "just another workstation." Soon after Apollo and Sun,

Silicon Graphics Incorporated (SGI) was founded to deliver high-performance terminals and workstations capable of displaying 3-D objects dynamically.

By 1988, faster, second-generation workstations were introduced based on the reduced instruction set computer (RISC) architectures of Apollo, HP, IBM, Intergraph, MIPS, and Sun. Ardent and Stellar introduced graphics supercomputers that provided both very-high-performance graphics and computation capability using vector processing and multiprocessing. These entrants became the forerunners of third-generation workstations capable of providing personal supercomputing.

By 1990, HP/Apollo, IBM, SGI, and Stardent had all introduced workstations of such power that they became known as superworkstations. With the cost of 3-D graphics dropping to affordable levels, permitting use by many professionals in technical fields, these workstations are beginning to supplant traditional supercomputing.

Nearly all the traditional mainframe and minicomputer companies regard the workstation as a critical product. However, despite the great numbers of firms in the business, a scant six of them provide 95 percent (by volume) of the workstations sold. Of these, two are 1980s workstation start-ups that have remained healthy and independent: Sun and SGI. The other four are established companies that introduced workstation products to serve their customer base, which was being eroded by the new form of computing: Digital Equipment Corporation (DEC), HP (including its Apollo division), IBM, and Intergraph. These big firms intend to become even bigger players in the workstation field. IBM, for instance, has stated (in its R6000 product announcement) that it intends to capture 30 percent of the workstation market by 1993.

The rampaging progress occurring on the workstation front does not mean that the lowly PC is a thing of the past, however. Far from it! In 1990, PCs with VGA graphics have about half the resolution of workstations and only display 2-D graphics, but by using Microsoft Windows software on a PC, much of the capability of workstations (including 3-D interaction) can be provided at a low cost due to the high production volume of PCs. By the mid-1990s, it is possible that the workstation market will decline into a niche, to be replaced by a range of high-performance PCs. Alternatively, the workstation could limit the PC's upward growth. Given the difference in the software that runs on the two environments (UNIX versus Microsoft's DOS and OS/2 evolving toward UNIX), the two are unlikely to merge.

BACKGROUND

The notion of a personal workstation is a matter not just of market application need but also of technology, sociology, and economics. Owning one's own computer has been the goal of designers and users since computers were first introduced. The earliest laboratory computers were used interactively and personally, even though they often cost millions of dollars. In the early 1950s, MIT's building-size Whirlwind computer (with CRT) was used to experiment with the first air-traffic-control system, do computer-aided design, and visualize scientific and engineering simulations—exactly what computers are still likely to be doing in the twenty-first century. Readers interested in an in-depth discussion of the emergence of workstations can refer to Goldberg's (1988) *History of Personal Workstations.*

In 1957, MIT and MIT's Lincoln Laboratory provided both the technology and the engineer training that led to the formation of Digital Equipment Corporation. DEC built the first small, interactive computers, which were the basis of the minicomputer industry. Its first computer, the PDP-1 (with CRT), was introduced in 1960 at a price of $120,000. This might have set DEC on the path toward building workstations, but it went on in the early 1960s to build large time-shared computers because of the economics of sharing, while forgetting the paradigm of one person/ one computer upon which the company was founded.[1] Similarly, it did not take the opportunistic path of building workstations based on Motorola's 68000 but instead waited until it had a VAX on a chip. By then, however, Sun was too firmly established.

In the late 1960s, the key ideas for graphics were being researched at the University of Utah by Dave Evans, Ivan Sutherland, and their graduate students under the sponsorship of DARPA (Defense Advanced Research Projects Agency). Evans and Sutherland company was created to commercialize this technology. The most important output of Utah and Evans and Sutherland was the generation of alumni who created workstations and graphics, including Jim Blinn (Jet Propulsion Laboratory); Ed Catmul (Pixar); Jim Clark (SGI); Charles Csuri, Phong Bui-Tuong, and H. Gouraud (who developed shading algorithms); Alan Kay (Apple); Martin Newell; and John Warnock (Adobe).

As is the case with virtually all technological shifts, the suppliers of graphics terminals connected to mainframes and minicomputers were unable to make the transition to become workstation suppliers. Such a transition would have required terminal companies to fund and become expert in computer systems and their application.

---

1. I accept much of the blame for this oversight, since I headed research and development at Digital from 1973 to 1983. When a computer is shared, the operating system's goal is to prevent a user program from gaining access to a terminal. With workstations, the major goal is to provide the best possible communication between the display and the program.

XEROX

Xerox's Palo Alto Research Center (PARC) built the first distributed LAN-based computing environment. Human-interface aids such as the "mouse" and "icons" were derived from Engelbardt's Augmentation Research Center at the Stanford Research Institute during the period 1964–1975. Although the PARC researchers, trained in computer science, were directed to provide a computing environment for the office, their main concern was providing a computing environment for themselves. Workstations and time-shared systems exemplify instances where the designers themselves were the first users or target consumers of the system.[2] They wanted a computing environment that they could own individually and that would therefore not degrade with more users.

The PARC workstation, based on Data General's Nova architecture, was called the Alto. Altos were interconnected via the first local area network, a 3-megabit-per-second ancestor of today's Ethernet. By October 1976, the first Altos operated in a network environment with applications, and the first user's manual appeared. In 1980, Xerox introduced the STAR workstation based on the Alto. Lampson (Table 12-1) has traced the ideas that influenced successor commercial computers. An account of PARC's influence on computing is also given in *Fumbling the Future* (Smith and Alexander, 1988).

The following are some observations based on the Xerox PARC story:

- Anytime a system can be built in which the designers are also the users, the system evolves much more rapidly, with higher quality, and to a higher state than with other types of products that rely on specifications.[3]

- The disadvantage of designing a product for oneself is that such products, though powerful, may not be easy for novices to use.

- Achieving success in the laboratory is no guarantee of success in the marketplace.

- Unless a large organization is already in the business in which new-product

---

2. Hewlett-Packard successfully incorporated this idea into its culture from the beginning, as "the next-bench syndrome," whereby HP engineers built instruments for use by their fellow HP engineers.

3. UNIX is an excellent example of such a system designed by computer scientists for users with a computer-science background. Because it was oriented toward technical users, UNIX provided an opportunity for other start-ups to develop a superior graphics user interface for humans.

Table 12-1. Descendants of Xerox PARC's Alto.

Engineering workstations	PERQ, Apollo, Sun, Tektronix, DEC
AI [artificial intelligence] workstations	Xerox 11xx, MIT Lisp machine, Symbolics and Lisp Machines, Inc.
Personal computers	Xerox 8065, Apple Lisa, Macintosh, Metaphor
Office workstations	Xerox 8010, Convergent, Apple Macintosh, Grid
Graphics terminals	BBN Bitgraph, Bell Labs Blit
Local area net[work]s	Ethernet/IEEE 802.3
Network protocols	DARPA TCP/IP, Xerox Network Services
Laser printers	Xerox 9700, etc.; Imagen; Apple Laserwriter
Printing protocols	Xerox Interpress, Adobe Postscript
Servers	3Com file server, Xerox 8044, Apple Laserwriter
User interfaces	Xerox 8010, Apple Macintosh, Microsoft Windows, ParcPlace
Editors	MacWrite, Microsoft Word
Illustrators	Xerox 8010, Apple MacPaint and MacDraw, Aurora Systems

Source: B. Lampson, "Personal Distributed Computing: The Alto and Ethernet Software," in *A History of Personal Workstations*, ed. Adele Goldberg, © 1988, by ACM Press. Table 2, page 331. Reprinted with permission of Addison-Wesley Publishing, Inc., Reading, Massachusetts.

research is carried out, the company will find it quite difficult to transfer new technology and products into either a new division or the mainstream of the firm.

- It is easy to transfer research results to start-ups if an entrepreneurial environment, such as Silicon Valley, exists.

- The major beneficiary of general corporate research is most likely to be those who leave and start companies.

THREE RIVERS' PERQ: THE PIONEER GETS THE ARROWS

The first start-up to use the Alto workstation idea was the Three Rivers Computer Company, located in Pittsburgh. In 1978, Brian Rosen, a former PARC researcher, rejoined the firm (where he had worked while a CMU student) to design and build the PERQ computer. The location seemed appropriate because computer scientists at Carnegie-Mellon University (CMU) believed in and proselytized PARC's distributed model of computing. Many of PARC's researchers were CMU alumni, and the computer-science community was tired of sharing large, overloaded, time-shared DECSystem-10s. Furthermore, several CMU Science Department members invested in the company, bought PERQ computers for the department, and did a substantial amount of software development for the PERQ.

CMU had outlined the idea for the computing environment in a 1979 report for a large research project, stating that "the era of timesharing has ended." Time-sharing would be replaced by powerful "3M" (1 million instructions per second, 1 megabyte of primary memory, and a 1-million-pixel screen) distributed personal workstation computers, like the models seen at PARC. The first PERQ was delivered in 1980.

By 1982, Three Rivers was delivering tens of computers per month and had an original equipment manufacturer (OEM) relationship to supply computers to ICL for the British and European markets. Although Carnegie-Mellon was developing a substantial amount of software for the PERQ, Three Rivers was unable to incorporate it into the product and hence had a technology-transfer problem. By 1983, workstations from other companies were all being fabricated easily and cheaply using the 68000 microprocessor. The PERQ was based on designing a more expensive computer using microprogramming, a premicroprocessor method of computer design. The firm ceased operations in 1985 after delivering about 350 workstations.

The following are some observations based on the PERQ story:

- Being first is no guarantee of success.

  In fact, being first is often a detriment if the wrong basic technology is used. Potential competitors benefit from seeing how to make the product a better way.

- Hiring people with experience in the computer industry to build a Pittsburgh-based computer systems company proved very difficult, even though CMU trains key people in the industry. Several software-only start-ups, such as Tartan Labs, were unsuccessful because their founders lacked good local role models.

In Pittsburgh, the infrastructure (e.g., manufacturing, marketing, legal, and PR firms) to support computer manufacturing and companies in the computer industry is quite small. If an area is to support a technology, it must build up a complete infrastructure that understands the industry and how it operates. Areas such as Austin and Boulder have built industries to support high-information-technology start-ups, whereas Pittsburgh's industrial infrastructure supports heavy industry, such as steel and petroleum.

- Transferring software from a university to a company/product is difficult at best, even though the survivability of the company and the efficacy of the product might depend on the transfer.

The best way to transfer software is to transfer the people associated with its development (e.g., Bill Joy brought the Berkeley version of UNIX, BSD 4.2, to Sun).

- A company must be able to translate its own vision of computing, which it usually has, into a vision that appeals to users and other third parties who might apply the product to solve actual problems.

PERQ was evidently unable to do this, since it was ineffective at securing either OEMs or end users.

- Usually, there exists a single technology path on which to base a product, and virtually every successful company follows that path. Those that do not follow the right path perish.

In the case of workstations, an open standard based on the microprocessor and UNIX was the correct path. PERQ was not based on the right technology and had to develop its own system. When the market finally began to open up, doing all that development proved too expensive and time-consuming.

- A general-purpose computer built in a mass-production fashion almost always wins against special architectures.

For example, two specialized LISP-language workstation companies formed during the early 1980s: Symbolics and Lisp Machines, Inc. LMI is defunct, and Symbolics is reduced to selling software, because traditional microprocessors provided greater performance at negligible cost.

- At DEC, I institutionalized the principle governing what to make versus what to buy: "Make what we sell, not what we buy."

If a part or product can't be sold competitively at the required level of integration, buy it. There may be other considerations, but this one is key, obvious, and often overlooked. The inability to make good make/buy decisions can become a fatal flaw for both new and well-established companies.

APOLLO

The concept for Apollo originated with several researchers and engineers at Prime computer, following the outline of the CMU Spice Project that was using PERQ computers. The idea was to replace the central minicomputer and its expensive graphics terminals with distributed personal, computing graphics workstations. Prime, however, rejected this notion because it believed itself to be in the minicomputer business. This attitude is reminiscent of Levitt's (1986) classic observation that "The railroads didn't understand they were in the transportation business."

In January 1980, Bill Poduska, one of Prime's founders, Mike Greata, of engineering, and Dave Nelson, head of research, left Prime to secure funding for a workstation company. The Motorola 68000, the first microprocessor to have the necessary characteristics for a workstation (32-bit address space), had just been announced. The Prime engineers, as MIT Multics alumni, had experience in time-sharing and virtual memory. They also had experience in distributed LAN systems, having introduced a proprietary LAN ring to interconnect Prime minicomputers.

Apollo's concept stage lasted about a month. The firm was incorporated in mid-February 1980, and about ten people began developing the product. The average age of the founders was over forty, and all had start-up experience. The two-month seed stage was self-funded by the three founders while they planned the company, wrote their business plan, and secured capital. During the seed stage, the team continued product design and project planning in various living rooms and kitchens. The team was melded together from the two cultures of research and development. On April 22, funding totaling $1.6 million was secured based on a six-page, handwritten plan (page 39), and the firm moved into its first building.

In March 1981, after ten months in development, the first two-node networked system was shipped to Harvard University. Apollo shipped $3.5 million (versus a planned $5.5 million), $18 million, and $80 million and went public with an initial public offering (IPO) in March 1983. One of its customers, Mentor Graphics, started up at the same time, using the Apollo environment to create an electronic computer-aided design (ECAD) system for logic designers. About half of Apollo's sales were to Mentor during much of its independent life.

By the end of 1983, with an annualized run rate of about $100 million, Apollo's market value was $700 million. Poduska claimed that sixty of the thirteen hundred people in the firm became millionaires. In early 1989, before HP acquired the company, Apollo had annual sales of $700 million, and its valuation was about $300 million.

While Poduska was the chairman and CEO, Charlie Spector joined from Digital as president. Following Spector's departure, Tom Vanderslice was brought in as president and CEO in 1985. Vanderslice had managed a division at General Electric unrelated to computers or communications and had most recently been at GTE working in telecommunications.

After a year of studying how to build higher-power workstations, Poduska left Apollo to form Stellar Computer (incorporated in January 1986), with the purpose of building a graphics supercomputer to attack 3-D problems that Poduska believed could be solved neither by Apollo's existing 68000-based product line nor by the new DN10000 architecture then under development.

In 1989, Vanderslice sold Apollo to HP after it began to decline and become unprofitable. Nelson left to start Fluent Machines, a company that would build a multimedia workstation.

The Apollo experience gives rise to the following observations:

- Understanding and mastering the technologies is what enables a start-up to remain healthy and meet its product development schedule.

  Nearly all the technology required to build the Apollo workstation environment was fully understood by the company's founders. Although they had not done it before, they did have experience and spent a significant amount of time building the basis for Apollo's technology (i.e., determining what to do and how to do it).

- When blending people (in this case, engineers) from several cultures, it is critical to have an integration period during which people come to agree on goals, constraints, and values.

  During this initial period, various members are likely to leave. But as a project is started, the entire team must agree on its direction! In fact, venture capitalists commonly insist that a new venture's founders have worked together before. The seed stage can accomplish this goal. Many successful start-ups require each new member of the team to spend up to six months on probation before finally being accepted into the company.

- An initial relationship with an OEM customer can be a serendipitous event to fuel a newly launched company.

Such an OEM is likely to be a start-up itself, since a large firm will probably not want to risk buying from a start-up until the new venture is well established.

- Although conventional wisdom holds that entrepreneurs should "never put risks in serial by basing a new start-up on another start-up," this observation is flawed.

When entrepreneurs want to found an innovative company, their search for new technology is likely to lead them to a start-up. Part of the reason Mentor succeeded was that it concentrated on software and left the hardware to Apollo.

- From the earliest experiences in computing, when General Electric formed several unsuccessful computer divisions, it became obvious that hiring a general manager from outside the computer industry to head a computer division is risky.

Apollo declined under the leadership of Tom Vanderslice. Steve Jobs hired John Sculley, an event that ultimately caused Jobs to leave Apple. Whether Apple has been and will be better or worse off without a visionary as its leader won't be clear until 1995, a decade after Jobs' departure.

- Beware of being overconfident when a new technology appears.

Having mastered past technology is no guarantee that a company will master future technology. Stellar was founded on a product architecture and custom complementary metal oxide semiconductor (CMOS) chips; the project took twice as long as predicted, both because mastery of new technology was required and because the company built the processor portion, which it could have bought.

SUN MICROSYSTEMS

PARC also inspired Professor Forest Baskett and Andy Bechtolsheim, his graduate student at Stanford, to build the Stanford University Networked (Sun) workstation, which became the basis for Sun Microsystems. Vinod Khosla was the entrepreneur who stimulated the founding of Sun. Vinod was employed by Daisy and was searching for technology to make an electronic CAD workstation. Vinod became convinced that a general-purpose design was required and would be used by many other engineers. In May 1980, he visited Stanford and saw Andy Bechtolsheim and the Sun workstation. Andy offered to serve as a consultant on the design for $10,000. However, Vinod convinced Andy to abandon his quest for a Ph.D. and help him start

Sun. Vinod has succinctly expressed a most critical principle of technology transfer as follows: "Given the choice of the goose and the golden egg, I'll take the goose."

By 1981, about twenty Sun workstations had been under test at Stanford for roughly a year. In February 1982, Vinod Khosla, Andy Bechtolsheim, and Scott McNealy founded Sun Microsystems. In June, Bill Joy, who was responsible for the enhancements to the Berkeley version of the UNIX operating system, joined Sun to head software. Scott had been Vinod's Stanford business-school classmate and was responsible for manufacturing at the first UNIX computer start-up, Onyx. The team's average age was twenty-seven. Several other companies—including Codata (defunct), Forward Technology (defunct), Cimlinc (formerly CADLINK), and Silicon Graphics—licensed the Stanford design, but none succeeded in building and marketing the original design.

The Sun Microsystems plan was six pages long, and it succeeded in getting the team $300,000, plus a $200,000 line of credit with an option on the next round of financing. The seed stage plan was to (1) fund the preparation of a proper business plan, (2) get a marketing person, and (3) make a prototype. A proper business plan was never written, but an operating plan was put in place. The group proceeded to start building the Sun workstation and selling it sans software, as a Tektronix terminal emulator, followed by a workstation running Unisoft's UNIX. The company turned a profit in September 1982, after a few months of operation, and has remained profitable almost continually since then.

In early 1983, Owen Brown, a former DEC regional sales manager, was hired as Sun's president to solve the marketing and sales problems and stayed for a year. Vinod remained CEO until 1984, when Scott McNealy took over that position. In the summer of 1983, Bernard Lacroute was hired as chief operating officer. Bernie had been at DEC, where he was then responsible for all communications products, including the development of Ethernet.

Sun's revenues for the first six years (1983-1988) were $8 million, $39 million, $115 million, $210 million, $538 million, and $1.052 billion. Sun went public in February 1986. By January 1989, Sun's revenue rate was running at roughly $2 billion, reflecting more than a doubling of size every year. The shareholder value of the company was roughly $1.3 billion, representing a 300 to 1 return on the investment.

Both Apollo and Sun emphasized relationships with third-party suppliers that would take their product into end-user environments, either by reselling with software or by joint marketing. Sun tended to emphasize reselling, and hence, its growth rates became significantly higher than Apollo's, even though Apollo had initial success with Mentor Graphics as an electronic CAD supplier.

The following are a number of observations based on the Sun experience:

- A product prototype that has been funded by a public research institution, together with the people who embody the technology, is an ideal start-up source.

  Digital Equipment, Silicon Graphics, Sun, and Evans and Sutherland all followed this pattern of technology transfer.

- Advanced development at another company can be a source of start-up technology, albeit this source is somewhat subject to possible litigation.

  Apollo came from Prime, and Stellar (Stardent) came from Apollo. Amdahl Computer came from an IBM laboratory, and Trilogy came from Amdahl.

- As a source of start-up technology, corporate research laboratories are even better than advanced development, albeit this source, too, is somewhat subject to possible litigation.

  The closer a start-up is to research, the higher the company's likelihood of producing more lasting technology. Many start-ups came from Xerox's PARC, including 3Com and Adobe.

- Although many recommend that start-ups build niche products for niche markets, as a rule, building nongeneral products that only solve a particular user problem is an expensive approach that often proves fatal to a firm that resorts to it.

  Of the three original and largest CAD companies (Daisy, Mentor, and Valid), Mentor has been the most successful, because it used Apollo workstations and concentrated on solving user problems, not on building just another workstation. By solving an overly specific problem while trying to maximize its return, a firm is likely to miss the larger market.

- A company that makes a product for a specific customer is doing so at very high risk, since the customer and its need may change and thereby invalidate the product concept.

  Wilson, a former head of General Motors, once observed: "What's good for GM is good for the country." In the high-technology industry, however, "What's good for Company X is, at most, only good for Company X."

- Technology transfer is very unlikely to occur without the transfer of key people.

  As mentioned above, Khosla has succinctly expressed this idea by stating his preference for taking the goose rather than just the golden egg.

- In cases where a product is available to a start-up right from the outset, becoming immediately profitable should be the goal!

  Start-ups that are fortunate enough to operate on this basis appear to have an unfair advantage. The basic circuit-design technology on which DEC was founded, together with the $70,000 initial funding that it received in 1957, were enough to make the firm profitable from the beginning. Apple started with minimal financing and became profitable, as did Microsoft.

- Profit is habit-forming.

  To ensure viability, profit must be the company's principal goal from its inception.

- If a hardware product is to be appealing to the ultimate buyer/user, it must be usable (i.e., include the necessary software) rather than having to be built up by the buyer/user.

  Therefore, relationships with other firms (called "strategic partnerships") are critical in order to finish the product, make it useful, and distribute it. These relationships typically follow one of three patterns: (1) the start-up and another company jointly market a system; (2) a third party resells the system in an OEM relationship; or (3) the system manufacturer becomes the system supplier and provides specialized software. Sun's revenues reflected the first two strategies, whereas Apollo primarily adopted the third approach.

- "Open systems" are more appealing to users than proprietary systems.

  Given Sun's university origin, the company operated to provide what appeared to be an "open system," whereby critical software interfaces were available from multiple vendors. Sun developed its Network File System (NFS) and made it available to all suppliers and, more recently, did the same with its processor architecture. SPARC was also licensed to a number of vendors. Only in this way can a lasting new computer class be established, because it has multiple sources of supply.

  Sun retained a number of critical interfaces, including its windows and network-sharing software. Sun may have failed to sponsor and make the standard in windows and most likely will have to follow the X Window standard, which was sponsored by MIT. Apollo created a richer, but proprietary network, initially in the style of the traditional industry. Thus, users entering the Apollo environment, Domain, appeared to become locked in.

- When designing products, a manufacturer must either make the standard or follow it.

  If a company tries to make the standard and fails, it gets to implement the system twice—the first time the company's way and the second time according to the standard.

- The rule that says "Only back experienced people" should not be followed blindly.

  A very smart team, even though inexperienced, may perform significantly better, be more dedicated, and remain together longer than a team of mercenaries that's done it once or twice before. If nothing else, by having a younger team than Apollo, Sun has survived longer and developed a substantially more interesting and vibrant culture that produces creative products.

OBSERVATIONS ABOUT FOUNDER INVOLVEMENT

Additional insights can be gained by contrasting the experience of founder-controlled companies with the experience of companies whose founder has relinquished control, as shown in Table 12-2. (A case in point is the fact that, in 1990, Apollo's founders have left the firm, whereas Sun's founders have all remained involved.)

The following are some observations about the impact that the founder's departure or continued participation can have on a high-tech venture:

- To create a company that will be successful over the long term involves a lifetime, not just a five- to ten-year commitment on the part of the founder.

  In 1990, three of the vital, working founders of Sun (Bechtolsheim, Joy, and McNealy) remain with the firm and are still bachelors. The founders are key leaders in various parts of the company and are able to help propagate the culture in a rapidly growing organization.

- When the founder responsible for the leadership and technical integrity of products leaves a company, it is likely to flounder and enter a state in which it sustains its user base but doesn't set off in any new directions.

Table 12-2. Founder Control in Various High-Tech Companies.

Firms Whose Founders Have Retained Control or Remain Involved	Firms Whose Founders Have Relinquished Control
AMD, Cypress, Intel, National	Fairchild, Texas Instruments, Motorola
Conner, Priam, Quantum, Seagate	CDC Disks, Maxtor, Shugart
Compaq, Dell	Altair, Apple, Commodore, Convergent
DEC, HP, Tandem,	CCI, DG, Harris, Pr1me, SEL, Wang
Silicon Graphics, Sun	Apollo
Alliant, Convex	Floating Point Systems
Microsoft	Lotus
Oracle	Relational Technology
Cray Computer	CDC, Cray Research
	Amdahl, Honeywell, IBM, Unisys
	3Com, Ungerman-Bass (now with Tandem)

Certainly, Lotus changed when Kapor left, and HP changed when Hewlett and Packard turned over the management to Young. In 1990, HP introduced a new management concept by appointing Morton as co-CEO.

- With a few notable exceptions, those companies that retain the founder enjoy a continuity of culture.

Founder-controlled firms tend to remain at the forefront, reflecting the founder's involvement, provided the founder has business and market savvy and is technically competent.

- A counterview of why an entrepreneurial founder leaves is that the company may for some reason have failed to meet his or her expectations.

Failure can involve lack of product or market, team, leadership, etc., and thus, the founder leaves as a reaction to the firm—a push, rather than the lure of a new venture. This scenario is particularly common among "chronic entrepreneurs," who continually drive to found new companies.

- Multiple, competitive companies are always created as each new technology or computer class is formed or as each new product type is introduced.

Table 12-2 illustrates the multiplicity-of-companies principle. Examples include Univac (now Unisys since it merged with Burroughs) and IBM in the early 1950s; TI and Fairchild, which started the semiconductor industry; DEC and SDS (now defunct) for minis; Cray and CDC for supercomputers; Apple, Altair and Commodore; Apollo and Sun for workstations; Alliant and Convex for minisupercomputers; and Ardent and Stellar, which created graphics supercomputers.

SILICON GRAPHICS

Silicon Graphics started up in the early 1980s to provide 3-D graphics terminals that were connected to minis and mainframes. By 1985, when more powerful 68000 microprocessors became available, they were expanded into 3-D workstations. The basic design for the Geometry Engine chip, which transformed polygons into a 3-D space, was completed in 1982 by SGI founder Jim Clark while at Stanford. Clark, an alumnus of the University of Utah, acquired the basic design ideas from his own thesis work and the powerful, highly pipelined Evans and Sutherland displays. In 1986, SGI adopted the MIPS architecture for its computational engine and began supplying a range of products from low-cost, diskless 3-D workstations to multi-processor workstations and computational servers.

STARDENT AND THE ELUSIVE GRAPHICS SUPERCOMPUTER

In January 1986, Stellar and Ardent (originally called Dana) started up in Belmont, Massachusetts, and Sunnyvale, California, respectively. The basic plan of both companies was to create a new computer class that would have substantially higher computing and graphics performance than existing workstations.

Ardent started with a $12.5 million first-round investment based on a plan put together by its seven founders during a month-and-a-half-long, accelerated, self-funded seed stage. Stellar obtained roughly the same level of funding based on a plan that had been in gestation for roughly a year.

Ardent's ten-page business plan, dated January 20, 1986, identified a number of risks that might jeopardize the plan. Table 12-3 shows the assumptions Ardent made in its plan regarding each of these potentially problematic areas and contrasts those assumptions with the actual outcomes.

In 1987, Ardent secured the second round of funding from Kubota Ltd., which took on the following functions: manufacturing the products in Japan, marketing in

Table 12-3. Assumptions Made in Ardent's Business Plan Versus Actual Outcomes.

Risk	Assumption	Outcome
Staffing	Would take 1–3 months.	Took 6 months.
Large-scale integration (LSI)	Looked hard, risky.	Not a significant problem but was a bit more costly than anticipated.
Software	Would be complex.	Did more than the plan: Operating system (O/S), compiler, and visualization software exceeded plan.
Hardware	Was not mentioned.	Required almost twice the originally anticipated engineering effort.
Customers	70% would be OEMs.	OEM strategy failed to materialize; had to build a sales force oriented toward end users.
Applications	Would be necessary.	Took much time and was costly. Users wanted more.
Offshore manufacturing	Was provided for in the plan.	Occurred and was much better than expected with Kubota.
Product cost	Would be $50,000.	Was over $80,000. Too far off plan. Major perturbation.
Other	—	First (beta) shipment was 5/88, not 7/87.

Japan and Southeast Asia, and developing software for mechanical design and manufacturing.

As a graphics supercomputer, Ardent's first product, Titan, was significantly more difficult to develop than anticipated, resulting in almost twice the development and product costs. However, the real flaw was introducing a first product that failed to demonstrate clear performance superiority, as discussed in Chapter 8. Although a second set of products overcame this shortcoming, the inadequacy of Ardent's first product inflicted very painful damage on the firm. According to Allen Michels, Ardent's founder and CEO: "You get one shot."

Rarely does a start-up get a second chance if it misses with its first product. The first product must be designed, sold, and delivered correctly. The only reason the company survived to merge with Stellar in October 1989 was that Ardent's Japanese partners had a basic faith in the firm and the market. Poduska became president and Michels chairman, and in 1990, Michels and Sanders left the organization.

The following are some lessons that can be learned from Ardent's experience with its graphics supercomputer:

- Although a start-up can count on a long-established company to be lethargic and noncompetitive, a high-growth firm less than ten years old is unlikely to let a start-up enter its space.

  Stardent underestimated the competitiveness of Silicon Graphics by classifying it with established companies such as Apollo, DEC, HP, and IBM.

- When attacking a walled city, a start-up shouldn't telegraph its intentions to the inhabitants by distributing promotional coffee cups, towels, and T-shirts. And it should avoid attacking two walled cities at once.

- When developing a high-risk, state-of-the-art product that has never before been created, a start-up's founders would be well advised to anticipate project surprises (by a factor of 2) in schedule, resource requirements, product cost, and specifications.

- When a new venture is entering a crowded market where the niches are small and perhaps hard to find, it helps to have a strategic partner with resources.

  Ordinary venture financing would probably have given up on Ardent after three years. Kubota is determined to be successful in technical computing and is prepared to invest for a long-term gain.

- A start-up must not skip the seed stage, especially if it is building a product that the world has never seen before.

  Detailed planning is essential. With a proper seed stage, Ardent would have either cut the product to fit the funding or made a realistic product plan.

DEC, HP, IBM, ETC., AND THE PERFORMANCE WARS

Mainframe and minicomputer companies have come to realize the importance of a distributed-workstation environment by watching Sun grow to over $2 billion in 1990 and take large fractions of their markets. By 1990, DEC and HP share less than half the market, and as the year has progressed, their share has dwindled even further. HP's divisional structure is organized to build and sell competitive 68000-based workstations. In 1985, HP began using its own RISC chips, and it bought Apollo in order to have a larger installed base of customers. DEC took longer to enter the market, given its need to have VAX-on-a-chip processors as its workstation engine. In 1989, DEC introduced a high-performance UNIX workstation using the MIPS RISC chip as its "Sun killer," followed by a faster version in the summer of 1990. Sun responded with its SPARCstation, and Data General entered the fray with a high-performance Motorola 88000-based workstation. In 1990, Evans and Sutherland made its first entry into the workstation market with a high-performance 3-D workstation based on the MIPS microprocessor to challenge its progeny, SGI.

In the late 1980s, IBM introduced several technical Unix workstations in the RT series (IBM's RISC architecture) and one based on the 68000. By 1990, none of IBM's products was powerful enough to appeal broadly to the technical and software-development community. Andy Heller, former president of IBM's Workstation Division, offered the following observation about the effect of having a long gestation period before a product finally becomes available: "Technology is like fish—the longer they stay on the shelf, the less desirable they become." In February 1990, IBM introduced a range of UNIX-based workstations and servers that is likely to retain a product edge for one to two years. These products are based on IBM's next-generation, superscalar RISC technology, which provides substantially higher performance for technical applications than ordinary RISC processors.

Given the push for performance as the differentiator, all companies have chosen different strategies for achieving supremacy. The multiprocessor approach introduced by Apollo, Stardent, and Silicon Graphics allows an arbitrary amount of power to be placed in a given computer. With several firms—such as DEC, Data General, and various Intel 486- based workstation companies—introducing such products in 1990, the 1990s will truly see the advent of parallel processing.

Some further observations on the performance wars:

• Large companies build every conceivable product as an advanced development project, often years ahead of any start-up.

These efforts rarely affect products and are often the basis of a start-up such as Apollo.

- When a new market opportunity appears, entrepreneurs should go for it with a start-up.

  Even if large, established companies are working on products, or have developed prototypes, in the area in question, these firms are lethargic and uncreative, and the likelihood of their producing a good product is very low in the short term (and sometimes even in the long term).

- Even if its products are mediocre, a large company will have a high market share.

  Large firms have a very big sales force and do not like to lose control of their relationship with a customer.

- Inevitably, all large companies will enter every large market area because their ego forces them to do so.

  This tendency represents opportunity, not competition, for a new venture. The large firms will either buy the start-up's products or buy the company itself, and if they don't, their competitors will.

- IBM always enters every product and market area and becomes a major winner (e.g., minicomputers, PCs, workstations, word processors).

  Rarely does IBM fail, as it did in home computing with the PCjr. When it does fail, it learns from its mistake and tries again. At some point, IBM will be a highly successful home-computer supplier.

WHATEVER HAPPENED TO JAWS (JUST ANOTHER WORKSTATION)?

With the introduction of the microprocessor and Ethernet, and the existence of a standard operating system, UNIX, over fifty more companies designed new workstations during the 1980s, among them Adage, Cadmus, Celerity, Lexidata, Lundy, MassComp, Megatek, Mosaic, Raster Technologies, Ridge, Sanders, Symbolics, Tektronix, and Vector General. The situation was similar to the late 1960s and early1970s, when ninety-two firms began making minicomputers (see page 175). Since there were fewer workstation start-ups than minicomputer start-ups, one might conclude that either it was harder to create a workstation company (true), the perceived market was smaller (true), or less capital was available (not true). Entrepreneurs and the venture capital community may finally have learned from experience. (Although the plethora of start-ups to make minisupercomputers and supercomputers in the 1980s for a very small market shows that the lesson about "too many start-up companies chasing a small market" was either poorly learned or soon forgotten.)

In October 1988, Steve Job's start-up (NeXT) entered the market with a 68000-family-based architecture. The workstation offered many incremental improvements over the Macintosh, including a built-in Ethernet, large CD ROM, signal processing for audio and fax input/output, the use of UNIX (through the MACH operating system), and NeXT Step, an improved graphical user interface. In October 1990, the second-generation products were announced, with RISC workstation performance, true color, and built-in video with compression. Most important, the second generation attracted numerous application programs for laboratory and desktop-publishing use, including multimedia and video. NeXT products, with sufficient marketing, could be a substitute for products from Data General, DEC, and HP/ Apollo, as well as Apple.

THE CLASH WITH THE PCs AND THE APPLE MACINTOSH

The IBM PC and its hundreds of clones present a threat to the workstation. The evolving capability of Microsoft DOS—with Windows 3.0 providing an easy-to-use, multitasking environment—will make the PC competitive with the UNIX-based workstations in the mid-1990s. Furthermore, the PC has accumulated almost a decade of software packages that system developers and users support.

What differentiates the personal computer from the workstation? Not much. However, workstations are already in the large-screen, multiprogrammed, distributed-processing space, but with more capability and more power, and they are less expensive. Intel 486-based PCs have comparable processing power. When PCs become available with large, high-resolution screens and the ability to carry out multiple tasks in parallel and also provide transparent distributed computing so that the network acts as a single system, workstation growth will be limited.

The future of the Macintosh is cloudy. It has only evolved in the most obvious fashion to use faster 68000 processors, larger memory chips, and bigger screens. It has a cadre of loyal users and software developers, although with the introduction of Windows 3.0 to provide a "Maclike" interface on IBM PCs, it is fundamentally doomed to a niche, with a rapidly dwindling market share and only modest or declining growth. Authors will continue to use Macintoshes until they switch to the PC, where a wider range of nonproprietary hardware, including portable computers, awaits them at much lower costs.

Although the Macintosh local area network, Appletalk, is inexpensive, it has only a tenth the bandwidth of Ethernet, the network most commonly used for workstation and PC distributed computing. Almost no capability exists for distributed computing, and because the Macintosh, like the PC, is locked into a particular CISC (complex instruction set computer) architecture, the Motorola 680X0 series, the prospects for an evolution in power are minimal. Because of the bus structure used in the MAC II series, those computers are more expensive than workstations, which have no external buses.

The moral: If Sun and other workstation vendors can establish really good channels of distribution, such as retailers, for their products, users will understand that workstations are a bargain compared to large PCs. Alternatively, PC makers (including Intel) may rise to the workstation challenge and begin providing powerful, low-cost PCs that challenge workstations.

THE 1990s: TECHNOLOGY STRIKES AGAIN

In the course of creating a workstation environment that would be competitive with a single shared system, a number of technologies were developed. One of those technologies, the X Window system, was developed to allow windows on one system to access another system using the local area network. In this fashion, a user can merely have a window terminal connected to an LAN that provides access to a time-shared system. Thus, still another approach that would be competitive with the workstation is the return of time-sharing in a fashion that's completely transparent to a user.

The ebb and flow among centralized versus fully distributed computing is a recurring theme in computation. Just as minis, PCs, and workstations (which made every user a computation-center director and system administrator) were an alternative to centralized computing, X Window terminals connected to servers represent a return to centralized computing services.

The group that developed UNIX at Bell Laboratories is using a new system, Plan 9, that is based on users connected via highly interactive, person-serving terminals that access central facilities for data and computation. Of course, such a system requires an excellent, high speed, worldwide communication network. Other technologies will also influence the evolution of the workstation, including high-definition TV and compressed digital video, enabling the development of "multimedia" computing.

CONCLUSION

Workstation companies are introducing lower-priced stations to be used as personal supercomputers for high-performance and 3-D applications. By 1995, the relentless reduction in the cost of memory, coupled with increases in processing performance, will force the workstation into the personal computer market space by default for nearly all but a few high-performance applications. Bill Joy of Sun Microsystems has predicted the "300M workstation" by 1992 and the "3G workstation" by 1995. Each of these workstations will provide 100 million and 1,000 million (giga-) instructions per second, respectively; carry out 100 million and 1,000 million(giga-) floating point operations per second; and have 100 megabytes and 1 gigabyte of primary memory.

Intel's 1989 announcement of the 80860 microprocessor and graphics processor chip as a "Cray on a desk" could have a great effect on technical computing, because it means a single chip can deliver both computational and graphics performance. In this way, the PC and the technical workstation could be merged by any development team capable of assembling a few chips together. This confluence of technology to make a technical workstation/PC using both the 486 and 860 chips would pit the UNIX world against the PC (DOS and OS/2) world. On the other hand, OS/2 is evolving toward a full-scale, general-purpose, multiuser operating system that will no doubt support both the UNIX and DOS programming environments. Thus, an evolutionary path for most PC users appears to exist.

In short, technology evolution beats revolution every time it can get there fast enough and do the job.

Chapter 13

THE FUTURE

The future can be viewed from several perspectives. Chapter 8 extrapolated from the past to provide a product overview of fifth-generation computing. Using this perspective, the evolution of hardware continues to be the dominant force in the creation of computer hardware products. The availability of hardware at a given price and performance level, in turn, paves the way for new software and applications.

The first section of this chapter presents the Intel view of the future. This is a good starting point, because Intel is the leading supplier of microprocessors, and hence, its plans *are* the future.

In *The Age of Intelligent Machines,* Ray Kurzweil (1990) provides an excellent overview and compendium of intelligent machines. His book includes a time line for the future, a portion of which is presented in the second section of the chapter. Ray's view is highly optimistic, because he sees the world in terms of possibilities.

That section is followed by one that offers my own, more conservative views. It summarizes what can be expected during the next decade, beginning with basic physical technologies (semiconductors, magnetics, etc.), and includes the application alternatives that will be made possible by new systems.

The last two sections of the chapter describe my view of the changes that can be anticipated in the mainframe, minicomputer, and supercomputer industries when cheap, powerful, and more ubiquitous desktop and other forms of distributed computing become available, as well as my ideas on worldwide competition.

These various perspectives on the future should be helpful to readers interested in identifying new business opportunities.

INTEL'S VIEW OF THE FUTURE

Intel provides the largest fraction of the world's computing power, thanks to the omnipresence of the Intel/Microsoft PC (aka the IBM PC). Because such a leader plays a dominant role in shaping the future, it is important for readers to understand Intel's view of what that future holds.

Intel characterizes the rapid change in computing performance as a function of time, as shown in Table 13-1, which compares microprocessors with larger machines of constant performance. Note that the first 8080 microprocessor, introduced in 1974, was roughly equivalent to the IBM 704 mainframe, introduced twenty years earlier. Over time, the microprocessor rapidly evolved to the point where it was only four years behind the large IBM mainframes. In 1990, the combined 80486/80860 microprocessor is equivalent in power to the largest minicomputer from Digital Equipment Corporation (DEC). Although the microprocessors listed sold for a few hundred dollars at most, the processor portion of all the "mainframes" shown in the table sold for between $100,000 and $2 million.

Figure 13-1, from Intel, shows how the computing power of a single microprocessor has crossed over to exceed the power of DEC's minicomputers in 1988 and is projected to cross over and exceed the power of IBM's mainframes in 1996. Figure 13-2, from the Gartner Group, points out the incredible disparity in the number of instructions that can be processed per second per dollar of hardware versus time for various computer classes, from mainframes to workstations, PCs, and pocket computers. For example, in 1983, a mainframe costing $2 million provided about 4 million instructions per second (i.e., mips), for a cost-effectiveness of 2 instructions per second per dollar. Eight years later, in 1991, a relatively low-cost, $2,000 personal computer delivering 2 mips provides about 1,000 instructions per second per dollar.

Although the evolutionary line of performance shown in Figure 13-1 appears to be continuous, the actual performance of the 80x86 microprocessor series has evolved in discrete steps. Table 13-2 illustrates how the clock frequency doubled over a three-year period, giving a 26 percent per year improvement, for each of the Intel products. The table includes the clock frequency not only at the time each microprocessor was announced but also at the end of the first, second, and third years thereafter, since design and process improvements often allow new versions of a microprocessor to be made available during the next several years after the first model is introduced.

Not only are microprocessors becoming more powerful, but the total number of chips (microprocessors and support chips) required to build a PC is rapidly declining, as shown in Table 13-3.

Although the cost of a particular computer will be substantially reduced by taking it from 170 chips down to 1 chip in less than a decade, greater functionality is also being incorporated into a given PC. Figure 13-3, from Intel, shows the various parts of a system

Table 13-1. Yesteryear's Mainframe Is This Year's Microprocessor.

| Intel Year | Micro Model | Mainframe or Minicomputer | | Delay |
		Year	Model	(In Years)
1974	8080	1954	IBM 704	20
1977	Z-80	1962	IBM 7094	15
1981	8086	1973	PDP11/45	8
	8088	1975	PDP 11/70	6
1984	80286	1977	VAX-11/780	7
1987	80386	1984 (1982)[a]	VAX 8600	3 (5)[a]
1989	80486	1985	IBM 3090	4
1990	80860	1986	IBM 3090/VF	4
	80486/80860	1990	VAX 9000	0

[a]The project was two years late to market.

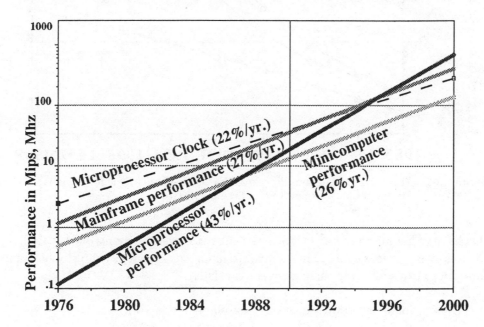

Figure 13-1. Performance Versus Time for Mainframes, Minis, and Selected Intel Micro-processors. (Adapted from a figure provided by Intel Corporation.)

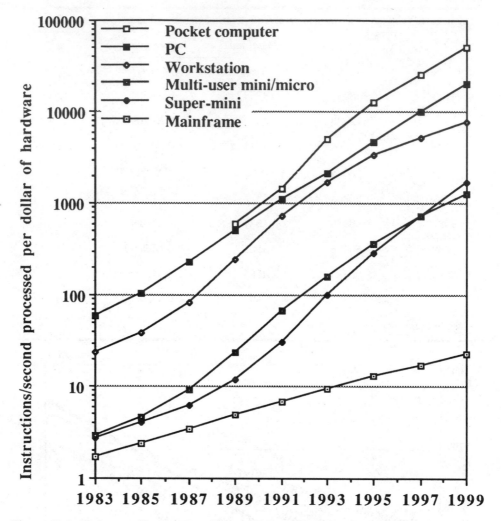

Figure 13-2. Estimate of Instructions Processed Per Dollar Versus Time for Various Computer Classes. (Courtesy of the Gartner Group.)

that have been integrated into PCs of a particular size over the course of time. Each of the following options evolved in a similar fashion, going from 100 chips[1] when first introduced to a single chip three to seven years later:

- The bus-interconnection scheme for controlling the chip set

- Graphics, with evolving speed, resolution, and functionality

---

1. This is the number of chips that can be placed on a printed circuit board for a PC option.

Table 13-2. Intel Microprocessor Clock Frequency (in Megahertz) Versus Time.

Microprocessor	Years After Announcement			
	0	1	2	3
8086	5	6	8	10
80286	6	8	10	12
80386	16	20	25	33
80486	25	33	50	—

- Communications modems and local area networks (LANs)

- Audio output

- Video output

- Speech output

Whether Intel will still be the dominant supplier of computers in 2001 remains to be seen, given the formation of consortia of suppliers to build chips and competitive systems based on MIPS's R-series, Motorola's 88000, and Sun Microsystem's SPARC architectures. Furthermore, if Microsoft's operating-system software becomes available outside of the Intel architecture, it could enhance the position of the three alternative suppliers. The fourth computer generation, beginning in 1978, has evolved based on de facto company-supplier standards from Intel and Microsoft. Having a sole-source monopoly for the microprocessor and operating system almost defies the open-architecture principle. Will the fifth generation continue to be defined by these company standards?

On the other hand, the supercomputer (Cray X architecture), mainframe (370 architecture), and minicomputer (VAX) and PC (80X86) machine classes have been dominated by a single architecture and supplier. Workstation architecture is still up for grabs in 1990 based on the use of the SPARC, MIPS, and IBM RISC (reduced instruction set computer) for executing the UNIX operating system, with no single manufacturer having more than a 50 percent market share.

SECONDARY AND TERTIARY MEMORIES AND PAPER COSTS AND SIZES (CIRCA 1990)

The decline in the number of support chips and the cost of microprocessors discussed above has been matched by a continued rapid decline in the cost of memory.

Table 13-3. Number of Chips in a Personal Computer Versus Time.

Year	Number of Chips in a Personal Computer (sans Memory)
1984	170
1987	70
1990	10
1993	1

Functional Integration

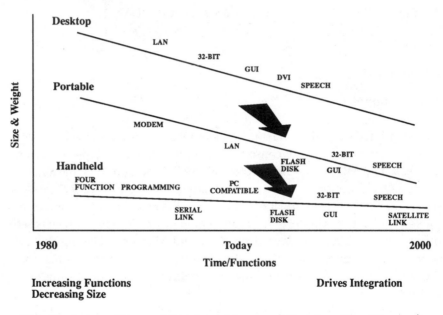

Figure 13-3. Evolution of Size and Weight and Increased Functionality of Personal Computers with Time. (Courtesy of Intel Corporation.)

Chapter 5 discussed the sharp drop in the cost of primary memory (the fastest memory most easily accessed by the processor), but the cost of secondary and tertiary memories has also declined rapidly. Modern storage media are cheaper than paper, as indicated in Table 13-4, which gives the storage capacity (in megabytes) and the price per megabyte of various memories in 1990.

Table 13-4. Cost Per Megabyte and Memory Size for Secondary Memories.

Media	Cost ($)/Megabyte	Megabytes Stored
8 mm tape	0.005	5000
4 mm (DAT) tape	0.01	1200
IBM 3480 tape	0.04	400
Write Once Read Memory	0.10	3200
CD ROM	0.20	620
Pulp paperback	2.00	2
5.25" magnetic disk	5.00	150–1200
Paper at $0.02/page	5.00	1.0–0.004

RAY KURZWEIL'S VIEW OF THE FUTURE

In *The Age of Intelligent Machines,* Ray Kurzweil (1990) offers his view of the future in the form of the following time line:

Early 1990s   A profound change in military strategy arrives. The more developed nations increasingly rely on "smart weapons" that incorporate electronic copilots, pattern recognition techniques and advanced technologies for tracking, identification and destruction.

Continuous speech systems can handle large vocabularies for specific tasks.

Computer speeds of 100 MIPS.

Application Specific Integrated Circuit (ASIC) technology makes writing chip programs as easy as writing software.

Mid-1990s   A multi-hundred-billion-dollar computer and information processing industry is emerging, together with a generation of ubiquitous machine intelligence that works intimately with its human creators.

Significant progress is made toward an intelligent assistant, a decision support system capable of a wide variety of administrative and information gathering tasks. The system can for example, prepare a feasibility report on a project proposal after accessing several data bases and talking to human experts.

Reliable person identification using pattern recognition techniques applied to visual and speech patterns, replaces locks and keys in many instances.

Accomplished musicians, as well as students learning music, are routinely accompanied by cybernetic musicians.

AI [artificial intelligence] technology is of greater strategic importance than manpower, geography, and natural resources.

Late 1990s   Documents frequently never exist on paper because they incorporate information in the form of audio and video pieces.

Media technology is capable of producing computer-generated personalities, intelligent image systems with some human characteristics.

1999   The several hundred billion dollar computer industry is largely intelligent by 1990 standards.

2000   Three dimensional chips and smaller component geometries contribute to a multi-thousandfold improvement in computer power (compared to a decade earlier).

Chips with over a billion components appear.

The world chess champion is a computer.

· · ·   · · ·

2020–2070   A computer passes the Turing test,[2] which indicates human-level intelligence.

COMPUTERS IN 2001

Since it takes roughly a decade for a technology to move from the laboratory to common use, every technology that will be employed in products by the year 2001 should be operating in a research laboratory in 1990. Extrapolating from today's research-stage technology, this section of the chapter examines some of the developments that can be expected by the turn of the century.

---

2. A person in communication with such a device could not tell whether he or she was communicating with a machine or with another person.

It is unlikely that any circuit technology such as optical switching will replace semiconductors, despite AT&T's impressive 1990 demonstrations that photons can perform logic operations. Although announced as a phenomenon, it is not yet operating as a system component in a research laboratory. Memory is critical, too, followed by the mastery of microfabrication of optoelectronic systems. The best use of optical computing would be in the design of a switching system in order to effectively utilize fiber-optic links. This will occur perhaps a decade before an optical computer is developed. Molecular computing is still in a preresearch proposal phase.

The mixing of electronics and biological processing to form the "biochip" has begun. These chips can be used as sensors and effectors. Thus, microelectronics will play an ever-increasing role as a bioengineer's component.

Semiconductor densities will continue to increase on their current trajectory. Various estimates predict semiconductor chip densities of over 400 million transistors, giving at least 100 million bits per chip (the Intel model) by the year 2000. Since the 1-kilobit chip of 1972, memory has quadrupled every three years—a phenomenon known as Moore's law (1975 version). If growth continues at this rate, the use of 4-megabit chips in 1990 would extrapolate to the use of 1-gigabit chips in 2002. Similarly, because a microprocessor with a cache requires about 4 million transistors, the largest chips will contain two to four microprocessors by 1995! Thus, the era of parallelism will be forced by technology.

The gains in magnetics and electro-optic storage are almost as impressive. In 1989, the most cost-effective disk was the 5.25-inch disk, which held 1.6 gigabytes and cost roughly $1,500. Assuming disk densities of all types continue to double every three years (an increase of 26 percent per year), such a drive would store over 25 gigabytes by 2001. Semiconductor advocates who continue to predict the demise of magnetics, to be replaced by semiconductors, will not see much replacement, except for notebook- and pocket-size computers. Magnetic disks offer an advantage by providing permanency. The vast amount of memory available to a user for transport on his or her person, at home, and in central and regional facilities is staggering.

If Seymour Cray continues to design computers, his clock rates may reach 4 gigahertz. This projection is based on a 1988 objective of the Cray 4 to achieve a 1-gigahertz clock in 1992 using gallium arsenide semiconductors. These high clock rates are leading to some really impressive computational capabilities. The Cray 4 was announced as a multiple, vector processor computer with sixty-four processors and was projected to reach 128 gigaflops. In 1990, NEC's SX-X44 supercomputer provided over 22 gigaflops when utilizing all four processors at a clock rate of over 500 megahertz.

At a more mundane level, the performance gains of "plain old processors" implemented as one chip are going to continue to be spectacular. Thanks to the simple, pipelined RISC architecture, a processor is as easy to build as a "test" chip for the semiconductor process. In the decade starting with 1985, performance has grown at the rate of 60 percent each year. Some of this performance growth has been due to architectural and design improvements, and some has been due to clock-speed improvements. Because the clock in a chip only needs to be propagated over a very small distance, clock-speed improvements have occurred at a rate nearly twice that of the larger Cray machines (26 percent a year versus 14 percent a year). The industry has come from a clock of 200 kilohertz in 1971 to 33 megahertz in 1989, and a speed improvement of 26 percent per year would mean that the 33-megahertz microprocessor would reach a speed of over 500 megahertz in 2001. However, as these microprocessors increase in speed to 50 megahertz, multichip packaging is required, so the rate of increase may slow slightly due to the need for increased clock lead lengths.

Like microprocessor clocks, local area networks have also improved in speed at a rate of 26 percent per year, a factor of 10 per decade. Ethernet operated at 10 megabits per second in 1980. FDDI operates at 100 megabits per second in 1990, and most certainly, 1-gigabit fiber networks demonstrated in 1990 will operate as networks in 2001.

Computer backplane buses have also improved at a rate of 26 percent per year. In 1970, Digital's 2-megabyte-per-second Unibus was the industry standard. In 1980, Motorola's VME bus operating at 20 megabytes per second was the standard. In 1990, various flavors of the Futurebus standards operate at 200 megabytes per second.

COMPUTER ARCHITECTURE(S)

By extrapolation, evolution will carry us into the twenty-first century doing things pretty much the same way we were doing them in 1990. This would mean that for high-performance technical computing, we'll be using faster, multiprocessor and multicomputer systems based on the computers we're just beginning to see from the plethora of start-ups aimed at developing high-performance computers based on parallelism. Although it is nontrivial to exploit the parallelism inherent in these structures, much progress is being made. The languages will have to change, but only after people start understanding the simple, parallel machines of the early 1990s that utilize only a modest number of processors. Just a few languages transparently support parallelism, and it's hard to imagine that users will switch very rapidly, given their conservatism and their interest in running dusty decks of Fortran (and Cobol). However, they must change in order to get the most benefit from parallel computers.

The Cray YMP introduced in 1988 operates at near its peak speed of 2.5 gigaflops on the Linpack benchmark when using all eight processors. Although Alliant parallelized programs first with its eight-processor FX 8 in 1985, the Cray YMP benchmark heralds the acceptance of parallelism in scientific computing and the beginning of a new, parallel era.

NEC's SX-X44 four-processor supercomputer provides a workload capacity of about three times the Cray YMP processor. Furthermore, the peak speed, using just one processor, is about 1.5 times higher than the Cray YMP using all eight processors!

By the turn of the century, parallel programming will become routine, either by evolving 1990 computers to be more transparent and easier to use, or by using explicit parallelism. Data-flow language constructs could be used to provide implicit parallelism if languages and training evolved more rapidly. In no case can compilers recognize that a problem may be inherently parallel. Users who program must be retrained in order to exploit parallelism, and computer science has yet to modernize its curriculum to include supercomputers. Otherwise, the "Do what I mean" (DWIM) paradigm would have to be "Do what is right" (DWIR), and that would be a superhuman computer.

MASSIVE PARALLELISM

The high-performance, general-purpose computers will have a high degree of parallelism, with each computer consisting of hundreds of processors in a multiprocessor with a shared memory. Several thousand computers that communicate via a fast switching network will allow multicomputers. In addition, computers that have a single instruction stream to process data in a massive number of processing elements can be built, patterned on Thinking Machines, Inc.'s Connection Machine idea. These computers will most likely provide a teraop, or 1 million-million (10^{12}) operations per second, of computing power. DARPA (Defense Advanced Research Projects Agency) has funded two such efforts, by Thinking Machines and Intel, to achieve high speed. Researchers and funding agencies believe a computer capable of 1 teraop is feasible by the year 1995.

It is unclear how much parallelism personal computers will have. This is because a single chip might have 100 megabytes of primary memory. Therefore, our whole personal database and all the programs we use today may be carried in our wallet, or in a pencil-like device. The interface to humans and to other systems is a crucial factor if the computer is to be widely used by a billion people.

THE VON NEUMANN ARCHITECTURE MODEL

Three alternative computer structures—single instruction massive data, multiprocessors, and multicomputers—are all simple extensions of the basic von Neumann architecture model of instruction fetch and instruction execute.

Neural-network computing is definitely *not* encompassed in von Neumann's model. Already, neural networks are being employed in a wide array of pattern-recognition applications, from speech synthesis to image recognition. Neural-network computing elements are likely to be used in conjunction with basic, general-purpose computers for such tasks as signature or handwriting analysis.

Systolic processing[3] may be used for signal- and image-processing functions at the computer's interface, although it is unlikely that special-purpose processors can compete with the rapid evolution of the RISC microprocessor.

OPERATING SYSTEMS AND THE HUMAN INTERFACE

Everyone hopes to see the advent of operating systems that are substantially more robust and easier to use than systems of the 1980s. Communication via voice and handwriting will most certainly become possible. The Apple Macintosh, which introduced Xerox PARC's method of control by means of icons instead of tedious commands, still has a long way to go in terms of ease of use. Many organizations are working on better graphical user interfaces, including all the workstation companies, the Open Software Foundation, and desktop-manager firms such as Visix. The NeXT desktop is perhaps the simplest and most complete with multimedia support. The Microsoft Windows interface for the PC is likely to evolve to reach parity with the Macintosh in terms of ease of use. Nevertheless, there is still room for start-ups to continue developing products that improve the human interface.

PERIPHERALS

Based on extrapolation from past progress, better input/output of all types will certainly exist. In particular, better human interaction is critical. The quality of screen images will rise dramatically and at a lower cost when high-definition television arrives. At the same time, low-cost, small liquid-crystal screens of all types are appearing just as the basic RCA patent on liquid-crystal displays expires. Higher resolution will also mean the production of realistic, three-dimensional graphics and images.

Hands and arms, legs, and much better eyes will become the most important new peripherals. These transducers will permit the construction of a whole new class of autonomous robots that can carry out simple tasks in the home, office, laboratory, and factory environments. The most useful, practical, and mobile robots are unlikely to be built by the year 2001, however, since such robots would need to "see" and "understand" the environments in which they operate.

---

3. The "pumping" of data through an array of processing elements.

PCs of nearly all sizes, from pocket to desktop, will have to include a fax and voice input/output. Chips from Intel (DVI) and C^3 for compressing video by a factor of 10–1,000 will ensure video integration with most computers by 2001.

HANDWRITTEN TEXT AND SPEECH

By the turn of the century, computers should be able to read text and communicate with us by voice, but unless more progress is made in speech understanding and computers come to have the ability to learn, they will still "feel" much like 1990 computers. HAL, in the movie *2001: A Space Odyssey,* may not be a bad model for how a computer might communicate, but a device with all of HAL's capabilities seems several decades away.

The most useful device I could envision would be a personal assistant notepad and database that would not only do everything today's PC does but also accept communication via voice, handwriting, and perhaps keyboard. Later on in the twenty-first century, such a device could listen and translate. It would plug into a conventional phone or be a cellular phone. This would represent the ultimate evolution of the plethora of virtually useless devices for the wallet, wrist, and pocket sold for $10 to several hundred dollars through specialty stores and airline magazines.

Computers would provide a more extensive public interface without the humans who currently operate systems in airlines, banks, insurance offices, and stores. Today, we stand in line to talk to these interpreters. Many of us would rather communicate directly with the computer system, when it can be made easy and powerful enough to use.

THE UNBOUNDED NETWORK

Cellular radio networks will make fully distributed computing available for use in any location without the need to plug in to a network. Such a network would allow any computer to call any other on a totally space-independent basis for computer and fax messaging, data access, and performing various tasks such as reserving cars or ordering merchandise.

The U.S. government's High Performance Computing Initiative aims at creating a network that will exploit the bandwidth inherent in fiber optics by the end of the decade to enable the research establishment in academe, government, and industry to communicate. Such an evolution would allow information to be transferred between machines at gigabit rates.

Fax traffic now constitutes about one-tenth of all telephone traffic and is growing rapidly. If specialized digital fax network providers came into existence, then computers might utilize such networks.

The Integrated Services Digital Network (ISDN) system, which was supposed to be available on a worldwide basis by 1985, might come into being to function as a "data highway" that would be available everywhere, including homes. The normal ISDN service (basic rate) provides mere 64-kilobit-per-second channels. Although this speed is adequate for documents of the 1980s, it is not sufficient to transmit the many color graphical objects required for remote, interactive computing. Primary-rate ISDN (1.544 megabits per second T1 carrier in the United States) or higher speeds, such as T3 (45 megabits per second) communication, are needed for the technical marketplace. A T3 network is likely to be the common mechanism for the interconnection of computers on a wide area basis by the end of the decade. The Synchronous Optical Network (SONET) being installed by the world's telecommunications companies is also a promising development. By all accounts, Europe and Japan will lead the United States in high performance wide area digital networks.

The availability of higher data rates and/or improved data-compression systems should result in the advent of home videophones using highly compressed video. Workstations will be the first to provide built-in computer and videoconferencing capability, because they can rely on fast local and wide area networks.

THE COST AND SIZE OF COMPUTERS

Computers will range in cost from a few dollars for those that can fit in someone's pocket to a hundred million dollars for those that are central to an enterprise or a laboratory. Whereas simulation stops at the molecular level today, these large machines will be able to simulate more of the universe, including interactions within the atom. Every person or organization spends some constant fraction of their budget for computing, just as they do for food or other necessities. Furthermore, the industry is segmented into companies that supply computers at every price level, from a few dollars to tens of millions.

THE DISAPPEARANCE OF PAPER

Computers with laser printers have enabled every PC user to become a publisher and continue the exponential increase in the production of printed matter. Paper must inevitably start to disappear as the archive-storage media, simply because the quantity of available information is becoming so vast that computers will be essential for tracking, finding, analyzing, and perusing it. This means that *all* information, including the enormous amount coming in fax form, will ultimately be captured and encoded, stored, and shipped around electronically, potentially minimizing the use of printed media. Printing should be reserved only for those occasions when the information contained in the machine cannot be used directly on-line. However, given the rise in the number of notebook-size computers, it will become feasible to start making nearly all information, such as books and periodicals, available in computer-readable form.

On the other hand, the amount of paper will rise rapidly as the ease of computer printing and fax proliferates among everyone, including schoolchildren. There will be a continued increase in the use of paper as the primary medium for applications requiring portability, such as entertainment (books and newspapers), information distribution (advertisements), and even the dissemination of information (memoranda) within organizations.

Electronic mail, though widely used within corporations, has failed to limit and substitute for fax because of the computing and communications industry's failure to create the necessary standards for interoperability. However, by 2001, one would hope for a common dial-up network for electronic mail that's as easy to use and accessible as fax.

With very large memories, and the ability to view and peruse information electronically, an environment could be envisioned in which there is much less paper and information is normally stored and viewed electronically because the image quality is higher than with paper. This scenario could become a reality by the early twenty-first century.

ARTIFICIAL INTELLIGENCE

In the past, artificial intelligence has been defined as a set of techniques not served by the mainstream of computer science. AI includes efforts to address very difficult problems such as understanding images, vision, natural language, and speech. It also includes the study of robotics and how robots can function autonomously. As an area of computing (e.g., expert systems) matures and becomes widely understood by the academic community, it is assimilated into the mainstream of computer science. During the late 1980s, expert systems using knowledge bases matured for practical, though not common, use.

EXPERT SYSTEMS

Many types of expert systems have been built for giving advice and for doing diagnosis and design, as described in Chapter 9. Writing programs to solve problems for a particular application domain, such as mechanical computer-aided design (MCAD), is not per se a new development, because much of the programming industry has been performing this function since computers were invented. Before the advent of "expert systems," however, programs were written in standard procedural programming languages, such as Cobol and Fortran. The "official" expert-systems programs are written using a rule-based approach, either by extending the LISP language with an inference mechanism shell (e.g., KEE or ART) or by using a new and unique language for rule-based programs (e.g., Prolog, OPS, or NEXPERT).

Unlike commercial and technical applications, which evolved rapidly because Cobol and Fortran standards were established by 1960, rule-based expert systems are still in the "sandbox" stage. Dozens of proprietary and unique languages exist for writing these programs. Rule-based programming is unlikely to grow very rapidly because the lack of standard languages will slow the industry's maturation. Thus, potential users cannot be trained easily by computer-engineering or computer-science departments. Furthermore, programs written on one system cannot be used on another system, and large systems cannot be built up from other systems.

If rule-based expert systems are to become a mainstay programming technique, all the major languages—including C, Cobol, and Fortran—must have extensions that include rule-based, inference programming. By the year 2001, the proprietary languages will become completely extinct if the industry is to grow and mature.

GREAT NEW APPLICATIONS

Although it is difficult to predict how the vast increase in processing power will affect science and engineering generally, its impact on the following specific areas is clear.

Animation

Large-scale computers, with their ability to compute realistic scenes, offer an alternative to traditional filmmaking techniques. The evolution of multimedia will permit the computer generation of cartoonlike actors that can be used within desktop publishing. Only in the twenty-first century will it become possible to compute real actors and real scenes.

Commercial and Transaction Processing

Although the preceding examples are from the technical marketplace, given a vast increase in transaction power, a revolution of equal proportions appears to be possible in the area of commercial and transaction processing. This can be accomplished through higher degrees of parallelism, obtained by using small disks, multiple fast microprocessors, and large memories. By 2001, a computer that never fails and delivers over a teraop is feasible. It will most likely be the center of enterprise computing and large transaction-processing networks used for banking and air travel.

Computational Chemistry, Including Biochemistry and Materials Science

Molecular modeling and computational chemistry have made possible the interactive design of molecules, using large-scale computers.

Computational Fluid Dynamics (CFD)

CFD, the basis of aerospace engineering, is also useful in designing buildings and automobiles. Horst Simon, of NASA's Ames Research Center, estimated that carrying out a simulation of a vehicle requires about 10^{15} operations (5 million grid points, 50,000 iterations, and 5,000 operations per point per iteration), using about 200 million 8-byte words of primary memory and about 10 gigabytes of disk storage. Table 13-5 shows several design activities, together with the turnaround time and computer speed required to perform each one.

Image Processing

Various disciplines, ranging from radiology and surveillance to weather forecasting, rely on the interpretation of high-resolution photographs and other image and signal sources. High-performance computers are finally making the use of digital images and image processing feasible, and the availability of satellite image data is transforming everything from military intelligence to urban geography.

Mathematics as a Generic Capability

The late 1980s saw the emergence of several programs that will have a long-term effect on the way computers are used. Programs such as MathCAD, Mathematica, and Matlab can deal with much of the college-level mathematics used in science and engineering. These programs are also the best way to train all students about mathematics, beginning with algebra in the upper elementary school. Fundamental mathematical competence is far more important than the ability to do spreadsheet programming. Making various forms of mathematics understandable to and usable by a much larger fraction of society could cause more change than spreadsheets, word processing, and electronic mail.

Mechanical Engineering

Over the last decade, a revolution occurred in semiconductors and digital-system design, with the advent of the ability to design and model large digital systems

Table 13-5. Turnaround Time and Computer-Speed Requirements for Selected Design Activities.

Design Activity	Turnaround Time (in Hours)	Computer Speed (in Gigaflops)
Proof of concept	1000.00–100.00	0.3–3.0
Design	10.00–1.00	30.0–300.0
Automated design	0.10–0.01	3,000.0–30,000.0

accurately. Furthermore, fabrication information can be sent electronically to factories for the direct production and testing of chips and physical interconnections. Thus, no physical prototyping is required, which at least halves the time between design and production.

Computers have been used to design all sorts of mechanical structures, from automobiles to spacecraft, and to perform a wide range of activities, from drafting to the analysis of designs, including crash simulation for cars. A designer can render high-quality images and show the objects in motion with the help of video. A vast increase in available computer power should provide mechanical engineers with sufficient computing capability to revolutionize mechanical design.

Under this design paradigm, it is possible to perform every facet of product design, including the design of the factory in which the product will be produced, without a prototype. Such a development could transform mechanical engineering and industries relying on the manufacture of physical parts. For starters, product quality would improve. The big impact would come from a drastic reduction in product-gestation time and in the size of the organization, which could be decreased by a factor of 5. Reducing the size of design teams has been shown to increase both product elegance and quality. In a totally computerized design and manufacturing environment, a team of no more than fifty could design a perfect car or other vehicle from the ground up, in under two years.

Personal Computers in 2001

The largest computers will continue to be used to explore the forefront of applications—applications that will later become feasible with a PC. Ardent's graphics supercomputer, introduced in 1988 at a price of $100,000, is an excellent model for the home computer of the year 2001 at a price of $2,000. Three-dimensional phenomena, from molecules to galaxies, will be simulated at high enough speeds to transform modern science from experimental to computational-simulation-based.

This paradigm shift will transform every facet of science, engineering, and mathematics, starting with the fundamental nature of education. Every home will have an unlimited laboratory in which to conduct experiments. As a result, children will learn in new ways, such as by using the Writing to Read program introduced on the PC, simulating all kinds of scientific experiments, and doing programming to develop logical thought. An educational revolution rivaling the replacement of the slate by the notebook is possible.

Robots for the Home

Given the eleven-year rule, useful robots for the home will probably not be available in 2001. Industrial and research robots are quite dumb, hard to program, and of limited use. Without significant advances in vision, planning, and understanding common sense, as well as some general ability to learn, it is hard to believe that robots will be very mobile (and hence very useful) around the home in the near-term future. Vision processing to rival human capabilities is estimated to require on the order of 10^{12} operations per second (one teraop) of computing power.

General Technical and Scientific Applications

With the vast increase in computing power reaching over a teraop, it will be possible to simulate very complex systems for such disciplines as atmospheric science and chemistry. This highly advanced simulation ability is needed in order to understand phenomena such as acid rain and the erosion of the ozone layer.

Visualization and Virtual Reality

Visualization is simply the ability to present a graphical view of a problem in order to enable a human user to gain insight into possible solutions. High-performance workstations provide the ability to generate photo-realistic models of all physical systems.

Virtual-reality environments take the form of a head-mounted, three-dimensional display that changes in response to the movement of the user's head, together with gloves or joysticks, all of which allow the user to position himself or herself within a three-dimensional space. Thus, the user can navigate through any three-dimensional area (in effect, "be anywhere") and look at anything at any scale, ranging from a molecule to a galaxy. Laboratories and start-ups have formed to provide interactive, virtual-reality environments such as these.

INDUSTRY RESTRUCTURING

Given the increase in microcomputer power and the reduction in price, as shown in Figure 13-2, an incredible performance-per-unit-price difference among the various computer classes must cause a major restructuring of the computer industry. Such a discontinuity alone could trigger a major recession, and the shift away from the minicomputer is most certainly behind the 1990 changes in the mini-based New England economy. Furthermore, portable operating systems and applications, both for UNIX and for MS-DOS and OS/2, have transformed hardware systems into high-tech, commodity products, with many suppliers providing essentially the same product.

Although the price of all the practical computers used today will be reduced to near-zero in 2001, parallel computers with more capability will come into being to maintain constant prices. In terms of quantity, however, the greatest growth will be in simple wallet, pocket, briefcase, and desktop computing, provided such devices can be made easy to use. All of these computer types are built with the same manufacturing techniques used in consumer electronics.

Figure 13-4 (by the Gartner Group) illustrates this growth scenario by showing the evolution in the number of computers sold in the various classes. Note that mainframes are projected to decline from their current population of fifty thousand. Workstations are the fastest-growing segment in the early 1990s and approach the installed base of all the shared minicomputer and microprocessor-based systems, including all local area network servers. The Gartner Group projects the emergence of powerful pocket-size personal computers that will nearly equal the installed base of the PC by 1999.

The message for start-ups is clear: very small, low-cost, new fifth-generation products present opportunities for new ventures, provided they concentrate on quality manufacturing, unique and important applications, and innovative marketing.

For the minicomputer and mainframe classes, the need to solve much larger problems involving more data will result in the emergence of more radical and specialized parallel computing for use in specialized local area network servers. Network computing is finally coming into being. The VAX computing environment, conceived in 1979, was formed as a hierarchy of three styles of computing, starting with mainframes operated as a central service, connected to distributed departmental minicomputers operated by specific groups, and terminating with personal computers and workstations operated by individuals. A modern follow-on to this structure is predicated on the evolution from a collection of centralized computers to fully distributed, networked personal workstations interconnected via high-speed local area networks, as shown in Figure 13-5.

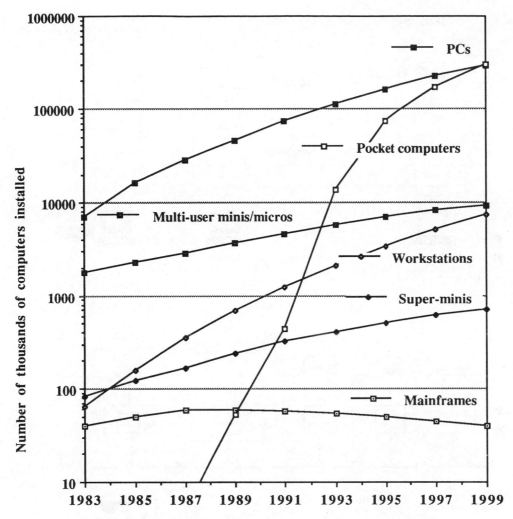

Figure 13-4. Estimate of the Number of Computers Installed in the Various Classes Versus Time. (Courtesy of the Gartner Group. Reprinted with permission)

CHANGES IN THE MAINFRAME AND MINICOMPUTER INDUSTRY

It is hard to believe that mainframes and large minis will benefit from the need for distributed computing, because of the considerable disparity in both performance and price/performance between mainframes and microprocessor-based computers, as was shown in the Intel scenario. Mainframes and superminicomputers have been slow to evolve, since they use expensive packaging for ECL. In contrast, complementary metal oxide semiconductor (CMOS) technology runs faster, because all the components are on

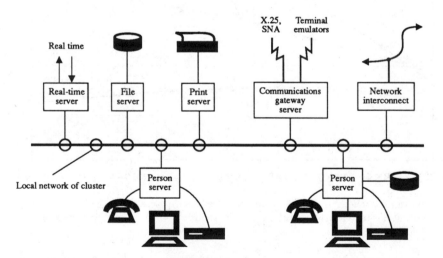

Figure 13-5. Evolution of Computing, from a Centralized Computer to Fully Distributed Personal Computers andWorkstations.

a single chip. Mainframe and minicomputer complex instruction set computer (CISC) architectures are more complicated and require arcane implementations that have historically had a gestation time of more than five years. Getting all the fast circuitry on one chip results in hardware that goes faster, runs cooler, is more reliable, and costs next to nothing. Differences in disk technology—from the large, expensive disks used in disk farms to the 5.25-inch format—also exacerbate the shift. Isn't it clear that expensive and slow has to lose to cheap and fast, especially if the development times and costs are also substantially less?

Even the large, die-hard users with lots of code locked up in "code museums" are beginning to understand that they must switch to an open-systems form of computing based on standards in order to get a better computing environment and at a substantially lower price.

The following CMOS micro-based alternatives all offer performance that equals or beats the old line of expensive mainframes and superminicomputers at negligible prices, thereby "niching" the existing hardware:

- PCs and multiprocessor PC servers from Compaq, etc.

- Workstations and servers from Sun, etc.

- Uniprocessor micros from Altos Computer Systems, MIPS, Motorola, NCR, Pyramid, etc.

- New network servers from Netframe, etc., using the Intel chips

- Multiprocessor servers and minis using multiple microprocessors from Arix, Digital, Encore, Sequent, Silicon Graphics, and Solborne

- Specialized technical computers from Intel and NCUBE, as well as a plethora of Transputer-based companies

- Front-end and back-end database servers from Teradata, etc.

For example, the Stardent 3000 is a quad vector processor multiprocessor delivered in November 1989 that sells for a tenth the price of a VAX 9000 yet almost equals it in performance. The DEC 9000, promoted as DEC's first mainframe, was delivered roughly one year after the Stardent 3000. The difference in the product-gestation time was a factor of 3 (two years versus six years to design each product). Digital claimed that it spent almost a billion dollars developing the 9000 (a factor of nearly 50 times what Stardent spent, excluding the microprocessor). Probably a thousand people were involved in developing the VAX 9000, whereas less than fifty people developed the Stardent 3000. Is it any wonder why America is losing its competitiveness and why start-ups must form?

It seems logical to anticipate a massive and continued shift in the industry's structure during the next decade, not growth for traditional minicomputer and mainframe products. Both of these markets have remained flat at about $15 billion per year.

Of the original BUNCH, Burroughs and Univac combined to make UNISYS, which is distributing UNIX products; NCR has switched to UNIX and the PC using Intel microprocessors; Control Data Corporation (CDC) has downsized its mainframe business and become a distributor of MIPS products; and Honeywell sold its business to Bull, a builder of UNIX products using the MIPS architecture and products. The lower revenues and reduced profits (or increased losses) at Alliant, DEC, DG, Encore, Hewlett-Packard, MassComp (now part of Concurrent), Prime, and Wang in the last five years, resulting in company downsizing, are not solely the fault of management but rather are the result of a fundamental technology shift. It is unlikely that these firms understand or know how to address the shift. IBM appears to understand and adapt to a changing market. On the other hand, the mainframe code museums hold most of the world corporate data as hostage.

Users are beginning to realize that proprietary architectures utilizing the wrong technologies mean higher cost and lower performance. Furthermore, key software suppliers have switched to writing applications for standards-based platforms.

This industry shift, which has been apparent since the mid-1980s, could, by itself, cause a major recession in the 1990s, as observed earlier. At the very least, the shift will be as dramatic as the movement of the textile mills from New England when new fabrics entered the market. Like the mills, New England's computer companies have begun a steady decline, which tracks the declining market for minicomputers. Kendall Square Research, a Boston-area firm building a large multiprocessor using CMOS technology, characterizes the inevitable decline of these companies in Figure 13-6.

CHANGES IN THE U.S. SUPERCOMPUTER INDUSTRY

When it was introduced in 1975, the first successful vector supercomputer, the Cray 1, provided power for general-purpose computation by having the highest scalar performance, together with a fast vector processor to provide an additional tenfold performance increase for problems involving matrix operations. In the 1990s, RISC-based workstations computing at near-supercomputer speed are more cost-effective by a factor of 10 to 20 for mostly scalar programs. Workstations such as IBM's R6000 perform adequately on "average" programs, giving an overall performance difference of only a factor of 3 or 4 between the workstation and the supercomputer. At the other extreme, massively data parallel computers from Intel, NCUBE, and Thinking Machines offer higher peak speeds than the supercomputer at one-fifth its price for highly parallel and tuned, vector processor applications.

The supercomputer is a protected species because of its use in defense, even though many of the functions it performs could be carried out just as well by alternative means. Furthermore, it has become a symbol of competitiveness, since the Japanese have begun

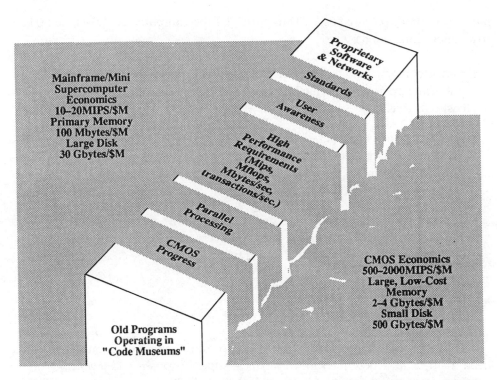

Figure 13-6. Fundamental Restructuring of the Computer Industry Brought About by Standards and Commodity Hardware. (Adapted from a figure provided by Kendall Square Research Group.)

making supercomputers with greater peak speeds than Cray Research or Cray Computer. A number of companies that tried to build supercomputers—including CDC's ETA, Denelcor, and Chopp—have withdrawn from this very small and overcrowded market. Supercomputing Systems, Incorporated, another Cray Research spin-off firm, is based on the traditional, vector multiprocessor supercomputer architecture. DARPA is funding Tera Computer Corporation to design a large-scale supercomputer. IBM is enhancing the scientific computing capability of its mainframe line. One, or at most two, of these multi-hundred-million-dollar development efforts will succeed and be profitable.

The amount of technical computing done with supercomputers per se is not very large, for many reasons, including high initial cost, complexity, training requirements, difficulty of use, responsiveness, and lack of visualization. It simply costs more to run most jobs on a supercomputer than on fast workstations or even personal computers. Minisupercomputers are a lower-cost alternative that has taken some fraction of the supercomputer's potential users. Thus, the U.S. supercomputer industry is being held to a billion-dollar level by:

- Minisupercomputers that are at least as cost-effective and provide high throughput. Minisupers built from CMOS microprocessors should prove to be the most cost-effective.

- Specialized, massively parallel computers such as the Connection Machine, which uses thousands of processing elements, and the Intel Supercomputer, built from 64 to 1,024 CMOS microprocessors, which provides exceptionally high performance at lower cost for vector applications.

- Personal computers, ordinary technical workstations, personal supercomputers, and superworkstations with a few microprocessors that perform the same tasks at one-tenth to one-third the speed, but at five to ten times the cost-effectiveness.

- Competitive machines from start-ups.

- Japanese supercomputers.

The U.S. supercomputer industry will decline by the year 2001, because it will have been "niched" at, as described above. Japanese supercomputers will supply the largest fraction of traditional supercomputing calculations due to the commitment by Fujitsu, Hitachi, and NEC. All three are vertically integrated and can develop the critical circuitry and packaging on which the supercomputer is based. The Japanese tend to see the supercomputer as the driving force or leading edge for building the fastest hardware in much the same way as automobile companies see building racing cars as advertisement. Furthermore, all of these companies can sustain any losses that are inherent in a small, but very-high-technology market. In the United States, only IBM is vertically integrated—but rarely does IBM sustain a loss just for show or to maintain its market presence.

WORLDWIDE COMPETITION

Provided that the U.S. venture capital community doesn't change significantly to become much more conservative and cease funding high information technology, the United States should retain its lead in *inventions* simply because it has such a fine machine for training a small number of creative engineers and scientists. Start-ups everywhere will continue to invent and to bring fundamentally new technology and products into existence.

Larger U.S. and foreign companies will still be synergistic with start-ups to adopt their inventions. The large firms that control over 90 percent of the engineering and scientific talent will continue to evolve slowly and to reinvent, instead of channeling creative energy into innovation by making the changes that would be required to do a given product or technology in a new but evolutionary way in order to make it dominate a market.

But the bulk of *innovation* will come from outside the United States, because the Japanese, for example, are not as plagued by the "not invented here" syndrome, which is endemic among most American and many European engineers, who tend to reinvent technology and products, often with poorer results than the original design.

With the economic unification of Europe in 1992, a broader, easier-to-access market may emerge. On the other hand, European suppliers might become more competitive in a world market. At the very least, Europe may take a more aggressive role as a global funder of start-ups. In the 1980s, Europe became effective at managing research and advanced development across national borders and between industry and academe. However, given the laws supporting lifetime employment in Europe, it is difficult to see how start-ups will form very easily there. Thus, the larger companies will most likely continue to count on slow evolution and invention coming from research. These advances will probably be small, as in the past. The only way large European firms will acquire big inventions will be to buy products from small companies or buy the companies themselves.

China and India—which have the world's largest supply of highly trained talent with mathematical, engineering, and scientific skills—are beginning to develop software for worldwide consumption. Since the development of much software requires minimal capital investment (often, only a PC), any country can become a significant software supplier because of the inherently "low barrier to market entry."

Japan will continue to excel in innovation and to become the dominant supplier in every market it enters. Japan will take the plethora of hardware and software *inventions* generated by the rest of the world and, by *innovation*, improve their quality, functionality, and performance, to substantially increase the size of the markets. In 1972, IBM invented the 8-inch floppy and used it to hold diagnostic programs for its large disk controllers. By the late 1970s, Shugart Associates started up and began the floppy industry, which evolved to the 5.25-inch-diameter floppy with more start-ups. In 1982, Apple adopted Sony's highly innovative and more durable 3.5-inch floppy, which has become the standard of interchange since 1985, with evolving increases in density, because the Sony floppy provided so much more than the first, simple invention and its evolution.

Because nearly all software products are developed by a method that is subject to process control and quality standards, the Japanese appear to generate software that is a factor of 10 better in terms of quality, as measured in defects per thousands of lines of code, and at a productivity rate that is a factor of 2 to 3 times higher, as measured in thousands of lines of code per person per day. This development environment is often called a software factory, and as with any U.S. factory, no one wants to work in one—certainly not America's creative software engineers.

Thus, over the next decade, when software products become better defined by standards (e.g., VHSIC's VHDL language for describing digital systems) and by well-developed algorithms and paradigms in well-defined domains (e.g., spreadsheets, electronic computer-aided design [ECAD] for very-large-scale integration [VLSI] design), Japan will dominate the software products market just as it dominates nearly all markets for physical goods. In any case, the software industry will remain only a small fraction of the entire high-technology industry until all computers cost just a few hundred dollars.

American engineers, coupled with the American MBAs who manage most U.S. organizations, will ensure the continued decline of the information-processing industry, because this deadly duo focuses on the human organization (and especially its political structure), not on the technology and product. The remaining bastion of American creativity, software products, may be eroded more rapidly than hardware. The highly disciplined, process-engineering nature of Japanese software engineering is antithetical to the U.S. software-engineering culture. As is the case with the steel-making industry, the old ways are too deeply ingrained in the culture to permit change. Thus, other countries will study and profit from the considerable body of knowledge about software engineering accumulated and taught by the U.S. academic establishment long before the United States does. Here, as in other aspects of engineering and manufacturing, the U.S. must switch its role from teacher to student and colleague.

CONCLUSION

This book has presented many technology and product ideas to stimulate the reader. I see almost unlimited possibilities for products extending well beyond the year 2001, just by extrapolating from the technology currently expected to be available. In this regard, the Kurzweil time line establishes many wonderful goals.

If any of the new-product development scenarios are to become a reality, however, it will most likely occur outside of the evolutionary product development process that is characteristic of established companies. Thus, entrepreneurs and venture capital must continue to exist. Hence, the opportunity for start-ups. If the reader is in a large organization and is trying to invent or even innovate, the challenge is to outperform the start-ups, the Japanese, and the rest of the world—all of whom are trying to build better products.

The last caveat of this book is especially important if the reader has gotten this far and is still determined to found a company:

Now that you've studied everything I know about technology, products, and start-ups; persevered and mastered a great new technology; demonstrated that it can be useful in a product that people are likely to buy; found a way to validate that there really is a market; and decided to start a company; the easy part is over—but the fun is just beginning.

BIBLIOGRAPHY

ARTICLES

Bell, C. Gordon. 1984. "The Mini and Micro Industries." *Computer* 17, no. 10 (Oct.): 14–30.

Carr, Robert. 1989. "How to Build Better Programming Teams." *Soft•letter* 6, no. 4 (May 1).

Gomory, Ralph E., and Roland W. Schmitt. 1988. "Science Products." *Science* 240 (May 27): 1131–1132, 1203- 1204.

Grayson, Paul. 1989. "How to Motivate Programmers." *Soft•letter* 6, no. 4. (May 1).

Lampson, Butler. 1988. "Personal Distributed Computing: The Alto and Ethernet Software." In *A History of Personal Workstations*, edited by Adele Goldberg, 291- 344. Reading, Mass.: Addison-Wesley.

Meindl, James D. 1987. "Chips for Advanced Computing." *Scientific American* 255, no. 10 (Oct.): 78–88.

Mendelson, H. 1987. "Economies of Scale in Computing: Grosch's Law Revisited." *Communications of the ACM* 30, no. 12 (Dec.): 1066-1072.

Rosenstein, James, Albert V. Bruno, William D. Bygrave, and Norman T. Taylor. 1989. "Do Venture Capitalists on Boards of Portfolio Companies Add Value Besides Money?" Working paper for a 1989 study.

Tarter, Jeff, ed. 1989. "Why Goliath Usually Wins." *Soft•letter* 6, no. 3 (June 15).

REFERENCES FOR THE ENTREPRENEUR'S BOOKSHELF

One or more of the following symbols appear before a number of the entries in this section of the Bibliography to indicate my recommendations for how these works can most profitably be utilized:

- •   A reference to own, understand, and use.

- Ω   A reference to own and read.

- +   A reference to outline, whose expert advice constitutes sound rules by which to operate.

Augustine, Norman R. 1987. *Augustine's Laws.* New York: Penguin Books.

Fifty-two tongue-in-cheek "laws" governing the production of high-technology, expensive, and unreliable military products. For example, "By the year X, only one airplane can be built because it will absorb the entire GNP." Contains many unfortunate, but empirically derived, laws and conjectures explaining the military-industrial complex. Evidence is given to indict the military-industrial establishment for incompetence. An essential work for any company dealing with the military.

• Baty, Gordon B. 1990. *Entrepreneurship of the Nineties.* Englewood Cliffs, N.J.: Prentice-Hall.

An excellent start-up handbook to supplement White (1977).

Bell, C. Gordon, J. Craig Mudge, and John E. McNamara. 1978. *Computer Engineering.* Bedford, Mass.: Digital Press.

• Brooks, Frederick P. 1975. *The Mythical Man-Month.* Reading, Mass.: Addison-Wesley.

A classic, useful book on programming that's also enjoyable reading. Essential if the start-up's technology is embodied in programs.

Burgelman, Robert A., and Modesto A. Maidique. 1988. *Strategic Management of Technology and Innovation.* Homewood, Ill.: Irwin.

See also Roberts (1987).

Ω Card, David N., and Robert L. Glass. 1990. *Measuring Software Design Quality.* Englewood Cliffs, N.J.: Prentice-Hall.

Cooper, Robert G. 1986. *Winning at New Products.* Reading, Mass.: Addison-Wesley.

Aimed at large companies. Contains some good advice and techniques for looking at products that a start-up can also use for product positioning.

+ Davidow, William. 1986. *High Technology Marketing: An Insider's View.* New York: Free Press.

> A fine book of stories. I recommend spending about two hours to outline the material and get the author's advice. The sixteen rules (i.e., questions, just like the Bell-Mason Diagnostic) presented in Chapter 11 ("Do You Have Marketing?") are worth understanding and following.

Ω+ Davis, Robert T., and F. Gordon Smith. 1984. *Marketing in Emerging Companies.* Reading, Mass.: Addison-Wesley.

> Contains good insights and much good advice about marketing and selling.

Deal, Terrence E., and Allan A. Kennedy. 1982. *Corporate Cultures: The Rites and Rituals of Corporate Life.* Reading, Mass.: Addison-Wesley.

DeMarco, Tom. 1982. *Controlling Software Projects: Management, Measurement and Estimation.* Englewood Cliffs, N.J.: Yourdon Press, a Division of Prentice-Hall.

DePree, Max. 1989. *Leadership Is an Art.* New York: Doubleday.

> An excellent book describing the culture of Herman Miller, Inc.

Drucker, Peter F. 1985. *Innovation and Entrepreneurship.* New York: Harper & Row.

> A work that should be read rapidly and outlined if time permits.

Ω+ Fairley, Richard. 1985. *Software Engineering Concepts.* New York: McGraw-Hill.

> Presents concepts that should be understood if the start-up is engaged in software engineering.

Gershman, Michael. 1990. *Getting It Right the Second Time.* Reading, Mass.: Addison-Wesley.

> Covers marketing dos and don'ts.

Gilder, George. 1989. *Microcosm: The Quantum Revolution in Economics and Technology.* New York: Simon & Schuster.

• Gladstone, David J. 1988. *Venture Capital Handbook.* New York: Prentice-Hall.

> An essential book on raising capital, with a good discussion of the business plan.

Goldberg, Adele, ed. 1988. *A History of Personal Workstations.* Proceedings of the History of Personal Workstations Conference (Jan. 1986). Reading, Mass.: Addison-Wesley.

•Grove, Andrew S. 1983. *High Output Management.* New York: Random House.

> An excellent book on how to manage and how to increase management productivity. It would certainly be great if everyone read and in some way practiced this kind of management.

Ω+ Grove, Andy. 1987. *One-on-One with Andy Grove.* New York: Putnam.

    Presents questions and answers about management.

Ω+ Humphrey, Watts S. 1989. *Managing the Software Process.* Reading, Mass.: Addison-Wesley.

    Essential for software-engineering management.

Ω JIAN. 1988. *BizPlanBuilder.* Los Altos, Calif.: JIAN Co.

    A template that can be used on a PC or Macintosh to write a business plan by revising and responding to material contained in the template, including spreadsheets.

Ω Juliussen, Karen, and Egil Juliussen. 1990. *The Computer Industry Almanac, 1990.* New York: Simon & Schuster.

    Contains very useful information about companies, organizations, markets, people, and products.

Ω+ Kawasaki, Guy. 1989. *The Macintosh Way: The Art of Guerrilla Management.* Glenview, Ill.: Scott, Foresman.

    Presents many critical rules for marketing products.

Kotler, Philip. 1986. *Principles of Marketing.* 3d ed. Englewood Cliffs, N.J.: Prentice-Hall.

    A traditional marketing textbook. Shows why MBAs can be replaced by a series of computer programs.

Kurzweil, Ray. 1990. *The Age of Intelligent Machines.* Cambridge, Mass.: The MIT Press.

Ω+ Levitt, Theodore.1986. *The Marketing Imagination.* New York: Free Press.

    The book on marketing. Reprints the classic "Marketing Myopia" from *Harvard Business Review* (July- Aug. 1960).

•+ McKenna, Regis. 1985. *The Regis Touch.* Reading, Mass.: Addison-Wesley.

    A great guide to all aspects of high-tech marketing.

+ McKenna, Regis. 1989. *Who's Afraid of Big Blue?* Reading, Mass.: Addison-Wesley.

    I recommend spending an hour to read and outline its two pages of advice.

Ω Nesheim, John L. 1988. *Startup: Founding a High Tech Company and Securing Multi-Round Financing.* Saratoga, Calif.: Electronic Trend Publications.

    Contains many details about what to do, along with numerous, clearly marked rules. This book is expensive, however, and most start-ups are unlikely to spend the several hundred dollars it costs.

Osborne, Adam, and John Dvorak. 1984. *Hypergrowth: The Rise and Fall of Osborne Computer Corporation.* Berkeley, Calif.: Idthekkethan Publishing Co.

Recommended reading to see what can go wrong in stage IVb, as a product takes off. Clearly illustrates the flaw of introducing a new product that can't yet be shipped while the company is still selling a product whose revenue is vital.

Peters, Tom J., and Robert H. Waterman. 1982. *In Search of Excellence.* New York: Harper & Row.

Presents a good discussion of corporate cultures in large organizations based on a survey of successful companies. Some ideas may be useful to a start-up.

Rifkin, Glenn, and George Harrar. 1988. *The Ultimate Entrepreneur.* Chicago, Ill.: Contemporary Books.

The story of Digital Equipment Corporation, a great role model for CEOs and for establishing corporate culture. Ken Olsen founded DEC in 1957 and led it to become the world's second-largest computer company, staying in charge longer than any other CEO.

Roberts, Edward B. 1987. *Generating Technological Innovation.* Oxford, England: Oxford University Press.

Contains many case studies. Any large-company bureaucrat managing research and development should understand its contents.

Rogers, Everett M., and Judith K. Larsen. 1984. *Silicon Valley Fever: Growth of High Technology Culture.* New York: Basic Books.

Helps in understanding the culture of employees, customers, and investors—if the start-up is doing business in Silicon Valley.

Ω Schlit, W. Keith. 1990. *The Entrepreneur's Guide to Preparing a Winning Business Plan and Raising Venture Capital.* Englewood Cliffs, N.J.: Prentice-Hall.

Worth owning. Contains lots of useful plan formats, definitions, and sources of capital.

Shim, Jal K., Joel G. Siegel, and Abraham J. Simon. 1986. *The Vest-Pocket MBA.* Englewood Cliffs, N.J.: Prentice-Hall.

Presents useful guidelines for understanding the subtleties of financial statements and financial decision making. Assumes that the reader is familiar with basic accounting principles.

• Silver, A. David. 1985. *Venture Capital: The Complete Guide for Investors.* New York: Ronald Press, John Wiley & Sons.

Explains how customers—i.e., investors—think when doing financing. *The* book about the venture capital community. Describes how the financing of funds and of companies works.

Smith, Douglas K., and Robert C. Alexander. 1988. *Fumbling the Future.* New York: Morrow.

> Story of Xerox's inventions in distributed computing and its attempts to enter the information-processing business. Useful for understanding the management of research and the technology-transfer process.

Ω Walker, John. 1987. *The Autodesk File.* Thousand Oaks, Calif.: New Riders Publishing.

> A great book on starting a software company. I recommend reading it and using its memos directly in managing a company.

• White, Richard M. 1977. *The Entrepreneur's Manual.* Radnor, Pa.: Chilton Book Co.

> Presents a wonderful set of rules for understanding and managing all aspects of a business (e.g., salespeople and how to close sales). Chronicles in an almost encyclopedic fashion many aspects of a start-up. Also contains a good discussion of building a plan.

INDEX

ACKNOWLEDGMENTS

Page 66. Numbered lists. A. David Silver, *Venture Capital: The Complete Guide for Investors*, copyright © 1985 by John Wiley & Sons, Inc. Reprinted by permission of John Wiley & Sons, Inc.

Page 96. Figure 5–6. Courtesy of Askmar and Frank Ura, Hewlett-Packard. Reprinted with permission.

Page 126. Summary of Brooks' Law. Frederick P. Brooks, *Mythical Man-Month*, copyright ©1975 by Addison-Wesley Publishing Company, Inc., Reading, Massachusetts. Reprinted with permission of the publisher.

Page 160. Extract. Copyright©1989 by *Soft•letter*. All rights reserved. Reprinted with permission.

Page 168. Figure 8–8. Courtesy of the IEEE Scientific Supercomputer Subcommittee, from "The Computer Spectrum: A Perspective of the Evolution of Computing." Reprinted with permission.

Page 201. Epitaph. Reprinted with permission from *UPSIDE Magazine*, Volume 2, Number 3.

Page 263. Quote by Arthur Rock. Levering, et.al., *The Computer Entrepreneurs*, New American Library, New York, New York. Reprinted with permission.

Quote by Don Valentine. Reprinted with permission from *UPSIDE Magazine*, volume 2, Number 4.

Page 300. The Gensym story. Reprinted with permission from Robert Moore, President of Gensym.